Successful Customer Relationship Marketing

Bryan Foss
To my wife Carol and my children Simon and Helen for always being there, and to the extended Foss family for their long-term interest in and support for my personal achievements.

Merlin Stone
To my wife Ofra and my daughters Maya and Talya, who somehow are still talking to me!

Successful Customer Relationship Marketing

New thinking, new strategies, new tools for getting closer to your customers

Bryan Foss & Merlin Stone

KOGAN
PAGE

First published in 2001
Reprinted in 2002

Kogan Page Limited
120 Pentonville Road
London N1 9JN
UK

British Library Cataloguing in Publication Data

A CIP record for this book is available from the British Library

ISBN 0 7494 3579 8

Typeset by Saxon Graphics Ltd, Derby
Printed and bound in Great Britain by Bookcraft (Bath) Ltd

Contents

List of figures

List of tables

About the authors

Bryan Foss

Bryan Foss is Customer Loyalty Solutions Executive within IBM Global Financial Services, and is currently leading an IBM business providing and integrating application-based CRM solutions for financial services companies worldwide. Typical B2C and B2B projects have included pragmatic customer management consulting (data warehouse and marketing database build, data analysis and data mining) and integrated customer campaign communications (including contact centre, Web and mobile e-business).

Bryan works primarily with key insurance and financial services companies globally, including large and innovative companies, composites and new directs. Prior to his global market management and solution development and delivery role, he was responsible for IBM's business relationship with the Prudential Corporation, worldwide, over a six-year period. Previous experience in financial services also includes a similar period spent working as IBM's technical management contact with American Express card and travel services, supporting all non-US operations.

His qualifications include an Executive MBA from London City University Business School focused on financial services marketing and CRM, Chartered Marketer and Fellow of the Chartered Institute of Marketing (CFCIM), postgraduate Diploma in Marketing (DipM), Chartered Engineer (C Eng Information Systems) and Member of the British Computer Society (MBCS), with Certified Diploma in Accounting and Finance (C Dip AF Certified Accountancy).

Bryan has represented IBM on the MBA advisory boards of City and Surrey Universities, is IT editor of the *Journal of Financial Services Marketing* and a co-author of Policy Publications' 'Close to the Customer' executive briefing series and the *Financial Times* CRM report. He contributed the 'Systems and Data' chapter to Merlin Stone's *Up Close and Personal?: CRM @ Work* (Kogan Page, 2000) and is a frequent presenter at CRM and financial services conferences in the UK and elsewhere.

Professor Merlin Stone

Merlin is the IBM Professor of Relationship Marketing at Bristol Business School – one of the UK's leading centres for academic research into relationship marketing and e-business. He is an Executive Consultant with IBM's Business Innovation Services, Finance Sector. He is also a director of QCi Ltd, specialists in customer management consulting and assessment, and suppliers of CMATÄ – the Customer Management Assessment Tool (software and benchmarks for assessing a company's CRM performance) – for which IBM is a leading agent.

His consulting experience covers many sectors, including financial services, utilities, telecommunications, travel and transport, retailing, automotive, energy and IT. His research is published in a series of IBM-sponsored briefings, 'Close to the Customer', which is published by Policy Publications. He is the author of many articles and 18 books on marketing and customer service. His latest books are *Up Close & Personal?*: *CRM @ Work* and *Customer Relationship Marketing*, both of which are sponsored by IBM and published by Kogan Page.

Merlin is one of the authors of QCi's report on the first two years of using CMATÄ, *The Customer Management Scorecard*, which is published by Business Intelligence and sponsored by IBM and Royal Mail.

He coordinates the IBM-sponsored Customer Management Group, a club of large customer database users, services suppliers and academics interested in this area. He is a Founder Member of the Institute of Direct Marketing and a Fellow of the Chartered Institute of Marketing. Merlin is also on the editorial advisory boards of the *Journal of Financial Services Marketing*, the *Journal of Database Marketing*, the *Journal of Targeting, Measurement and Analysis for Marketing*, the *Journal of Interactive Marketing* (the journal of the Institute of Direct Marketing), and the Journal of *Selling & Major Account Management*.

He has a first-class honours degree and doctorate in economics.

List of contributors

IBM contributors

Julie Abbott, EMEA Influencer Manager, BI Marketing

Edward Ben-Nathan, Senior Consultant, Global Consumer Packaged Goods Industry

Kumar Bhaskaran, Enterprise Solutions Research, E-commerce and the Supply Chain

Mark Cerasale, Management Consultant

Kevin Condron, EMEA Marketing Manager, GBIS

Colin Devonport, CRM Market Manager, IBM WebSphere

Steve Dickey, Manager, IGS E-business Enablement, Relationship Management and Strategy

John Griffiths, Senior Consultant

Rich Harvey, W W Financial Services Sector Executive, Sell & Support Solutions

Richard Lowrie, Global Thought Leadership Executive, FSS

Alla Main, E-business Consultant

Jonathan Miller, Senior Solutions Specialist

Doug Morrison, Senior Consultant, Business Intelligence, IBM Global Services Australia

John Mullaly, Industry Consultant, Travel & Transport

Brian Scheld, Managing Principal, IBM Business Innovation Services (Global Services)

David Selby, Senior Data Sciences Consultant

Harvey Thompson, Managing Principal, Customer Relationship Executive Consulting (now retired)

Richard Whitaker, Global Integrated Marketing Communications Manager, Travel & Transport

Other contributors

Alison Bond, Partner, ABA Research

Francis Buttle, Littlewoods Professor of Customer Relationship Management, Manchester Business School

Dave Cox, Managing Director, Swallow Information Systems Ltd

Chris Field, Retail journalist

Tess Harris, Marketing Director, Specs2go Ltd

Liz Machtynger, Senior manager, Customer Management, Mummert + Partner UK Ltd

Richard Sharman, Manager, Siemens Ltd

Roy Sheridan, Managing Director, Viewscast Ltd

Dania Spier, Consultant, KPMG

Michael Starkey, Senior Lecturer in Marketing, De Montfort University

Tim Virdee, European Sales Director, Consodata

Paul Weston, Director, QCi Ltd

Neil Woodcock, Chairman, QCi Ltd

Preface

The last few years have seen an outpouring of books and articles on the subject of customer relationship marketing (CRM). During these years, we have carried out a programme of research, sponsored by IBM and other companies, examining different aspects of CRM – overall and in specific industries.

The research is led by Merlin Stone, strongly supported by Bryan Foss and others at IBM and the Directors of QCi Ltd, specialists in customer management consulting and assessment. This research has been published in various ways including white papers and articles in the academic and professional press.

We felt that it was time to publish this material in one book, partly because so many people ask us whether we have brought all our work together. This book is therefore an edited summary of our thinking on a variety of topics in CRM. It covers most topics and all sectors. Much of our research has concerned the financial services sector, and we decided that because we had so much material on this sector it merited a separate book (our next publishing project), although financial services examples still occur frequently in this book.

The theoretical and empirical foundations for this book are contained in two previous books of which Merlin Stone is co-author. These are: *Up Close & Personal: CRM @ Work*, by Paul Gamble, Merlin Stone and Neil Woodcock (Kogan Page 1999), and *Customer Relationship Marketing*, by Merlin Stone, Neil Woodcock and Liz Machtynger (Kogan Page 2000). The most recent empirical work that our extended research team has produced is *The Customer Management Scorecard*, by Michael Starkey, Neil Woodcock and Merlin Stone (Business

Intelligence 2000) – a report that summarizes the outcomes of our work with QCi's Customer Management Assessment Tool (CMAT). Some of the scores from CMAT are also analysed in this book.

This book is divided into four sections, as follows:

1. Knowledge of CRM and customers.
2. Strategy and technology.
3. Implementation.
4. Sector studies.

The detailed coverage is as follows:

PART 1. KNOWLEDGE OF CRM AND CUSTOMERS

This part considers some key issues that relate to how companies interpret and make use of data about customers.

Chapter 1 defines CRM as a series of processes, and shows how the quality of CRM can be measured, and then correlated with business performance.

Chapter 2 contains a study of the extent to which CRM data is used in practice.

Chapter 3 focuses on strategic data analysis for CRM. It considers two of the key dimensions of marketing data analysis – customer and product, and some approaches to segmentation.

Chapter 4 covers data mining. It defines data warehousing and data mining, considers how it can be used in CRM and gives some examples of patterns of customer behaviour discovered through data mining.

Chapter 5 contains a comprehensive listing of the kinds of analysis required for successful CRM.

Chapter 6 discusses the issues involved in sharing customer data within the value chain, including reasons why companies should or should not share customer data, and the results of a survey on this question.

PART 2. STRATEGY AND TECHNOLOGY

This part examines how our view of CRM is being altered by e-business thinking and by new technologies for managing customers, wherever they are. However, the classic areas of CRM technology (eg call centres, customer database) have not been covered in detail, as these are covered comprehensively in our previous books.

Chapter 7 is an updated version of our original chapter on systems in *Up Close & Personal*. It focuses primarily on CRM systems architecture and systems integration.

Chapter 8 investigates how e-business (not just the Internet) has affected the way we think about customer management. It probes areas such as virtual exchanges and electronic hubs, and considers new approaches to market segmentation.

Chapter 9 describes an approach to aligning the value that a company gives its customers with the value it obtains from them – the customer value management (CVM) approach.

Chapter 10 examines the impact of wireless technology and mobile phones on customer management, in particular how this technology collapses the impact of distance even further.

Chapter 11 examines the re-emergence of smart cards as a technology for customer management, as credit card companies adopt smart cards as their solution to fraud, and as digital TV companies use smart card technology as their key to customer identification.

PART 3. IMPLEMENTATION

This part considers some of the most important issues involved in translating theory and technology into the reality of improved customer management.

Chapter 12 analyses one of the most intractable problems for global companies – how to extend an approach to customer management across the world.

Chapter 13 examines the importance of people in customer management, and reviews some recent research on the problems companies have in recruiting and managing people whose job it is to improve customer management.

Chapter 14 examines some aspects of managing CRM programmes.

Chapter 15 examines some of the problems companies have in managing marketing communication campaigns in a world of CRM.

PART 4. SECTOR STUDIES

This part covers some of the most important issues facing companies in particular sectors when they try to implement CRM. The sectors are:

- Travel (Chapter 16).
- Airlines – as a special case within the travel industry (Chapter 17). This chapter includes a substantial discussion on frequent flyer programmes (FFPs).
- Retailing (Chapter 18).
- Automotive (Chapter 19).
- Durable and other infrequently bought goods (Chapter 20).
- Utilities and telecommunications (Chapter 21).

The book concludes with Chapter 22: Where next for CRM?

Acknowledgements

Bryan Foss

I am grateful for this unique and long-term opportunity to work with CRM thought leaders and best-practice implementers across the world. There are too many to name here, but you each know who you are and the contribution you keep making to successful CRM.

My appreciation goes to all the contributors to this book (both IBM colleagues and many others) and our associated papers in the Policy Publications 'Close to the Customer' series. Also to Henry Stewart conferences and their publications, especially the Journal of Financial Services Marketing.

Working contact with the executives and practitioners of many large financial services companies in many places and cultures has provided me with the opportunity to learn some of what works and why it works with customers. In particular, I have valued engaging with those who strive for practical solutions in customer management and are willing to commit their personal efforts to this goal - often far beyond the direction and boundaries of their own company.

I have also valued the opportunity to work with IBM's key CRM alliance partners and those companies and individuals who have informal working relationships with myself and often with joint clients, especially the members of our UK customer management group. There should be no barriers to sharing best practices and our individual contributions to successful CRM.

During my MBA and CIM work, I have come to understand the value of academic contribution to these business issues, finding many techniques and much existing material that shows that these problems are not always new. In particular, my connections with individuals from City and Surrey universities and the CIM has helped me substantially.

Finally, I have valued the many years that I have worked with Merlin, and the extended working and personal contacts network he has shared with me - ensuring that any spare time available is quickly devoured by an exciting new project or idea related to successful CRM.

Merlin Stone

Many of those who have helped me are contributing authors — and of course I thank them for their help over the years, as they all became co-authors because of a strong relationship based on ideas. A few others need to be mentioned for specific contributions. They include Mike Wallbridge, formerly of BT and now of Bermuda Telecom, who sponsored my work on campaign management, as well as being the most important career-influencer and helper I have ever had; Joe Stephenson of UPS, who sponsored my work on the globalization of CRM; Ian Cox of Mondex, who sponsored my work on smart cards; Tim Virdee of Consodata and Kevin Condron of IBM, who sponsored my work on data sharing; Ron Mathison of Cathay Pacific, who has continued to develop my knowledge of airline CRM; and Steve Byrne of IBM, who continues to help me to develop ideas in digital marketing and branding. Clients who have been particularly helpful and influential to my ideas recently include Barclays, Boots, Bentley Motors, BP, Britannia Building Society, British Airways, BT, Close Wealth Management, Homebase, the Jigsaw Consortium, John Lewis, NatWest, Norwich Union, Orange and Swiss Re. James Lawson, Editor of *Database Marketing*, Peter Bartram of Policy Publications, Daryn Moody of Henry Stewart Publications, David Harvey of Business Intelligence and Howard Kendall of CSM-Europe have been the report and journal publishers without whose constant harassment over deadlines I would never have managed to sustain my output. I'd also like to thank my manager at IBM, Paul Clutterbuck, who has supported me in the development of this book; the Dean of Bristol Business School, University of the West of England, Professor Charles Harvey, who has given me the ideal academic context within which to work — supported by Professor Clive Nancarrow, Professor Martin Evans and Dr Alan Tapp; and the team at the Chartered Institute of Marketing, who have lately been so supportive of my work. The directors of QCi Ltd have, of course, been part of the team that has helped me to develop much of the material for this book. A special mention goes to Phil Anderson of Citigate Dew Rogerson and Clare Looker of Fishburn Hedges, who have taught me what good public relations is!

Finally, the various general sponsors of my research over the years — IBM, Acxiom, the Royal Mail — deserve special mention, as without them I would surely have not been able to develop material of the breadth and depth included in this book.

Part 1

Knowledge of customer relationship management (CRM) and customers

1

Defining CRM and assessing its quality

Merlin Stone and Neil Woodcock

CRM is a term for methodologies, technologies and e-commerce capabilities used by companies to manage customer relationships. Traditionally, companies have developed databases to capture customer information including such details as customer profiles, demographics, products purchased and other items of interest. This data is used by management, salespeople, service personnel and others to determine market trends, customer preferences, service and maintenance required by customers, and so forth. Many companies have managed to capture and archive this customer data in servers and mainframes. However, the extent to which they have managed to transform this data into value varies dramatically. The frequency of failure or poor performance therefore makes it unsurprising that few companies have successfully leveraged fully the relevant new technologies, including smart cards. However, it is early days yet.

The figures confirm the significant increase in spend. For example, the Hewson Group estimates that the year 2000 saw 70 per cent growth of European market for CRM software applications and services direct from software vendors to US $1.3 billion. Unless otherwise stated, this and other figures are for application software and services direct from vendors including e-commerce. These applications are defined as those that are customer facing and allow acquisition, retention, management, trading with or service of that customer. Overall spend including third party services (including integration and implementation services from third parties or supporting technologies such as computer–telephony integration or data warehousing and analysis) was over US $3 billion. Further growth of 100 per cent or more is forecast for 2001. Implementation resource is forecast to be at a premium in 2001. This means that no matter how coherent CRM strategies are, the resources to deliver them are scarce. It is not uncommon in enterprise-level systems for the ratio of overall implementation cost to exceed 4:1 or even 5:1.

There are two main drivers of the growth of CRM. The first is the fact that customer acquisition and retention have become top management priorities. This additional dimension of business strategy has not come to the fore just because systems suppliers and management consulting firms have promoted the ideas. It is because senior managers realize that this is a dimension of competitive strategy which if managed well can lead to much more profit, but if managed badly can lead to the loss of best customers, missed opportunities in developing customers, and high costs of customer acquisition and management. These all affect company profitability.

The second driver of the growth of CRM is the trend towards e-business and the increasing importance of the Internet as a customer-care and sales channel, which has brought a feeling of uncertainty to companies. Poor identification of the value model has led to many companies suffering very high customer acquisition costs. Adding a new channel has created problems for old channels. So companies have been looking for approaches which help them integrate old and new ways of managing customers, in particular an increasing demand for an integrated view of the customer, and a switch in spending on IT from increasing back-office efficiency to improving front-office effectiveness.

However, the rush to CRM has created many problems. Many companies are very disorganized in their approach to CRM, with responsibility being diffused among many competing groups. Tactical rather than integrated solutions are common. Large companies often fail to understand the requirements of scalable, multi-channel strategies, so start with an approach that works in one channel and collapses in another.

In addition, despite concerns about customer privacy and security, these are actually poorly managed in most companies. Throughout Europe, most large companies are not compliant with data protection law because they have no process for being so (eg undertaking a proper data protection audit and having a process for repeating it). It is only through an audit that companies discover the full extent of the customer data they hold and the quality of that data. When companies do audits, they usually discover that they are holding far more data than they thought, at far lower quality. The data is rarely concentrated on one database, except in relatively simple businesses (eg single product or single channel). If as a result of doing an audit, a company becomes compliant (or nearly compliant) with the Data Protection Act 1998, a year later it may well have become non-compliant. This is likely to be because someone has set up another customer database that is not properly tied to the first and has records that overlap with it. This makes it more or less certain that one or other customer record is incorrect! Hence the importance of regular audits. Many companies do not record the declarations made to customers whenever they capture customer data. If a company does not know, it should refresh the declaration by sending the data to customers and asking them to sign a fresh declaration, or it should restart its data collection process with clear separation between old and new data. It is not sufficient under the law for the consumer to be referred to declarations – they must be visible at the point of data collection. For example, asking a customer to click on a data protection item on a Web site is not enough. At a minimum, a summary of the terms must appear, with the detail available for reference by clicking.

Finally, although most of the effort required to improve customer management is implementation effort, there is an acute shortage of the relevant skills – those involved in getting systems to work properly, and those involved in using the systems to manage customers.

There is a largely unspoken assumption among senior managers that a focus on CRM is conceptually desired, but actually may not be the panacea that it is often heralded to be. There is a commitment to it (at least verbally and within 'mission' statements) in boardrooms all over the world, but when margin pressures increase, the focus from senior management can often become myopic – leading to a focus on short-term financial measures. This myopia is often illustrated by a loss of focus on key customer management measures in the areas of customer behaviour, attitude and long-term value and less of a focus on good customer service and service standards, which begin to slip. This, together with the impact of a squeeze on costs and a shift in focus towards productivity (rather than a more balanced effectiveness and efficiency), often results in the demotivation of the people who deal with customers. For these reasons, the customer experience degenerates and a downward spiral of volumes, margins and motivation may be perpetuated. To win the hearts and minds of senior managers and convince them that good customer management is important, especially in tough market conditions, it is important to be able to answer the fundamental question: *Is business performance related to how well a company manages its customers?*

To answer this, we need first to determine the quality of customer management and then how well the company performs in business. Then we can carry out some analysis and interpret the findings. The methodology used here was first developed out of QCi's consulting experience in 1996, is robust and objective and has been refined since 1996 through experience and by leading practitioners and academics. QCi and its partners have carried out over 150 customer management assessments, but used the 21 most recently implemented at the time this chapter was written.

THE CMAT MODEL

The model encompasses all of the essential elements of practical customer management. It assumes you know what market you are in and where you want to be – but that is all it assumes. This model defines the **scope** of customer management and is shown in Figure 1.1. Let us examine its main elements.

Analysis and planning

Customer management starts with understanding the value, behaviour and attitudes of different customers and customer groups. This includes:

- **Value**. Best defined by profitability or margin, it can be measured in terms of actual value (database), realistic potential value (database or research) and future or strategic value (customer is in a segment which is, for instance, increasing in value). You cannot extract value without investing in your proposition to that customer. We look for some application of 'cost to serve' and efficiency in determining strategy.
- **Behaviour** analysis will look at retention performance (absolutes or indices) for different value cells, the type of customer you are acquiring and the share of wallet you get from the customer (your penetration).
- **Attitudes** will look at realistic surveys around what the customer looks for in a supplier and how well you match up versus the competition.

Once value, behaviours and attitudes are understood, planning can start for the cost-effective acquisition, retention and penetration of the customer base. We look for sales and marketing plans that reflect specific retention, acquisition, penetration and efficiency objectives at customer or product group levels.

The proposition

The understanding derived from analysis and research will help identify groups or segments of customers who should be managed. The next step is to define the proposition to each of the segments and plan the appropriate value-based offers. This is done through focused 'needs' research, mapped against the values and behaviours discovered during analysis. The proposition is normally defined in terms of brand; price; service; transactional interactions; relationship; logistics; product; and for each element of the proposition a service standard is defined in terms that can be measured. It must involve all functions within the operation that impact on the proposition and customer experience – it cannot successfully be developed by marketing and imposed on the organization. The proposition must then be communicated effectively to both customers and the people responsible for delivering it.

Customer management activity

This is the delivery of the customer management. Plans and objectives, based on the retention, acquisition, penetration and efficiency findings of the analysis, and the needs of the customer groups, drive activity throughout the customer life cycle from prospect,

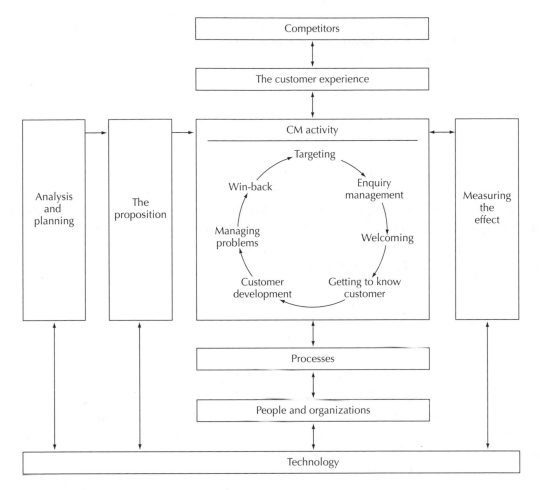

Figure 1.1 QCi's CMAT model of customer management

through new customer and on into mature customer. This will involve the day-to-day working practices of the marketing, sales and service support functions within the following key areas:

- Targeting of acquisition and retention activity.
- Handling of enquiries.
- Support for new and upgrading customers.
- Getting to know customers and how they want to be managed.
- Account management (service, billing, technical support, field, third-party telephone).
- Identifying and managing dissatisfaction.
- Winning back lost customers.

We look for the application of specific key practices (eg targeting high lifetime value, having a 'no blame' culture for complaints) in each of these areas.

People and organization

People deliver the activity. We look at what the organization does to identify and develop competencies and how well leadership supports the customer management objectives of the company, within an organizational structure that enables good customer management. Clear, understandable objectives linked to the overall business goals and employee satisfaction are two key elements that we look for here. Suppliers support the organization with the skills not available internally, or with skills that are non-core. We evaluate the practices the company has put in place to ensure that suppliers are sourced, briefed, managed and evaluated taking into account customer management requirements.

Measuring the effect

Measurement of people, processes, profitability, proposition delivery, channel performance and customer activity (eg campaigns) must underpin the vision and objectives as well as enable the assessment of success and failure. Identifying performance versus plan will enable the refinement and redefinition of future plans and activity. We also look for processes that allow policy and activity plans to be altered based on dynamic measurement.

Understanding customers' experience

Customers experience customer management activity across all of their 'moments of truth'. It is important to understand from customers' answers to questions like:

- How well are we doing?
- What can we improve?
- What do competitors do better than us?

These questions should be asked about each key experience customers have with you, especially the ones that they rank as most important. We need to look not just at measuring satisfaction but trying to get at what defines true customer commitment to your organization.

Information and technology

Information and technology underpin the whole model. Information needs to be collected, stored and used in a way that supports the strategy, the way people work and the way customers want to access the organization. Technology needs to be used to enhance the way that customers are managed (from analysis to data at point of contact) and enable, rather than disable these core customer management practices. Integrated CRM strategies require integrated systems.

CMAT METHODOLOGY

So how is the model used to assess how good a company is at managing customers? Each company undertakes the assessment seriously and expects to obtain both a realistic picture of the way they manage customers and a clear set of recommendations. The assessment is not a 30-minute question and answer session with senior management, this is a two- to four-week in-depth assessment of the intention and reality of customer management in the organization.

Typically, a trained assessor will talk to and observe 30 people in an organization (normally a specific business unit) from senior managers to sales staff. When QCi or one of their partners carry out an assessment they ask over 270 questions (looking for specific practices) across the model to understand what goes on. The questions and answers are built into the CMAT software tool for easy recording of scores, recommendations and notes and for speedy assessment analysis and comparison. During the interviews, trendy, vague or unfamiliar jargon in the questions is avoided because the purpose is not to confuse, generalize or show off knowledge of the latest tools and techniques but to be clear and specific about proven sensible practices. Questions are asked of people responsible for setting policy and ask questions of the 'doers' – for instance customer service staff, field salespeople, telemarketers and so on, so that comment can be made on the intention of the policy makers and the reality of what happens. There is an insistence on seeing evidence where appropriate and to ensure that the practice or behaviour in question is widespread and not isolated. In this way a realistic picture of how the company operates is obtained.

As an illustration, the example screen in Figure 1.2 illustrates a question from the analysis and planning section, together with the compliance text (guidelines for the assessor) and answer options. The maximum score for this question at the time of writing was 750 (it was one of the high scorers). In this fictitious example some organizational commitment and progress towards achieving a real recognition of retention, acquisition, penetration and efficiency (the three revenue drivers and the cost driver of a business) has been seen in the plan, and some progress in moving this from plan to action. To obtain a full 750 score wider organizational commitment (behaviours and measures) to improving retention, acquisition, penetration and efficiency would have to have been seen. The Compliance tab text is a reminder to the trained assessor as to what he or she needs to look for here.

After the assessment, the findings are presented in detail to senior company management. In 100 per cent of assessed cases, the results, however derogatory, were accepted by client management as a fair reflection of their customer management capability.

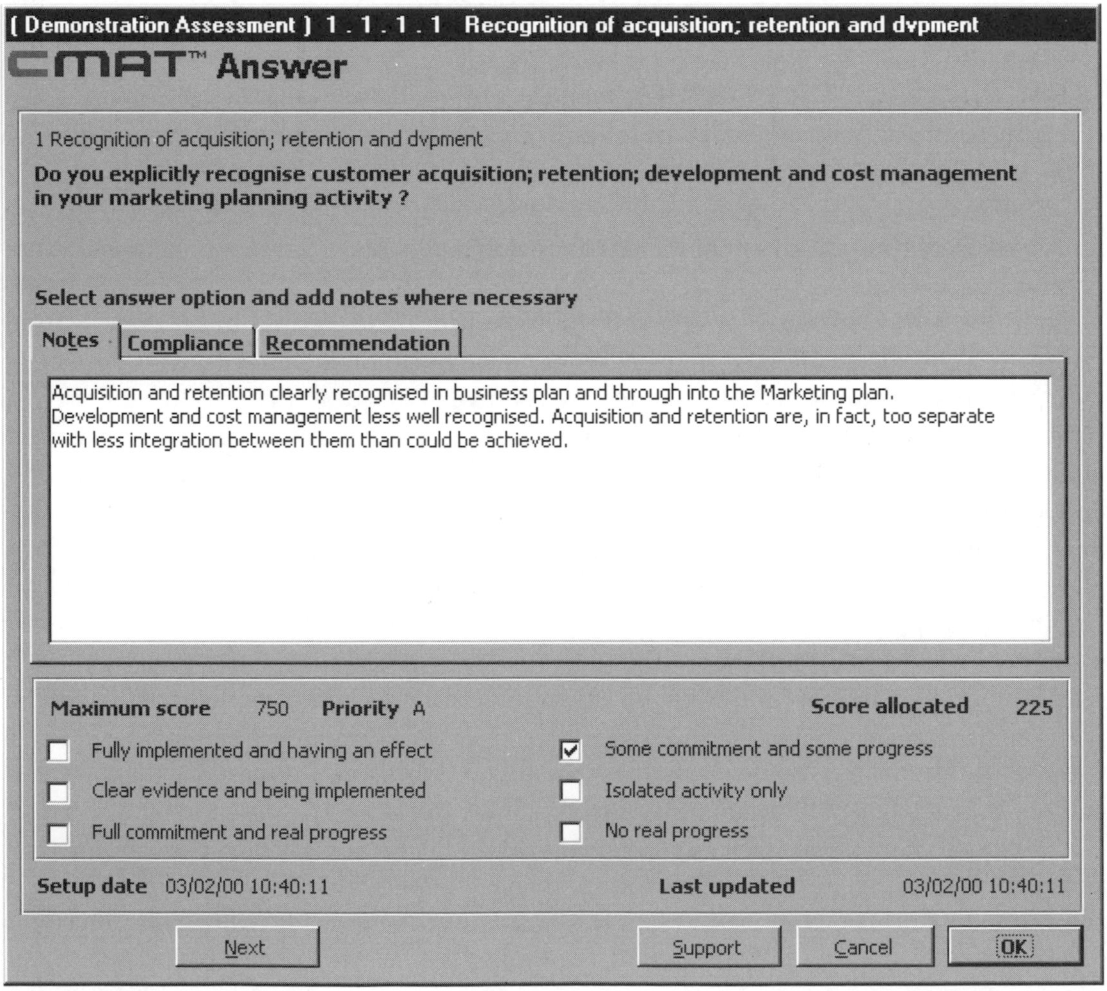

Figure 1.2 Example screen from CMAT

CUSTOMER MANAGEMENT PERFORMANCE

The standard of customer management in the UK and nearby countries is disappointing (see Table 1.1). Most people suspect this statement to be true and, through CMAT, we now have the evidence to prove it and can explain why. Exaggerations at seminars by consultants and some client companies may give a false impression of the reality of the situation.

In the UK and mainland Europe, where most of our assessments have been carried out, the standard is not good, with basic business practices being ignored and often replaced by overcomplex conceptual approaches to customer management. The CMAT assessments carried out in Asia-Pacific and the United States show no particular improvement. Interestingly, the difference between management intention as to how customers should be managed and the reality of how they are actually managed is great.

From the scoring process above, each of the companies could be ranked against their performance overall *and against each element of the model*.

THE MODEL USED TO DEFINE 'BUSINESS PERFORMANCE'

Good business performance is not always what it seems at first sight because, for example:

- Corporate financial juggling often produces a set of performance figures designed to present an impression to the City, stakeholders, a possible acquirer and so on. Stock market performance, for instance, is one pointer to success but needs to be treated with caution.
- Overall market dynamics may be very different in different markets. If the market conditions are tough (eg low demand, high competition, introduction of substitute products) then the company performance may look poor in financial terms but it may

Table 1.1 CMAT scores at time of writing

	Average score	Range
Overall	**38**	**28–45**
Analysis and planning	30	23–40
The Proposition	38	18–46
People and Organization	47	32–63
Information and Technology	47	39–52
Processes	43	5–70
Customer Management Activity	36	25–49
Measuring the Effect	40	17–54
Understanding the Customer Experience	20	6–37

actually be good in comparison to the performance of its competitors. Conversely, in a growing market a company's performance may look good but may actually be poor in relation to its competitors.

- Market capitalization is another confusing area – particularly with companies involved in some form of e-commerce, where valuations on companies appear to bear little relationship to the underlying financial performance and inevitably involve a substantial element of speculation!
- A company may be operating in an environment with unusual competitive dynamics, such as a market following deregulation. Utilities companies are a typical example of this. This can paint a confusing picture of business performance.

Needless to say therefore, rank-ordering companies in terms of business performance is not straightforward, not least because there is no single, recognized set of criteria from which to work. For this reason, the services of a panel of five independent experts were engaged (with no fees involved) and they were asked to use their experience and judgment to examine the business performance of the companies in question.

Each panel member was asked to rank the companies in terms of their business performance, from 1 to 21. The aim of the research was to identify whether the business performance over the year in question would be judged as successful by a variety of businesses experts as follows:

- financial specialist;
- business specialist;
- senior business manager;
- senior business manager – industrial marketing;
- senior business manager – consumer marketing;
- senior partner in an accounting firm;
- senior independent business consultant;
- sales and marketing director;
- business unit head of a senior client-side multinational company;
- VP of a US multinational company.

This may be, perhaps, for the way the company has generated sustainable sales and/or profit, gained market share, bucked a sector trend, produced a healthy return on assets, performed well for the shareholders in a tough environment and so on. We were less interested in those aspects of business performance that depend on how well the company's investments (eg property investments) have done, or the increase in asset value that may be unrelated to the business the company actually carries out.

QCi commissioned Lee Associates Chartered Accountants to provide much of the data from accounts, and Web searches were carried out for other data (eg sector performance).

Data used in the comparison had to be as common as possible across all of the companies. Some data was gained from the client during or after the assessment and was correct at time of assessment. 'Growth data' attempted to compare data for the 12 months before assessment to the assessment date. In practice, the data obtained could rarely be that precise so data around the assessment period was used. Ancillary profit and loss report data was provided to the panel for use if required.

The data used to judge the 'business performance' was based on a combination of the following criteria:

- percentage sales growth;
- percentage pre-tax profit growth;
- sector growth (sales);
- the company's estimated market share growth (volume percentage versus competitors);
- whether the company met its own objectives;
- percentage return on assets;
- percentage return on shareholders' funds;
- independent comment, from sector analysts.

Following a set protocol and working independently from one another, the panel rank-ordered the companies from 1–21 (with 1 denoting the strongest performance and 21 the weakest). Panel members were allowed to adjust the final position to take into account unusual factors such as product substitution, significant new entrants, deregulation, market or acquisitions and mergers. The panel members were unaware of the customer management scores of the companies. If there was a statistically significant agreement between the experts, a reasonably reliable ranking would be obtained, if not we would have to think again. The agreement between the panel members is shown as a set of pair-wise correlation coefficients in Table 1.2.

Table 1.2 Level of agreement among panel members on business performance rank-ordering task

Panel Member	1	2	3	4	5	Average Business Performance
1	1					
2	0.78	1				
3	0.83	0.83	1			
4	0.66	0.71	0.88	1		
5	0.84	0.78	0.93	0.91	1	
Average Business Performance	0.89	0.89	0.97	0.90	0.97	1

The table shows a significant level of agreement among the panel members as to what constitutes 'business performance'. The rank scores for each company were subsequently added together to provide the basis for a final, aggregate rank ordering of the companies. This is the measure of business performance which is used in the analysis presented below.

THE COMPANIES ASSESSED

Although they would of course be interesting to the reader, the names of the companies who took part in the study cannot be revealed. All companies who undergo a CMAT assessment are guaranteed confidentiality – apart from anything else if companies knew that they were going to be part of a public beauty parade it would make the objective assessment of their capabilities that much harder! However, an understanding of the type of company involved in the study is essential and in most cases the sector, size and geography of the assessed contact can be revealed. The reader should be aware that the 21 were companies that paid a significant fee for a customer management assessment – they were not especially selected for the research.

The 21 companies used in the study were all assessed in the last 15 months and the assessments were carried out on a UK or mainland European business unit. Increasingly, QCi and their partners are assessing companies across the globe and for some multinational companies they are carrying out pan-European and even global assessments across a number of business units. QCi will soon be in a position to sensibly produce sector, country and sector/country benchmarks and will report on these comparisons some time during next year – early results here look fascinating! The companies used in this study were from the sectors in Table 1.3.

In terms of size, each of the assessed companies would be considered to be in the top 500 companies in Europe and had marketing budgets of millions of pounds sterling. All except one are household names. We predict the odd one out will become a household name soon!

Correlation analysis

Figure 1.3 shows a scattergram comparison of business performance ranking against overall CMAT score. From this base data, correlation analysis provided us with the insight required to determine if there was a relationship between business performance and customer management.

The correlation result was calculated at 0.8. A score of 1.0 would of course be a perfect correlation and with this research approach we would accept correlations better than 0.4 as being statistically significant – 0.8 is therefore a very convincing and exciting correlation.

Table 1.3 Companies assessed

Finance, Banking and Insurance	12
Utilities	2
Distribution	2
Manufacturing	3
Other	2

For the 21 companies studied then, the positive correlation between good business performance and good customer management is clear. The business interpretation is simply that: companies that manage customers well using sensible, observable, well-implemented business practices are very likely to be good business performers. Conversely, companies that do not set up good customer management practices are likely to be poorer business performers.

It is common to confuse a correlation with a cause. The analysis cannot say for sure that customer management caused good business performance, all we can say is that good business performers are likely to show good customer management practices and vice versa. There are doubtless other reasons outside the scope of this study for the effect that is seen as excellence in business performance. Some of these (eg the quality of the CEO, the power of the brand, a world-beating product) may also correlate as well as customer management or better, and we make no claims as yet to having any quantitative research on areas outside of the CMAT model.

Interestingly, the least correlation (companies furthest away from the line) occurred with companies operating:

● in fast-growing markets, where the company is acquiring business and producing excellent returns almost despite itself (this may raise questions over the sustainability of this growth);

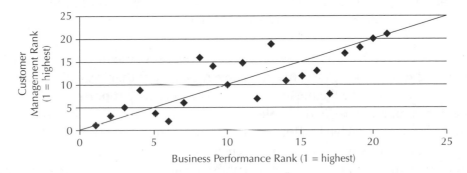

Figure 1.3 Scattergram of overall CMAT rank versus business performance rank

- in recently deregulated sectors with abnormal competitive dynamics, where business performance can actually look good even though the observed customer management practice was poor;
- in very tough, competitive markets, where business performance may appear poor despite relatively good customer management practice.

However, even in these companies the correlation between customer management and business performance was significant. It was the *degree* of significance that was different.

What areas appear to have most impact on business performance?

Looking deeper into the data, an understanding can be gained of the elements of customer management which have the largest correlation with business performance (see Table 1.4). The results are fascinating!

All of these correlations were positive and statistically significant, with some areas having a greater correlation with business performance than others. This indicates that the most important elements are (in order of importance):

- People – a clear winner! Having the right leadership, customer management competencies, people with clear objectives related to customer management and well-managed suppliers appears to have the biggest correlation with overall business performance.
- Measurement – regularly measuring actual performance against specific customer behaviours, not just high-level financial targets, *and* having the policy deployment processes in place to action the results from the measurement also correlates well.
- Customer management activity – actually doing something! Implementing some sensible customer management practices such as targeting high lifetime value customers, managing enquiries well and quickly, welcoming new customers and proactively monitoring the initial transactions with your company, handling complaints well and learning from them, etc, has a positive correlation.

Other positive, but interestingly *less* positive, correlations include IT and processes. Information and technology underpins the whole model – but that's exactly what it does – it *underpins*, it does not *drive* the business model. This finding supports our intuition and experience: if a company has good people, a clear customer management strategy, a clear proposition and measures what it's doing, then IT can be an essential enabler. If it does not, IT may actually be a costly hindrance to good customer management. The same can be said of process management. Well-documented, continuously improved processes must make business sense – but in support of the business model not as an end in itself.

Table 1.4   Business performance versus each area of CMAT model

	Correlation with Business Performance
Overall CM Performance	0.8
Planning and Analysis	0.6
Proposition	0.6
People	0.8
Information and Technology	0.5
Processes	0.5
Customer Management Activity	0.7
Measurement	0.7
Understanding Customer Experience	0.29
	(rounded to 1 decimal place)

Our interpretation of these findings is as follows:

- Companies are not particularly smart in the way they manage customers.
- There is a significant prize (worth many millions of pounds for the companies assessed) to be gained by focusing on improving the way they manage customers.
- The approach to improvement involves examining a holistic view (see the essential principles listed below) of customer management (eg looking at all of the areas covered by the CMAT model described earlier) and prioritizing a series of actions designed to improve the whole CRM model. If you look at the scope of the CMAT model, the internal sponsor of this holistic review must be a reasonably senior manager who can encourage cooperation between departments.
- To have maximum impact on business performance, our analysis shows that most companies need to focus improvements in three critical areas (in this order) of the model:
  1. Working on the leadership and the development, management and motivation of people and core suppliers.
  2. Developing clear customer management measurement criteria and 'actioning' processes.
  3. Carrying out some practical, sensible customer management activities.
- Companies should develop and introduce customer management systems to *support* the model; to enable good people to carry out customer management activities to manage the customers they need to manage and then to provide the measures to show whether profitable customer behaviour is being influenced; ie IT developments should support the clear business process, not drive it or overcomplicate it.
- Companies should not overly focus on process development and improvement. This can cause organizational focus to shift from an external, customer, viewpoint towards

an inward focus that can often stifle good business practice and absorb 'organizational energy'. Most companies could focus on simplifying what they do and the way they do it and consider the key principles of customer management summarized below.

● Companies should maintain focus on demonstrating and encouraging good customer management behaviour even when market conditions become tough.

To many experienced observers, the essential principles listed below may be common sense and we certainly have no right or intention to claim any ownership of them. However, they may prove useful as a high-level checklist for determining the path towards improved business performance. They are as follows:

● Have you adopted a holistic model of customer management that makes sense to you and your organization (eg the CMAT model) and used it to plan your customer management approach?

● Have you worked to understand customer value and behaviour, and determined which customers you actively want to manage, and which you don't?

● Are you clear, as a whole organization, about your core (profitable) customer's core needs and how these needs can be delivered efficiently without error, in a way that allows the customer to enjoy the experience?

● Have you set up and do you measure the service standards defined in the proposition?

● Do senior managers reinforce basic customer management principles, show that they care about customer service and cascade clear people targets related to retention, penetration, acquisition and efficiency objectives?

● Are your people and supplier competencies and activities aligned with the achievement of the only four things that matter – retention (often through excellence in customer service), acquisition, penetration and efficiency? This is a leadership issue as well as a target and remuneration issue.

● Do you listen to and act on the feedback from your employees? On balance, are they happy at work?

● Have you influenced the key job roles in your or your suppliers' organizations (not necessarily customer facing) that influence the customer experience? Have you ensured that they are competent to enhance the customer's experience?

● Do you have a system plan to support the holistic customer management approach?

● Have you identified the everyday core processes and policies, especially those which impact on customer experience? Did you check that they are robust (nothing falls through the cracks), customer friendly (customer perception) and measured (internal compliance against set standards). Have you done this for your company and your customer-facing suppliers?

- Does the technology actually support the business model, or does it hinder good customer management? Have you checked that the enabling systems are not over-engineered?
- Is the customer experience of your overall proposition monitored and are any issues quickly identified and remedied?

If the answer to all the questions above is 'Yes', you are likely to be a good business performer. Without wanting to borrow the now overused political slogan, there is a clear benefit to be gained by returning to common-sense customer management. Focus on good sensible business practices – it makes good business sense!

2

Integrating customer data into CRM strategy

Merlin Stone, Julie Abbott and Francis Buttle

INTRODUCTION

This chapter describes the results of a recent empirical study designed to reveal the level of deployment of customer data in CRM strategies. Today, technologies such as data warehousing and data mining allow companies to collect, store, analyse and manipulate enormous volumes of data. This can be important for marketers trying to provide better service and more satisfaction to the customer than competitors. But are these technologies in general use? Much of the CRM literature assumes that companies have extensive customer databases, populated with clean, usable data, collected on a regular basis and used to ensure customers are satisfied. This chapter questions this assumption. Participants in the study were from various industries, but with a high proportion of technology-based businesses. All the companies surveyed were embracing CRM to some degree but the level of implementation depended on the industry, and the size and age of the company in question. Small, niche players are furthest along the way. Large, older mass-market companies appear slower to change. None of the respondents report having a completely up-to-date, clean and usable set of customer data or a fully implemented CRM strategy.

LITERATURE REVIEW

Basic issues

Kotler (1999) discusses the creation and management of customer databases stating that 'one key use of the computer is to manage the prospect and customer database'.[1] He looks forward to 2005 and predicts that by then all companies will have moved to CRM, making heavy use of data. This implies that CRM is currently in its infancy. When companies truly embrace CRM, managing the customer database will be a small part of what is needed from the available technology. Data will be central to the business and will be routinely mined for insight and information which will then be rapidly and appropriately deployed. This theme is taken up by McKenna (1997) who focuses on the speed of information dissemination and communication: 'Managers hoping to serve them must work to eliminate time and speed constraints'.[2] Customers expect the right information (or marketing communication) at the right time and become dissatisfied if this is not achieved. It is not clear if marketers today are ready to do this.

Reichheld (1996)[3] stresses the importance of data for measurement purposes as companies strive to achieve customer loyalty. 'It's hard to overestimate its importance in determining the future course of a business... Measurement turns vision into strategy and strategy into fact'. Of course it is not just measurement per se that matters but the right measures. 'The gateway to the loyalty revolution is developing the right kind of measurement system', he writes. Buttle (1996)[4] echoes this. Companies 'are now beginning to talk about share of customer (in addition to share of market), economies of scope (as well as economies of scale) and customer loyalty (instead of brand loyalty). Share of customer, a reference to the percentage of an individual's annual or lifetime purchases that is won by a company, is employed as a measure of (C)RM performance'.

Clearly, customer data also has relevance for the marketing planning process. Although Kotler (1999)[5] discusses different types of plan that need to be developed and their contents, he does not detail the computer power and data needed to execute the planned strategies effectively. Fifield (1998)[6] discusses how customers are changing and the need for marketers also to develop and change, mostly by working cooperatively with customers. This requires customer insight and affirms the need for strategic planning that is flexible.

In stark contrast, Mintzberg argues (1994) that plans and 'planning itself breeds a basic inflexibility in organizations, and so a resistance to significant change'.[7] This would significantly hinder the move to CRM by established companies who are firmly entrenched in their current strategies and planning processes. We could therefore expect to see that small, young companies are faster to embrace CRM. Thurbin (1998) shows how new ways of strategic thinking deliver benefits to the organization. Information is always the key: 'Successful organisations are becoming increasingly reliant on being able to create new knowledge – at the same time it is imperative that they make the best use of the old!'[8]

A central activity in CRM strategy is exploiting customer insight and information to create profitable customer relationships. As Buttle writes (1996), 'Marketing is no longer about developing, selling and delivering products. It is progressively more concerned about the development and maintenance of mutually satisfying long-term relationships with customers.'[9] He concludes that, 'Enduring relationships with customers cannot be duplicated by competitors, and therefore provide for a unique and sustained competitive advantage'.[10] This is a view endorsed by Tzokas and Saran who also comment that 'relationships henceforth developed with customers become core competencies of the firm which, owing to the uniqueness of the individuals involved, become non-imitable by other firms.'[11] Furthermore, according to Grant and Schlesinger (1995), 'achieving the full profit potential of each customer relationship should be the fundamental goal of every business. The logic is as simple as it is compelling: Profits from customer relationships are the lifeblood of all businesses.'[12]

A key message in CRM is that in mature markets, the cost of keeping a customer is far less than obtaining a new one. Kaplan and Norton (1996) write, 'Clearly, a desirable way for maintaining or increasing market share in targeted customer segments is to start by retaining existing customers in those segments.'[13]. This is an objective helped immensely by holding the right information about customers. Related CRM performance measures are share of wallet (or customer spend) and customer lifetime value. These need accurate historical and forecast data. In the words of Christopher, Payne and Ballantyne (1991), 'Increasingly, organizations are coming to recognize the opportunities for using database marketing whereby the profiles of existing customers are analysed to correlate their demographic and other characteristics with their purchase patterns.'[14]

Customer relationships and the knowledge needed to sustain them are the focus of our research. Stone (1998) discusses how to set up the database as well as the processes and management policies around it. He describes different data types and explains why each is needed. 'As a general rule,' he writes, 'the more information a company has, the better the decision.'[15] This is the heart of our research question – how many companies are embracing CRM and implementing the processes and technology needed to ensure its success?

Industry insight

A number of studies have explored the degree of CRM development and implementation across industries. As Buttle (1996) argues, 'Although the shift to [C]RM is widespread, it is occurring more rapidly in some sectors and industries than others, facilitated by fundamental cultural shifts within organizations, powerful databases and new forms of organizational structure.'[16] One recent survey by Cap Gemini and IDC (1999) on CRM adoption in 300 large enterprises found that 'almost half of the companies surveyed were still in the planning stage of the [CRM] project...'[17]

A number of studies are dedicated to single industries – especially the *Close to the Customer* series.[18] This has papers on industries such as retail, airlines, utilities, automotive, insurance and banking. The briefing on airlines (Stone, 1999) observes that there is 'no doubt that the honours for international service success have gone to those airlines which have decided *which* customers they want to deliver top-class international services to'.[19]

McKinsey's report (1997) into banking indicates that this industry is at the forefront of the CRM revolution, but that there is still room for improvement. 'In particular, customer acquisition and management processes will have to be adapted and channels co-ordinated'.[20]

Technology

As customer numbers increase and/or companies become larger and more remote from customers, technology is increasingly important to CRM strategy development and implementation. Many papers address the use of technology, particularly in the area of data management. Several of these are on the Web at sites such as www.ibm.com, www.ncr.com and www.crm-forum.com. O'Connor and Galvin (1996, 1997) describe many aspects of marketing's use of IT including data warehouses and databases. They are great advocates of technology. 'IT is so powerful in marketing because it is enabling organisations to build powerful personal relationships with their customers and to understand their needs.'[21]

According to Stone, Sharman *et al* (1997) 'Although the term 'data warehousing' is becoming a popular term, not many marketing managers really understand what it means, and fewer have experience of real warehousing projects. Most companies – even those experiencing major gains- – still consider themselves to be learning how to use it.'[22] This indicates a gap between installation and successful use of the available technology. This is confirmed by Shaw (1998) who believes that 'the amount of information held on customers today is truly startling' but goes on to say that 'the average British household receives over 100 items of direct mail annually... with over half of these thrown away unread'.[23] This suggests that although there is a wealth of data available, it is not being used effectively to improve the return on investment.

We are seeing a huge growth in the purchase of database technology needed to enable CRM. One recent study has traced investment in IT to support CRM. In 1998, IT spend worldwide was computed at US $2 billion, in 2001 estimated at US $5 billion and by 2005 is forecast to be US $10 billion.[24] 'Overall, organisations have invested and are continuing to invest in accessing and sharing information in areas of their business where benefits are immediate – eg marketing.'[25]

Although different authors express different viewpoints on CRM, all argue that IT and the wealth of data available are accelerating the overall pace of change. They all agree that better information is fundamental in moving from transactional marketing to CRM, increasing loyalty and keeping the right customers, resulting in better profits and lower costs. But, do marketers have and use large, clean customer databases? Are they all trained in the theory and practice of CRM, and empowered to use it effectively? Or, does reality reflect McDonald's comment? 'Too many companies believe that all they have to do is collect large amounts of… data and they will finally be able to meet those (ludicrous) cross-selling objectives. Ah, the power to annoy more customers, faster and at greater cost – heaven!'[26]

THE QUANTITATIVE STUDY

Research question

Our basic research question, derived from this literature review, was as follows: To what extent are companies collecting, storing and manipulating customer data in order to develop and implement more effective CRM strategies?

From our literature review we hypothesized that, although technology now allows enormous amounts and diverse types of data to be held, with sophisticated methods of interrogation, marketers generally have neither the level of data nor the tools to exploit the potential. Indeed, we felt they may not even be aware of some of the tools, eg tools to allow complex segmentation, tighter product or campaign targeting and the control of those campaigns. This shortcoming must be inhibiting the speed of implementation of CRM strategies.

Data collection

The research was conducted in two stages, an e-mail survey of 40 respondents from UK industry, followed by face-to-face or telephone interviews with a subsample of 20 e-mail survey respondents. Data was collected from heads of marketing departments or groups. The e-mail survey was designed to collect more quantitative data that could then be used in conjunction with the second set of qualitative responses. Three respondents gave their permission to be short case studies, which are to be published later. Some additional research was done via the Internet to enhance the case study data.

Respondent demographics

Of the 40 respondents, 66 per cent came from an IT, software or services company. Other sectors included manufacturing, marketing consultancy, retail, utilities, petrochemicals and not-for-profit. The companies ranged from those with a global presence (62 per cent) to those who concentrated on serving the UK market. This was matched with an employee or company presence in the served markets – the main anomaly being one luxury goods company that had a global presence but was staffed entirely from the UK. Of the companies with a global presence, 95 per cent were well established (over 25 years). Others working globally were new companies with IT offerings.

Over 55 per cent of the respondents worked for companies with an annual turnover of over £500 million. Of these, 20 per cent operated solely in the UK and were spread across retail, utilities and finance sectors. Typically, the companies with a high turnover had a large number of employees and were long-established companies (older than 25 years and with over 5,000 employees). One exception was a company in the insurance sector with a turnover of £500 million and with between 1,000 and 5,000 employees, all based in the UK. It is under 25 years old and well known for revolutionizing its industry. This company did not take part in the second stage. The sample companies were predominantly business to business, although around 25 per cent had some consumer focus. No FMCG companies were represented.

Most of the respondents have worked for their company for less than 10 years (70 per cent), 15 per cent for between 10 and 20 years and 7.5 per cent for between 25 and 30 years. A further 7.5 per cent declined to comment. All were from marketing or customer service departments and 17.5 per cent of them were directors or general managers. A further 37.5 per cent were managers – either of people, products, customers or markets/programmes. The balance were professionals from specialist areas in marketing, for example marcoms and channels. Most had been in these roles for less than 2 years (55 per cent).

Of those giving their gender, 57.5 per cent of the respondents were male and 35 per cent female. Most people were in the age range of 26–45 (80 per cent), only 2.5 per cent were younger, and the rest between 46 and 55. There were various qualifications among respondents, including MBAs and professional degrees – mainly in engineering, marketing or other business subjects. The majority (62.5 per cent) had some marketing qualification – from the CIM advanced certificate, to an MA. Again, this figure was skewed due to a high take-up of CIM qualifications within the IT industry.

RESULTS

Marketing department information

We investigated the breadth of responsibilities of marketing groups within respondent companies. As Table 2.1 shows, the top three areas of responsibility were planning/strategy, brand management and advertising/PR. These are all concerns of traditional marketing departments. Database marketing and market intelligence were ranked equal fourth.

Table 2.1 Marketing department responsibilities

Responsibility	Position	%
Planning /Strategy	1	77.5
Brand Management	2	72.5
Advertising/PR	3	70
Market Intelligence	4	62.5
Database Marketing	4	62.5
Field Sales	6	57.5
Direct Marketing	6	57.5
Customer Service	6	57.5
Telemarketing	9	55
Relationship Marketing	10	52.5
Telesales	11	47.5
Call Centre	12	37.5
Other	13	20

Had CRM been a major responsibility in marketing departments we would have expected associated activities to be cited more frequently. However, database marketing, direct marketing and relationship marketing are all subordinate to the traditional areas of responsibility. Only 20 per cent of companies had other types of marketing group: Web enablement, events, marketing communications, pricing, new product development, after-sales service and design. Almost 70 per cent of the sample felt that their links with product developers were at best only good – half of these were only fair or even poor, and only 15 per cent thought that they had an excellent relationship with the product developers. The time spent with customers varied dramatically. Only a quarter of marketers spent time with their customers on at least a weekly basis.

We asked about the types of campaign that marketing departments managed. As Table 2.2 shows, certain types were more popular than others. Although all the respondents work for companies that are embracing CRM and feel that a benefit of better data is improved targeting, the top campaign type did not involve data-based targeting. Even if specialist magazines, newspapers and journals are chosen for editorial campaigns there is still no control over the audience who read them. This result may reflect on the industries in the survey – over 70 per cent were from IT-based companies and the press are key influencers in this sector. It may also show that companies are now aware that customers have more faith in articles written by the press than supplier-sourced marketing material.

Targeted mailshots were second with 85 per cent of the marketers using this tactic as opposed to only 47.5 per cent who do mass mailings All of the latter also do targeted mailshots. Less than half of this 85 per cent are confident that only 50 per cent of their data is accurate and should be used for targeting (but which 50 per cent?). This could lead to a lot of potential wastage, increasing costs and potential customer dissatisfaction.

Table 2.2 Campaign types

Campaign Type	Position	%
Editorial	1	90
Targeted Mailing	2	85
Trade Shows	3	82.5
Conferences	4	80
Press Adverts	5	77.5
Seminars	6	75
Telemarketing	6	75
Customer References	8	72.5
Offers and Discounts	9	67.5
Roadshows	9	67.5
Executive Events	9	67.5
Other Adverts	12	65
Hospitality	13	62.5
Telesales	14	60
Web-based	14	60
Focus Groups	16	57.5
User Groups	17	52.5
TV Adverts	17	52.5
Mass Mailing	19	47.5
Packaging	20	40
Loyalty Schemes	21	32.5
Competitions	22	30
Other	23	12.5

One way to increase the quality of data is to motivate or reward customers for giving their details, via competitions and loyalty schemes for example, but both of these are at the bottom of the campaign-type list.

Traditional events and shows were still favoured by the majority of the respondents despite the huge expense and often poor turnouts, but using customers as a reference was also popular. Over 72 per cent of the marketers use this tactic. Web-based campaigns are used by the majority and we can expect this to rise. However, the different forms of advertising were ranked lower in the list than expected – although this could be a factor of the industries represented in the survey. Many different campaign types were employed, with 67 per cent of the marketers using over 50 per cent of the campaign types listed in the table.

Customer interaction

Over half of the companies in the survey used a mix of mail (including e-mail), intermediaries, and direct contact (including face-to-face and telephone) to access their customers. Direct methods of customer contact were used by 95 per cent of respondents; 65 per cent used intermediary channels.

Brand or customer management?

Around a third of respondents worked for companies (or divisions of a company) with a single brand, and at the other end of the scale 17.5 per cent had 'numerous' or 'too many' brands within their company/division or felt that the question was not applicable to them. Over 60 per cent had between 1 and 10 brands within the company/division as a whole. When looking at the number of brands that the respondents' marketing groups had responsibility for, this changed the picture with nearly 50 per cent looking after a single brand and a further 40 per cent looking after between 2 and 10 brands. Nearly two thirds of respondents worked in a group that was responsible for all of the brands within their company/division. From the respondents' job titles it appeared that marketers still focus on brand rather than customer management.

Budgets and targets

Over half of the respondents worked for companies that had an overall marketing budget in excess of £5 million per annum, and 27 per cent were in marketing groups that also had a budget in this category. The company marketing budget was carried by 15 per cent of the respondents. Apart from one exception, these respondents worked in a marketing group that was responsible for all the company's brands and so it could be expected that they would hold this budget.

Revenue was cited by 80 per cent of respondents as the top target; 57.5 per cent cited profit as one of their targets – but awareness and market share were cited more than profit, by 60 per cent of respondents. A third were targeted with increasing their share of customer spend/wallet and another third with reducing attrition (65 per cent of these wanted to do both). Over half were looking to increase market penetration despite the (supposed) higher costs of this as opposed to keeping current customers (55 per cent of this latter group also were targeted on reducing customer loss).

One-eighth of the respondents had all seven of the targets mentioned in the questionnaire, ie increased market share, profits, revenue, awareness, share of customer and new market penetration and reduction of customer attrition, while 10 per cent had six of the seven.

Measurement

We asked respondents to list the metrics which were employed to assess achievement of the targets. Cited frequently were sales (80 per cent), lead generation (65 per cent) and expense–revenue ratios (60 per cent). There was then a fairly big drop to customer loyalty

(42.5 per cent), customer lifetime value (20 per cent) and improved share of customer spend (15 per cent).

It would appear that even if marketers are adopting CRM, their metrics are out of alignment. Perhaps colleagues in other functions such as sales, finance or accounts, or senior management still require reports in terms of short-term measures. However, it just may be a reflection on the newness of CRM within the company – that the understanding is there but the business processes have to catch up.

Three-quarters of respondents had some sort of computerized tracking/measurement mechanisms in place and 60 per cent had many systems rather than one. This may just be a reflection of the size of the company, but does also suggest a level of complexity that could lead to error if care is not taken.

Databases

The customer database was owned by marketing in 65 per cent of responses; 17.5 per cent said it was owned elsewhere in the company. The balance had no database that they were aware of and used other company or external data. Of respondents with a database, 55 per cent used external or other company data as well as their own customer data. This either shows a lack of confidence in the accuracy of the customer database, or that more complex types of data are needed for some types of campaign.

It was shown that 80 per cent of respondents used their database in campaigns, with over 40 per cent of respondents accessing it on a daily basis. A further 25 per cent accessed it on a weekly basis, and a steady decrease was shown as the access frequency reduced – 15 per cent monthly, 10 per cent quarterly, 2.5 per cent every 6 months and 2.5 per cent annually.

The databases range from less than 1 year old (10 per cent) to over 10 years old (20 per cent) with the majority being somewhere in the middle (52.5 per cent). The vast majority of the data comes from marketing or other internal sources. However, 45 per cent of respondents did purchase external data; 72.5 per cent input data from campaigns, 15 per cent from loyalty programmes, 60 per cent from sales team input and 62.5 per cent from purchase information. Only 20 per cent held competitive information. This clearly shows that the majority of databases in the survey have multiple information sources.

Only 10 per cent of respondents had total confidence in the accuracy and quality of their data; 32.5 per cent had confidence that it was accurate 75 per cent of the time, and the same percentage again were confident of 50 per cent accuracy; 7.5 per cent had little or no confidence in the data they held. But, as was seen earlier, 80 per cent of respondents still use the data for campaigns.

As Table 2.3 shows, the more traditional types of data are commonly, but not universally, held. This would suggest that, despite the acknowledgement of the importance of data for CRM strategy development and implementation, it is not yet implemented everywhere.

This could be for many reasons, including lack of buy-in from the rest of the company (a culture change is often needed for CRM), lack of technology or budget to run campaigns to collect this data, or simply the sheer difficulty of getting it.

Marketing tools used

There are many computerized tools that can help marketers run effective campaigns through customer databases. Table 2.4 outlines the better-known tools and the percentage of respondents currently using them. This shows the huge take-up of the Internet within marketing, but the tried and trusted spreadsheet is still used by most. Other tools to help the onset of CRM such as data mining, campaign management software and call centres are gaining ground, but some of the more specialized analytical tools, such as data mining, are still only used by a minority.

Table 2.3   Data types held

Data Type	Position	Percentage of Respondents with this Type
Basic Customer Information	1	75.0
Campaign History	2	62.5
Other Historical Data	3	60.0
Buy Patterns/Purchase	4	50.0
Market Information	5	42.5
Competitor Information	5	42.5
Forecasts	7	25.0
Other	8	10.0
Don't know	9	2.5

Table 2.4   Computerized tools for campaign management

Marketing Tool	Position	Percentage using this Tool
Spreadsheets	1	87.5
Internet	2	82.5
Data Mining	3	70.0
Personalized Printing	4	65.0
Call Centre	5	60.0
Planning	6	45.0
Campaign Manager	7	42.5
Online Data Analysis	8	30.0
Decision Support	9	27.5
Other	10	7.5

The effect of data on marketing

We asked respondents how important they felt data to be in contemporary marketing management. A massive 92.5 per cent of respondents agreed that more data would help marketers. However, 5 per cent believed it did not and 2.5 per cent declined to answer. A few people added the comment that better data was needed – not just more data. Table 2.5 shows that data has made a difference to how marketers work since 1995.

Many respondents commented on the influence of data. Illustrative comments follow:

> Now it is much more targeted.

> I still do not believe that we have got enough data to enable us to do all of the things on the list although I wish that we had.

> Things are not a great deal better because as well as the data collected, what is needed is a different approach to customers/markets by the company.

> We are going in the right direction, but slowly.

> Quality of data isn't any better now than before.

> Our ability to customize offers is affected by other areas.

> Targeted marketing is the most important point.

> Cleaner, more easily accessed data is also a benefit.

Moving to CRM

The majority of respondents were currently implementing CRM (55 per cent), with 2.5 per cent saying there was no need for CRM in their company. The other respondents were evenly divided, with 12.5 per cent each for 'always used CRM', 'have used CRM for

Table 2.5 How data has influenced marketing practice since 1995

Difference from 1995	Position	%
Targeted Marketing	1	80.0
Segmentation	2	65.0
Keeping the Right Customers	3	47.5
Trend Analysis	4	45.0
Increased Loyalty	5	42.5
Customized Offers	6	32.5
Increased Share of Customer	7	27.5
Other	8	10.0

some time' and 'looking at CRM'. Only 20 per cent of respondents said there would be little or no change in company policy needed to move to CRM, 2.5 per cent said it would be a complete change and 70 per cent thought that significant changes would be needed.

Table 2.6 shows why the companies are moving to CRM. It is obvious from the answers that most are adopting CRM because they believe it is good for business. This is not to suggest that they do not care about their customers, but they prioritize business requirements. Respondents were asked how important successful CRM deployment was to business performance. Table 2.7 suggests that for the majority, CRM is deemed extremely or very important.

Despite the claimed importance of CRM, only 17.5 per cent of all respondents believed that their company understood their customers very well. However 70 per cent felt that they had some knowledge. A minority (15 per cent) felt that they had little or no understanding of their customers. Successful CRM implementation, including perhaps one-to-one marketing, requires closeness to customers. The results show that the majority of the sampled companies have some way to go if they are to fully embrace the accepted view of CRM.

Table 2.6   Why move to CRM?

Why move to CRM?	Position	%
To increase profits	1	45.0
Will lose business if do not	1	45.0
Technology allows it	3	40.0
CRM is customer focused	4	35.0
Due to customer demand	5	32.5
Data allows it	6	30.0
Competition are doing it	7	27.5
Not moving to CRM	8	7.5
Other	8	7.5

Table 2.7   The importance of CRM

	%	Position
Extremely	37.5	1
Very	32.5	2
Somewhat	17.5	3
A little	2.5	5
Not at all	5.0	4

Conclusion

CRM is an important area of activity. Some 80 per cent of respondents said that they were embracing CRM – either implementing it at present, had been working this way for some time, or had always worked this way.

Respondents believed that the amount of data that marketers now have is of benefit. Around half believed that the data enabled them to keep the right customers, improve customer share and/or increase customer loyalty. A majority of around 62 per cent said it helped them to improve their marketing, getting to the right audiences via better segmentation, targeting and improved trend analysis coupled with better offers.

The majority believe that CRM is key to the future performance of the company. However a large majority do not understand their customers well enough today. This was compounded by over 50 per cent having very little direct customer contact and running the more 'traditional' campaigns – mailshots and events.

All respondents agreed that the customer data held is not as good as it should be. Interestingly, the IT companies often hold less accurate data than others. There is an imbalance between respondents having only 'some' degree of confidence in the data yet reporting that it is critical to CRM success.

The link between marketing and product development is weak in many companies, but on the whole is better than that between marketing and customers. Interestingly it was the IT respondents who reported weaker links than other companies. The implications of this are that marketing is not always seen as an integral part of the new product development process (which in the CRM world should be customer driven) and that some companies are too introspective.

If it is true, as many claim, that 'what gets measured gets managed', then full CRM adoption may be difficult to achieve. Currently, measurement and target systems are typically based on the traditional areas such as revenue, leads and expense–revenue ratios, rather than share of customer and loyalty.

THE QUALITATIVE RESEARCH

In this section, we report the results of the qualitative part of the study. Seventeen companies are investigated. Three short case studies are presented. We find that clean customer data is essential to successful CRM performance and that technological support for data acquisition, analysis and deployment is not widespread. Although clean customer data enables CRM strategies to be both more effective and more efficient, not all companies are investing in improving data quality.

Most of the companies in this part of the research are IT companies. Others include a new business start-up, a not-for-profit organization, utilities, manufacturing, luxury goods, services, petroleum companies and a marketing consultancy. The research focused on three areas: database, CRM and general marketing.

Research question

Our basic research question was as follows: to what extent are companies collecting, storing and manipulating customer data in order to develop and implement more effective CRM strategies?

The research was conducted in two stages, an e-mail survey of 40 respondents from UK industry and follow-up face-to-face or telephone interviews with a subsample of 17 e-mail survey respondents. The aim was to elicit more qualitative insights into CRM implementations. Three informants gave their permission for us to write the short case studies that appear later in this chapter. Some additional research was done via the Internet to enhance the case study data. Our methodology was guided by Yin's recommendations for conducting qualitative research (1994).[27] Further details of research methodology appear in our earlier paper. We report the general findings from the 17 follow-up interviews, supported by insights provided by particular illustrations.

Database/data management

Our goal here was to understand better the content and deployment of marketing databases within companies. We consider access, data accuracy and how the database is populated.

Successful campaigns due to better data and the long-term view

The overwhelming finding is that segmentation and targeting of customers and prospects based on clean and accurate data are the keys to success – regardless of the campaign tactics employed. There were examples of inaccurate data causing expensive wastage and a marked lack of success, and others of enhanced effectiveness and efficiency based on reliable customer data.

An employee of a database-marketing agency cited savings of 'over 250 per cent' by using good quality data. He advised investment in cleaning and improving the accuracy of the database. Databases, he suggested, should be based on customers rather than products. This should precede profiling and targeting activity. This can give major increases in campaign responses and a return on investment of between 400 and 1,200 per cent depending on the industry and campaign type.

The main campaign types benefiting from better data are direct mail and Web (viral) campaigns. All of the successful campaigns mentioned by respondents were highly targeted and the majority also returned more data that was used to improve the database still further. For example, a luxury car manufacturer's product launch campaign employed Web advertising, coupled with mailers to current customers, then a product brochure timed to arrive the morning of the launch.

Respondents cited a number of campaigns specifically to collect data. These mainly took the form of incentives, questionnaires and Web site registrations. Others included making sure that call centres get the correct information on the customers, data cleaning exercises (often through third parties that can tele-clean) and making sure that responses from all campaigns are added to the database (and that these campaigns generate the correct data needed).

All of the respondents agreed that better data is one, but not the only, key to success of marketing in the future. How the data is used and understood is also crucial, along with the correct analytical tools. Individual comments included:

> People don't understand how critical data is yet.

> Knowing how to use data and exploit it for marketing terms is the issue.

> Data gives us an edge.

> We also need the people with the right skills around the data.

Database usage

Few of the respondents actually accessed the database themselves. It was either a task for another department or someone who worked for the respondent. Monitoring data accuracy is therefore difficult.

Regardless of who actually accesses the database, the reasons for access varied from campaign-specific information (usually to segment/target) through to analysis, tracking and cleaning. The quality of the data appears to be improving slightly over time. However, marketers' expectations are increasing at a faster rate, giving the impression that the data is actually less accurate then before. A minority of respondents was happy that their data was clean and accurate. They were in the luxury goods and not-for-profit sectors, where traditionally targets market are smaller. One respondent from a services company has just finished a successful major exercise to increase data accuracy, based on an incentivized mailing to the customer base.

It is typically the marketing and front-line customer-facing departments (such as sales and customer service) who are responsible for changes to the data, the momentum of which has increased since the inception of CRM. Some CRM proponents advocate the sharing of some customer data between companies in the same industry (for example on 'bad' customers). This practice is not yet widespread. None of the respondents admitted to doing this, although some share basic data with business partners, usually for joint marketing purposes. However, one respondent in the utilities sector mentioned a governing body that insists on customer data being passed across if customers move utility suppliers.

Technologies and tools employed

Around half of the respondents have implemented new technology to aid data collection or run their campaigns, with the balance trying to make better use of what they already have. The technologies are a mix of new databases, data warehouses and marts, call centres, campaign managers, data analysis tools (such as OLAP and mining) and data capture facilities (scanners, etc). E-mail, Internet and other electronic communications (such as Lotus Notes-based team rooms) are also reported.

Surprisingly perhaps, it is the non-IT companies that have invested in technology to help with marketing. Table 2.8 shows the number of affirmative answers given by the respondents (17 in total) to a question asking which technology-based marketing tools they were aware existed, they used today or had used in the past.

As expected, spreadsheets were ranked top, but the Internet also shared this position. Call centres were next, but the specific tools designed to help marketers be more effective (campaign managers and data analysis tools) and make better-informed decisions, were lower ranked. This perhaps shows that budget holders still do not accept what marketers can achieve with the right tools.

Table 2.8 Technology tools employed to help marketing

	Use Today	Are Aware of	Have Used in the Past	Rank
Campaign Manager	4	13	7	8
Spreadsheets	16	17	17	1
Personalized Print	10	16	13	4
Data Mining	9	16	11	5
OLAP	7	16	8	7
Call Centre	12	17	17	3
Internet	16	17	17	1
Planning	8	16	10	6

Data-improving routes to market and CRM

Having more (and in some cases better) data has enabled companies to adjust their routes to market. Customers are matched with the best channel for both their, and the company's, needs. For example, lower-value customers are serviced through lower-expense channels, such as telesales or business partners rather than field sales. This cuts the expense–revenue ratios, enabling the field force to concentrate on the high-yield customer base, increasing profits while maintaining coverage across the entire customer and prospect base. Some companies have always worked in this way so no change has been necessary. Younger firms have embraced new channel technologies such as the Web and call centres from the outset and so have not made any changes.

As the data quality improves, databases are playing a greater part in CRM implementations. Virtually all the respondents acknowledge this. Some maintain that the database underpins the whole CRM enterprise. They also suggested that their own databases had some way to go before the theory of CRM and the practice meet, but that efforts were being made to move forward as fast as possible. Some commented that the database and communications around it needed dramatic improvement before it would be effective.

CRM

Our goal here was to understand both the marketer's and the company's viewpoints regarding CRM and whether they feel they are adequately prepared. (All of the respondents were implementing or already using CRM.)

The database

Having agreed that the database is an integral part of CRM, only four respondents said their databases would not need changing. Most noted that significant changes would be needed. The nature of this varied, from simple cleaning to adding to the complexity of the data (adding new areas of information such as wallet share, derived attributes and behavioural data for example). More flexibility was needed along with better structures and more simplified access.

Although most of the respondents identified different areas for change, the consensus position was that the databases did not hold the right type of information to allow marketers to understand their customers well enough to segment and target properly. This was also adversely affecting the strategies and tactics employed.

Half of the companies had started to make changes to the database, mainly by aiming to understand what was needed and then to look for sources of missing information. Some felt that a culture change was needed to really make this happen on the scale needed, and that it was happening in too small a way today.

Channel changes

Over 50 per cent of the respondents said that there would be no changes to channels linked to the implementation of CRM. Some did not know but the rest (around 35 per cent) said that changes were taking place. These were mainly in the area of value (eg low-value customers moving to low-value channels or special personal service for high-value/top customers, call centre implementation and usage of business partners for fulfilment). The channel strategies were being reviewed and better use of technology, for example the Web/phone, for customer dialogue was starting to be used.

Personal beliefs

The respondents were asked what could be done as far as data and CRM were concerned in their company to ensure greater marketing success. Three main themes stood out – they need to:

- Understand and get closer to the customer base, see customers as individuals. There may need to be a corporate/company culture change to do this.
- Improve the quality of the data and database and the commitment from the top to ensure this happens. This included using the latest technology to analyse the data and access the customer and prospect base.
- Make marketing more pervasive across the company. Marketers need to get out of their individual areas and talk to others to gain credibility and make sure that messages are consistent. This again may need a culture change.

All of the answers showed that things needed to happen and commitment was needed from people at the top of the company to ensure that it did. Some respondents were in a position to push harder for change than others.

This was shown by the answer to the next question: 'Are you being held back in any way on this?' Funding and executive commitment to database development and CRM are the main barriers to change that marketers are experiencing. Some respondents felt that time was also an issue – mainly because other areas of the business took priority.

Everyone believed in the importance of CRM to some degree, the differences being whether it is right for that particular company, industry or marketplace. One informant said: 'It depends very much on the business and need, rather than being a universal panacea.'

The respondents were asked if their company was implementing CRM because they genuinely believed in putting the customer first (assuming profits would follow), or if it was being implemented for reasons internal to the business. All but the not-for-profit organization and start-up company said the latter.

General marketing

Our goal here was to find out how respondents would like to see marketing change in their company. The answers differed widely but most could be given a CRM interpretation.

It was felt by many that marketing must be accepted across the company as the core strategic force for the business rather than short-term sales support. Marketing has to show it adds value in order to be taken seriously and permeate the whole business. Customer relationships and channel strategies should re-examined, and integrated marketing communications deployed across channels.

Finally, worries about data quality need executive attention for some respondents, with the correct enablers and funding put in place to ensure fast improvement. This means better technology to access the data, analyse it and drive campaigns.

Conclusion

Although companies are beginning to embrace CRM, there is much room for improvement. Some companies are more advanced than others. These tend to be newer companies operating in niche markets where there is a lot of choice for the customer. Larger, established, mainstream players find the changes harder to make and although the principles of CRM are accepted as sound, the practical implementation moves at a much slower pace.

Many of the respondents queried whether their companies were adopting CRM really for benefit of customers (in the confident belief that profit would follow) or as a 'me too' strategy to combat competition. There was a widespread belief in CRM – but with an acceptance that the customer will know which companies really cared about them and which were paying lip service to the concept.

Overall, most of the companies were moving to improve their data and customer focus. Marketing is not highly regarded in the slow-to-adapt companies.

CRM CASE STUDIES

This section contains three short case studies from survey respondents. The individual cases were chosen because of their diversity and relevance to the research question. Names have been removed to preserve anonymity where requested.

Case Study 1 – Start-up company

This case reports a new business start-up. It focuses on the beliefs of the board members in respect of customer data, CRM and customer service.

BACKGROUND

This company was set up two years ago under the Young Enterprise Scheme. It is based in a school near London. There are five board members. All but one were studying for GCSE exams at the time of the research. The exception is the MD's father who is in business separately. He is on the board only to take on any activities that have to be performed by someone over 18. Everything else, including all business decisions, is undertaken by the teenagers. The company employs several sales representatives in the same age group. They are friends of the board members and work for the company part time.

The company's mission is to set up and run Web sites for customers. At present the operation is based in and around London due to time and travel restrictions. The board members are not old enough to drive and must rely on public transport. However, the sales reps are based in major cities across the UK and Ireland as well as Brussels, Paris, Berlin and Jerusalem. The company has a turnover of between £1 and £2 million and is making a profit.

BUSINESS PHILOSOPHY

This is a very young company run by young entrepreneurs who are trying out their business wings. They practise what they learn from the textbooks in their economics and business studies classes and therefore understand (and believe) the theory of CRM and use it daily in their business. They started with a penetration pricing policy to enter the market. They have experienced a sales growth rate of 40 per cent per annum across the two years that the company has been in existence. This is expected to slow now. They are committed to customer service as the company's sales director said: 'We are a small company so we have to focus on service, and when we look after our customers it does help business.'

PRODUCTS/SERVICES

The company designs, establishes, promotes and hosts Web sites for customers. There is a Web design team of five who have a capacity of 15 Web sites a month (depending on complexity and time/exam constraints). An external company is subcontracted if demand cannot be fulfilled.

BUSINESS/MARKETING STRATEGIES

The main strategy is to develop relationships with their customers. This promotes repeat business and recommendations. The board is in the process of launching a parent company to the three companies in their portfolio, one of which aims to be the first no-monthly-fee Web hosting service in the UK. A major review of business and marketing strategies had just taken place. This enabled the board to study the customer feedback and data and decide how best to move forward to achieve their business goals of increasing awareness and entering new markets while giving the best service to their existing customers in order to retain them. The result of the review was that the company would rebrand and relaunch in September 2000 when it planned to diversify into new markets.

FINANCIAL OBJECTIVES

The main objective is to have profits increase by 10 per cent year on year; 60 per cent of this will be retained into a company university and car fund for the directors. The remainder is reinvested into the company.

MEASUREMENT

The company measures its performance in terms of customer satisfaction, sales, revenue and whether it is meeting its profit objectives.

MARKETS

Today, half of the company's customers are in and around London. It markets to small and medium businesses that want to go on the Internet. However, the company targets customers worldwide and as two of the board are multilingual, Web sites can be set up in German and French as well as English. The remainder of the customer base is in the rest of the UK and mainland Europe – accessed due to contacts made when two of the board members lived there. The United States is a future target market.

CUSTOMER PROFILE

There are 18 repeat customers on the books, who have had their sites updated or who have bought new sites. Most of the customers pay a variable monthly fee dependent on the services they use. Most customers are small to medium-sized businesses with a sizeable number being start-up companies. Others are individuals who want their own Web site built and dot.com companies.

ROUTES TO MARKET

The main channels are the company's sales force, Web site (including e-mail) and promotions. Those involved also make use of the telephone and have face-to-face meetings whenever possible. The employees of the company are all based at their family homes although the directors do work from school occasionally.

MARKETING TACTICS

Campaigns are based on the Web – especially those asking for responses from prospects and customers – in order to get better data. Telephone promotions are also used. Other promotions include linked Web sites, e-mailshots and attending a small number of trade fairs (a maximum of two per annum.) Marketing spend is quite low – no details were given.

DATA/DATABASE USAGE

The database is company-wide, holding a variety of data, including customer and company data, customer feedback, personal information, buying patterns and competitor information. There is also general information on the markets. The directors each access the database on a 'need to know' basis – exam constraints stop this happening more often although there will be an annual review and analysis of the database in the summer holidays. At the moment the data is mainly used to look for new markets and improve customer service but members of the board believe that it can be used in a better way and this will be part of the summer review. The data is seen as being very useful in order to facilitate business decisions and market in the most effective way possible. It is employed mostly in the planning process and to review previous campaigns and services. This allows the board to enhance services where necessary and put the most relevant marketing and sales tactics in place.

CONCLUSION

The team are committed to giving a personal, tailored customer service as well as sustaining growth in their company. They realize that in order to achieve the latter (and make profits), they must concentrate on the former, making sure that after-sales service and contact are as good as pre-sales. They are a very impressive team and have already achieved a lot in their first two years of trading as well as keeping up with their studies and plans for university.

Case Study 2 – Not-for-profit

This case concentrates on database matters as they influence the CRM strategies of a not-for-profit organization. The information was supplied by the marketing director.

BACKGROUND

This ecological organization relies on supporters in their subscriber database for revenue. Since 94 per cent comes from individuals, the marketing department is dedicated to meeting these supporters' needs. Direct debits are the most common method of payment (used by 70 per cent of subscribers) and a paperless direct debit system was recently set up which passed the stringent scrutiny of the clearing banks. The organization was the first in the sector to take paperless direct debits.

THE DATABASE

The database was moved from card index files to computer in 1982. A lot of the original data was still in existence until fairly recently, causing problems due to the constraints imposed by 1980s technology (eg null fields full of asterisks). This has now been cleaned and the constraints removed. All new data entered uses a comprehensive set of rules to ensure accuracy and allow flexibility. For example, new subscribers will be asked for date of birth rather than age, as well as telephone number and any e-mail address. Whenever anyone talks to a subscriber, the current details are checked and reconfirmed. As the organization is entirely dependent on the data it is forced to keep revisiting the data integrity.

THE DATABASE TEAM AND TECHNOLOGY

The marketing database team set the data objectives. They are very focused on getting the right data and using appropriate forms of analysis. They use the latest technology including data mining, analysis and e-commerce. Only data that is necessary and can be made use of is collected, and this is under constant review by the team. A good team is considered vital as it vastly improves the understanding of the information held within the database. The team keeps abreast of technology to ensure continued success, for example the re-engineering of the database to allow the validation and change of e-mail addresses. As external agencies are used for telemarketing, excellent e-commerce facilities are necessary. E-mail is the primary communications method between the organization and the agency, and is becoming more important in contacting subscribers.

CRM

The database is essential to the organization's CRM strategy. It is used to maintain supporter relationships and slow attrition, which are two significant drivers of revenue, and achievement of the not for profit goals. The organization has always worked in this way and the database was built around this understanding. Genuine care for supporters is what drives the organization and it would be unacceptable to employ CRM strategies for business reasons alone. CRM is something the company employees believe in but they think that the expectations are too high today and it is set for failure. They believe that the CRM ethos is strong in this organization, but that companies generally need to be realistic about what can be achieved. In this organization, everything must be more tailored to the individual subscriber as it is totally dependent on its supporters and must meet their needs.

ISSUES

The main issue is that of budget. Keeping the database up to date has a low priority as supporters want their contributions to go to mainstream campaigns. Salaries are another concern. They are lower than within industry. People who are there typically want to work for the organization because they subscribe to the ideals. (This can also be a benefit as everyone will be working together towards the same goals.)

DIFFERENCES FROM THE COMMERCIAL SECTOR

The marketing director has some experience of the for-profit sector. Marketing gives confidence to the other parts of the organization by delivering the vision and receiving the subscriptions. This also adds a lot of value and makes it easier to open up internal communications channels. The marketing director believes that the commercial sector still has a problem with marketing as it is not seen to have value, credibility or trust, and marketing's objectives are often dissimilar to other departments' within a company.

Case Study 3 – Luxury goods manufacturer

This case focuses on the role of data in yielding CRM success.

BACKGROUND

This manufacturer of high-value luxury goods has been in business since the early days of the 20th century, is based in the UK and relies on a worldwide network of dealers as its route to market. Its name epitomizes high-quality motoring and, although it has recently been the subject of a takeover, and therefore has new objectives (such as production rising from 1,200 to 15,000 units a year), it is still reliant on its small customer base at present.

CUSTOMER BASE

The customer base is global but quite small and niched. Customers are wealthy individuals or companies who use the goods to make a statement about their own brand (for example the Peninsula hotel in Hong Kong). Many customers own several residences and have a lifestyle that includes yachts, aeroplanes and even their own sports teams. The company partitions customers into two segments: the main customer base and key accounts (top customers, including some of the world's richest people). It treats those buying new and used goods in the same way. Most purchasers of new goods were once owners of used goods. The rebuy cycle ranges from once every 20 years to several purchases in a single year.

CUSTOMER RELATIONSHIPS

Customer relationships are paramount for this company. This is accepted at every level in the organization, with all employees taking a great pride in their workmanship and ensuring the highest-quality product and service. After-sales service is as important as pre-sales because customer loyalty is a high priority, with repeat purchases as the target. The customer service line goes direct to the experts at the manufacturing plant to ensure that the customer gets the right answer first time. The company makes sure that it knows enough about its customers to ensure that the correct type of service and offers are given. Product launches are executed in a personalized way, to ensure the best response. Personal managers are also employed from other luxury goods companies whose sole job is to interact with the customers. A benchmarking exercise was recently undertaken to measure performance against aspirational brands and companies (eg Krug, David Linley, Amex Black Card, etc).

Many customers live in the in the Middle or Far East. Different cultures and conventions present challenges to the customer service team as they ensure that the highest-quality service is given without adversely impacting cultural sensitivities. For the marketers, one problem that arises is simply that of names. From an occidental perspective, customers in the Middle East often have long and complex names. It is crucial to get them right. Customers are proud to own the products and are very loyal to the company. Therefore knowledge of them is critical and data is fundamental to this.

DATA AS A FACTOR IN CRM

The database is central to keeping the customer relationships. Accurate personal data is critical. Purchase histories are maintained for at least 20 years and this is being extended as more information is obtained. Each unique item manufactured in this time frame can be tracked. The data base currently holds around 50,000 active customer records and 30–40,000 products. The company is now trying to go back even earlier with the ultimate aim of knowing the whereabouts and 'life' of each of the units it has manufactured since its inception. The data is collected and kept up to date mainly by personal interactions with customers and dealers as well as from campaigns and customer satisfaction surveys. Every respondent to the survey gets a personal letter of thanks or a visit from a customer manager. The database is used daily and any problems quickly addressed to ensure minimum disruption. There are no specific cleaning exercises done. Instead customer records are dealt with on a personal basis.

COMMENTS

This long-standing company genuinely cares for its customers and has learnt over the years that it is critical to keep them loyal. Therefore CRM measures have long been used and proven. This has been relatively easy with such a small set of high-profile customers. Time will tell if this can continue once output increases tenfold and less costly products become part of the range. This will open up the market and bring in a new set of customers who may need a different approach. The new owners of the company are mainstream and not used to dealing with customers in an individual fashion and this too may be a concern for the current employees of the company.

CASE STUDY CONCLUSION

The three cases were similar in that the companies targeted customers who in the main were individuals or small businesses rather than large corporates. All three focused clearly on customer needs and delivery of high-quality service to exceed expectations and promote loyalty. Although they were different in age and industry, they all served a niche market. This is something that larger, mass-market companies find more difficult to do due to the size of their customer base. However, it is likely to become more necessary as customers become more sophisticated and the Internet channel expands, bringing with it a huge increase in the amount of data collected.

Notes

[1] Kotler, P (1999) *Kotler on Marketing*, Simon & Schuster, London

[2] McKenna, R (1997) *Real Time*, Harvard Business Press, Boston, MA

[3] Reichheld, F F (1996) *The Loyalty Effect*, Harvard Business School Press, Boston, MA

[4] Buttle, F (1996) in *Relationship Marketing: Theory and Practice*, ed F Buttle , Paul Chapman Publishing Ltd, London

[5] Kotler, P (1999) *Kotler on Marketing*, Simon & Schuster, London

[6] Fifield, P (1998) *Marketing Strategy*, Butterworth Heinemann in association with CIM, Oxford

[7] Mintzberg, H (1994) *The Rise and Fall of Strategic Planning*, Prentice Hall Europe, Hemel Hempstead

[8] Thurbin, P (1998) *The Influential Strategist*, Financial Times Pitman Publishing, London

[9] Buttle, F (1996) in *CRM Theory and Practice,* ed F Buttle, Paul Chapman Publishing Ltd, London

[10] As above

[11] Tzokas, N and Saran, M (date unknown) Value Transformation in CRM, www.crm-forum.com

12 Grant, A W H and Schlesinger, L A (1995) Realize your customers' full profit potential, *Harvard Business Review* reprint 95503, HBS Publishing, Boston

13 Kaplan, R S and Norton, D P (1996) *The Balanced Scorecard*, Harvard Business School Press, Boston, MA

14 Christopher, M, Payne, A and Ballantyne, D (1991) *Relationship Marketing*, Butterworth Heinemann, Oxford

15 Stone, M (1998) Building customer focused data, *Close to the Customer* series, Policy Publications, UK

16 Buttle, F (1996) in *CRM Theory and Practice*, ed F Buttle, Paul Chapman Publishing Ltd, London

17 Petrissans, A (1999) *Customer Relationship Management: The changing economics of customer relationships*, Cap Gemini and IDC white paper, IDC and Cap Gemini, EMEA

18 See for example, Stone, M (1998) Targeting high value customers, *Close to the Customer* series, Policy Publications, UK

19 Stone, M (1998) Targeting high value customers, *Close to the Customer* series, Policy Publications, UK

20 Adolf R, Grant-Thompson S, Harringtom W and Singer M (1997) What leading banks are learning about big databases and marketing, McKinsey and Company, www.crm-forum.com

21 O'Connor, J and Galvin, E (1996, 1997) *Marketing and IT*, Pitman Publishing, London

22 Stone, M, Sharman, R *et al* (1997) Managing data mining in marketing Part 1, *Journal of Targeting, Measurement and Analysis for Marketing*, **5** (2) pp 125–50, and Part 2, **5** (3) pp 247–64

23 Shaw, R (1998) *Improving Marketing Effectiveness*, The Economist Books in association with Profile Books, London

24 Meta Group/Infact Research, 2000

25 IDL (2000) 2000 European Business Intelligence Report, IDL on behalf of IBM, Harpenden

26 McDonald, M (2000) On the right track, *Marketing Business*, 29 April, CIM, Berkshire

27 Yin, Y K (1994) Case study research: design and methods, *Applied Social Research Methods* Series, Vol 5, rev edn, Sage Publications, Newbury Park, CA

3

Strategic data analysis for CRM

Merlin Stone and Bryan Foss

Many companies have not determined how to deal with the rapidly increasing volume of data about customers now being recorded in and about their businesses, through research, operations or external data suppliers. Here are two examples:

Consumer goods retailers – retailers can now obtain reports about the purchasing of individual products by specific customers, usually within a few hours of purchasing taking place and sometimes online. In its most extreme form this can include the results of promotions mounted through mobile phones.

Utilities, financial services and industrial marketing companies – managers in these industries now have comprehensive databases which record not only purchases but also sales enquiries, responses to promotions and a mass of detailed data about customers.

These examples illustrate two of the key dimensions that exist in marketing data analysis – product and customer.

THE PRODUCT DIMENSION

Companies which do not know the identity of their final customers, while applying customer management disciplines to their immediate direct customers (eg retailers), must use product management to get the best results. We call these the 'product optimizers'.

Their own and market data on price, promotion, inventory levels and movements, and shipments is used to determine the optimum marketing and distribution policy. Their data is organized along the product dimension, and the key analysis task is to make sense of the possibly daily millions (eg for a grocery brand leader) of transactions in which their products are involved. There are many companies that organize data by product and focus on marketing efforts which aim to increase demand for specific products – Gillette is one example, aiming to increase regular shaving, perhaps to twice a day.

THE CUSTOMER DIMENSION

Companies that can manage their customers as individuals or small groups need to become expert in analysing customer data, to answer questions such as:

- Which customers do I want to market to, and which not?
- How do I want to manage my customers?
- Which products and services would I like to sell to particular kinds of customer?
- At what price would I like to sell, through which channels of distribution, and when?

These questions apply whether or not the contact is managed directly or through an agent. The key requirement is that the individual final customer is known to the supplier (eg the business person buying an airline ticket through a travel agent). The data requiring analysis situation is typically in-depth customer data, combined with transaction and promotional response data. We call these organizations the 'customer optimizers'.

THE HYBRID CUSTOMER AND PRODUCT FOCUS

Some companies are hybrid product and customer optimizers. Many service retailers (eg retail finance organizations) can identify their final customer individually, but must also work hard to optimize product marketing in order to make the best use of their sales capacity. Some retailers focus entirely on product-optimizing merchandising, but others have discovered that individual customer management is now possible through store cards (credit, debit, loyalty). In practice, most companies are hybrids to some degree, requiring both product and customer optimization.

One of the most fascinating aspects of applying data mining in hybrid situations is that we often end up rewriting history! This is because we discover that what a company had considered to be purely a classic marketing mix problem, eg product, advertising campaign, store location, turns out to be a customer acquisition and/or retention problem. Some examples are given below:

Symptom – Falling capacity utilization for an airline on an important route.
Cause – Frequent flyers who took up most of the capacity on that route had been specifically targeted by a competitive airline.
Symptom – Falling traffic in a retail store chain.
Cause – Failure to recruit younger customers for key product ranges, and consequent ageing and falling value of the customer base.
Symptom – Failure by a photocopier company to achieve sales targets for a low-volume copier.
Cause – Market share falling in smaller, fast-growing businesses because of poor representation in dealer outlets.

Given this risk of completely mistaking the nature of the strategic problem, the key strategic question can be stated as follows. How can you manage the vast flow of information that you have at your disposal so as to:

- understand what is happening;
- take control (as fast as possible) over what is happening;
- gain advantage over your competition?

The answer to this question differs according to whether your company is a product or a customer optimizer, or a hybrid (when the answer is a combination of the two). It also depends on the particular situation of your company. However, the answers for each type of organization have in common the need for what we call a decision analysis framework.

DECISION ANALYSIS FRAMEWORK FOR PRODUCT/ SERVICE OPTIMIZERS

Here, the volume of data flow is so great that the key need is to distil from the data, which usually comes from many sources and at different intervals, the scope and scale of any required management action. In many cases, management does not have a clear idea of the possible full range of required actions, so these actions are simply not taken, with the result that product/service decisions are not optimized. For example, a customer recruitment response might be required to address an apparent failure of a new product to reach its targets.

In the decision analysis framework for product optimizers, management actions are classed as in Table 3.1. Table 3.2. gives a simplified example of this for a packaged consumer goods supplier.

Table 3.1 Classification of management actions

Action	Change Required by the Action
Nil Action	No change required to operating decisions, operating parameters within which operating decisions are taken, marketing and sales policies, or longer-term strategies
Operating Action	Change required to adjust one or more variables (eg inventory levels) within existing operating parameters
Operating Parameter Change	Change required to parameters which normally determine operating actions (eg the lower limit to inventory which triggers replenishment)
Policy Change	Change required to a marketing or sales policy (eg a promotion should be terminated, an advertisement should be rerun)
Strategic Change	More fundamental change required (eg a product withdrawn or relaunched)

Table 3.2 Packaged consumer goods example of decision analysis framework

	Operating	Operating Parameter	Policy	Strategy
Trigger Issue	Cash flow slows	Short deliveries to retailers	Promotional coupon return rate too high relative to sales	Continally declining sales relative to category
Data Combination which Revealed Need	Invoice totals Payment totals	Orders Shipments	Sales ex-retail Retail ex-orders Coupon return rate	Sales trend Category sales trend Usage and attitudes and research
Key Indicators	Days sales outstanding	Order fulfilment ratio Inventory level	Coupon–sales ratio	Share of category
Diagnosis of Cause	Delayed payment by key supplier	Replenishment level set too low	Malredemption ratio abnormally high	Weakening brand values
Action Required	Pressure to pay	Increase replenishment level	Kill promotion if possible. Do not repeat	Reposition or withdraw brand

This classification of management actions can be combined with a categorization of decision areas to produce a clear statement of requirements for the analyses to be undertaken. For example, for an FMCG supplier, the decision areas might be categorized to include, among others:

- packaging;
- manufacturing and inventory volumes;
- distribution strategy and tactics;
- standard costing and pricing;
- promotional pricing;
- promotional offers;
- settlement terms;
- media advertising;
- product range definition;
- individual brand/product definition and positioning.

Each of these decision areas has its own list of trigger issues and the resulting analysis requirement.

Our conclusion is that to make the most of the much-increased flow of data available to them, product optimizers need to:

- Determine in advance all the possible trigger issues they might be faced with.
- Identify the possible diagnoses of the reasons for these issues.
- Use data mining to identify likely patterns in the data which might indicate these diagnoses, and also to identify any missing diagnoses.
- Use their reporting systems to set up an overall approach for triggering management action, which allows senior marketing management to focus on the most serious (not just strategic) issues, and automates as far as possible the process for managing other issues.

Obviously, this represents a major investment, but unless it is done, there will be an increasing tendency for marketing management to revert to the days when they spent too much of their time contemplating screens and reports, and too little on making the right policy decisions. Data mining must not be carried out for its own sake. In the same way that a specific ore (eg gold or diamonds) might be mined, data mining only provides a return on investment when used to address some strategic business objectives. Releasing these forms of tool to crawl through a data warehouse with the hope of finding something 'interesting' only ever finds 'fool's gold'.

THE CUSTOMER OPTIMIZER

One of the key requirements for success is the company's ability to classify customers into different groups to be managed differently, either tactically or strategically. Our research suggests that organizations that are most successful in this area have developed a hierarchy of segmentation, as follows:

- contact management;
- analytical segmentation;
- response segmentation;
- strategic segmentation;
- delivered loyalty segmentation.

Contact management

This is using data at the point of contact with the customer to improve the management of the individual customer. It usually uses the output of the segmentation categories described below to change the action or response of the company (eg alter the telemarketing script, accept or refuse a customer). Initially, contact management may be based on simple analytical segmentation techniques, but over time usually matures to be directed by response segmentation (or predictive scoring), supplemented by analytical segmentation for an improved understanding of relevant wants and needs.

Analytical segmentation

This is the use of customer and market information to identify that there are indeed different groups of customers with different profiles, needs, etc. This approach often starts with very broad questions such as 'What kinds of customer do we have, what is their behaviour, which products or channels are the most successful?'

The segments that are identified in this way may never be subjected to different promotions, policies or strategies. For example, they may be aggregated into a target market for a promotion. The main criterion for the successful use of analytical segmentation is that any resulting strategies work overall, because they are based on in-depth understanding of customer needs. Analytical segmentation often provides the foundation for the other three types of segmentation.

Response segmentation

This is the identification of different groups of customers for targeting particular promotions. A given customer may belong to a whole series of different segments, according to the objectives of individual promotions. The key criterion for the success of responsive segmentation is the success of the individual promotion (ie whether response rates met expectations, whether final purchases hit target). In direct marketing, apparently small differences in response rates can make a very big difference to profits, so a segmentation approach that delivers such an increase can be a key source of competitive advantage. Put simply, a 0.1 per cent increase in the response rate means a 5 per cent increase in sales if the response rate was 2.0 per cent before. As costs will not usually rise 5 per cent, it means a much larger increase in profit.

Response segmentation has become increasingly important in the last few years. Best-practice direct marketing depends upon tight targeting of customers and careful building of customer databases to ensure high-quality data. In some industries, direct marketing practice has taken a step backwards because so many companies are crossing industry frontiers and targeting each other's customers. Banks are offering insurance, and insurers are moving into banking, as are retailers. Everybody is offering credit cards (9,000 at the last count in the United States). Previously monopolized state industries are being broken up and the resultant companies are all competing for the same customers. They all see direct marketing as the answer to their prayer.

In these circumstances, unless there is amazing increase in the propensity to respond, or to buy direct, response rates are more likely to fall than rise. The need for improved targeting is key as better targeting will be the only way to make direct marketing pay. Simple predictive modelling is likely to give way to more complex modelling based on classification techniques, achieved through data mining.

Strategic segmentation

This is the identification of groups of customers who need in some sense to be handled differently. This should be driven by a study of key performance indicators to provide the maximum benefit. For example, in mass-market financial services, it is particularly important for suppliers to identify the following two groups: loan customers who are likely to be higher credit risks (in which case they are usually only accepted as borrowers at an interest rate which covers the risk premium); and mortgage customers who are likely to be rapid switchers (eg of mortgages), in which case they may only be accepted for loans with higher penalties for earlier cancellation.

Conversely, low-risk or infrequently switching customers will be targeted and marketed to intensively, and particular attention might be paid to the quality of customer care they receive.

The core idea of strategic segmentation is to ensure that each actual or potential customer is allocated to at least one strategic category, membership of which carries certain implications for the marketing policy likely to be directed towards them. Also, one should avoid creating too many categories, with attendant risks of: **overlap** (a given customer being subjected to too many marketing initiatives or restrictions, which have to be resolved by prioritization rules); **over complexity** (because of the number of segments that need to be addressed with different marketing policies).

While this approach can sound exciting in theory, real implementation examples have often created customer dissatisfaction because of the inherent mixed messages. A particular issue of importance for both strategic and loyalty segmentation is the movement of customers between categories. The best example of this is life cycle category. For example, a mother with very young children will be in the market for disposable nappies (diapers) for two years after the birth of each child. During pregnancy, the mother can be considered about to enter a strategic segment – as a current buyer. So the supplier's main strategic segment is women in the late stages of pregnancy and mothers of children under, say, two years old. But when the child is trained, the mother moves into another segment – as a candidate for other products and services, as well as a potential recommender to others.

Figure 3.1 shows customer value relative to the most frequent purchasing for one child.

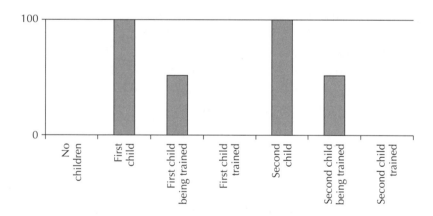

Figure 3.1 Strategic segments for a nappy/diaper supplier

Figure 3.2 shows a similar chart for frequent flyers. Here, the vertical axis indicates the propensity to fly relative to the most frequent flyers. The strategic segment of greatest importance to the airline are those who will become the hyper-flyers. Data mining can be used to predict who these will be.

The same competitive pressures that apply to direct marketing apply to strategic segmentation. Companies are trying to target their products and services accurately. The

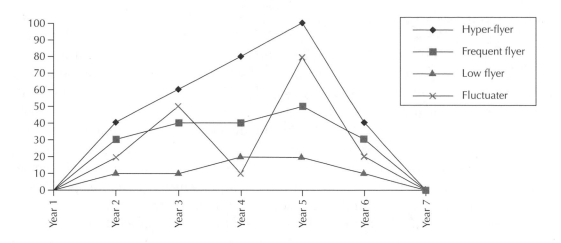

Figure 3.2 Strategic segments for an airline

ultimate aspiration is often expressed as 'the market segment of one', implying that the entire marketing mix can be attuned to the individual. Realistically, large companies are finding the concept of 'mass customization' more helpful. This involved designing the marketing mix with a high element of modularity, combined with the ability to 'package' the offer individually, eg by changing the information that forms part of it. The simplest example of this is the personalization of communication.

Mass customization is attractive because products and services can rarely be changed quickly to meet the needs of different segments. Product and service features are usually determined as part of a strategic process (although of course modularization allows some flexibility). Tightly defined strategic segmentation – in which the characteristics of customers who make up particular target segments are defined in some detail – is becoming more common, as products and services are targeted at smaller segments. Older methods of segmentation, based upon quite large groupings defined using broad socio-demographic or economic characteristics, are giving way to more tightly defined segments, often defined through data mining.

Where life cycle segments hold the key, you need to be able to identify not only which customers are already in the high usage segment, but which customers are likely to move into them, and when.

For both response and strategic segmentation, senior management is starting to ask that investigative work, questioning the definition and value of segments, becomes part of the routine of the marketing department rather than a once-for-all exercise which determines marketing policy for years to come.

Delivered loyalty segmentation

This is a special case of strategic segmentation, and consists of the identification of particular groups of actual or potential customers whose loyalty is critical to the supplier. This criticality normally relates to the volume and profitability of business coming from this group of customers, but may also be related to other variables (eg political sensitivity). Identification of this group is followed by the development *and* implementation (or 'delivery') of a practical marketing approach. This may include branding, relationship management (through whichever channels are appropriate), promotional management and systems support, which work to draw that group of customers into a special, long-standing, mutually committed and transcending relationship with the supplier.

The components of delivered loyalty segmentation are usually no different from ordinary loyalty programmes. What is different is the focus of the company upon the segment and commitment of resources to managing the segment profitably and well. Perhaps the most important feature of such segmentation is the degree of commitment of the organization to the segment. This means that the company must be fully committed to the segmentation approach.

The systems and management characteristics of these four kinds of segmentation are summarized in Table 3.3.

THE SYSTEMS AND MANAGEMENT INTERFACE

So far we have identified the need for managers to anticipate in some detail the kinds of analysis they need to perform on marketing data. But how can management act to achieve improvement in data analysis? Our view is that the answer lies in:

● how the business requirement for data management is specified;
● the consortium of systems and software suppliers used;
● business requirement.

Here, our recommendation is quite simple. It is only too common for large companies, in specifying their requirement for marketing and sales systems, to omit the analytical dimension. This leads, as we noted earlier, to this requirement being tagged on at a later stage. This in turn may mean that some kinds of data are neglected altogether, such that collecting, storing and analysing them is difficult. The analytical dimension should therefore be included – down to the level of detail suggested in this briefing, for product and customer optimizers.

Table 3.3 Segmentation characteristics

	Contact Management	Analytical	Promotional	Strategic	Loyalty
Technical Approach	Expert systems and data mining should be integrated into response management system	Can be left to expert systems and data-mining approaches	Expert/data mining approaches may be used, but test results are key Predictions can be based on data mining	In-depth business understanding required to define issue. Data mining may lead the way to discovery of new segments	In-depth businesses understanding required to define issue. Data mining can be used to identify segments that respond best to loyalty initiatives and which initiatives produce best long-term result. Data mining can also be used to preduct loyalty propensity
Senior Management Involvement	High costs, so must understand immediate profitability gain from improved customer management	Not required except to ensure that capability exists	Required if promotions are a large share of marketing budget	Important in defining areas of strategic focus	Absolutely critical because of subsequent commitment to comprehensive loyalty management approach
Customer Contact Implications	Dialogue is more relevant 'Right' customers dealt with better – eg right products offered. 'Wrong' customers deleted quicker	Depends on conclusion	Customers experience correctly defined and targeted promotions	Customers may be required to give more information and should find that they are being offered more appropriate products and services	Customers who are loyal or who have the propensity to be so experience more integrated management, whatever the contact point and whatever the product or service

Systems and software suppliers

Customer and market management systems, most broadly defined, are normally the result of the work of a range of suppliers. Their work typically covers the areas specified in Table 3.4.

This consortium of suppliers is usually put together very carefully over a period of years, so companies are reluctant to disturb it. Our conclusion is that the appropriate analytical software is often omitted from this carefully constructed consortium, or introduced too late and without the management insight to ensure that analysis provides the required solid foundation for business success.

Table 3.4 How suppliers support customer management

Hardware	From mainframes to PCs and including operating system, networking and printing support
Telecommunications	To connect sites, customers and suppliers
Database Software	To provide the structure within which data can be entered, updated, extracted
Transaction Software	To handle the flow of product and service to the customer and payments from the customer. More recently includes integration software
Marketing and Sales Software	To support the acquisition and retention of customers (in some cases this overlaps with transaction software)
Analytical Software	To extract and integrate data held on other software, often benefits from the existence of sound industry data models for integration and consistency
Data	Data about the external world (eg markets, customers) to match with company data, enhance it and in some cases to help interpret it
Facilities Management and Bureaux Services	To carry out work done by some of the above and by the company's managers (marketing and/or systems)
Consultancy and Systems Integration	To integrate the whole, using tried and tested techniques to accelerate the completion of staged projects at reduced cost and risk

As more new CRM and other systems are added within a company's operations, it becomes increasingly difficult to integrate and synchronize changing data. Through experience of such projects, new techniques are becoming available which enable consistent mapping of data between 'legacy' systems and new CRM systems, enabling data to be successfully integrated for reliable analysis and use. However, few companies are so far deploying these reusable data integration methods, skills and tools across their organizations, as most continue to drive projects which stand independent of each other from both business and IT perspectives.

THE QUALITY OF DATA MANAGEMENT

In this section, we consider the findings of CMAT (see Chapter 1) concerning customer data management. The scores are listed below, and they show a fairly poor situation.

Internal information sources

Have you fully researched what customer and associated data is available to you from internal resources? **59**

Have you fully researched what customer and associated data is available to you from external suppliers? **47**

Data quality standards for imported data

Do you have published quality standards and checks for all imported/bought-in data? **50**

Understanding of data feeds

Do you fully understand what each piece of information on each system feed means and how it has been derived? **54**

Transaction system feeds

How frequently is customer information fed from key transaction systems? **42**

Third party channel data

Do you have a clear policy agreed with third party channels regarding the customer information that they will provide to you? **42**

Record source storage

Is the source name/reference stored on your customer database for each new record added? **47**

Implications of data protection legislation

Do you fully understand the implications of current and planned data protection legislation in all of the countries in which you have customers or prospects? **54**

Customer information plan

Do you have a comprehensive and accessible customer information plan covering information value; acquisition priorities; information management and usage? **16**

Information quality standards

Is there a clearly documented set of customer information quality standards that apply to your customer-related data? **28**

Historic information quality measures

Is information quality formally measured against the information plan with measures being stored and used to monitor improvement? **21**

Information quality incentives/sanctions

Do customer management people have any incentive/sanction relating to information quality on the customer database? **27**

Data library for the customer database

Do formal data dictionaries/libraries exist for your main customer databases? **55**

Documentation of core customer information

Is at least the core customer information clearly documented in a way that can be understood by non-systems people? **30**

Company record validation

How frequently are key customer/prospect records validated to ensure that they still exist? **27**

Mailing returns

Is information about mailing returns and unsuccessful outbound calls always fed back to the central customer database promptly and are transactional systems updated? **44**

Information archiving strategy

Is there a clear strategy on what information can be archived and at what stage? **47**

Availability of the customer database

Is the customer database accessible to all staff whose role involves significant customer contact in a way that matches their needs? **33**

Indirect access to the customer database

For individuals who do not have direct access to the customer database, is there a process to enable them to work with the information indirectly? **38**

Information match to channels

Can customer information be represented on your customer management systems in a way that links with your channels, proposition and strategy? **31**

Storage of planned activities

Can planned activities for customers and prospects be stored on the customer database? **25**

Database contact strategy link to communications

Does the contact strategy recorded on the customer database actually drive all the communications with that customer? **23**

Protection of records from updating

Can individual records be protected on the customer database to prevent them being changed by feeds from other systems? **48**

World Wide Web integration

Has the customer database been developed/upgraded to store and use information on customers which enables full benefit to be gained from the World Wide Web? **24**

Our conclusions from this analysis is that the drive to acquire more customers and to implement more and more data-driven applications very quickly means that most companies have not dealt very well with data issues. This is reflected clearly in other CMAT scores. The score for all topics related to the acquisition of new customers is 50, which contrasts with that for managing existing customers of 33. Similarly, the score for developing new systems is 52, while that for current systems is only 32. It can therefore be argued that we live in a world of customer data chaos.

CONCLUSIONS ON STRATEGIC DATA MANAGEMENT

- The analysis required by product optimizers and customer optimizers is different, but many suppliers now realize that they have to do both.
- Companies should recognize that they will normally need to consolidate and synthesize data from different sources (internal, commissioned market-research, generally available market data, etc) and functions (marketing, sales, finance, customer service, manufacturing, etc).
- A successful approach to analysis requires the company to define the key analysis dimensions in some detail, and then to ensure focus on a few areas which can be backed by management action.
- The needs of different users vary, and different users will require different tools to support their different management actions, but this must not lead to data being dispersed to different users so that the capability for coordinated analysis is lost – hence the need for central consolidation of data to facilitate reporting to all parts of the organization.
- This approach will be much facilitated if the data and analysis requirement is defined as part of the wider business systems requirement, and if the consortium of suppliers is built around this concept.
- Without the underlying data being in order, many conclusions will be invalid. The CMAT scores show that much work remains to be done on data.
- When deploying data mining tools start with a clear business understanding and identified business problem. Do not expect data mining alone to be a 'silver bullet'.
- Successful joined-up business processes require joined-up IT systems and underlying data structures.

4

Data mining and data warehousing

Merlin Stone, Richard Sharman, Bryan Foss, Richard Lowrie
and David Selby

DEFINITION AND KEY CHARACTERISTICS

A simple definition of data mining in marketing is: extraction of previously unknown, comprehensible and actionable information from large repositories of data, and using it to make crucial business decisions and support their implementation, including formulating tactical and strategic marketing initiatives and measuring their success.

This definition may sound rather technical and long-winded. However, we so often encounter misunderstandings about what data mining is and how it is used that we decided that we needed to make it absolutely clear what we mean by it.

Our definition stresses the following aspects of data mining:

- Extraction of information.
- Large data repositories.
- Formulating initiatives.

Extraction of information

Methods developed to analyse and interpret scientific data have been able to achieve remarkable insights in specific scientific fields. However, in the past it was hard to apply them to very large data sets. These methods often originated with small, well-defined experimental tasks. Today, using modern IT, we can apply them to large-scale problems.

Large data repositories

The key characteristic of commercial data is its volume. Millions of individuals, in thousands of separate locations can perform hundreds of transactions each, in a short space of time, resulting in billions of countable events. For example, a frequent supermarket shopper may visit one outlet and buy 60 items, and the next day visit another outlet and buy 50 items. National retail chains have hundreds of thousands of such frequent shoppers. These transactions generate hundreds of millions of data items each week. Tracking and understanding this customer behaviour involves building complex and sophisticated operational systems. Similar systems are used by other large organizations, such as banks, insurance companies, airlines and manufacturing companies. Until recently neither the data nor the means to process it were readily available.

Sometimes, these large data volumes arise not from millions of customer or transactions in a short period of time, but from fewer, more complex cases, possibly stretching over years. So business-to-business marketers with hundreds or thousands of customers may find the techniques described here as useful as a consumer marketer with millions of customers. The same applies to markets for more complex consumer financial services, such as pensions and life insurance. In fact, some of the most interesting findings are based on identifying new patterns of behaviour among a few hundred customers which the company believed it understood well!

Formulating initiatives

Determining strategies to manage customers, products, outlets and the like can be aided by a more complete understanding of the current and past activities of customers. In some cases business strategies are almost entirely based on sophisticated analyses of past behaviour (eg some trading systems in financial markets, mail order campaign targeting).

For example, an insurance company can analyse its customer portfolio and recent transaction history to determine the typical profile of customers who take out policies, but then lapse (fail to renew). The lapsing group can be assessed for the desirability of their business. Marketing initiatives can be planned to prevent future lapsers, or win back previous lapsers. Three key points arise from this simple example:

- **There is a clear-cut and important business problem to be solved.** Customers who fail to renew insurance policies create high costs, in terms of marketing, selling, agent commission and policy administration. Such costs can consume the value of the first premium. If the policy is not renewed costs cannot be recovered later. Of course, this must be set against the increased risk of a claim being made, as the policy is held for a longer period.

- **There is an information rich environment.** Insurance companies routinely use large data bases for operational administration, and maintain comprehensive information on their clients, the products they buy, and the nature of claims. This may be held on separate computer systems, using different operating systems and incompatible database architectures. However, a comprehensive and consistent database of all information can be achieved through a data warehouse. Note that the data needed to solve a particular business problem need not be owned by the company. Other data from public sources, and complementary sources may be used. Indeed, while current data is often enough for a company to start with, it is usually skewed towards administrative information and will usually need to be enhanced to support new customer management initiatives.

- **The means to modify the situation exist.** If it can be shown that the pattern of lapsing customers is related strongly to other factors, then some remedial activity can be undertaken. For example, lapsing might be more prevalent in certain geographical locations, where agents from another company may be active. It might be related to demographic factors: for example, customers of a specific age and social group. Or lapsing could be related to changes in economic factors, such as unemployment or interest rates, which affect customers' ability to support payments. If such factors can be identified, the insurance company could take specific actions to remedy the situation, such as targeting its marketing activity, improving agent training, introducing products with different payment profiles or deferrable payments, or giving inducements to particular customers groups to renew at favourable rates.

WHY USE DATA MINING IN MARKETING?

The aim of data mining is to obtain a sufficient understanding of a pattern of market behaviour to allow *quantifiable* benefits to be derived from changes in behaviour suggested by the analysis. This involves: learning previously unknown facts about market behaviour; answering specific questions, including forecasting questions.

Of course, you cannot always finalize your expectations before data mining starts, as the results usually determine what can be done. However, you must not overestimate your company's capacity to change. Marketing budgets may be set for a year ahead, and with them, plans. New promotional initiatives may have to displace existing ones.

Data mining is not a miracle science. In deciding whether to use data mining, you must develop a clear view as to *how* you are going to use the output, in policy terms. Far too many data mining projects have been undertaken on the initiative of IT departments. These usually result in lots of interesting findings but no action. Companies with large customer bases, with a reasonable degree of stability in the marketing staff and in their marketing services suppliers, should have a wealth of knowledge about customers in the heads of their people and in reports on their past activities. Data mining will often confirm their beliefs, but add a more quantitative or practical edge – eg specifying the size of a long-suspected segment, identifying which customers belong to it. Some deductions are reasonable, such as buying behaviour depending on socio-economic status, and these are the ones where one should collect data to investigate.

So, data mining starts with the idea that companies hold a lot of data about their businesses, but do not have full understanding of what is happening in detail. By 'digging' in the data it is possible to 'mine' the nuggets of buried information. This simple approach is relevant mainly to companies which have a lot of readily available information, but have done little analysis of it. In these cases almost anything discovered will be interesting and of use to the organization.

But data mining is more than simple data analysis. It is the understanding of a business environment, such that relevant questions can be answered by the use of the appropriate data analysis tool on the properly selected data. As such, data mining is a machine-aided consultancy activity which requires:

- Understanding of your industry conditions.
- Appreciation of specific factors that apply to your company.
- Familiarity with a wide range of analytical tools.
- Ability to present extracted information in informative ways.

Data mining consultancy can advise you on what can be determined and how to interpret it, for example:

- what can be learnt from particular types of data;
- the answers to certain questions about the data;
- the way to collect new data to answer other questions;
- the limits of what can be learnt.

What data mining is not

Myths about data mining abound. One is that it is trivial, because it is just running a few off-the-shelf tools. In this view it is business-as-usual because it is:

- just exploration;
- simple use of off-the-shelf packages;
- merely fancy graphical user-interface tools.

Another myth is that mining is the answer to a maiden's prayer because it will unlock everything a company needs to know. According to this view, it is:

- the way to run the whole business;
- the reason you should install a data warehouse;
- the single factor that will give an enterprise its competitive edge.

Myths like these often arise because data mining is fashionable, so much so that many suppliers of analytical software call their products data mining. This can be very confusing, but the reason for this is that data mining is simply at one end of a continuum of methods, from simple counts and tabular analysis, through to discovery data mining – techniques which can simply be 'turned loose' on a data set to identify relationships. Data mining is in our view a consultancy activity, supported by statistical techniques. These techniques do not require hypotheses to be specified beforehand but do require enough understanding of the business situation to ensure that the data is in a form which will yield useful results. However, some data mining techniques work better with hypothesized findings, because hypotheses determine which data should be analysed and in what form.

What data mining offers to marketing

Most users of data mining are already quite advanced users of other data analysis methods. This simply reflects that the culture of the company is one of investigation and curiosity, based on a belief that business decisions require complex data sets to support them and the tools to analyse them. Some of these companies have operations research units staffed by qualified statisticians and business analysts. Others use external suppliers for these skills.

In some cases (eg in insurance and banking), the use of statistical techniques to handle risk (used by actuaries in insurance, credit analysts in banking) has been part of the culture for years (although this does not always transfer smoothly to marketing analysis). For these companies, data mining is an evolution of previous scientific method, not a revolution which upsets it. Many users of data mining complement it with standard statistical and even tabular analysis.

Of course, the exploration which is characteristic of data mining software has been made possible by advances in computing, in particular massively parallel processing. Put simply, this allows data processing at very high speeds – for example, comparison of very large numbers of attributes of cases, to see which cases are similar. In particular, it helps marketing managers in the following ways:

- It helps them understand and predict likely customer actions in a complex (multifactor) world. For example, data mining was used to show how some frequent flyers had fluctuating frequencies of flying, while others had a relatively smooth pattern of flying. This meant that the former were at risk of 'demotion' within the scheme, despite the still-high lifetime value to the airline.
- It helps them discover customer groupings which would be hard to discover using theory-based hypothetical work, for profiling, needs analysis and focused actions. For example, a life insurance company discovered a low-risk group of smokers within the high-risk group of all smokers. These were customers who were prudent in every other way – except that they smoked. These customers could be retained by a lower premium.

What questions do companies want answered?

The last few years have seen many companies applying data mining to their marketing data. These applications are designed to answer a variety of questions. Here are some examples:

Customer-based questions

- What kind of customers does your company have?
- How do they behave?
- Which customers are more desirable and which less?

Product or price

- Which products are bought together?
- When is the best time to sell a product?
- Which combination of tariffs yields the maximum revenue?

Distribution and communication routes to market

- Which campaign design works best?
- Which distribution channel is most effective?

Combinations of the above

- Which customers are most responsive to which communications for which products?
- Which customers with low lifetime values can be deterred by higher prices?
- Is it possible to identify groups of customers, within groups that were considered homogeneous, that can be managed more profitably and/or less riskily?

Some examples of data mining activity in marketing

Here are some popular types of data mining activity which are encountered in practice, with a short description of the type of business problem associated with it:

Customer gain and loss analysis

Why have some customers have been gained for certain products, and others lost? Variation in behaviour may be random, or it may correlate with business trends, economic or social factors, or the activity of competitors. A first step is to understand which types of customers are unusual, and then to explain the factors which contribute to their behaviour.

Customer migration

What factors cause customers to move to different products? Their buying pattern may show that they buy one particular product followed by another (eg after buying a dress the customer buys matching shoes in 70 per cent of cases). The linkage between product types, and the susceptibility of a customer to follow a sequence, could determine how items should be placed in a store, or which customers to target in a marketing campaign.

Customer solicitation

How effective are marketing campaigns in reaching the right customers? Increasing campaign yield (eg the number of positive responses), or decreasing the cost of finding new customers can bring substantial savings. The propensity of customers to buy certain products can be used to predict future behaviour for new products.

Customer response analysis

What causes customers to respond to a campaigns? A customer segmentation can determine what types of customer exist, and a propensity analysis can determine which types are most likely to respond.

Promotion analysis

What are the results of a marketing promotion? Which customers bought particular products, and why? The key task is to explain observed behaviour in terms of a mix of customer and product types. This can be achieved by comparing the segmentation of customers before and after the promotion in question.

Purchase analysis

What types of products and services are specific customers buying? Simple divisions into characteristic types of purchase can be achieved by segmenting customers into groups. More sophisticated studies can involve determining the linkage between different types of purchase.

Seasonality analysis

How does the purchasing profile change during the year? Seasonal patterns in products (certain soft drinks and popcorn in the summer, hamburgers in the winter) and in strengths of links between products can be studied.

Priority analysis

What order do customers prefer to buy products in? This is an application of product link analysis.

Customer loyalty

Which factors cause a customer to remain loyal to a company or product? Customer loyalty and lapsing are two sides of the same coin.

Cross-selling

What additional products could be offered to existing customers? The propensity of customers to buy a product can be used to infer how they will respond to new cross-selling opportunities.

Niche market determination and target marketing

What segments of customer populations exist or which have specific buying patterns which have not be previously identified? The existence of numerous, often small, previously unidentified and possibly high-value (or low-value!) segments can lead to the provision of new products or services. For example, finding a small group of older drivers with fast cars that were costly to repair but had very few accidents led to a special insurance offering for vintage sports car enthusiasts.

Channel of communication and media analysis

Which channels do particular types of customer prefer to use? Do their preferences vary for inbound and outbound communications? The rise of telemarketing in insurance is revolutionizing the market by changing the channel through which customers buy. The exposure for a company which is not yet using telemarketing can be assessed once some evidence has been accumulated. Some customers have a strong preference for mail, as they can control the contact better. Who are these customers, and how strong is their preference?

Channel of distribution analysis

Which channels are different types of customers using, when and for what products? Which would be most suitable, given customers' geographic location? What is the optimum number of branches to cover the market? How should deliveries to trade customers be planned?

Basket analysis

What associations are there between products – within the shopping basket, between products bought in the same week, month or year? This is the classic application of product link analysis to determine dependencies between otherwise unrelated activities.

Is data mining essential to answer these questions?

You do not *have* to use data mining to answer the kinds of questions listed above, but the more complex the question, and the larger and more complex the data set, the more likely it is that data mining will shed additional light. Data mining not only helps you find better answers, it also makes it easier for you to find these answers. In a competitive market, particularly under changing market conditions, profitability is often closely related to the speed of solving multiple problems. The sheer variety of possible applications of data mining is a problem. So we recommend that before embarking on a data mining project, you decide exactly how you expect the outcomes of your analysis to relate to marketing strategy.

BASIC METHODOLOGY OF DATA MINING

The basic steps of a data mining analysis are data collection and cleaning, data analysis and presentation of the results.

Data issues

Types of data covered

The first answer to the question 'Which data should I mine?' is simply 'Whatever you have which is likely to be relevant to the business problem and may give business insights if analysed effectively'. Most of this data is transaction data (ie data collected at the time of sale of the product). Often only a part of the available data is captured and retained at that time. This data is primarily product, not customer data. Response data may also be available. This includes campaign responses, survey or research data, and complaint data. Data on customers – how to access them, their characteristics, etc – may be collected during transactions and responses, or by a special collection effort. It may also be sourced externally.

Volumes of customer interactions and resulting response and transaction data vary dramatically by type of business (eg retail, where card holders may transact daily, compared with insurance where there may be one transaction a year). In some cases, data will also be held on the relationship (eg renewals of contracts). This data can be supplemented with external sources (eg demographic, geographic, lifestyle, etc). Combining one or more product sources may provide more insights into customers and the relationship between customer and company, and also on past customers and relationships.

The steps typically involved in data mining are:

- data collection and warehousing (extraction, transport and loading);
- data cleaning, merging and purging, grouping (including householding);
- variable redefinition, and transformation;
- new data collection – typically items revealed as missing;
- data mining – often in several steps as 'internal clients' learn about type of results that can be achieved;
- data visualization;
- new requests for analysis, additional information to be collected and analysed;
- assimilation;
- planning – including action and monitoring, and decisions about whether to move to online rather than batch usage.

Time and space dimensions

Traditional market segmentation approaches tended to be rather weak when it came to understanding how customer behaviour varied over time and space. This is partly because adding these dimensions exploded the complexity of the data analysis. The increased availability of geographical data (where a customer lives, where he or she has bought) and the ability to map it and show changing mapping patterns means that marketing managers are becoming more demanding when it comes to understanding the spatial dimension. Where time is concerned, time series analyses often led to simplification of the specification of the problem because of the difficulty of handling complex sequences of behaviour. The difficulty in both these areas was not that the statistical techniques could not handle them in theory, but that their introduction multiplied the complexity of the problem and made it hard to implement hypothesis-led approaches.

One of the main justifications for the data warehousing approach is that too often companies lose historical data. For example, a customer's new address overwrites the old one. As prediction usually involves analysing current *and* past relationships, commitment to a data warehouse should also involve commitment to keeping slices of the database 'frozen' for analysis. The simplest example of problems caused by failure to keep frozen slices would be if a retailer tried to understand why a customer bought at a number of different branches without knowing that the customer had lived at three different addresses!

Where the data may be

The data required for mining could be:

- so far uncollected;
- collected but on paper rather than on a system;
- within the appropriate business unit, in one or more systems;
- in other business units in the company, on paper or in one or more systems;
- outside the company, but in one or more business partners within the value chain (eg suppliers and/or distributors);
- available from a public or group (shared-data) source.

The next part of this paper shows how companies are approaching organizing data for analysis through data warehousing.

The data warehouse – organizing the data for analysis

Although the term data warehousing is becoming popular, not many marketing managers really understand what it means, and fewer have experience of real warehousing projects. Most companies – even those experiencing major gains – still consider themselves to be learning how to use it.

To get the best results from data mining, you should start with an available computerized data set. Whatever the variety of sources from which it is compiled, it should be consolidated into a data warehouse for analysis, to ensure consistency across different business uses. If you have already established and implemented a clear business data model, then most of the required data should be available in the right form.

A key benefit – consistency

Many marketers are surprised by the simple gains made by warehousing. Not only are counts of strategically significant variables made more easy (eg the number of lost customers), but it also it enables a common 'language' to be used across marketing and IT, (eg What is a customer? What is a lost customer? What is a product? etc). The definitions of these variables are at last clarified – they have to be for the warehouse to be constructed. Table 4.1 gives some examples of some of the terms that are used rather loosely in marketing and for which data mining forces a tighter definition.

Once an agreed definition has been achieved, it becomes the 'corporate' definition. This removes one of the problems that is so common among users of large marketing data sets – agreement about the meaning of data.

Stages of construction of a warehouse

A warehouse should be constructed through the key stages of:

- audit (of sources and needs);
- design (logical and physical);
- extract of data from sources;

Table 4.1   Definitional consistency

Examples of Terms	Examples of Definitional Issues
Customer	A customer ranges from someone who transacts very infrequently with a company to one who transacts regularly. Some customers may still have a financial relationship with your company even if they have not made a single purchasing decision in favour of your company for a long time eg 20 years for some pension policy holders, several years for car owners who use non-franchise agencies
Lost Customer	Is a lost customer one who has stopped buying? If so, how do we know, particularly if the product has a long replacement cycle?
Loyal Customer	There are degrees of loyalty. In some cases, loyalty is binary – ie the customer buys from one supplier or another (eg the only family car, house contents insurance). In other cases, the customer may buy from several companies (eg detergents)
Cross-buyer	Does this mean buying several products at the same time or within a specified interval, or at any time, even if the customer no longer has the first product when he or she buys the second?
Satisfied Customer	Satisfaction is usually measured through surveys, with a scale ranging from very dissatisfied to very satisfied. In many cases, the middle point of the scale is labelled 'satisfied'. Does this really mean that the customer is satisfied, or that that are neither dissatisfied nor very satisfied (a very different way of looking at things – as they may be completely indifferent!)
Frequent user (eg flyer)	At what level of usage is a customer considered to be a frequent user? How long does he or she need to be in this category to be regarded as in it for a significant period?

- enhancement of data by addition/matching/analysis, etc;
- deduplication of data (hard or soft);
- loading data into the warehouse.

The update becomes key, determining how data is transferred from its sources into the warehouse on a regular basis, maintaining the currency and quality of data. Some data will be transferred back from the analysis data sets for operational use, eg segment indicators, propensity scores (for individuals), handling algorithms (for groups).

How closely are data warehousing and data mining linked?

A common mistake is to assume that the data warehousing work required to create the database for data mining to be applied is an integral part of data mining. Once a data warehouse has been created, many methods of analysing it can be used. It is not unusual to find that the data warehouse allows the company just to count certain frequencies for the first time. For example, an airline was able for the first time to identify all members of its frequent flyers programme who worked in specified large corporations, simply because the data warehousing operation led to a standardization of employer codes and company names.

Once this has been done, each user group can select their own most appropriate analysis tools to meet their needs. It is highly unlikely that one analytical approach will meet the needs of the many different marketing users. However, this requires an 'open' or 'non-proprietary' approach to storing data, enabling an open choice of tools, access and business use across all a company's departments.

The importance of metadata

As we shall see later, most data warehouses used in marketing are not 100 per cent comprehensive – the data warehoused is selective. It is chosen because hypotheses indicate that it is likely to be useful. A further issue is that much data in data warehouses is transformed ie not in the same form in which it appears in the source system. For example, most airlines do not hold data about 'day return behaviour', ie those who fly out and back in the same day. This behaviour has to be inferred from basic ticket purchase and user data. But in the data warehouse, it is important to have a variable indicating whether customers fly 'day return' often, because it means that they are less likely to use hotel services (unless as part of a special offer to encourage them to stay overnight).

Therefore, an important concept in warehousing is *metadata* – broadly speaking, data about how the warehouse has been developed which may include:

- which new variables have been created, from which existing variables (eg interpreting a flight out and back on the same day by the same customer as a day return);

- what formulae have been used to create the derived variables;
- how often tables are updated;
- how much data is in the warehouse.

There are different views about how to approach warehousing for data mining. Although we have stressed that it is important to start with analysable data sets that you have, there is a view that you must create a data warehouse with as much (within reason) data as possible. This is because data mining always leads to more questions, and if you haven't got the data to answer the questions, then the warehousing and mining exercise may be a waste of time.

One response to this is that companies don't want to create more questions, but rather want to move to take actions quickly. Neither approach is right or wrong. All we can suggest is that warehousing and mining are not once for all activities. That is to say, management learns from the experience. A data warehouse created as an archive to be analysed (rather than as an online warehouse which is continuously updated – a much more expensive proposition) will yield conclusions not only about which policies should be followed, but also about which additional data should be added to it. As creating an archive warehouse is not that expensive for large companies, you should not try to resolve this issue a priori.

Should the warehouse be online or batch?

Of course, every marketing manager would like to have all possible data in its most recently updated form immediately accessible and analysable. In practice, this is very expensive, and few companies take this approach, though some of those that do derive immense commercial benefit from it. In some cases, the data warehouse is accessible by customer-facing systems for constant adjustment of contact management to meet individual customer profiles. Data marts (see below) are often incorporated into customer-facing systems.

Right at the other extreme are companies that decide on a one-time sample data warehousing and mining activity, or those that just use data mining on their existing marketing database. This is often the first step in a long process of moving forward to a more sophisticated approach. However, if you feel that your company's understanding of the fundamental characteristics of its customers is relatively weak; or that your company has a poor record of acting upon segmentation findings, then we recommend that you start with a relatively simple approach, identifying stable strategic and response segments. Stability can of course be determined by repeating the warehousing and mining approach over an appropriate interval. The length of this interval depends upon the rate of change in your market. This is determined by factors such as:

- length of time a given buyer remains in the market (eg about five years for the typical frequent flyer);
- how fast customers move into and out of strategic segments;
- brand loyalty and customer attrition (will your customers be a totally different group in three years' time?)

The relationship between the data warehouse and source systems

We find it useful to distinguish five types of databases which hold marketing data, as shown in Table 4.2.

Table 4.2 Definitions of database types

Database Type	Basic Characteristics	How it is Used and Other Characteristics
Master Customer File	This holds the basic details identifying and allowing access to the customer, ie name, address, telephone numbers	It is often held within another database. In companies which transact directly with their customers (eg banks, mail order), it is held within the transactions database. For businesses which do not transact directly with their final customers, but through agents (eg airlines, FMCG), or where transactions are anonymous (eg retailers – although this does not apply to those with customer loyalty and credit cards) it is more likely to be held on the customer database
Operational or Transactions Database	Used to manage sales and service transactions with customers	There are usually several of these in most companies, perhaps used to manage transactions for different products or services
Customer Database	Provides a single, current, view of the customer – policies, relationships (household, family, commercial, etc)	This is built from operational data, which has been merged, cleaned, de-duplicated, sometimes using semi-automated or even manual processes, and often dependent for its quality on a highly skilled database administrator. It may be supported by customer notes. It may have different interfaces and will almost certainly be used by many different people, eg tied or franchised agents, telemarketing personnel, mailing houses. It should have smooth access to its source operational systems and becomes the accepted source of quality information about the state of the company's customer inventory
Marketing Database	Supports business and marketing planning. It provides a view of the business over time, because it holds details of current and past customers, and campaign prospects	It is used to drive campaigns and assists tracking of prospects and proposals. It tracks and supports the development of customer relationships over time. It is this database which may include data from external sources – lifestyle, psychographic and demographic, any segmentation codes, responses to test campaigns, questionnaire responses, etc. It is here that campaign selections are likely to be held, and any scoring algorithms. Note that some operational data may not be here, as it has been found not to be useful for marketing purposes. Note also that segmentation codes and scoring algorithms may be written back into the customer database, as they will be used at point of sale to a) determine which segments new customers belong to and how the customers are to be handled b) calculate appropriate, customized prices
Data Warehouse	This contains data from many of the above databases and possibly from still further databases, eg customer service (complaints and compliments)	This is constructed either for analysis or to provide a master standardized data set which other applications can use

It is dangerous to confuse these different types of database because they have very different processing requirements. For example, the customer database is interactive, accessed by all customer-facing staff. It is being updated constantly, increasingly seven days a week, 24 hours a day. Very limited time is therefore available for back-ups and implementing any changes required – which is why, once established, customer databases need to last for a long time. A customer database may be 'thin', just holding basic customer data. Or it may be 'thick', holding account balances and perhaps even recent transaction histories. This contrasts with the marketing database, which will also hold past customers and current and past prospects, and will also be enhanced with many other data sets, as described above. It is usually accessed in batch mode, for campaign selections, analyses and the like. This would prevent the interactive response required for the customer database. The aim of the marketing database is to encourage learning through analysis, trial selections and test campaigns. If a company were to try to do this on a customer database, either the time would simply not be available, or it would start to impede use of the customer database in dealing with customers.

These different databases require different types of database software to manage them. Their requirements for security, back-up, auditing, interactive and batch performance are very different. To our knowledge, there is as yet no product that optimizes all of them. Nor is it simply a matter of choosing software. Integration expertise is also required.

Warehouse hierarchies

The language of data warehousing is developing very quickly. Many companies have realized that the need to assemble data for a particular application is as great as the need to assemble it for the whole corporation. Putting it simply, there is no need to involve the whole corporation in data warehousing if there are clear signs that a particular area will benefit from it. This approach has led to the idea of the departmental warehouse or 'data mart' in transatlantic parlance. This is no more nor less than a warehouse built to meet a specific business need. Examples might include:

- All the data associated with identifying why customers retain or cancel insurance policies.
- All the data associated with identifying why people start and stop frequent flying.
- All the data associated with identifying which supermarket products are bought together by which kinds of customers.
- All the data associated with identifying which customers respond to which kinds of promotions through which media.

Initially, they were called functional warehouses because they met the needs of one function, eg marketing, or human resources. However, as we learn more about data warehousing, we are realizing that even within a function, there is enough complexity to warrant mini-marts, or sub-departmental warehouses. Of course, the eventual dream is one of consolidating all these mini-marts and marts, but the practicalities often indicate otherwise. In very large corporations, getting a consistent view about analysis and policy priorities within marketing is no easier than developing a consistent view across functions.

Data marts and mini-marts are easier to justify, build and maintain. They do not require consensus on technical issues such as data definitions and data ownership. They also allow implementation to be tuned to the needs of the users, so issues such as ownership and practical application tend to be less of a problem. Of course, even if your IT department works behind the scenes to try to ensure data compatibility by including the functional data warehouse in the corporate or departmental data model, there is still the risk that users will force the pace and always make the choice in favour of speed and against data compatibility.

This approach also enables the warehouse to be built in stages, with each addition fitting comfortably rather than adding complexity. Additions can then be prioritized and justified by business need.

BASIC TECHNIQUES OF DATA MINING

Data mining techniques are often classified as being either *discovery-led* or as *hypothesis-led* (also known as *verification-led*).

Discovery-led

This is the usual situation for new data mining users, as the first question is usually: 'How can the data I have help me solve my business problem(s)?' The aim is to use self-organizing methods to determine the nature of variation within the data, without preconceived ideas as to how the data might be organized. Thus, a company might believe it has three customer types – average customers: 'run of the mill' takers of the service or product; very good high-value customers; and bad customers: debtors or defaulters. A marketing campaign might aim to reduce defaulters while increasing cross-selling to high flyers. A discovery-led analysis of the data might show that there are several types of high flyers with different needs, or that defaulting is related to particular factors, to which some parts of the general group are also susceptible. The commonest approaches here include predictive modelling, segmentation and resegmentation (the latter involving successive reselection of segmentation variables as more is learnt about customers), deviation detection and link analysis.

Hypothesis-led or verification-led

This is the conventional approach of standard querying, reporting and statistical techniques. A hypothesis is formed as to which types of customer have which characteristics (eg those making them good prospects, those making them vulnerable to competition), and a test performed to see if this view has significant support from the data. While this approach is still valid, it does have the drawback that the hypothesis has to be invented before it can be tested, often requiring sophisticated understanding of both the data and the potential of various tools. Also, a hypothesis-led approach can lead to critical issues being missed. The hypothesis may be confirmed, but it may not be in the best form or as complete in coverage as it could be. However, later on, hypotheses come into their own as discovery techniques start to suggest new areas for hypothesis formation.

It may be better to use discovery-led procedures to identify potential hypotheses, and then to focus on particular factors for testing. For example, a general segmentation of customers into retail buying groups could suggest that there exists a large group of elderly couples on low incomes. The hypothesis that this group also correlates with those who take up low-premium insurance policies could then be hypothesized and tested.

Basic data mining operations for hypothesis or discovery-led work

Basic data mining operations can be classified into the generic activities of:

- correlation;
- segmentation;
- propensity.

These activities are defined below. The division between these three is not fixed – there is overlap between them. Some authors give a different division, although there is a good general agreement that this is an informative way to consider the various types. Within each type there are many individual methods, and each method may be applied to a number of different business problems. Note too that each method can be used as part of a discovery approach or a hypothesis approach. For example, we could ask 'Which factors are related to each other, and how well, and which are more related to each other than to other factors?' (Discovery-led), or 'Is factor X related to factor Y, and if so, to what extent and how significantly?' (Hypothesis-led). It is the sheer volume of the data that pushes companies towards discovery-led approaches, because of the difficulty of determining which factors to hypothesize about!

Correlation (or association, or sequencing – if over time)

How does one factor relate to another? Or, more generally, how does a group of factors relate to some other group of factors. Simple correlations (whether linear or some other form, eg algebraic, rank) between two factors, usually with an associated confidence factor, are the easiest to understand. Income correlates with the propensity to buy retailer own brands. But whether higher income causes this behaviour is a different question, not answered by that analysis, but suggested by it. The hypothesis that higher income causes more buying of own brands may depend on a psychological argument about a diminishing need for the reassurance provided by a manufacturer's brand.

In retailing this is known as 'basket analysis', for obvious reasons. For example, an association model trained on transactions in a retail grocery store might learn that there is a group of identified customers who buy bacon with eggs. The store might want to place bacon and eggs close together for customer convenience, or far apart to ensure that the customers see other products that they might be tempted to buy. Customers found to buy gin and tonic might be offered coupons for a different gin type when they buy tonic. Sequencing is association over time and is a key area for applying data mining, as if buying or response behaviour is very frequent (eg grocer retailing, frequent flying), then data mining is required to explore possible patterns.

Segmentation (or classification)

This involves defining classes and assigning individuals to a particular class based on one or more criteria. For example, a set of customers can be classified according to age, or according to home location. It typically tells us little about the members of the resulting groups as there is still high variability in each group. Multi-dependency classifications can be created by techniques such as neural nets, which learn to discriminate between individuals based on a composite view of their behaviour. For example, a neural net trained on product-buying activity could learn the past behaviour of customers and be used to predict if new ones would or would not buy the product.

Cluster analysis, or clustering, is a generic term for forming groups generally by bottom-up methods (grouping similar items together using some numeric criterion of proximity), and seeing what groups emerge. The groups are chosen such that they maximize the differences between the groups, while minimizing the differences within each group. There is no prior decision on which groups might exist, or which factors may be important. Relational analysis is used to associate similar customers and put them in the same group. It is a particular method of clustering, and uses Condorcet scoring (see below) to define similar items, and a particular ranking strategy (block seriation) to sort the items once it is known how similar they are.

A method of ranking preferences was first proposed by the Marquis de Condorcet at the time of the French Revolution for electing the least unacceptable politician, and has been adapted to the task of choosing the least controversial clustering of customer groups. The characteristics of each group can then be examined. For example, a segmentation of bank customers might show that older, retired couples in the UK have smaller mortgages than middle-aged couples with children. Very often the segments found do not correspond to exact definitions, as are found by a data enquiry. They do however show tendencies that all the members in a group follow to some degree.

Segmentation is a much-abused term, and carries with it the dangerous implication that once grouped, all customers within the group behave in the same way. In some companies or industries, the use of the term implies the use of certain determining variables (eg geodemographic, industry sector), even though these may not be the most important dimensions by which customer behaviour differs. Segmentation is the process of separating out groups of customers who are similar (but not the same). Some segmentation methods presuppose that the number of groups is known, and try to find them. Other methods assume that only large groups are important and try to find all such groups. Some methods require an estimate of the typical members of the group, and attempt to find all the other less typical members, other methods try to find the typical members at the cost of including some who are not typical.

Propensity (including prediction and scoring)

Given certain types of things, what can be expected for the remainder ? This type of analysis can be considered as an extension of either correlation or segmentation, but is often used in different ways. For example, 'How likely are policy holders to lapse?' and 'Do buyers of toothpaste also purchase razors?' can both be phrased as propensity questions: 'What is the propensity of X to be associated with Y?' Special techniques exist to do this type of study, and there are applications in diverse areas such as market basket analysis, and customer loyalty.

Propensity involves the process of learning what are the important factors that predispose to a particular type of action, such that a numerical score can be assigned to some event. This is typically done by fitting an optimization function on the multi-dimensional data, and measuring the difference between a given individual or group and the general behaviour of all the groups. For example, a predictive model fitted to the lapsing behaviour of an insurance company's customers can assign a numerical probability to the likelihood that some group of customers might lapse. The size of the group can be used to calculate the risk to the company, and the features of the group to plan a marketing plan aimed at retaining those customers.

Prediction (or propensity modelling) of likely customer actions and characteristics (eg to lapse, to remain loyal, to be stable, to buy more, to be profitable) is the key to financial services scoring and direct marketing, but the same mindset is transferring to many other areas of marketing. In many cases, companies want to apply these ideas at the point of contact with the customer (eg so that appropriate offerings can be made at the point of contact). The ability to do this has been enhanced by the use of telephone channels and laptop computing (eg for financial services sales staff) – they both allow additional data to be collected from the customer and input into a scoring module. Of course, there needs to be appropriate and efficient scripting to support the staff member handling the customer.

Identifying 'key questions' and logic structures for scripting is critical to effective use of customers' telephone time and maximizing sales and profitability. Scripting can now be much more dynamic and dependent on customer responses. It can also use latest version of algorithms which can be easily modified on a regular (learning) basis. In financial services, this is also necessary to conform to new regulatory requirements (eg for fact finds, where there is a need to demonstrate that the quality of data collection is high, and that needs analysis and financial advice are appropriate). Penalties for not conforming are such that a channel or business could be closed down by the regulator overnight!

Following prediction should come testing. This is usually a sample-based marketing activity to validate the prediction – or discover where it does not work. Data mining techniques can be easily adapted to this process. From discovery of several segments of high-value customers can be built a model to predict high-value customers, and then to test whether the prediction proved accurate when applied to new customer data sets.

Figure 4.1 is a simple flow chart describing these issues is shown below, though note that many of these approaches are used in parallel or sequentially.

WHEN TO USE PARTICULAR TECHNIQUES

A good start point is simple counts and percentages, particularly if the company has had no previous access to the data because of the absence of a data warehouse. This also provides a cross-check for more complex analysis techniques later. Each marketing user will have his or her own analyses to conduct. Direct marketers, for example, will want to analyse frequency, recency, amount and category of purchase.

There is an argument that statistical hypothesis-based techniques can be omitted, as discovery data mining techniques will create and test hypotheses automatically. However, these techniques can be used to statistically test the discovery models built through data mining, to increase confidence in the results. Discovery techniques can be used at any or all stages – but as part of the complete approach. Data mining techniques are not rocket science and can be used at any stage. Even if a company wants to identify just three or four simple segments, these are better developed using data mining discovery techniques than assuming that standard marketing approaches (eg based on geographical or social segmentation, or product purchasing) will provide a good foundation for segmentation.

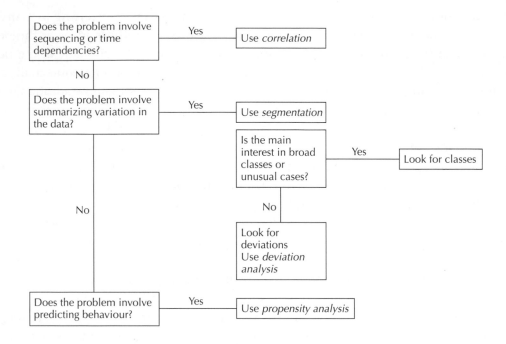

Figure 4.1 Choosing techniques

Simple tools still need to be used in combination with discovery data mining to extract and prepare data for analysis, provide check-counts, etc. Also, after the discovery analysis, some tidying-up may need to be done before acting on the data (eg if a segment is primarily, but not all, elderly people, the company may want to extract exceptions before running a targeted campaign addressing elderly customers' needs). Making data analysable can include:

- joining data (eg about same customer or situation);
- improving data quality, where inconsistencies occur over time;
- construction of new fields (eg counts, derived indicators, etc);
- removal of fields which are inappropriate or misleading to an analysis.

CURRENT DATA MINING AND WHY WE KNOW IT WORKS

There is a new enthusiasm for understanding of customers, needs and required actions – often driven by extreme market pressures (eg the 'insurance war'). Some (eg retailers, airlines and some banks) are now collecting client transaction data for analysis. However, many companies have yet to achieve this – but are keen to achieve early benefits from analysis of existing data sources (primarily legacy systems, holding product rather than customer information).

Some companies are specifically going to their customers to collect new data via survey, then analysing it as quickly as possible for customer insights. This gives them better understanding of clients and is based on the idea that if we can segment our customers (perhaps only a few simple segments), understand them (perhaps through segment-focused research of their needs), and apply different offerings to their segmented needs, then we should have happier and more profitable customers! Understanding may be helped by modelling scenarios of interdependence (eg if we reduce price of product X by 5 per cent for specific customers, what is the effect on volume, cost recovery, profit, and on the business risk profile?).

It is just such questions that companies are starting to highlight in publicity designed to show the financial markets how competent their managers are. Companies highlight their data mining projects in annual reports – to demonstrate that their innovative actions are paying off. More importantly, these younger customers have a high expected lifetime value.

Industries which use data mining in marketing include those which have recently either: started to develop very large additional data sets, perhaps because starting to use direct techniques in integrated operations companies (eg utilities, retail cards); or have been gathering these data sets for some time and are now in situation where better analysis is more important (recent competitive pressure) or have realized that data holds clues to competitive advantage (eg frequent flyer programmes, retail product data).

Major user industries therefore include:

- financial services (banking and insurance);
- retail and distribution;
- telecommunications and utilities;
- travel and transportation.

Back to hypotheses

It is worth noting that – for a smart marketing manager – nearly all these findings are ones which could have been expected, if only there was time to formulate the relevant hypotheses. What we find is that busy marketing managers rarely have the time to do this, as they tend to be drowned in operational problems. However, the kind of gains achieved from data warehousing and mining projects when they do make the time to develop hypotheses indicate how essential it is to make the time. This is especially so when it is taken into account that most warehouses are data marts or mini-marts, in which the company has made a positive choice about which variables to warehouse. Clearly, it is only possible to make sensible decisions about which variables to warehouse if the criteria for choosing includes the kind of hypotheses that marketing management wishes to test. For example, basket analysis by itself of limited use. It only pays off in the context of category management and assortment planning. A grocery store knows that people who buy lettuce and tomatoes may also buy bacon. But proving that those who buy a head lettuce tend also to buy tinned vegetables is not so obvious a pairing.

Problem stories

However, for every one of the success stories mentioned above, there is one (and usually several) problem stories. Companies have learnt what data mining is through various media but have not fully understood how to use it to support specific strategies. By itself, the analysis is not worth much. Unsuccessful data mining assignments are often due to lack of investment of time, resource and intellect in defining the business issue or opportunity.

In financial services there has been much segmentation work, scoring, etc, over many years, and so it has been possible to put data mining into a well-established perspective. So, projects have been defined as outcomes of a discussion of business issues, usually involving those responsible for creating or sustaining business together with IT staff. In such assignments, data has invariably been an issue. Much of the data had to be extracted from legacy systems on flat files and then worked on to make it meaningful. This requires considerable input from business managers, to help determine the valid attributes.

Senior management commitment is very important as without it a small data mining project can easily be dismissed as an interesting piece of technical analysis. In most cases, outside consulting expertise has been needed to assist the company to use the mined information and to get value from it. This is because so often users of the information will not be experts, eg customer contact staff who will have to be trained to manage the 'new' type of information or 'sell' from it (for example, identify at point of contact whether a customer fits a new category unearthed by data mining).

As we have mentioned above, the data issue can usually be addressed by building a data warehouse from which appropriate data can be drawn, and which becomes the platform for all future information requirements. For companies with such warehouses, data mining should be fairly easily incorporated into their strategy/activity to manage customer value. Results vary tremendously, but if the project is properly defined initially and has a team of company staff and external marketing and data experts working on it, with knowledge of what is to be done with the information and systems in place to do it, the outcome can be very productive and can even set the company safely on the road to managing customers differently, eg by CRM.

QUANTIFYING THE BENEFITS

Interestingly, detailed studies with numerical results are rarely undertaken, although as experience of the possible returns grows, it has become possible to estimate the gains prior to commissioning the work. Much data mining today is still done for reasons of curiosity and sometimes prestige! The main questions which the potential data mining user should ask include the following.

The likely exposure if the business problem is not solved

If the likely exposure is high then a data mining investigation is strongly indicated. But if the exposure is low, and an urgent solution not indicated, a data mining investigation aimed at simple discovery can still be worthwhile. Here, the aim is to build up confidence that the tools being used do produce interesting and believable results with available data. The user will be ready to react if the exposure increases arise, and if unexpected results occur during discovery early actions can be taken to assess any exposures.

The likely benefit of changing policy using improved knowledge

Suppose that a 1 per cent improvement in customer loyalty or market penetration, etc, can be obtained, what is the benefit? Companies with tight profit margins often find that a small improvement is very significant as it is multiplied over many cases. A retention project with a non-life insurer showed that each 1 per cent increase in retention percentage was worth more than £1 million per annum straight on the bottom line! Most companies interested in and capable of data mining also have very large customer databases, or product portfolios, so that small improvements in managing them leads to sizable profit increases or new business opportunities.

The cost of not doing enough analysis to gain useful understanding

Major analyses of large customer or transactions databases take some time, but sample investigations can be carried out quickly. The factors to bear in mind are:

- How quickly is the answer required?
- How precise does the answer need to be?
- Will the enquiry be repeated, or is it unique?

The answers to these questions determine how much should be spent on each project. Finding accurate answers to new problems in a hurry is costly. However, the amount and detail of the data mining can be adjusted on an almost infinite scale to the needs and capabilities of the requester.

Benefits likely from integrating decision support into policy making

This may be hard to assess, as business processes change over time, and the relevance of a given type of business decision may not be constant. A change in business process such as method of data collection (eg telesales versus third party agents), or introducing new technology (eg smart cards versus magnetic cards for customer loyalty schemes) may change the cost–benefit ratio of a particular business decision. If market penetration is high the opportunity for increased market share may be low. For example, if the risk attached to a higher-than-average lapse rate increases, a continuous process of assessing lapse risk may be justified, while continual resegmentation to understand market share may not.

The following additional questions may be asked.

'What behaviour should I expect, taking into account the general behaviour of my own customers?' This can usually be answered from the company's own data. This type of question has been successfully dealt with and good techniques exist.

'What behaviour should I expect, taking into account the general behaviour in my target market, or of customers in general?' This is harder to answer as it requires detailed knowledge of market-wide factors, or even factors outside the target market. This is unlikely to be readily available in the depth needed for data mining. Our recommendation is therefore to start with comparisons within the customer base. Note that this restricts the likely benefit of customer-focused data mining to companies that already have large customer bases and good data on them.

THE IMPORTANCE OF VISUALIZATION

The need for visualization

Data mining is an advanced technique, and its results are complex. It identifies groups of customers and patterns of behaviour. These patterns are derived from analysis of possibly hundreds of variables, and are therefore not usually amenable to presentation using standard statistical techniques – ranging from tables of raw statistics or of derived statistics such as correlation coefficients to one or more multivariate equations. Visualization techniques for simple univariate data and multivariate data when there are not too many dimensions include bar charts, pie diagrams, vector plots, box-and-whisker diagrams and so on. Graphs and 3D surfaces are popular for low-dimensional data. Higher-dimensional data, such as customer records with 20 factors, are not usually easy to visualize.

The advantage of visualization over more direct tabular, or numeric, displays is that the shape of distributions which do not fit typical patterns can be more easily understood. For example, a factor that correlates well with 10 per cent of the data items in a set may be seen only as noise from the point of view of a statistical fit. However, when visualized it might form a particular group of outliers, which might in turn suggest a new type of analysis to identify this small but interesting group.

Some types of analysis techniques can do a very good job of partitioning the data into interesting subsets, but provide little in the way of explanation as to why the particular sets have been chosen. In some cases the explanation may be self-evident, or more easily understood when properly visualized. In other cases, the reason that a particular member has been placed in a given set is often not obvious. The role of explanation-based methods is that they attempt to extract *rules* from the data which can be used to justify the placement of the item. For example, a neural net classifier may divide customers into good and bad prospects for telemarketing. Or for a cross-selling analysis, a fuzzy logic rule induction process may be able to extract the explanation that a given customer has been classified as *good* because he is a high-earning, middle-aged, conservative-preference person. Especially in cases such as credit scoring, there is often a need (sometimes a legal requirement) to justify why a service is given (or denied) to certain customers.

The central benefit of visualization is that huge amounts of data can be reduced to key messages which can be understood very quickly by the busy marketing manager. Our experience of working with marketing managers is that although they may agree the importance of improving analysis, they are often unable to dedicate the time required to understanding its outcomes. 'Understanding' is not identical with 'viewing output'. It means taking the output and interpreting it in the light of what the manager knows about customers and the marketing mix. If the process of taking in the output can be shortened, then more time can be devoted to understanding its implications. In many cases, it is unwise for more senior management to try to delegate understanding to more junior managers, because it is precisely the senior managers' experience and wisdom that needs to be combined with the output for true understanding.

Of course, the easier the output is to absorb, the greater the danger of oversimplification. For this reason, data mining should be treated as a learning exercise, in which the marketing 'brain' is learning:

- How to understand new customer groupings and ask further questions about patterns (groups, behaviours, etc) identified.
- How to test the answers by developing new marketing strategies and tactics.
- How to return to the underlying data to understand the situation case by case.

A visualization technique

A good example of the visualization process is that used by the IBM product Intelligent Miner. This shows an exploration of a particular customer's data, to find the natural segments that its customers belong to. According to whether the variable concerned is continuous or discrete, it describes the segment characteristic as a roundel (the centre roundel is the segment distribution of the variable, the outer circle is the population), or a histogram (where the outline is the sample and the solid is the population). It lists the variables in order of their importance in differentiating the segment from other segments. The relative size of each segment is clearly indicated by the width of the band on the left. This simple visualization technique allows managers with little of no knowledge of statistics to grasp the essentials of the data mining findings. Our experience in meetings with these managers is that it quickly transforms their attitude to data mining – it is no longer seen as a black box technique. But more importantly, they can immediately see the business conclusions and are spurred to action. In one case, a high-value segment was identified which responded very little to promotions, because the displayed product purchasing pattern was completely at variance with the products supported by promotions. The manager went away to redesign his whole promotional programme.

LEVELS OF INVOLVEMENT IN DATA MINING

Some companies are reluctant to start data mining because they cannot see how long, or how complex the operation will be. Others start with grand plans of analysing everything only to be disappointed when progress is slow. Here we show how to minimize exposure to failure, while maximizing the comfort with the success of the work done.

The importance of a clear programme for using results

In general, a clear programme for using outcomes is the key. The company must have some idea of what the analysis is for, and how the answer fits into the business process. Given this, the way to control risk and maximize benefits is to start with small-scale samples which can be easily analysed, and increase the scale and applicability as experience builds. Here are four suggested levels of involvement.

Exploratory investigation

An exploratory investigation into data with reference to some particular question. This may involve no more than a few days' work to establish the credibility of the methodology, and to indicate the likelihood of producing the sort of answers needed by the business. The objective of the operations is to agree the approach, the methodology and the tools, and to plan further work.

Business question solution

This involves a substantial piece of work to establish definitive answers to particular questions. Typically a large amount of data is extracted and processed, either as offline data, or in a data warehouse constructed for the purpose. Considerable care is applied to extraction and cleaning of the data, and a number of different aspects of the same problem are investigated. The work takes several weeks of effort by a dedicated data mining person, usually in collaboration with an industry specialist. The result is a definitive report on the factors affecting the business question, and on which judgements for future business activity can be based.

Repeatable process

The data and methodology now exist to repeat processing in a given area of need. The need now is for a process to manage it. Thus, customer resegmentation may be needed weekly in a supermarket. A solution which can be used by company staff of the appropriate skill level to repeat a specified analysis, eg daily, weekly, monthly, etc, is now needed. Components of the data mining tool-kit can be set up to access data from a business data warehouse which is continually updated from operational databases. This requires additional programming and systems integration over and above the data mining insights. Its objective is to create an industrial-strength repeatable process to solve one or more limited business problems.

Decision support infrastructure

This is a total solution, including hardware, software, consultancy, design and implementation to implement a new way of analysing marketing data – in effect a form of process re-engineering. This usually involves creating data warehouses for specified purposes, integration and cleaning of data from many sources, and selecting data mining tools for both discovery-led and hypothesis-led analyses.

Generalized and specific decisions

There are, however, two basic kinds of decision that can be supported by data mining. One is what could be called the generalized marketing decision – for example, on which groups of customers to focus, what to offer them. The other is the specific customer decision – what to do with a specific customer, particularly when the customer is in contact with the company. While much of this briefing has concerned the former, use of data mining for the latter is becoming increasingly common, particularly in inbound telemarketing situations, where a decision has to be made what to offer the customer, or even whether to offer anything at all to the customer. Here, data mining can be built into the software, allowing frequent or even continuous reanalysis of the results of customer contact (eg which kinds of customers are contacting the company, which kinds of customers are accepting the offer) to determine how the next customer should be treated.

SYSTEMS AND PROCESSES

Architecture

A data mining architecture is one which gives a framework within which the enterprise can plan and manage its data collection and analysis techniques. It is related to an architecture for data warehousing – for creating and maintaining a company's data assets so that it can mine data. Data mining will logically fit in a layered system structure shown in Table 4.3 and illustrated in Figure 4.2.

Table 4.3 System structure for data mining

Data Warehouse	Provides data access and manipulation functions. It handles problems of extracting and synchronising data
Data Mining Analysis Functions	Provides kernels for the generic data mining analytical functions (eg segmentation)
Data Mining Analysis and Visualization Layer	Provides interactive analysis and visualization tools for an analyst to use
Data Mining Application	Provides operational support for data analysis functions which need to be repeated at intervals, for example weekly, or monthly analysis of buying behaviour, etc
Marketing and Sales Applications	Data mining is often an analytical support for a marketing or sales process, eg direct marketing campaigns. Products such as Target from CPM incorporate a data mining module, allowing the outcomes of data mining to be translated directly into campaign targeting, telemarketing scripts or triggering individual customer contacts based on facts about customers gathered during the marketing process (eg via questionnaires). This applies particularly to situations where scoring is an integrated part of the marketing application. At an earlier stage of the marketing cycle, data mining techniques can be used to improve data quality (usually in a data fusion module)

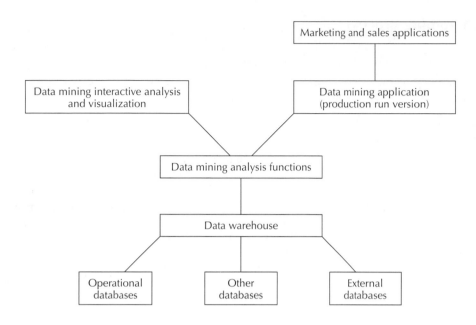

Figure 4.2 A schematic view of the relationship between data mining and a data warehouse

System bases for data mining

These may include the following.

Workstation basis

These typically have very good GUI and visualization. They are often limited in the size of problem they can tackle, speed of execution and robustness. Such tools are good for exploration and presentation, but not for repeated process work.

Mainframe basis

These typically have industrial strength, and scalability, but lack visual and interactive interfaces. Such tools are good for production use, but difficult to use for exploration and investigation.

Client–server basis

Where each part of the systems architecture plays its role (eg *client PC* or similar) displays data, and provides nice user-interface; *server* (eg mainframe or dedicated parallel processing computer) analyses huge quantities of data.

The data mining process

The operations shown in Table 4.4 are used in a data mining analysis of a customer database. The operations are usually in this order, although some steps may need to be iterated to achieve a good analysis.

Table 4.4 Data mining operations

Data Collection and Cleaning	**Extract** data from customer databases	• Identify the information required for the study • Extract it from the customer database
	Map data field to variable names	• Establish correspondence of data fields in records to names specified in data description • Title file for fixed records, no method for free-form data • Check mappings
	Construct tables for analysis	• Relational database type operations for combining various sources of information to create suitable set of data to analyse, eg **join project, select, abstract** • Create new variables by algebraic operations on variables • Create new cases by splitting/combining cases
	Substitute data values	• Proper treatment of missing values, bad values, etc • Select out-of-range values • Convert text/numeric items • Scale/reformat fields (eg dates, amounts, etc) • Input preprocessor does some functions
Data Analysis	**Process** data tables	• Perform a range of statistical functions on the data • Segmentation, etc
	Compare analyses	• Interpret evidence for/against hypotheses • Compare various different analyses • Use other statistical packages to validate, etc
Data Visualization	**Visualization** of results	• Demonstrate interpreted results by visual methods • Show segmentation pictorially
	Report generation	• Determine format of reports likely to be acceptable • Identify possible reports • Prioritize reports by business need • Include reports at various levels – from fundamental data analysis (eg counts), through missing data, to advanced segmentation

MANAGEMENT RECOMMENDATIONS

In this chapter we have reviewed our experience of being involved in data mining projects. Table 4.5. identifies some key points for managers to take into account before or during data mining projects. The reasons for the recommendation or issues highlighted by it are summarized in the right-hand column.

Table 4.5 Recommendations

Recommendation	Reason/Issue
Tools and Techniques	
1. Use the right tools for the problem and establish modest gains, but beware of wasting effort on fruitless avenues, or overambitious projects	It is easy to become very enthusiastic about the techniques, when there may be no major commercial gain. Aiming too high may lead to poor performance relative to goals, but this could lead to unjustified abandonment of the approach
2. Avoid techniques that are not scalable (as samples will not normally be representative enough)	It is sensible to start with smaller amounts of data to prove the concept, but as the variety of patterns in the data is likely to be large, it is unwise to assume they are exactly replicated in larger data sets
3. Avoid tools which do not yield business insights and are 'black box'	Many managers have tried using neural techniques by themselves, and this has led to dissatisfaction because the reasons for outcomes are not understood. But such techniques have their place alongside other techniques which provide results where causation is more transparent
4. Understand that data will only tell so much, taking the company one step further forward, confirming some things that are known and discovering others	Outcomes often appear self-evident in general terms, but bring much greater precision, eg not just that there are many customers like X, but precisely how many, and who they are
5. Don't jump to conclusions – create hypotheses and investigate them thoroughly (eg through customer focus groups or market research) before acting	Very often, the first results look so plausible that managers are happy to take them as final conclusions – but there may be other factors at work which need to be probed
6. Measure the value, identify further improvements and reapply the approach to gain further benefit	This ensures that the approach is not vulnerable because it delivers no business benefit. Good analysis is just the first step to improving business results
7. Use a clear methodology, including which techniques will be used and how and where they can be applied.	This ensures that all involved in the project know what is going on, have a good opportunity to understand it, and have their concerns or objections dealt with
Project Management	
1. Make the approach business-driven, focusing on a key issue or business opportunity to gain	As with all systems projects, it is best to focus attention on areas of agreed priority. This does not make it more risky, because the approach can be tried on a small sample of data within the priority area
2. Use an audit and/or workshop to determine what data is appropriate and can be used for this business issue	This is one of the best ways of ensuring that all staff with an interest in the project outcomes are consulted beforehand, and that they contribute their expertise to help define which data should be analysed and in what form, eg in creating the data warehouse
3. Get real sponsorship from senior management, to guarantee positive motivation and action	Data mining projects commonly produce nice analyses which are not taken further. The sponsorship should come from conviction that the approach will deliver important results

Table 4.5 *continued*

Recommendation	Reason/Issue
4. Ensure that senior management understands that the learning is not just about the data, but also about how the company approaches it, and that mistakes will be made along the way	First data mining projects are tough, for various reasons, ranging from poor data and demonstration of lack of business priorities, to revelation of poor understanding of customers. However, if this is accepted at the beginning, staff are more likely to continue cooperating as the project continues
5. Use professional resources from within the company and suppliers, ones that understand the business problem and the data available	The team is critical – an unbalanced team, with too strong a representation from either IT or marketing staff or supplier, may lead the project to focus on one aspect, eg the data problem, rather than on the need for business results
6. Define 'deliverables' from the analysis exercise to provide the business professionals with the decision data they need	This might be segmentation which yields a much improved response rate, or which provides the strong basis for a new product specification. Without such a basis, the analysis can go on forever
7. Ensure that the necessary funds and priority are allocated within each involved department (eg marketing and IT, etc)	There is nothing so wasteful as a project which runs out of money half way. Careful definition of goals and development of the project plan by experienced professionals gives the basis for firm budgeting. The budget should then be committed
8. Develop a team approach, rather than one in which experts go away and come back with results	This ensures that successive redefinition of approach – common in data mining projects – is always undertaken with business input
9. Make sure that the required marketing concepts, eg in CRM, the ideas of customer acquisition, retention, and development, are well established	If the analysis turns out major problems in conceptual areas that are not understood, the pay-off will take much longer. This does not mean that these areas should not be pursued, but it does mean that pay-offs in areas that are understood should be sought
10. Understand the real costs of the approach (usually dominated by time of skilled staff)	The big devourers of staff time include data preparation, gaining input from staff about the business situation, and interpreting the results
11. Create a vision for the longer term, but take practical time-delimited project steps to achieve real business benefit at every stage	If the project is seen as a one-off and not a new way of understanding customers and markets, it will not get the support it needs
Suppliers 1. If necessary, use outside consultants that can contribute possibilities and proven methods and show other companies where mining has worked	This is not a sales pitch, but a recognition that experience of working in and managing data mining projects increases the speed and cost-effectiveness of future projects

Table 4.5 *continued*

Recommendation	Reason/Issue
2. Use an experienced business partner (total solution supplier), at least to start with, including for the provision of practical consulting/ experience in this business area, supported by a wide range of technical analysis skills and tools (and of course data warehouse, end-to-end design, etc)	Problems are rarely confined to one area – they usually include data preparation, agreement between different marketing staff about what needs to be analysed, project definition, and so on. With an experienced supplier, many problems can be anticipated and dealt with before they become serious
3. Select a business partner/s to work with on a long-term basis, rather than shopping around at every stage	Switching suppliers increases the costs of the approach, and decreases its reliability, because learning is lost, while company staff have to spend more time briefing suppliers and getting used to working with them

5

Analysis requirements

Merlin Stone

This chapter is different from the other chapters in this book, in that it contains a listing! This listing was produced because in so many CRM consulting projects, one of the key requirements is to get marketing managers to think clearly about the kinds of analysis and reporting that they would need to carry out on their customer information. There is no implication that any company needs to do all, or indeed any, of this analysis. However, for companies that have decided that they need to do more analysis in this area, it gives a pretty comprehensive checklist. This provides a basis for discussion of:

- What the value of the analysis or reporting is.
- What actions might be taken as a result of what might be found.
- What business benefits would arise from those actions.
- A conclusion as to whether the analysis or reporting is therefore worth undertaking.

So, this is a fairly comprehensive listing of some key data analysis and reporting requirements needed to establish and improve customer management, in either a direct or an intermediated environment. In the latter case, reference is made to the supplier and retailer, irrespective of whether the latter is actually a retailer as conventionally described, or another kind of agent. Of course, it does not cover all kinds of analysis – CRM has become such a widespread discipline that it is impossible to anticipate all requirements. However, the idea is that a company might take this as a starting point, using the structure to develop more ideas, and then filter them down to the profitable ones (rather than just generating an unstructured wish-list).

Each section is covered by:

- Identifying the objectives.
- The general analytical requirement, ie what needs to be identified from the analysis to support the objectives.
- The detailed types of analysis to be carried out to fulfil this requirement.

Under detailed types of analysis, it is assumed that both absolute and comparative statistics (eg growth rates, comparison to overall figures, regional/area league tables) are needed. In most cases, a control group is required to check effectiveness versus the no-action option, and take out the effect of independent changes (eg general growth trends, effect of other promotional efforts, competitive actions). The analysis must also cope with discontinuous variables, which are critical in analysing both time series and cross-section data. Examples include competitive actions (product launches, sales and other promotional campaigns) and qualitative variables (eg changes in the supplier's marketing and sales policy). Where possible, these variables should be standardized and indexed, so that they can be treated quantitatively, but this may not always be possible. Treatment of these variables requires some creative thinking, but must be dealt with, given the importance of the cross-section approach in interpreting performance.

PRE-RELATIONSHIP PLANNING

This applies to planning the set-up of different relationship types and identification of groups of customers to be managed in significantly different ways, either by supplier, retailer or both.

Objectives

To determine what are the main variables by which relationship types are to be defined, for example:

- contact media (sales force, telemarketing, mail, catalogue);
- contact frequency;
- information exchanged during relationship;
- positioning of relationship (branding, value-added, etc);
- buying behaviour, as measured by FRAC (Frequency of purchase, Recency – of last purchase, Amount bought – volume and/or value, and Category bought, ie types of products);

- loyalty – actual share, state of mind (ie what does customer think about the company versus the competition), propensity to be loyal (eg does customer always buy at the lowest price);
- estimated lifetime value.

To determine what is the optimum number and types of relationship the supplier is to offer. This is determined by:

- variety in customer needs and behaviour patterns (eg how varied are their needs and behaviour – the greater the variety, the greater the need to manage customers in different groups);
- the supplier's ability to manage a number of different groups (ie the supplier's relationship management capabilities – systems, procedures, skills, etc);
- competitive policies (eg if a competitor has defined a group to include customers of particular strategic importance to the supplier and has found a good way to manage relationships with them, then the supplier needs to improve on this).

To determine the boundaries between relationship types. Boundaries may be fixed in terms of, for example:

- amount and category of spend over a particular period (actual and/or potential);
- industry types;
- customer relationship needs (eg a customer may request a different kind of relationship, or prefer contact via a particular medium).

To support testing of the different levels of incentives, benefits and customer commitment (eg minimum spend level, giving of information via questionnaire) that are optimum for each type of customer group, relationship management must be not only effective, but efficient. Investing too much cost in a particular relationship may cause it to become unprofitable. As a relationship is launched and then extended to cover more customers, its cost-effectiveness must be measured in terms of return on investment.

To determine what the possibilities are of customer dissatisfaction for those on the borderline of relationship types (eg those just placed in a category with lower frequency/intensity of contact but requiring the benefits of the next level up). This is achieved by analysis of expenditure (volume/value) of those just on different sides of the relationship dividing line.

To determine what kinds of promotion are most likely to pull customers into their 'best fit' relationship type.

Analytical/reporting requirement

Whether there are significant clusters of customers, measured by, for example:

- amount and category of spend (FRAC, estimated lifetime value);
- relationship need;
- contact media/ frequency, etc;
- buying behaviour, including loyalty (note that loyalty/share data may require collection of data by customer contact staff or commissioning of research).

How far these clusters overlap.

Whether the clusters are 'real', in the sense of being significantly different from other groups of customer, durable and not spurious or accidental. Durability will be demonstrated through time series analysis, to find out whether pattern of behaviour persists and/or is developing in right direction.

Whether the clusters are large and actually/potentially profitable enough to be managed as a separate type.

Whether there is a match between relationship need of each cluster and the kind of relationship that the supplier is likely to be able to deliver.

Detailed analysis/reporting required

FRAC versus loyalty, overall and for each industry type; past time series on this, and estimated lifetime value; contact histories (contacts made and results), overall and for different categories of FRAC, loyalty, product, industry, etc.

CONTINUING RELATIONSHIP MANAGEMENT

Objectives

To determine whether the quantitative and qualitative boundaries between customer types remain the optimum.

To determine whether the relationship offered (contact media and frequency, level of benefits/incentives offered, information given/required) remains the optimum.

To identify which types of sales initiative and promotion work best for different customer types.

To identify opportunity areas for achieving customer migration to higher-spend types.

Where boundaries between customer types are changed, to identify which customers should be targeted for move to particular other types.

Analytical/reporting requirement

Whether the clusters as defined at initiation of CRM are still appropriate and, if not, what the new clusters should be.

Numbers of customers affected by any change in boundaries between customer types.

Which methods of contact and promotional types work best for customers affected by change.

Key trends in demographics of each type of customer (numbers of customers who fit definition, volume/value of purchasing, etc).

Evolving customer service and relationship needs of each customer type.

Detailed analysis/reporting required

Continuing trends in FRAC versus loyalty, overall and for each industry type and for major product categories; trends in contact histories and responsiveness to contacts (as measured by FRAC), overall and for different categories of FRAC, loyalty, product, industry.

CUSTOMER RECRUITMENT, RETENTION AND COMPETITIVE DEFENCE

Objectives

To provide clear definition of which customers who are not currently in a relationship with the supplier should be targeted for recruitment, taking into account their quality, creditworthiness, likely persistence, etc.

To identify which customers are most at risk of or actually experiencing declining spend or completely inactive relationship with the supplier (taking into account past frequency and recency of purchase) and the reasons for this.

To identify which actions (contacts, offers, etc) are most likely to prevent these customers from reducing or cancelling their commitment to the supplier and which actions are most likely to regenerate their commitment.

To identify numbers and types of non-spending customers and evaluate the results of campaigns designed to stimulate them into use.

To evaluate the requirement for actions to stimulate customers who only buy rarely or customers gained from competition into continued purchasing activity.

Analytical/reporting requirement

Different ways to segment actual and potential customers by potential or actual propensity to become, remain or cease to be loyal to the supplier and then to support prioritization of segments for marketing treatment.

How these segments should be best addressed to achieve the supplier's objectives of recruitment and retention.

How to link retention to service level improvements prompted by use of customer satisfaction data.

Lifetime patterns of purchasing and promotional responses of different types of customer, from the moment they decide to become members, and the associated lifetime values.

Detailed analysis/reporting required

Comparison of customer base with external data on opportunity, to identify unaddressed customers; FRAC trends versus loyalty and versus research/questionnaire data on perception, service levels, etc.

PRE-LAUNCH PROMOTIONAL PLANNING AND POST-CLOSE ANALYSIS

Objectives – pre-launch

To identify, using where appropriate forecasting approaches, which sales and media promotions/types of promotions should be mounted or discontinued, including:

- which kinds of customer should be included;
- through which channels should they be addressed;
- with what marketing and financial targets and measurement criteria (ranging from response rates to lifetime values);
- with what volumes and timings;
- with what incentives;
- covering which products/product types;
- in which geographical areas.

Objectives – post-close

To assess success of each campaign and campaign types.

Analytical/reporting requirement

Which promotions/type of promotions worked, and which did not (as calculated by spend versus control group and in detail – changes to FRAC and estimated lifetime value against promotion cost).

For which regions and types of customer targeted did they work.

Which channel/media proved the best for each promotional type.

Detailed analysis/reporting required

FRAC and estimated lifetime value, for different customer types, before and after promotions.

ANALYSIS DURING PROMOTION OR SEQUENCE OF PROMOTIONS

Objective

To identify whether actions should be taken during period of promotion (eg extend or curtail, repromote to boost response).

Analytical/reporting requirement

Which variables are diverging (positively or negatively) from their planned levels, and why (likely to apply to outbound volumes, enquiries, order levels (overall and by category).

Detailed analysis required

Time series on contacts, enquiry levels and FRAC during period of promotion; incentive planning and control.

Objective

To determine and monitor optimum level of promotional incentives, overall and for each customer and product type.

If volume discounts are provided, to determine what is optimum level for different customer types.

Analytical/reporting requirement

Relationship between variations in incentive on the one hand and FRAC and loyalty over different time periods (eg short term and long term).

Customer recruitment, retention and lifetime value in the longer term.

Effect of qualification levels on motivating customers to achieve them.

Detailed analysis/reporting required

Comparison of FRAC and estimated lifetime value with customer groups provided with different levels of incentive.

PRODUCT PROMOTIONS

Objectives

To provide data to optimize product promotion plans (which products or product types, areas, customers, etc) and to evaluate product promotions after campaign close.

To provide data in a coherent form to any business partners in promotions.

Analytical/reporting requirement

Effect of promotion on sales and spend of different customer types.

Effect of promotion on promoted customers' spend on product or category.

Identification of product types not yet promoted likely to benefit from promotion.

Selections of customers/customer types likely to be responsive to particular product promotions.

If media are to be used, media types likely to bring best results.

Detailed analysis required

FRAC and estimated lifetime value for individual products and product types, for different customer types, before and after promotions.

PRODUCT RANGE

Objective

To support identification of which products or product types are most attractive to customers in different types of relationship.

Analytical/reporting requirement

Which products and categories are most attractive.

Likely future patterns of spend of customers on existing and new product categories.

Detailed analysis/reporting required

Trends in FRAC on existing products; customer need data gathered by researching customers.

PRODUCT MANAGEMENT

Objectives

To identify what sales, profits, inventory, claims, payments, debt levels, etc, are optimal for supplier, retailer or both. This includes conversion rates to sale/take-up where this is split into two stages.

To identify situations in which product sales, profits, inventories, claims, payments, debt levels, etc, have departed from plan/normal levels, and why.

Analytical/reporting requirement

Actual levels and trends in product sales, profits, inventories, claims, payments, debt levels.

Detailed analysis/reporting required

Sales, profits, inventories, claims, payments, debt levels for different time periods, in different business units, areas, customer segments, etc, actual versus forecast/plan.

DIALOGUE MANAGEMENT

Objective

To increase frequency of contact and responsiveness of customers to contact, for different types of customer.

To identify the longer-term effects on dialogue achievement and loyalty of the combination of marketing initiatives undertaken by the company and its competitors.

To investigate potential improvements to long-term dialogue with customers (eg newsletter, magazine, catalogue, telephone enquiry point, etc).

Analytical/reporting requirement

Contact patterns of different types of customer (frequency and type of contact by them, responsiveness to contact by the company).

What kinds of marketing initiatives work best to stimulate responses, short term and long term.

Detailed analysis/reporting required

Quantification of frequency and intensity of contacts in both directions; correlation of contact analysis with FRAC and estimated lifetime value.

MARKET RESEARCH

Objectives

To develop a deeper understanding of the characteristics and behaviour of customers.

To support all other requirements identified in this framework by providing quicker/deeper insight into analytical requirements.

To identify dimensions/areas of marketing activity which have not been covered by any of the other functions, or opportunities/problems relating to existing marketing activities.

To create/acquire, manage and interpret new sets of data which will support the requirements identified here (eg questionnaire data, geographical information system data, external data, customer service data).

To recommend limits to effort to recruit customers into a relationship (as a proportion of total customer base).

Analytical/reporting requirement

It is not possible to be specific about the requirement, except that it will include nearly all the other requirements mentioned here. The most important requirement here is a general one, ie the ability to move quickly between and combine a variety of different kinds of analysis (eg slicing and dicing the data, performing statistical analyses and tests, viewing graphs and tables). In addition, market research plays a critical role in determining which external (eg market, economic, social) data needs to be sourced for analysis alongside in-house data.

FINANCE

Objectives

To determine the costs, revenues, gross margins and profits resulting from any individual past or planned customer-addressed marketing activity or arising from particular groups of customers, overall and for particular area, channels, product types, etc.

To permit evaluation of future marketing plans.

To permit evaluation of entire relationship management schemes (eg loyalty).

Analytical/reporting requirement

All performance parameters of relationship programmes, translated into revenues and costs:

- recruitment;
- establishment of different relationship types;
- promotions and promotion types;
- customer profitability analysis and lifetime value.

Patterns

This section involves current patterns, forecast future patterns, and divergences from expected/current patterns.

Detailed analysis/reporting required

All the analyses specified in this document, translated into costs and revenues.

OPERATIONS

Objectives

To assist in the evaluation of general performance of marketing/sales channels.

To assist in the evaluation of success of individual customer contact staff/areas in capturing relationship management opportunities, relative to the potential of their catchment area.

To assist in the evaluation of customer service levels delivered by different operations and channels.

Analytical/reporting requirement

Penetration level of achievement of relationship relative to potential, for each area, member of staff, etc.

Responsiveness to promotions compared to target, for each area, member of staff, etc.

Responses to and implication of responses to any customer satisfaction questionnaire.

Detailed analysis/reporting required

FRAC and contact and response data analysed by area and member of staff.

CUSTOMER SERVICE

Objectives

To support the planning, monitoring and controlling of customer service so as to ensure that customer satisfaction is optimized, sustaining relationship and spend.

To allow the interaction between perceived and delivered customer service levels and performance (overall, for particular areas and channels, for particular customers and customer types and, where appropriate, for product categories which are more service intensive, eg requiring more information/advice) to be understood.

To assist in determining which customer service measures are critical for performance.

Analytical/reporting requirement

Trends in customer service levels.

Interaction between customer service levels and performance (overall, individual areas and channels, customer types and individual customers).

Effect of initiatives to improve customer service on perceived customer service and thence on performance.

This area may require the introduction of a customer service questionnaire to establish customer perceptions, plus some monitoring of key parameters of delivered customer service (eg time to answer, wait for problem resolution).

Detailed analysis/reporting required

FRAC versus customer satisfaction for different customer types; trends in customer satisfaction for different customer types, areas, channels.

STRATEGIC AND MARKETING PLANNING AND CONTROL

The measurement, understanding and stimulation of customer behaviour should form a critical part of strategic and tactical marketing. An integrated overall picture needs to be developed and integrated into normal planning and implementation procedures. The role of the market research function in developing the required integrated understanding is critical.

Objectives

To develop an overall picture of status and trends in the behaviour of customers and the supplier's relationship management performance, and the causal relationship between this and all relevant variables (eg marketing actions, competitive actions, general economic and social trends).

To develop from this picture a view of prioritized opportunities and threats.

To identify which strategies and programmes offer the best way of capturing opportunities and neutralizing threats.

To support the quantification of the benefits and costs of these programmes and the subsequent measurement of their achievements.

To help identify/forecast deviations from current/expected trends and identify reasons for them.

Analytical/reporting requirement

The most significant characteristics and trends in the supplier's relationship management performance.

The most significant characteristics and trends in external factors (market, social, etc).

The implications of these trends for performance in the short, medium and long term, including a variety of what-if scenarios.

The marketing initiatives that have been most successful in supporting positive trends or neutralizing serious threats.

Detailed analysis/reporting required

Top-level statistics (current and time series) on FRAC, loyalty, lifetime value and customer service – overall and for each customer group, versus estimates of same achievements for competitors; demographics on customer types and how they are changing (numbers, demand for product category).

DATA VENDING/PARTNER POLICY

Objectives

To allow easy implementation of different selection criteria.

To allow easy demonstration of the effect of different selection criteria on the numbers and types of customers selected.

To provide easily understood summaries of data on selections.

Analytical/reporting requirement

This is slightly different from other categories, as the objective is not marketing policy but data provision to data agents or business partners. The requirement is therefore summarized in the objectives.

Detailed analysis/reporting required

As per customer needs.

Part 2

Strategy and technology

6

Sharing customer data in the value chain

Merlin Stone, Tim Virdee and Kevin Condron

Much of the focus of data-related discussions about value chain management is on how data about products and services (prices, availabilities, etc) can more easily flow up and down the supply chain using e-technology, helping customers towards the end of the chain serve themselves better. However, it is also clear that the more that suppliers further up the supply chain know about customers further down it, the better they can serve those customer needs. Put simply, customer data is valuable to more than the supplier immediately facing the customer. An example of this is the willingness of suppliers in a market to share negative data about their customers, including those that do not pay or are fraudulent in their activities. While there are many such examples of negative (or risk avoidance) data being shared, there are very few occasions where positive data is shared within a market or value chain. In order to probe the subject of valuing and sharing data more deeply, we carried out two studies.

VALUE OF THE CUSTOMER DATABASE

The first study was a simple survey focusing on the extent to which companies valued their customer data. The logic of this part of the study was that in order to understand companies' attitudes towards sharing customer data, we needed to understand the extent to which they valued the customer data they already had. Of course, this is not a necessary connection. Companies can refuse to deal with other companies precisely because they do not know the value of these assets.

This study was conducted via e-mail to 250 supplier and client organizations. The client organizations were asked whether they formally valued their customer data, not necessarily for the purposes of valuation in their accounts, but at least for the purposes of making decisions about whether to invest further in acquiring or maintaining customer data.

ATTITUDES TO SHARING DATA

The second study was an in-depth qualitative study of nine major organizations and their attitudes to sharing customer knowledge with their value chain partners. We used as a research instrument a rather (too) long e-mail questionnaire, which we believe reduced the response rate. We can only excuse this because our study is the first significant attempt to research an issue in which we have been involved since our earliest work on the UK direct insurance industry.[1] Therefore, these results are not presented as typical, but rather for what they are – how nine major companies view cooperation in the area of customer knowledge. However, this qualitative study gives us a clear view of what the main issues are in this area. These can now be researched by a quantitative study.

Before reviewing the results, it is sensible to review:

- The different ways in which companies can share customer knowledge.
- The theoretical justifications for cooperating or refusing to cooperate in sharing customer knowledge.
- The factors that influence why individual companies might or might not want to share customer knowledge with their business partners.

VALUE OF CUSTOMER DATA

Research on the valuation of customer data produced some results that we believe would be regarded as astonishing by most proponents of the idea of managing customers through data. It showed that almost no companies formally valued their customer data. Given the amount of investment dedicated to the building and maintaining of customer databases, as a medium that is an alternative to other ways of managing customers, this is surprising. In our view, this is like building a marketing factory with no understanding of the rewards of doing so, or of the asset value thereby created.

The results are given in Table 6.1. Usable responses were received from 47 companies (a few other responses took the form of a discussion of the issues, but were not usable for this survey). This showed that most companies do not value their customer databases. Particularly surprising was the number of specialist data analysis houses who said none of their clients did. How should we interpret these results? Of course, formally valuing the stock of customer data so far accumulated is not a necessary condition for getting value from the data. However, our understanding is that while many companies can show that they can use data cost-effectively to achieve results that contribute to the bottom line, it is rarely possible for companies to say whether creating (and maintaining) the data in the first place was worthwhile (whether or not it was!).

There are two ways of measuring the value of a customer database: the opportunity cost or alternative cost method; the return on investment method.

Opportunity cost method

Here, the idea is that customer data is best valued by what it would have cost to achieve the same marketing results by other means. For example, a relevant calculation might be what it would cost through advertising, list rental, and customer service to achieve a particular increase in contribution. In our view, most companies do not have the data and systems required to support such a calculation.

Return on investment method

This requires calculating the full acquisition and maintenance cost of data, the full cost of using the data (eg customer contact costs), and setting it against the contribution achieved by using the data. The key question here is whether this should be done on an average or marginal cost basis. An economist's recommendation would be that the value is best measured on a marginal basis. For example, if we collected another customer record, what would it cost to do so, and what contribution would we make from it. The benefit of this method is that whatever the actual historical cost of collecting the data, it would be valued at replacement cost (the cost of collecting another name now) and current value (what use can be made of the record now).

This marginal return on investment method of valuing data is the more feasible, as many companies do know the marginal acquisition cost of data and the marginal benefit of using data. Applied to the whole database this would give some estimate of value. The problem here is to distinguish between an average and a marginal name. Clearly we cannot use a true marginal name, as a company ought to have most names it wants already on its database. So it should look at the cost of acquiring a name that is of average value (ie average responsiveness, average resulting purchasing).

Table 6.1 The value of data

Company Type (C=client, S=supplier)	No	Yes	Don't Know	Can do Calculations
C Charity				1
C Financial Services				1
C Mobile Telephony Service Provider				1
C Retail and Travel Services				1
C Retailer				1
C Consumer and Business Services	1			
C Consumer Services	1			
C Logistics	1			
C Mobile Telephony Services Provider	1			
C Travel	1			
C Automotive	2			
C FMCG	2			
C Petrol	2			
C Retailer	2			
C Financial Services	8			
C Automotive		1		
C Financial Services		1		
C Utility		1		
C Consumer Services		2		
C FMCG		2		
C Publisher		2		
Total Customers	**21**	**9**		**5**
S Analysis House			1	
S Systems Supplier	1		1	
S Customer Database Bureau	1			
S Database Bureau	1			
S Direct Marketing Consultant	1			
S Retail Consultancy	1			
S University Expert	1			
S Analysis House	4			
Total Suppliers	**10**		**2**	
Overall Total	**31**	**9**	**2**	**5**

A short-cut to this answer would be to look at the external price of data of equivalent quality. In some cases, where there is a ready market in customer data and most companies would use it to do the same thing (eg customer acquisition), this would be a good measure. But where the customer base is loyal to a particular supplier and represents the outcome of years of managing customers well, external valuation in this way would clearly be inappropriate.

Conclusions on data sharing

This is not the place to investigate database valuation models in detail. Most of our respondents did not do it either way! The practical implication of this is that if and when companies decide to share data, they are unlikely to have a solid financial basis for calculating the basis for any payments to be made, or indeed whether it is worth doing.

WAYS OF SHARING CUSTOMER KNOWLEDGE

The ways companies can share customer knowledge are influenced by:

- the type of data;
- sharing process (eg level of detail, timing of transfer and access, hosting);
- data protection legislation and industry conduct guidelines.

Let us consider each of these in turn.

Types of data

These are the commonest types of data relating to customers likely to be of interest to partners:

- demographic and lifestyle data, including interests;
- product preferences;
- media preferences and responsiveness;
- buying behaviour – transactions (what, where, how often, etc);
- complaints, merchandise returns, claims, risk management and exposures;
- mode of payment;
- use of loyalty scheme;
- product data – inventories, orders of partner's customers;
- product movements within the company;
- promotional outcomes – redemptions, sales;
- promotional plans, targets, performance and histories – what works, how well;
- revenues and profits from customer relationship.

Our research shows that the closer we get to the purchases of individual consumers, the more reluctant companies are to share data. They seem to be much keener to share data such as demographic and lifestyle data, which can be gathered and sourced from trusted third parties. However, as knowledge of what customers buy needs to be compared with what they could buy if the products and services were available to them, opportunities are being lost. It is as if each partner believes that they know best in this area.

Sharing process

The level of detail with which data is shared can be aggregated or at individual level, and sometimes a halfway house, with data made available in very small customer segments, or perhaps some made available at individual level, but with other data grouped. In general, the more detailed the transfer, the greater the perceived risk, although less risk is usually perceived when it comes to lifestyle and demographic data.

Timing of transfer (or access by one partner to another's data) can vary from online to batch. It seems that here systems incompatibility can raise issues, although this may be an excuse!

Hosting may be by swapping, ie each partner imports the other's data, partially or completely via a third party. Most respondents to our survey clearly felt comfortable with the role of a trusted third party.

Of course, the role of a third party is already well established in the data vending market, typically in the supply of lifestyle and similar data. This includes:

- standard list rental, where the role of brokers as experts in managing data acquisition is well understood (eg selection criteria, data quality, control of contractual terms);
- tagging of client databases by data suppliers – adding data to an existing customer or prospect file;
- prospect pool supply – finding prospects that match a client's existing good customers, or in its negative form, identifying prospects to be avoided because they match a client's 'bad customer' profile;
- one-off data pooling – assembly of an overall customer/prospect file from various client and external sources;
- outsourced management of a customer or prospect file.

However, this description of the role of the third party focuses on the operational procedures for bringing data together. Many clients have found that the involvement of an experienced third party brings benefits of a different order. Before investigating these, however, we need to focus on the different skill and knowledge sets and capabilities that might be resident in a third party or with a client, and the types of companies that supply them. This is because the third parties are of many different types, with very different core skill sets. However, each company may have added to their core additional capabilities that can overlap with those supplied by other companies. Indeed, the market opportunity in customer management, combined with intense competitiveness, has led many companies to position themselves as generalized suppliers of customer management capabilities.

The main skills, knowledge and capabilities required for data-based customer management are:

- strategic analysis/planning/audit/review of customer management activity;
- strategic IT planning for customer management;
- customer data analysis – for all purposes from understanding customer base to analysing results;
- determining data requirements for customer management;
- customer information management systems selection and implementation;
- gathering consumer data from a non-transactional source (eg questionnaires, guarantee data);
- extracting customer information from client transactional sources;
- campaign planning;
- selection management;
- media planning – including new media;
- outbound communications management;
- response handling and fulfilment.

These tend to be resident in the following types of company:

- data analysis houses;
- lifestyle data suppliers;
- list brokers;
- database management bureaux;
- direct marketing agencies;
- response handling and fulfilment agencies;
- IT hardware suppliers;
- IT systems integrators;
- software suppliers;
- management consultancies;
- client direct marketing departments (or similar) – often including data exploitation staff;
- client IT departments.

The important points to understand about the third parties are: the nature of their core skills/knowledge/capabilities; their main business model(s), ie how they make their money (eg through sale of staff time, software, data access, service usage).

The main choice facing the client is the management advantage of reducing the number of suppliers, against the advantage of using the best of breed for each task. However, in some cases this problem is dealt with by outsourcing customer management activities to one or more companies, leaving them to select partners for provision of specialist skills, knowledge or capability. Given the complexity of the above, many companies have realized that selecting suppliers to help in customer management is a critical decision, which should therefore be handled as a coordinated supplier selection process, rather than as a series of one-off decisions. The mistake many companies make, our research has shown, is to assume that the choice of customer management system is the most important choice. Good systems working with poor data, processes and implementation programmes usually lead to very expensive ways of managing customers that do not please the finance director!

The practical implication of the above is that where a company is considering involving a third party in any area of customer management, and particularly where that involvement may lead to intense inter-working with other suppliers or to data cooperation with other peer companies, a key selection criterion should be a strong track record of working professionally and (usually) quickly within a wider team.

Data protection legislation and industry conduct guidelines

Data protection standards have typically varied by country regulation and privacy expectations and culture. In some cases these are supplemented by the business conduct guidelines of an industry or market, for example in insurance and banking. More recently Europe has aligned its data protection legislation; this applies immediately to new business processes, systems and database developments, but has a delay time for existing systems to conform. Demand is increasing in some markets (eg in the United States) to tighten regulation which can protect individual privacy as data use and sharing becomes more prevalent.

Rules of importance for value chain management include: how the data was collected, for what purpose and with what expectation and approvals by the customer; assured currency and relevance of the data; data sharing within the company or group and with value chain partners; retention of the data in identifiable or anonymous form; customer data held in other forms (eg paper files).

Data protection legislation has become a key management issue for all new and existing processes and systems. A poor understanding of options can constrain a company's ability to use customer data competitively, while infringing legislation can have dramatic and expensive impact on company brand, create legal actions and constrain future operations. To remain in control it is important to understand (and perhaps influence through recognized bodies) current and planned data protection legislation. Prioritized plans must be put in place to address these issues for each new and existing system or database.

Arguments for sharing customer knowledge

The main arguments for sharing customer knowledge include:

- Improved targeting of marketing strategy.
- Improved targeting of marketing communications.
- Improved/more relevant content of marketing communications.
- Improved product planning.
- Improved pricing.
- Reduced costs of data acquisition.
- Reduced costs of data processing.
- Reduced media advertising.
- Reduced direct mail expenditure.
- Increased responsiveness to changing market conditions.
- Gaining an advantage over competition at the same level of the value chain.
- Bargaining more effectively with other value chain partners (eg divide and rule).
- Reducing market risk.
- Learning/skills transfer.

Our respondents focused primarily on improved targeting, cost reduction and competitive advantage.

Arguments against sharing customer knowledge

The main arguments against sharing customer knowledge include:

- Increased complexity of the marketing process.
- Increased marketing costs.
- Increased problems with data management.
- Conflict caused by mismatch in objectives/types/pace of marketing/sales process.
- General conflict of interest.
- Conflict of interest over customer ownership.
- Conflict of interest over data ownership.
- Temporary nature of some business relationships.
- Systems incompatibilities.
- Legal complexities (regulatory, data protection).
- Data security.
- Political difficulties.
- Skills shortage – data analysis.

- Skills shortage – data management.
- Accentuating marketing skills difference between partners.

Most of our research respondents stressed issues relating to lack of alignment – skills, processes, systems. Conflict of interest was also raised.

What influences sharing of customer knowledge

The reasons for or against sharing data include the following.

Sector-specific issues

These may be regulatory, but can also be cultural (eg a history of conflict, or to do with the product – an intermittent purchasing cycle can give the retailer the upper hand because the supplier becomes more remote from the customer).

Competitive situation

This includes factors such as how many major companies are competing on each side of the market, their size distribution, their relative competitive strengths (eg products, distribution, branding). These factors tend to determine the risks if competitors get hold of information that has been shared. For example, if the customer list of a weak company gets into the hands of a strong company, then the latter will be in a good position to mount a competitive attack.

Relative strengths and weaknesses of different partners

This can apply to areas such as customer knowledge management or IT – where sharing with a partner perceived to have a greater or lesser capability can lead to perceived risk of better/worse exploitation of data and consequent problems with customers or competitors. Skills and systems compatibility problems can have their origin here.

Particular marketing/sales approach of the different companies in the supply chain

This includes in particular the extent of use of targeted marketing. In many distribution chains, it is not uncommon for the level nearest the customer to be involved in direct marketing. However, this is changing, particularly as the economics of managing high volumes of customer data are not necessarily favourable to this approach.

Perceived costs and benefits of sharing

These are usually determined by the partners' views about the above factors. Our research shows that there is little doubt about the general benefits – the issue is whether it pays the particular companies, and whether the partners can work with one another cost-effectively.

Availability of trusted independent intermediaries to help

Our research shows that third parties are generally trusted with demographic and lifestyle data, some of which may have been contributed or collected on behalf of specific partners. In financial services, this trust extends specifically to transaction data (eg credit cards).

Relationship between prospective partners

This includes strategic agreements to meet other objectives, and of course trust.

RESEARCH ON DATA SHARING: THE CASE STUDIES

The sectors of the nine companies surveyed are given in Table 6.2. The detailed responses from these companies are not given, as this would compromise confidentiality. Therefore, only the main issues are highlighted.

The utility

This utility is a regional utility, responsible for the marketing, customer administration and customer service for electricity, gas and fixed line telecommunications. Its business partners are, perhaps surprisingly, other utilities, as it may sell its electricity to be distributed through their networks, but it is also interested in partnership with directly competitive

Table 6.2 Companies participating in data sharing research

National Newspaper Publishing	1
Automotive	1
Packaged Consumer Goods	2
Utility Supply	1
Leisure Retailing	1
Rail Travel	1
Transportation and Retailing Services	1
Data for Businesses and Consumers	1

companies (ie those who also market energy rather than distributing it). Its marketing priorities can be summarized as increased targeting and search for more cost-effective distribution channels. Its attitude to the sharing of data is that it is not interested in selling data but more interested in strategic data exchange to meet effectiveness and efficiency objectives. It is particularly interested in exchange of data with direct competitors, as this helps in risk reduction. The main kind of data of interest here is payment practices of customers. This is an issue that we have explored in our earlier researches.[2] These researches focused on how bad customers could cause utilities problems by moving around, leaving a trail of bad debt or late settlement. However, because of the conditions under which its data was collected (as a former area monopoly) it sees particular data protection problems in the legal area. It sees that increased data sharing might lead to problems due to different skills mixes in the sharing companies, as well as possible systems problems. The company considers itself well served in terms of the systems, analytical and reporting capabilities available to it, with a customer view of the data warehouse, campaign management systems, etc. It is already matching data coming from a variety of electronic environments (the Web, mobile) with its customer data.

Packaged consumer goods – Company 1

This company is a very large supplier of alcoholic drinks. Its business partners are specialist and generalist retailers. It maintains a strong focus on classic market-wide branding and marketing communication, but its focus on targeting and optimizing the value of particular target customer segments is increasing. Its focus on Web activities and direct sales to consumers is also increasing, and it is expecting much-increased communications activity through the Web and e-mail. It believes most of its data is of interest to retailers and vice versa. There is an expected imbalance in the areas of transactions and orders (where the retailers' data is of strong interest to the company). Some data exchange currently takes place, but there is a strong reliance on data from specialist third parties. The main perceived benefits of data exchange lie in improved competitive advantage, marketing planning and targeting, and reduced marketing costs. However, systems incompatibilities and shortage of data management and analysis skills can be a problem. The company's systems and data management capabilities are good as far as batch analysis is concerned, but its ability to exploit this through online work with staff or customers is not strong. It has routine reporting for some area, but there is a weakness where sales and promotional response data is concerned.

Packaged consumer goods – Company 2

This company is a very large supplier of a broad range of packaged consumer goods, with its target market therefore being mostly women with families. Its business partners are retailers. It has its own customer database and is using it to achieve more targeted marketing, while maintaining a strong focus on product branding and retail distribution. It is particularly keen on areas such as optimizing segment value and finding cost-effective direct channels of communication and distribution, and is also focusing on electronic channels – particularly the Web, mobile, and digital TV. It is interested in data exchange in virtually all areas except product inventories. Again, strategic partnerships are a prerequisite for data exchange, and even here it would prefer to limit these to more data such as demographic and lifestyle data. This company is quite advanced in the types of analysis it performs on its data, such that its marketing decision makers are dedicating greater budgets to the direct channels that its database supports.

Leisure services company

This company is one of the UK's largest leisure retailing companies, but it also produces some of the products sold through its leisure outlets. Its partners are other producers of products. Its marketing focus is both across the board and targeted, with more targeted methods expected to increase. In terms of media, the biggest increases are expected in the area of the Web, e-mail and mobile, followed by digital TV. Where it comes to the company's interest in partners' data and its perceptions about its partners' interest in its data, the strongest focus is on leisure interests, product and media preferences, promotional responsiveness and purchasing data. In general, relatively little data is exchanged with partners, and there are strong concerns about confidential sales and promotional response data falling into competitive hands. However, the company's willingness to exchange data is increasing, though not in the area of transactions and responsiveness. Exchanging data in summary form is very acceptable, but again not about transactions or responses. Third party data is found to be useful, and willingness to share is much enhanced if the data is hosted by an independent third party. The benefits of exchanging data are seen to be mainly in the area of improved targeting, reduced marketing costs, reduced market risk and competitive advantage. Likely problems are in the area of poorly aligned marketing/sales processes, systems incompatibilities and skills. The company is well provided for when it comes to data warehousing, analysis and campaign management, but its reporting capability is incomplete.

Travel and retailing services company

This company supplies a variety of services to travellers, including retailing. Its business partners are providers of travel services and retailers who take space on its locations. Its marketing is therefore both general, in the sense of focusing on all customers in its target market, and targeted. It expects its use of e-mail, the Web and mobile telephony to increase a lot, with digital TV also increasing. Most kinds of data are of interest to it, and most of the data its partners have interest it. Transactions, demographic, preference and responsiveness data are of interest to the company, as are product movements, orders, inventories and the like. Promotional, plans, performance and histories are also of high mutual interest, and these determine sales performance. The current situation on data sharing is mixed. Trust in relation to exchanging different types of data varies according to type of data, with in general less trust in the area of sales and response. Summary data is an area of stronger performance, where there is exchange. Being able to demonstrate improved profitability is the key to data sharing. Third party demographics and lifestyle data is considered a valuable supplement to customer data. The benefits expected from data sharing are less than with other respondents, with less benefit of all kinds expected, but also fewer significant problems. The systems situation seems less complete, with only a few of the basic capabilities required for data exchange and subsequent professional use of the data in place. Much reporting is ad hoc rather than routine.

Rail company

This is a local rail company, which sells rail services and packaged holidays direct and through ticketing and travel agents. Its marketing approach combines general marketing to its whole customer base with an increasingly segmented approach. Its use of targeted media such as mail, e-mail and the Web is increasing, but not radically. Its interests in partner data and beliefs about its partners' interest in its own data are more or less evenly balanced. The exception to this is in the area of complaints, where it believes it would like to know more about its partners' data than it believes its partners would like to know about its data. In general its preference is for data to be exchanged within strategic agreements. There is less trust in the area of exchanging transaction and response data than lifestyle and demographic data. Profitability and improved targeting are the main justifications for data exchange, particularly for data it might receive from its partners. Skills, systems incompatibilities and conflict over data and customer ownership are seen as barriers to exchange. The company's systems, data analysis and reporting infrastructure are reasonably strong, except in the core area of customer database.

Automotive supplier

This company supplies one of the premium automotive brands. Its key commercial focus is on cost-effective and more targeted distribution, but also more targeted product design. It is expecting to use more of all targeted channels of communication, particularly telephony of all kinds, digital TV, and the Internet (e-mail and the Web). Its business partners are car dealers, and it believes that all categories of its own data is of interest to its partners, and that all categories of their data are of interest to it. Its partnership relationship with dealers is strong, and it exchanges data within strategic agreements with them. Targetability and profitability are the key justifications for this data exchange. However, systems incompatibility is an issue for this company. In terms of technology, analysis and reporting, the company feels it is well provided for (eg data warehouse, campaign systems) with one area of weakness being in the bringing together of mobile and Web-derived data with its existing sources of customer data.

National newspaper

This company publishes one of the UK's main daily newspapers. Its intermediaries are newspaper distributors, particularly major wholesalers and retailers. Its marketing approach is broadly mass market, but the targeted element is growing. It is broadening the range of products and services marketed to its customers. In line with this, its media usage is broadening. It is increasing usage of the main direct media in selling to existing customers – particularly via direct mail, e-mail and the Web. Purchasing, promotional responsiveness and customer service data owned by retailers is of particular interest to this company, relative to its perception of intermediaries' interest in its own data. Most other data it perceives to be of high mutual interest. Strategic agreements are necessary before this company would engage in data exchange, and it is reluctant to extend this to transaction and response data because of issues of trust. However, it does buy data from its partners. The company is happier with exchanging grouped data. It also believes third party data sources are a valuable addition to its data. The main benefits of exchanging data are seen as improved targeting and responsiveness to market conditions rather than cost saving. Systems incompatibilities and differences in marketing skills are seen as particularly important barriers to data exchange. Its systems and data capabilities are reasonable but there are significant gaps, particularly in terms of online availability, which would make it difficult to engage in some aspects of data exchange.

Data supplier for consumers and businesses

This government-owned company sells its data in various forms (eg publications, digital supply) to organizations and individuals. Much of its output is sold through booksellers and newsagents, who are its business partners. Some of its major customers are utilities and telecommunications companies. Its marketing approach is both mass market and targeted. The main changes it sees to marketing methods are catalogue marketing and the use of the Web. The company expects to be using more of most channels, including direct mail, ordinary telephony, digital TV, e-mail and the Web. Most types of data are of interest to it. It believes that partners interest in its data is mutual, with any imbalance being due to its retailers ability to identify buying behaviour, promotional redemption and the like. In general the company is a recipient of data, but would be keen on full data sharing where profitability and targeting could be improved. Barriers to exchange include its own skill levels in analysing and managing data and systems incompatibilities. In the systems and business intelligence areas, it perceives it has significant weaknesses.

SUMMARY OF CASE STUDY FINDINGS

This study was a qualitative study. Yet the responses were on the whole consistent. They are as follows:

- In general, companies are happy to exchange data about general customer characteristics, but reluctant to do so about topics such as sales and promotional response.
- Where exchanging this kind of data, companies are likely to do so only in the context of a strategic agreement, backed by trust.
- The role of third party suppliers in supporting data exchange is important.
- The main benefits of exchanging data were targeting, competitiveness and cost reduction.
- The main barriers were perceived differences in analytical skills and to some extent process skills, plus perceived problems with systems incompatibility.
- In one case perceived legal barriers were important.
- The quality of the respondents' systems and business intelligence capability varied significantly, with some claiming an ability to report in nearly all areas, with others admitting significant limitations.

BUSINESS IMPLICATIONS

The picture that emerges is a slightly confusing one. Behind it, we suspect there is uncertainty about the appropriate models of cooperation between suppliers and intermediaries in an increasingly digital age. However, there is hope. The questioning of retailer loyalty schemes is taking place at a time when product suppliers are becoming increasingly expert at understanding their markets, and reaching out more directly to consumers as our survey highlights. It shows that sensible product suppliers can look in a detached manner at whether they are really getting increased customer value out of the investments they make in formal customer knowledge. However, our research into whether companies actually value their customer data has produced some disturbing results. Although it is clear that getting value out of data does not depend upon valuing the data, it is also clear that lack of confidence in valuing the data indicates some vulnerability.

This was a relatively small study, though we hope it is evident to the reader that a lot of thinking has been going on – by authors and respondents. As nearly all the respondents saw data exchange as an important way to improve profitability, our earlier researches into the implementation of new approaches to customer management, suppliers and intermediaries considering data cooperation should consider:

- Which of their partners they can trust, or how risks can be contained.
- Which partners would be interested in strategic partnership
- What the possibilities are for joint customer management strategy.
- Where simple data cooperation is better than formal cooperation on customer management strategy.
- How such a partnership might affect other aspects of marketing strategy – branding, product/service specification, pricing, distribution arrangements, marketing communication.
- What enabling infrastructures (systems, data, processes, measures) are needed to provide their own capabilities and to support cooperative capability developments.
- People implications – everything from joint decision making to training, and in its most advanced form, whether a cooperative organization should be established.
- The required implementation programme, including piloting and testing, to ensure that results are positive and that risk is controlled.
- How third parties might help broker such an arrangement.

Notes

1   Stone, M, Foss, B and Machtynger, L (1997) The UK consumer direct insurance industry: a role model for relationship marketing?, *Long Range Planning*, **30** (3) pp 353–63

2   Stone, M *et al* Managing customer service in utilities (December 1997); Building customer-focused data (November 98); Managing good and bad customers (July 1999) – *Close to the Customer Briefings*, Policy Publications, UK

7

Integrating customer management systems

Bryan Foss and Merlin Stone

INTRODUCTION

One of the major problems in implementing customer management systems is that the process rarely starts with a clean sheet of paper. In this chapter, we consider an approach to customer management system design, and then describe how to integrate different customer management systems. CRM systems need to be integrated to support the integrated business processes required to maximize return on investment.

To avoid reinventing the wheel and incurring additional cost and time it is important to use a comprehensive, proven, industry model. The model helps to achieve goals, by encouraging the formation of a detailed plan which covers every relevant aspect of IT across the enterprise. This plan is the overall systems architecture. The main components of an IT architecture are described in Table 7.1.

THE CRM ECOSYSTEM

The leading customer loyalty analysts – including Meta, Datamonitor and Bloor – refer to CRM ecosystems. They apply the analogy of a closed ecological loop (such as the Amazon rainforest or the Pacific Ocean) to CRM. As prerequisites to achieving a 'closed loop' CRM ecosystem, these analysts have identified three forms of integration:

Table 7.1 Components of an IT architecture

Component	Description
Context	A plan that conveys basic requirements, guidelines and constraints. It may itself be an output of a higher-level architecture such as a business plan so there is input here from the business vision statement
Frameworks	A multi-layered approach to developing the architecture in stages. Typical frameworks consist of a series of elements and levels that can be envisaged as a grid. Elements include computing systems, communications systems, data management and applications software. These are then specified with increasing degrees of precision as initial parameters are translated into policies, models, plans and procedures. This is how integration is achieved by ensuring that each part of this 'grid' fits to the next part. For example, the area of data management might proceed from defining data assets, through to requirements for use, access control and storage. It would not be possible to use, say, data warehousing or data mining without thinking through the implications for other elements
Components	Commonly accepted objects that make up building blocks. The purpose of architecture is to define and arrange these. Within these the architect will define hardware, software, people, and decisions processes
Interrelationships	Relationships between objects are based on some sort of modelling. The purpose is to evaluate the effect of varying relationships between components so as to maximize synergy and interaction. We look at customer to customer links (processes), the flow of decisions, the proximity of functions, data dictionaries and indexing (of databases)
Models	There is a need for standard components or interfaces to act as guidelines for developers and for aesthetics. If they do not like the look and feel of software, they might not use it
Architects	The people who turn visions into reality and provide the link between concept and implementation. They must identify and meet the needs of users so as to produce executable plans. Users are often not directly involved in systems development so architects must link information services (IS) with business managers. A data warehouse is an expensive waste of money if nobody wants to use it because it is too complicated, slow or unwieldy. In this example, the architect would be the CRM project manager

- Collaborative CRM – where channels or touch-points share and use information about customers.
- Operational CRM – where each channel or touch-point directly accesses the organization's back-office systems for straight-through processing.
- Analytical CRM – where the integration of customer, financial and marketing information allows more focused, effective and profitable information analysis and directed activity across the organization.

The result of applying and integrating collaborative, operational and analytical CRM is closed loop CRM. This is when a continuing learning loop – a virtuous circle – is created that delivers increasingly effective activity in each area. Additional customer information is acquired and stored at every interaction, while the organization's customer knowledge is deployed and redeployed to optimize the value of each relationship. The common enabling factor in all these forms of CRM is integration – which we deal with later in this chapter.

A key element in systems models for CRM is whether the data can be traced from business requirements to source and to other uses of the same data. Systems models should therefore provide for easy integration of best practice, one-off applications into an integrated systems approach. For example, a new profitability reporting application can identify and share data from earlier projects, requiring only previously unused data to be incorporated. Even project change costs can be reduced as additional databases may be modelled and mapped with overall consistency.

The complete full cycle architecture produces an operational business system. In the past, decision support systems were considered as non-operational IT. Only transaction systems were seen as operational. The production of reports for decision making was regarded as having only a loose connection with day-to-day business operations. The feedback loop through decision, action and measurement was not fully implemented. Current systems provide for timely, one-to-one campaign management, rapid product customization and for yield management (product repricing based on demand management). These features depend on constant market intelligence and rapid decision-making affecting both operational and non-operational systems.

BUILDING A 'FULL CYCLE' SYSTEM

The complete data cycle is complex. If the start point is considered to be sources of data mostly from customer interactions we then need to manipulate this data in various ways. It has to be combined from different originating points, transformed and analysed before being used for business decisions. Once implemented, decisions produce further customer interactions which have to be measured. The cycle is illustrated in Figure 7.1 (over):

- Data is sourced from customer or partner contacts, legacy systems and external data sources.
- A common data store such as a data warehouse or data mart is designed and built for all selected, cleaned and structured data.
- Customer data is then analysed using online analytical processing (OLAP) and data mining tools. These produce customer scores which forecast the probability of responsiveness to different kinds of marketing campaigns and likely profitability within actionable customer segments.

- Planned customer dialogues and contacts are then optimized for maximum return.
- Marketing campaigns are designed and executed based on these plans, with contact follow-up activities.
- The campaigns are evaluated individually, against each other and against plan.
- Learning and new knowledge is internalized into processes and campaign improvements.

This implies neither that the systems solution should be defined in detail at the start, nor that the whole system must be built before benefits are obtained. It is designed and built in stages. Focus on the development of a specific capability usually provides a basic definition of systems and data needs. With this focused approach, the IT implications of the early stages are often much smaller than expected. For example, not all legacy system data needs to be extracted, cleansed, structured and analysed. A narrow focus on business requirements will normally delimit quite a small subset of data that reduces timescales, effort, cost and risk. As an example, a cross-selling project may only require details of current product holdings, specific buying indicators, potential profitability and risk. Quite often a subsequent project phase will then need only small additions to the data already available and in use. Much customer data will prove to be common to many new capabilities. In this example the same data is likely to be common to retention or target acquisition projects. In the worst case, only limited additional data will be required. It is not necessary to build the complete cycle systems and data, with all feedback mechanisms, to create the first learning loop. Interim feedback mechanisms can be created to enable rapid learning capability.

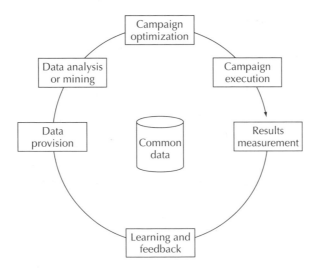

Figure 7.1   The learning/development cycle – campaign example

At a high level the architecture and approach looks very similar, even for different industries. At a more detailed level, experience shows that there are many variations in the type of customer data required, where it is collected, the volume, type and frequency of customer interactions, the relative need for rapid decision making, the type of action that results and the improvements gained. These differences must be reflected in industry data models and applications, and by using sound and experience-based decision making techniques during implementation. Consulting and delivery methods are available to assist here which take into account the systems available to speed implementation while reducing costs and risk. A good CRM systems architecture and approach will draw on many years of previous implementation experience while retaining the flexibility to customize the approach in each project.

The planning approach or architecture should not determine preset business or data cycle times. Rather it should enable incremental improvements in cycle-times as customer management capabilities develop. In this fashion, an initial campaign management capability may begin with well-planned bi-monthly promotions to large customer groups. Through the learning process, an understanding of actionable segments and key customer buying or lapsing events can be derived. As experience and understanding of managing customers improves, it becomes more practical to make just-in-time marketing responses to individual customers, which should result in an improved return from each project. For example, a home improvement retailer in the UK realized (unsurprisingly) that customers tended to make multiple and repeat purchases when a house move, building extension or major redecoration project was under way. Using loyalty discount cards to encourage customers to identify themselves ('hand raising') at each store visit, the company was able to recognize rapidly the likely project type from what was bought. They were then able to offer customers incentives to spend more of their project budget in the store through targeted promotions. New customer servicing activities were also introduced to support the marketing scheme in an integrated manner.

The systems solution will continually evolve and different data items will be identified as key at different stages. Responsiveness, cycle speed and personalization are likely to increase dramatically, although cycle volumes may change as the most appropriate data is identified. One financial services provider aiming to cross-sell additional products initiated a data mining exercise to identify the attributes and needs of previous cross-buyers. Additional customer information was obtained through research before this knowledge was used in the call centre to customize the conversation (or script) flow during a dialogue. Using simple decision tree logic, and rules derived from data mining, it was possible to identify the most appropriate product offers by intelligent questioning of callers. Specific additional data captured during the telephone conversation and supplemented by follow-up calls to selected customers helped complete an understanding of key buying indicators.

Significant differences may be identified either within small customer segments or across large customer groups. While the systems and data architecture should be able to support the management of differences across many small segments, it is not usually advisable to implement this feature. The basic architecture should however enable planned, continual systems changes in response to both trials and operational use.

For a successful system, two key requirements should be considered. First, a sound system architecture for the complete solution. This includes development and management of linkages and feedback loops to ensure a seamless transition between business processes.

Second, the use of an existing industry data model. This can save substantial time and cost in both the short and long term. A fairly complete, well-tried model will have been applied many times in different projects, gaining content and rigour from each application. Such a model can underpin the 'build in stages, use in stages' systems approach, as the required data for each stage has an integrated structure. Even when additional data items are identified, such as new customer attributes, there is normally an obvious place for them to be added within a proven model.

Although the data supporting customer contact management are very similar across industries (after all, these are usually the same customers), data supporting the management of profitability (of customers and products) is usually unique to each company. For example, in an industry like financial services, the management of good and bad customer risk plays a larger role than in, say, retail.

The data model often introduces a common, agreed business language for the first time. For example, the terms 'lapsed customer', 'product' or even 'customer profitability' may well have been in general usage previously but they will need to be defined exactly if they are to be employed by a computer-based system. While these definitions may appear 'obvious' to different managers, big differences often emerge between and within business departments, between business managers and IT managers and between merged or international companies. A common language is important to successful CRM as this requires the business to act in a consistent manner. There may also be legal or cultural implications for the use of terms in the data model. These are important to a company when implementing a global programme. It is easy to underestimate the eventual in-house build cost of such a model, which can often be purchased for much less.

It is crucial to be able to view all data by customer, this is after all a customer database. In many cases, the customer may not be an individual but a household or other buying group. Such groups are the basis of what the financial services industry calls a party database. A party database seeks to capture and represent data about all relationships relevant to the contact life cycle. It is equally important to retain views of data by product, channel or intermediary. This is sometimes forgotten in the rush for a 'customer' database. A practical system will enable any or all of these views to be exploited as required. A great deal of learning and expertise of this sort can be imported through a bought-in system.

When models are designed and built in-house, a step at a time, there is often a need to restructure periodically. For example, in one project it was very unclear at the early stages where profit data should reside within the database. Using an established system helps avoid the costs associated with unnecessary data complexity introduced insidiously as a result of gradual learning. In another project the importance of the household buying group was not documented in the initial systems requirements. It was identified and added to the model much later. Due to this late, major change the database survived only a few years before yet more unexpected changes required a fresh start to control unnecessary complexity and cost. The impact on the business project timescale, on delayed development of customer management capability and on eventual ROI was substantial.

UPDATING CURRENT IT SYSTEMS

Extending the role of transaction databases

During the 1980s, when many companies focused on efficiency of operations, most IT investment was in transaction systems. The major purpose of transaction systems was to provide clerical support. Its aims are to reduce costs, improve consistency of performance and provide management control. In the 1990s and beyond, these transaction systems are now being asked to do a quite different job. Newer transaction systems provide a wider range of support. The new-breed direct sellers, in areas such as financial services, pioneered them. They are now required to support swift product innovation and flexible product construction and billing. For example, in the automotive industry they support the sale of customized, mass-produced cars and individualized financial packages.

The move from a product, to a product and customer focus, has usually led to the development of a common customer database in front of or alongside legacy transaction systems. This customer (or party) database is transactional, as it supports contact with the customer in daily business operations, for example in the call centre or behind the Web site. The implementation of a separate front-end customer database enables new contact management capabilities to be implemented without replacing other administrative systems in the short term.

Some early implementations of this sort of front-end database are little more than indexes, pointing to customer data held within multiple legacy systems. With only a customer index and a unique customer reference such as a credit card number, name or date of birth, it is usually possible to identify whether the customer has an existing relationship with a company. The product holdings of that customer can then be found even though the details may be spread across a number of legacy transaction systems. This is not a perfect method and does lead to some duplication when new records are created. Mr J Smith may describe himself as Mr J T Smith next time he calls and this necessitates periodic de-duplification. This type of customer data reconciliation is very difficult, if not impossible, to carry out in real time while handling the customer.

Over time, developments of the transaction database allow for consolidation of common customer data so that each record is held only once. Common data can then be removed from the legacy systems or updated as a shadow or copy of the single customer view database. Other data relevant to the management of the customer may then be added, for example customer value or potential value indicators. A contact log is especially important as this is required to manage the customer across multiple contacts. Otherwise, each contact is made without reference to the others. Both customer and company expect all relevant contacts to be taken into account in the relationship, whichever channels they take place through.

The customer database is designed for rapid access from a number of different channels or channel applications rapidly to support individual customer contact. For example, immediate and simultaneous access may be required for Internet and call centre enquiries, as a transaction may start in one channel and move to another.

It would not normally be appropriate therefore to use the same database for analysis. The data structures here would be designed for performance, rather than for ease of use for report production. For technical reasons, the performance of this type of database is likely to be poor when used for analysis. Performing an analysis would degrade daily operational response rates. In addition there is a need for more historic and supplementary data for analysis. Consequently it makes sense to have some separation of data structures, storage and use between the transaction and information systems.

Enormous improvements can, however, be made to customer contact systems such as those in call centres, sales agent support systems and retail point of sale systems without major changes to the underlying legacy systems. Once a transaction customer database is in place, legacy systems can be replaced over time, as illustrated by Figure 7.2.

The hands represent integrated contact systems and required support data. Channels might include any or all direct or indirect contact methods based on different technologies. The transaction database is used directly or indirectly to support and coordinate all customer contacts dynamically. The brain represents integrated decision and learning systems, sometimes called business intelligence systems. It draws on both current and historical data. Analysis might include segmentation management, campaign planning, contact management, profitability management, knowledge management and other applications. The link to action may include direct customer contact, agent or dealer management or product development. Administration represents product support, administration and legacy systems.

In the CRM ecosystem the hands provide collaborative CRM, the brain is analytical CRM. Integrating these together and with the administrative and transactional systems (sometimes called 'legacy') creates the closed loop that completes the ecosystem.

This architectural approach is becoming common to CRM systems in many industries. Consumer and market pressures are driving most if not all industries to enable multiple contact channels where previously a few major channels existed. For example, in the auto-

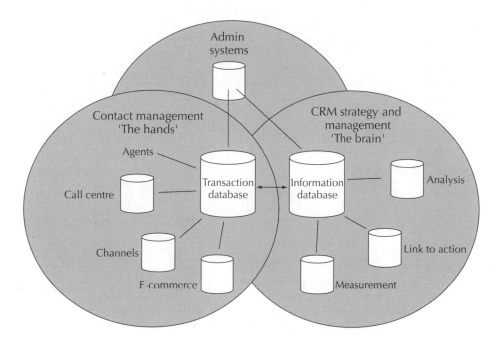

Figure 7.2 Relationship between transaction and information databases

mobile industry, previous dependency on a tied dealer channel is opening up to allow multi-franchise dealers and direct customer contact through e-business or call centres. At the same time a much broader product mix is becoming available across those channels, with the addition of many new financial and physical services aimed at the development of the same customer base.

Supporting hybrid channel management

Many projects now aim to utilize channels cooperatively (or in collaboration) to achieve greater revenues through a hybrid sales and marketing approach (see Figure 7.3). New business can be pre-qualified by mail or through a call centre before the sales team gets involved. Customers can review or amend their business arrangements electronically as they decide. However, although products like mortgages can be arranged over the Internet, personal contact is often required by the client during the process, for assistance or even just for reassurance. This hybrid channel approach requires a common service centre to coordinate prescriptive (outbound to customer) and responsive (inbound initiated by customer) contacts.

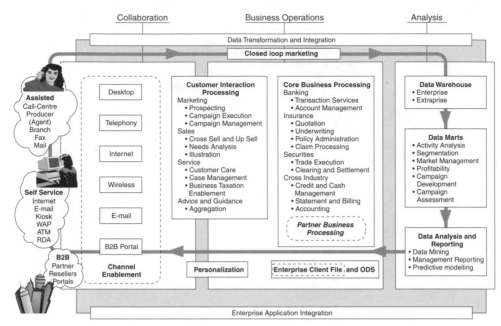

Figure 7.3 Multi-channel and closed-loop customer management example

Customers may deal with the company through any mixture of channels that they prefer. Typically, they may visit a local car dealership to inspect vehicles or get information but purchase the car direct over the Internet. In this environment, it is important that a common database is available behind these different channels to ensure consistency. This will support the same basic actions, identify the customers, understand their current arrangements and customize responses to what we know of them from the contact log.

The contact log provides a record of all outbound and inbound customer contacts, through any contact method including using the Internet, e-mail, mail, telephone and others. It can be considered as part of the transaction database or may be held alongside. It will also be duplicated within the information database or data warehouse, when required for mining or analysis.

The costs and complexity of such systems are usually significant due to the many links with multiple product administration systems and customer contact channels. The business case is only likely to succeed if customer service managers have substantial budgets and power. The financial benefit of improved customer service is not usually easy to justify, unless it is provided as part of a full cycle project. Financial benefits are usually couched in terms of revenue increases from cross-selling opportunities. It is usually not easy to establish the value of these revenues in the short term so a focus on retention efforts can be a stronger base for development and learning. As a result, projects usually start with stand-alone systems in campaign management or in the call centre. Inevitably these need to be integrated with other systems eventually. The transaction database then becomes a key component in that integration. If it is overlooked, dramatic consequences may arise in contact coordination which are only too evident to the customer.

These systems investments concentrate on the ability to act. They are developing the hands, arms and legs of the organization. However, we cannot manage customers effectively without a brain. The brain in the IT systems process is the other major investment area. The integration of these capabilities is key.

BUILDING THE BRAIN

Until the mid-1990s, decision support systems were something of a second-class citizen. Often there was no obvious link between data analysis, decision making, and operational actions. Nor was there a link between action and measurement. More recently, the importance of customer management strategies has become apparent and there is increasing focus on the use of information to understand customers and build relationships.

This capability goes under a variety of labels including decision support system (DSS), market intelligence system (MIS) and the more recent business intelligence (BI) or analytical systems. These systems support the organizational decision making and learning. The enormous quantity of business information produced by transaction systems has to be interpreted by business managers in some way to direct future efforts towards CRM goals. Without effective intelligence, the business's capacity to act is greatly reduced or wasted. For example, effort may be made trying to cross-sell unprofitable products to unprofitable customers, or to acquiring and retaining bad customers. Transaction systems with the capability to implement new products rapidly, or to customize existing products, cannot be exploited without understanding what customers will respond to. This understanding emerges from the BI brain.

The role of the data warehouse

The brain is built around another customer database, the data warehouse. This database is the partner of the transaction database and exchanges data with it. A data warehouse is generally structured for performance, in terms of ease of access, fast analysis of large data sets and efficient report generation.

Prodigious amounts of data are required for the statistical and operations research routines used by a data warehouse. Comprehensive historic data is important so that the past can be used to predict the future (which is not always possible if sudden changes in trend occur or where customer behaviour is very erratic). Nevertheless, past responses to marketing campaigns are often used as an indicator of future behaviour. How much historic data needs to be held becomes clearer over time and depends upon the nature of the data and the volatility of the market. Detailed transaction data is usually required to gain insight into buying events. Storage systems can now hold enormous data sets which ever faster processors are able to analyse in a cost-effective manner. The costs of storage and processing power continue to drop rapidly, improving the economics of this sort of exercise. Historic data can usually be removed from transaction systems once a data warehouse is in place, which saves duplication of this data.

Accurate data timing in the transaction database is central to the reliability of the data warehouse as this forms the basis of sales and other time-based reports in previous periods. One UK bank predicted that existing account holders would be more likely to take loans if they had a large account balance from a recent credit transaction. In fact the bank was only recognizing borrowers *after* the loan had been paid into their accounts, subsequent to loan approval! In a similar case, a property insurer predicted that claimants were likely to have had a recent survey. Of course this turned out to be a post-claim survey. Careful interpretation of timed data is obviously vital.

Generally the data warehouse will hold much more data than any other, even more than the transaction database. Not only will it hold historic data but supplemental data such as geo-demographic, lifestyle, risk data and the developing contact log. It may even hold potential prospects and will grow over time as relationship priorities develop. Many large companies are building and using these strategic data warehouses to provide the BI to drive marketing strategies. While smaller versions of these, known as data marts, were (and are) being built as experimental or development tools, they were often incompatible with other enterprise systems. While a data mart provides some tactical benefit there is often no way to proceed towards an integrated capability without replacing it completely.

One common example of a component now understood to be a specific data mart is commonly referred to as the MCIF (marketing customer information file). During the 1980s many companies in the United States started to create MCIFs, in isolation from other system components, in order to build a basic campaign management tool. Sometimes they were developed without even the involvement of the IT department. Effective system performance however requires the full cycle architecture to achieve the right level of integration and inter-operation.

As customer information is acquired and the data warehouse develops, it makes no sense to hide this valuable information away within a few internal departments. New PC-based tools and other technologies are making ready exploitation of this data more viable. Most PCs now have standard Web browsers readily available as the primary user interface. These tools enable easy database access from almost any PC. Appropriate data can then be made available from the data warehouse to branches, business partners and even customers. Regular reports, for example by sales territory, can be distributed automatically, enabling security-protected 'drill down' by authorized users so they can better understand the reason for out-of-line business indicators. It is this technology which underpins the use of KPIs (key performance indicators).

Reporting tools can then work on an exception basis, identifying and broadcasting reports only when KPIs are out of line. This push technology enables broadcast data to be sent to almost any device including a Web site, an e-mail address, a fax machine, a laptop computer, a mobile phone, a pager or a PDA. Such data services are becoming recognized for their value in managing business relationships.

Combining analysis and action

There are major differences in the way operational or transaction data and information or decision support data are managed. If these differences are ignored in the basic architecture and in feedback mechanisms, then major problems occur for large scale usage. For example, in a marketing campaign the pre- and post-analysis of data is informational, while campaign execution and response management are considered operational. Yet only together do they form a complete closed loop process.

More recently systems-automated or direct linkages are being created from information to transaction systems (from the brain to the hands). For example, the actual mailing of targeted leads derived from scoring by the data warehouse can be distributed over the Internet to sales agents and to the call centre which is then ready to handle customized campaign responses. Batch data movement processes or common messaging hubs can provide this integration function.

It is not only data such as scores and offers which can be passed in this way. Knowledge in the form of algorithms can be passed too. This knowledge can be used to make the call centre scripts dynamic, varying both questions and answers to callers according to their enquiry, thus supporting call handlers 'intelligently'. Response management, product customization and pricing can then be driven more effectively. Algorithms and customer information can be used in real time to respond to customer needs and likely profitability. This enables the sales agent or call centre to act in real time, making better decisions about how to manage their relationship with the customer. It becomes especially valuable for decision making as the customer starts to initiate the higher contact levels associated with transparent marketing.

Meanwhile, the contact and transaction systems add more information to the data warehouse about customer responses and purchases, in turn improving the knowledge handling algorithm even further. In other words, more iterations yield more data which improves relationship handling which produces more interactions, and so on, exploiting the closed loop as a learning loop.

The importance of feedback from transaction to information systems to measure the effect of previous decisions is now recognized, at least as an objective. However, there is much lower understanding of the need for feedback at the modular level. For example, scoring customer data is a reusable systems module that can prepare for marketing campaigns or personalization support through several different channels. If customer scoring is to be used as an independent, modular activity this must be incorporated within the design, ie within the systems architecture, so that scored data is passed to, say, contact optimizers or campaign execution tools. In the same way, mail contacts need to be passed to the active contact log, responses and purchases need to be made available to the campaign evaluation process and so on. The importance of a well-thought-out architecture, with sound informational and operational feedback loops quickly becomes apparent.

The difficulty of integrating these feedback links into a complete system design should not be underestimated. Even with a proven architectural approach, this is a major implementation problem. Systems complexity quickly escalates, which is not only expensive but can become a major constraint on further development work. While a number of companies have now developed integrated CRM system strategies, there are very few examples of companies that have achieved more than the first few stages of implementation successfully. The race is therefore very open and the winner may well reap substantial reward in the form of competitive differentiation..

Route maps or IT cookbooks are just beginning to emerge which encapsulate the growing years of experience from both successful and failed projects and especially the potential role of pilots, prototypes, staged build and outsourcing. As more fast-start assets of this sort become available, the cost, timescales and risk of large CRM project implementation will reduce. Experienced CRM skills are in short supply in every industry and geography. The use of an agreed architecture and project method can help ensure that available skills are used to best effect. In addition, it becomes practical to utilize other, less experienced developers as part of the project. A broad mix of many different technical skills will be required but there is a tendency at the moment to specialize on one topic such as change management, data quality, call centre operations and so on. As there are few hybrid skills available, architecture and method assume greater importance in terms of leveraging and coordinating expertise to best effect.

THE IMPACT OF MERGERS AND ACQUISITIONS

Companies recently merged, or with merger strategies, may encounter special systems and data challenges, not just in creating a strong strategy but in ensuring practical implementation. Mergers within a country or market can often delay evolving CRM programmes by two to three years. This is due to the increased complexity of integrating marketing postures, differences in the operational management of units such as call centres and the added complexity of integrating IT systems and databases. From many perspectives, the most valuable asset of a modern enterprise is the knowledge (in the form of expertise) and the information (in the form of databases) which it owns. If this is to be recognized, the 'predator' company's first steps when considering a merger or acquisition should be to devise ways of retaining key personnel in the target company and ensuring that the information services of the two enterprises can be combined at reasonable cost.

The merger objective is often market share and cost reduction so that immediately after the fusion of the two companies there is a flurry of cost reductions. Product rationalization is often the basis of the cost reduction exercise so as to enable processes and systems to be simplified. However, this can quickly backfire. Indeed, it has been known to result in almost the complete loss of customers from the target company, as products and services which attracted and retained them are removed.

An alternative approach is to analyse the two sets of databases for common customers and for differences. Building a strategy for the management, retention and growth of the merged customer base provides a better starting point for positive rationalization. In practice, there are very few examples of mergers being tackled in this manner. Many companies miss this one-time opportunity and can take years to recover. They may even claim that merger activities have made them too busy to consider CRM issues.

Global or cross-market mergers are usually carried out to gain additional market access. This is still the most usual approach to becoming a more global player. In this scenario the challenge is to gain benefit in other ways from the merged company. For example, a global financial services company may intend to replicate its CRM projects between markets, so as to leverage its marketing capabilities through parallel learning. Alternatively, or additionally, central resources may be shared to reduce operating costs. If financial responsibilities are then delegated to country or market level, the CRM programmes will only be able to benefit where there is a cooperative management structure and a strong project champion at the highest level. In short, whilst the rewards of integration may be very high for a merged companies, the execution of strategy is considerably more difficult to achieve than it first appears.

INTEGRATING CUSTOMER MANAGEMENT SYSTEMS

The benefits – to companies and customers – of customer management are fairly clear in most industries, particularly when customer management strategy is based on a well-thought-out model of customer management and when the implementation programme is carefully planned and managed. However, few companies anywhere have overcome the technical barriers to achieving the full potential of customer management.

From a systems point of view, the key is integration of the many systems that a company uses to manage different aspects of its relationship with customers (and increasingly that customers use to manage their relationships with the company). Integration allows data arising and used in many different types of interaction, in many channels and for different products and services to be brought together and transformed into valuable and accessible customer information.

The reason for this is that many companies develop their IT infrastructures organically over decades, adding systems to meet particular business needs as they arise. This means that many companies have systems that were conceived during the 1980s or even earlier, running alongside ones implemented in the 21st century. The older ones are usually referred to as 'legacy systems', although in many cases they are critical operational systems without which the business would collapse. The technologies and computer languages that these use are completely different from those used in newer systems, and there are formidable obstacles that make it very difficult for these systems to communicate with each other. In many cases, because companies have over the last few years introduced several CRM systems to meet the needs of different channels or products, even these systems cannot share data easily.

To improve the consistency, productivity and benefit of customer management, data must be derived from many incompatible systems and turned into useful information that can be used to build a complete picture of each customer. It requires specialist knowledge, combined with experience of previous projects, to transform data resident in many systems into actionable information that can be used when managing a particular customer. The information is used to ensure that:

- The right product is offered to the right customer at the right time.
- Where the product can be customized in any way (eg features, pricing), it is done in such as way as to optimize the customer's lifetime value and profitability to the company.
- The business has the resources, at that moment, to close and fulfil all the deals that will flow from the offer.
- Customers are managed in a way that optimizes the cost-effectiveness of each channel.
- Senior and middle managers always have what they need to make the best informed strategic decisions more quickly than their competitors.
- In its most advanced form, that customer knowledge is used by every layer of management, from the CEO for strategy development, across sales, marketing, operations and financial management, uniquely providing an integrated approach to CRM from the CEO right through to the database administrators who enable all the above to work.
- Collaborative working takes place across departments and channels, especially in areas such as customer retention and new product development.

Data where it's needed… when it's needed

Integration involves more than unlocking data that is imprisoned in many legacy systems. Just as important is the ability to move current data around the business. Particularly now, with customers being offered and choosing to use a variety of touch points, it is important that some forms of data are updated instantly.

Of course, not all areas of business are time-critical, requiring immediate access to up-to-the-minute information. Where this is not required, data can be batch-processed using traditional ETL (extract, transform and load) techniques. But where customer management requires a customer view that is up-to-the-minute, it is important to make sure that, say, the branch, the call centre, the Web site and the interactive television service all show the same information at any given moment.

There are two methods of transporting and transforming this data, and most companies use different combinations of both. A traditional ETL model can be used. Data is moved in batches, often in overnight or even less frequent runs. This is appropriate where there is no penalty in users accessing out-of-date information, eg for budgets or end-of-month figures. The other approach is to update in – effectively – real time, and is the preferred model where customers or customer-facing staff use the information, or where data is being employed in time-sensitive activities.

If the latter approach is used, a company can use advanced middleware, eg messaging software such as IBM's MQ series, to interchange data immediately between many different systems and then make it available to all channels, in real time. This software acts as a hub, accepting messages from one system and employing XML (extensible mark-up language) technology to make these messages intelligible to all the others. This approach has several additional benefits:

- It can greatly reduce time to market, allowing new functionality and products to be integrated into the business and launched very quickly.
- It provides a company with a single, comprehensive view of each customer.
- It facilitates superior workflow practice when a prolonged interaction with an individual customer is required.

When theory meets practice

Closed loop CRM may not be readily achievable by every company – or even desirable. Companies seem to have a number of requirements in this area. Those that are confident about their customer management strategy, perhaps already having deployed a number of CRM systems, may only need to customize and implement a further component, such as a Siebel, Kana, S1 or ChannelPoint package. At the opposite end of the continuum are companies with no customer management infrastructure at all. They may require a complete solution from a single source. Most companies fall between these two extremes. They have deployed some customer management systems, but now require objective analysis and advice to feed into the continuing process of evaluating and re-evaluating their customer loyalty strategy. The first step in any such process is to make a realistic appraisal of the current position and align this with their strategy, such as the process described in Chapter 1. Then follows program development, using roadmaps and techniques described in Chapter 14.

Simplifying data migration and integration

This section looks at simplifying data migration and integration in financial services customer loyalty projects.

The process of migrating, integrating and consolidating data is littered with obstacles. It often causes serious slippage in project timetables – and equally harmful budget over-spend. Frequently, projects fail to deliver the anticipated business benefits, simply because the quality of the data they produce is too suspect to be useful. Worse, some projects are never completed at all. The reason for much of this is unpredictability of the integration process. Until recently, the investment in time and money required to assess the issues involved has been so great that it has been unfeasible to gain a full understanding of a project's scope and scale until the migration and integration team is well into its work. Even then, there is no guarantee that unwelcome difficulties will not arise unexpectedly. What is certain is that often up to 50 per cent of a project's cost and time can be taken up by the data migration and integration effort.

When you can't start from scratch

A primary objective of a customer loyalty initiative is to build as clear a picture as possible of each customer, through a continuing process of acquiring and using information. For most projects, the richest source of start-up information is the historical data stored in the company's legacy systems. These databases may contain transaction histories for different sorts of products or services (including ones for which the customer is no longer active), responses to various direct marketing offers, customer service queries (complaints, requests for information), core customer data, product subscription records, and so forth. Generally speaking, all of the different sources of data are likely to have been constructed at different times, for different purposes, and often using different tech-nologies. The challenges of transforming such varied data into usable and valuable infor-mation are formidable. Conflicts can be as basic as having the same data presented in different length fields in different databases. More seriously, data with the same meaning may be recorded differently in various systems, resulting in varying degrees of reliability. Some data may not even match its original document description. When this 'semantic drift' and 'data mutation' arises, assessing the value to be placed on each source takes on a central significance.

As the business issues that drive customer management initiatives become more acute, the ability to migrate and integrate data quickly and cost-effectively delivers an increas-ingly critical competitive edge. Below, we describe the methodology used by IBM, just to give the reader a sense of the technical complexity involved.

Data integration methodology

Here is a suggested methodology:

1. Use specialist tools to analyse and profile the content, structure and quality of the source data, and to produce a normalized data model. The process is carried out three-dimensionally (down columns, across rows and between tables) and permits the selection or customization – in consultation with the customer – of the data model that the new application will use.
2. Use the source data model thereby created to map to the design of the new target data model. This target data model has been designed and customized to address precisely the business requirements of the new CRM project, and may be based on one of a number of industry database models. From this mapping, batch data transformation and load routines can be generated using ETL techniques to pre-load and/or to batch or synchronize regular changes between these databases. It is also at this point that issues regarding the quality of data can be identified and the data cleansing criteria defined.
3. For interactive updating, use specialist messaging software to allow an immediate interchange of information. Here data transformations are carried out by adapter programs that carry data between the source system and the messaging software's read and/or write messaging hub. XML formats are loaded into the target mapping function created in Step 1. Use a specialist tool to map between the source model and the XML format to generate a data transformation design. This design can then be encoded as a hub adapter for the application to converse with any other through this common hub.

These new tools and methodologies work equally well for data migration (when the source data is being merged with, or moved to, an existing database in a one-time operation) and for data integration (when the target application or data warehouse is being freshly constructed, and then continuously synchronized).

Using traditional manual analysis techniques, 50 per cent of an average migration and integration project's labour costs are typically expended on data analysis, while 30 per cent go into development, and the remaining 20 per cent into the actual movement of data. When specialist data integration tools are used, the data analysis element is typically slashed to 15 per cent of the original labour budget, saving up to 35 per cent overall. As importantly, a similar impact can be expected on the time required to execute the project. None of these figures takes into account the cost of aborting analysis and integration work that cannot be brought to fruition owing to complications that remain unforeseen well into a project timetable – an all too common experience when using traditional techniques. When the Standish Group published its *Migrate Headaches* report in 1999, it suggested that only 17 per cent of e-business initiatives requiring corporate systems integration were wholly successful. It reported that 49 per cent overran, and a full 34 per cent failed, meaning that projects were twice as likely to fail than succeed. It is in order to contain and manage these risks better that many experts advocate treating data migration and integration – along with data cleansing – as a discrete sub-project within a CRM implementation.

Using specialist software tools continues to provide savings well after the data migration and integration project has been completed. Because the analysis has been done on an end-to-end basis, a good base of meta-data (higher level data, derived from original data, usually by combining different data elements) can be defined. This, together with the actual process can then be reused for subsequent projects. For example, if the initial project is to build an operational customer file, the meta-data and process can be reused during the development of the informational customer data to go into a data warehouse or mart.

There will be very few occasions when a data migration and integration project results in a closed database containing only historical records. There is almost always a need to refresh the data on a continuing basis. The mapping and profiling carried out as part of the original work will allow new data to be synchronized continuously between the source and target databases.

CONCLUSION

Integrated systems are required to support integrated business capabilities for customer management. New capabilities can be added alongside existing systems and integrated to provide improved ability to gain return on investments. These developments can be prioritized and carried out in stages if a consistent approach is deployed which reuses skills, methods and tools against a common architecture and roadmap. A closed loop operation can be developed in one business area or for one customer management objective and extended to others. Over time the CRM ecosystem is developed by combining collaborative (multi-channel) and analytical capabilities through operational integration.

8

The intelligent supply chain

Merlin Stone, Kumar Bhaskaran and Colin Devonport

INTRODUCTION

Developing an effective e-business means handling a whole range of supply chain issues. This chapter focuses on the data, processes and systems that companies need so that the various supplier–customer relationships in an electronic supply chain work effectively. It investigates the extent to which removing different parties – vertical integration and/or disintermediation – increases net value to suppliers or customers, when it does not, and the costs and benefits to final customers. It considers how redefinition of a supply chain or market can cause you to change your place in the virtual supply chain. It also covers some aspects of the systems and data support you need to make the new supply chain work. Finally, it provides an extensive case study on one of the biggest barriers to improving customer management through e-chain techniques, namely the sharing of information about customers.

In this chapter, we use the term e-chain to refer to the situation in which one or more members of the supply chain connects, using e-business technology, with a member of the supply chain that is above or below them, and may even be one level removed from them, eg a supplier's supplier or a customer's customer. This connection may be direct, or indirect (eg via the systems of the supply chain partner immediately above or below them. It may be via a third party agent that provides the connection process). It may also be automatic, ie with no human intervention other than that of the initiator (eg a manager in one company viewing or securing inventory from a supplier's supplier).

E-chaining is not a new idea. Even in its most advanced form (connecting with companies one level removed), in airline inventory, intermediaries have been able to secure inventory (seats) for customers in this way for some time. So it has been a (relatively) small step to allow customers to do it themselves through an intermediary Web site such as Travelocity. However, it is the extension of these techniques into other areas, such as insurance quotations, that is causing our views on how to manage customers to change.

Of course, sharing information and improving processes in the supply chain is how leading companies have operated for some time. Many have also realized that it is not the adoption of technology per se that is important, but how leaders use it to share supply chain data to improve mutual management of the chain. It is the widespread use of e-business techniques that have increased the opportunity for doing this and extended it beyond a select group of large companies prepared to pay for the development and maintenance of a proprietary infrastructure into an e-market.

REDESCRIBING MODELS OF CUSTOMER MANAGEMENT

We start by reconsidering our conclusions about best practice in customer management, and seeing how they also apply to supplier management by customers. A key part of this is our concept of customer management models. Elsewhere we have stressed how the model by which any part of the supply chain relates to the next level down (its 'customers') has a dramatic effect on the optimal types of information flows between the parties in the supply chain. The business model of customer management is also the most important determinant of business intelligence requirements, closely followed by the particular strategy followed within the model. Let us consider how these customer management models look when we focus on the supply chain angle. As we shall see, e-technology not only makes most of these models more feasible and cost-effective, but it also makes it easy to combine models.

One to one

In this model, the company gathers high volumes of data about the individual and tries to adapt its entire offer as closely as possible to the individual customer's needs. In the age before e-business, this model tended to work for managing quite large customers, where the costs of doing it are likely to be paid by the benefits. Of course, this model is also followed in personal services. However, in the e-world, mutual customization becomes much easier. Suppliers have found that one of the best ways of using e-technology to reduce relationship set-up and management costs is to allow customers to provide data, design and run relationships. When the relationship is between a large business as a customer and its suppliers, the very way in which the process is set up can be one-to-one (ie the customers tell or show the supplier how they would like to trade using e-technology). In the case of the new business-to-business exchanges and e-markets, groups of customers are doing this to groups of suppliers.

Transparent marketing

The company gives as much control of the offer as possible to the customer. This is best viewed in the context of certain other models. We have already seen above how customer control can lead to one-to-one supplier management. It can also radically improve the effectiveness of CRM, because instead of suppliers trying to gather lots of data about customers and determine the right offer, customers can specify the type of relationship required, and when change is appropriate.

Classic CRM

In this model, customer data is used to group customers to allow them to be managed in a limited number of segments with significantly different offers for each segment. E-technology makes it possible for customers to validate or refresh the supply of customer data more frequently and more accurately, and also to select different modules in the relationship offer, which are appropriate to the value they see. These additional interactions can keep the relationship on track much more effectively.

Personalized communication and targeting

The offer is similar to all customers, but modified slightly to allow basic personalization, and targeted appropriately. This applies particularly in mass markets, where the costs of gathering the information used for customization, and then ensuring its quality and maintaining its freshness, are high, and margins on subsequent sales can be very low. So, perhaps paradoxically, allowing customers to specify which of a standard range of products should be considered, and when, can lead to dramatic cost savings. Meanwhile, the information relationship can be highly customized, so customers get much more relevant information about the different standard offers available. Targeting becomes self-targeting.

Top vanilla

Here, a best of breed but standard offer is made to all customers. This has proved to be one of the most popular and profitable business models for the Web world, best demonstrated by low-cost service operations (airlines, car hire, telephony, utilities). Here the customer just registers and buys, or simply sets up an account. The customer can decide whether or not to buy again, and the supplier may find that keeping this model as simple as possible pays. Making it more complex, (eg by giving customers an incentive to come back other than through the inherent benefits of the product or the service), can overcomplicate matters. At worst, it can lead to inappropriate expectations of privileged service. The other side of this is, of course, top vanilla customers are easier to deal with because they know what they want, when they want it and what they are prepared to pay for it. Indeed, it is arguable that one of the successes of low-cost airlines selling over the Web is to educate customers to become top vanilla. This may include reducing their expectations about 'frills', knowing how to use the product or service optimally, and so on. For this reason, some top vanilla suppliers will start with relatively large call centre operations, then migrate customers to the Web as they learn how to buy and use.

Pure spot selling/buying

This is closely related to top vanilla. This is because if you are selling spot, based on best value at the time, it is hard to succeed without a top vanilla model. However, it can be done, as you can spot-sell at lower quality by setting a lower price, or of course combining this with the auctioning model. Spot-buying is characteristic of many markets, and such markets perform best when the market has perfect information – on both sides, suppliers and customers know who is in the market and have information available about supply and demand. This is what the Web and e-markets can provide.

Spot selling/buying within a managed roster

The company focuses on getting on to the customer's roster, and then offering best value. This is effectively a combination of CRM and pure spot-selling. CRM is the process by which the supplier is put on the customer's roster (and of course vice versa). The latter process is very important, as it is easy to lose control in a spot market. Selling a large deal to a spot-buyer who turns out to be the customer from hell, because you do not know much about them, is not a good idea. Not only is there financial (eg credit, order cancellation, fraud and abuse) and service risk, but transaction costs may not be zero (eg there may be substantial tendering work). From the buyer's perspective it is easier to select and manage a small number of buying relationships, at the same time enabling multi-sourcing to operate effectively, providing preferential relationship benefits and negotiation opportunity.

Spot selling/buying via an agent

Here agents make choices on behalf of customers and suppliers. The aim for the supplier is to get on to the agent's roster (if any) and then deliver best value. The aim of the customer is to ensure that the agent has all the information about the customer necessary to secure the most appropriate supplier and deal. The big difference between the e-world and the old world is that the cost of holding the roster of customers and suppliers and offers or requirements (gathering and maintaining the information) collapses. The main investment is the set-up cost for the system to hold it (this includes security aspects), plus marketing of course.

Channel partnership

In this model, suppliers work with channels/agents to create and manage relationships, and customers agree to allow agents and suppliers to cooperate in managing them. Here, as in the model above, the most spectacular development is the emergence of the Web agent, which interfaces between the suppliers' and customers' computers. In this model, data about customers and their needs, orders, etc, and about suppliers, their offers and ability to supply, can be exchanged so as to optimize provision to the customer.

Classic models

We have emphasized that classic models of customer management are also thriving in the e-era. In fact, in some ways, we would argue that sticking to a classic model and e-enabling its supply chain can be the best options of all.

One example is in retailing/agency – by ensuring that data about inventory flows freely between product suppliers and retailers (from manufacturers stock through to point of sale transactions), retailers can focus 100 per cent on classic retailing, ensuring that the right stock is in place and moving quickly off the shelves, or in the case of service products, ensuring that customers select the correct product and that take-up of products proceeds smoothly (eg documentation, fulfilment, service delivery).

Another example is in sales force management – particularly for complex products and services, e-chain techniques allow salespeople and customers to cooperate using supply chain data to deliver best service to customers.

MOVING BETWEEN MODELS

In much of our work we have focused on the relationship between two partners in the supply chain – the customer and their immediate supplier. However, as e-business technology develops, an interesting phenomenon has emerged. In many industries, the classic supply chain has been partly or completely exploded. Cosy CRM-style relationships between one or more sets of suppliers and customers down the supply chain are replaced by a series of apparently chaotic relationships, in which the CRM model is left behind, to be replaced by a mixture of spot-buying, auctioning and partnered CRM. This can either be within companies, or between parts of the same company. See Tables 8.1 and 8.2 for two examples.

Table 8.1   Moves in airline models of customer management

1980s and before	1990s	2000 and beyond
	CRM for higher value customers, but only basic alliances	CRM for higher-value customers, now including extensive alliances
		Personalized communication and targeting for leisure and low-value business customers
Product and yielding-oriented agency marketing	Mass marketing for leisure travel, product-oriented, with agencies managing customers during the sale	Auctioning for all customers
		Low-cost top vanilla approach for less service-sensitive and more price-sensitive customers

Table 8.2   Moves in general insurance (car, property) models of customer management

1980s and before	1990s	2000 and beyond
	Personalized communication and targeting, including cross-selling and customer retention work	Highly customized Web quotations available, direct or through agents, making reverse auctioning principle (bidding for customers) more explicit
Product and risk-oriented agency marketing	Early partnership CRM between insurers and major agents, eg banks, affinity organizations	Mass marketing of top vanilla products through retailers, eg travel insurance

As these transitions are made, there have been these general trends in information and data management:

- Product and inventory data has become available online, to customers and agents, so that customers can identify precisely what they can have, when and at what price, and so that suppliers can allocate products or services to customers. In its latest form, this allows customers to book individual service appointments by access to the scheduling systems of service companies.
- Advanced allocation systems and their associated rules have had to be developed to ensure the optimum match of supply to demand. This includes auctioning software and online yield management systems.
- Online matching of data already held about customers and suppliers and new data supplied during any interaction have become critical. These enable suppliers to determine whether the customer is 'good' or 'bad'. Customers can also use similar techniques, perhaps using third party databases to identify whether suppliers are appropriate (eg likely to deliver on time, whether their product is of the right quality). Both parties can also update their own records online (eg a supplier profile with a customer, a customer profile with a supplier).

However, note that making transitions between models does not always imply gathering and maintaining more of all kinds of data. For example, an airline that decides to follow a bifurcating strategy of CRM for high-value business flyers and top vanilla for low-cost flyers may end up throwing away lots of data about low-value customers.

REDESCRIBING GENERAL MANAGEMENT REQUIREMENTS

Our research has also shown that choice of customer management model is one of five very important general management areas of focus in implementing customer management. If one of these focus areas is poorly addressed, then even the clearest thinking and decision making about models can be wasted. These areas are listed below, together with the effect that supply chain e-business makes on them. Note that the major change is that we are now looking both ways – not just 'down' to customers, but also 'up' to suppliers. The recent spate of announcements concerning business-to-business exchanges in industries such as automobile, electronics and aerospace industries indicates that customers are more than ever before engaging in explicit e-chain policy making for supplier management.

Customer/supplier management strategy

From the supplier's point of view, this was defined as where you want to be, with which customers, products, channels, etc. However, exactly the same applies to customers managing suppliers. One of the recurring themes of this series has been the extent to which e-technology helps customers determine which suppliers they want to use and how they want to use them. E-technology has collapsed the costs of searching and subsequent inter-action. This includes:

- supplier identification, whether through e-directories or simple Web-searching;
- supplier evaluation and selection (eg through taking up references, checking stock position);
- supplier management (ordering, setting up and tracking logistics, receiving invoices, paying).

This liberates customers to diversify their models of supplier management, as we shall see below.

Customer/supplier management model

In the customer sense, this was defined as managing customers through recruitment, development, retention, to improve net value. E-technology has made it easier than ever before for customers to adopt the 'customer-side' of some of our new models of customer management strategies such as spot-buying, reverse auctioning (getting suppliers to bid for customers). Gone are the days when suppliers could hope to manage customers according to the old rules of account management, in which 'best' customers got the most attention and the best service. Now, the expectation is that all customers should get the best, most cost-effective service. Of course, there is always scope for the supplier to attune the product or service to the customer, but increasingly e-technology allows customers to do it them-selves, and at best cost. However, this does not necessarily imply commoditized pricing. By good use of business intelligence to understand and even predict which customers want what, suppliers can ensure that they get the maximum yield from the way they have organized their particular supply chain. Auctioning is just one form of yield management. For example, instead of having to guess what price levels customers are prepared to pay for immediate availability, customers can be asked to bid.

Interestingly, this new flexibility in supplier–customer relationships does not imply the death of CRM. Supplier search and management costs may have fallen, but they are not zero. Not all suppliers (or customers for that matter) are equally competent at managing their mutual interactions. So classic CRM techniques can still be used in managing the cycle of the relationship – the process by which a relationship is set up is just a lot faster and more efficient. It is also worth noting that a truly mutual relationship that is possible using e-tech-nology is more self-protecting than one in which there is opaqueness between supplier and customer, lags in the transmission of information, and few ways for customers to tell suppliers about problems, changed needs, etc.

Customer/supplier management enablers

This includes data, systems, processes and measures that support/ensure the delivery of strategy and model. Of course, in the new version of the e-chain, these systems may be shared, or are at least Web-enabled. In business-to-business situations, suppliers can view the level of stocks of their products held by their customers, while customers can see the state of their suppliers' inventory of products these customers need. Third parties involved in moving material between the two may provide views on progress. However, one area of real problems is when a customer and supplier both have views of mutual customers further down the supply chain. As Chapter 4 showed, there are real barriers to information sharing in this area, often due to lack of trust.

People in customer management

One of the constant themes of our research is that the people involved in setting up new ways of doing business between suppliers and customers are usually poorly briefed and managed, in terms of their accountability, training, communication, etc. They are often poorly supported with current and accessible information too. These issues also apply to individual business initiatives (eg marketing campaigns) within a customer–supplier system. Although many aspects of e-chain management are taken over by computer, and substantial information and process support can be provided through Intranet systems, there is still room for human skills, decisions, activities and therefore errors.

Customer management programme

In customer management, much of the focus of discussion is upon what it will be like when the approach to customer management has been changed, rather than on the process of changing the system. Our research has repeatedly shown that lack of a proper change programme leads to severe problems of poor coordination and waste of resource. The same principles apply to e-chain change. Moving from managing suppliers via conventional media and processes to e-chain techniques also requires a coordinated sequence of projects (a change programme), varying in breadth and depth, with cumulative, transferred successes and learning, shared infrastructure/capability development, and with testing and piloting built in.

E-COMMERCE AND SUPPLY CHAINS

Evolution of the supply chain and the emergence of e-markets

Supply chains are business models, such as those depicted in Figure 8.1, that integrate information and decision within and between multiple trading partners to form an extended value chain (e-ValueChain) offering goods and services to customers. The e-ValueChain (see Figure 8.2) consists of a core set of business processes that coordinate planning and transactional applications based on shared information across functional and enterprise boundaries.

The e-ValueChain processes include:

- PDM (product data management) for requirements, design, development and introduction of products to market faster;
- ERP (enterprise resource planning) to maintain an integrated view of enterprise resources such as inventory and financial transactions such as sales orders and purchases;

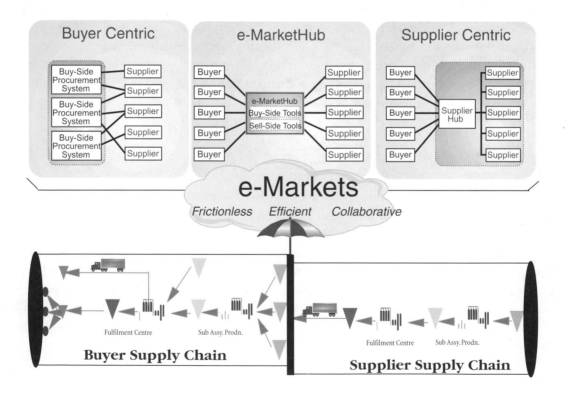

Figure 8.1   E-market categories

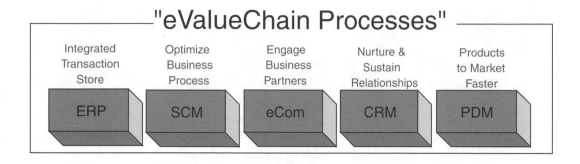

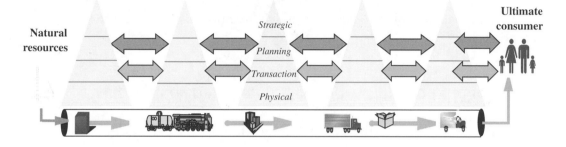

Figure 8.2 The e-ValueChain

- SCM (supply chain management) to plan, schedule and manage production, distribution and delivery;
- CRM to provide customer service, maintain, and nurture customer relationships;
- E-Com (e-commerce) to engage business partners including suppliers for procurement, customers for selling, and other logistics, financial and service providers.

The e-ValueChain vision is to create an ultra-responsive, efficient and profitable business model via integrating core business processes and enabling frictionless commerce between businesses. Electronic marketplaces or e-markets represent the technology and market driven transformation of the supply chain to e-ValueChain. Current business trends point to four graduated levels of e-business capability that highlight the overall trajectory of transformation of the supply chain to e-ValueChain. Each individual level encapsulates a new business-to-business model. Levels 2–4 introduce a variety of electronic marketplaces that collectively represent e-markets. The levels are as follows:

- Integrated supply chain: repositioning the enterprise to do e-business by moving from paper to electronic transactions and providing information visibility in the supply chain.

- Dynamic supply chain: extending the enterprise to take advantage of aggregation economies generated by buy-side (e-procurement) and sell-side (e-store) online markets.
- Electronic hubs: compressing the multitiered supply chain through online exchanges (e-Hub) that concentrate supply chain execution and logistics services and generate value and economy for the trading network of businesses.
- Virtual corporations: enabling collaborative, frictionless commerce across e-marketplaces (e-ValueChain) in discovering business partners, optimizing business processes, efficiently executing transactions, and reaching a global market.

What are the capabilities of the e-business models, mentioned above? How are they shaped by e-markets?

Repositioning to conduct e-business (integrated supply chain)

In 2000, only 1.9 per cent of the overall business-to-business activity in an economy as advanced as that of the United States is expected to be transacted over the Internet.[1] The e-marketplaces that have enjoyed wide press to date have been largely for low-margin and low-touch commodity items (eg office products). Core supply chain processes and primary markets remain to be the huge future potential for e-markets (expected to be US $500 billion by 2003). This is not surprising as most businesses are striving to change their traditional supply chains to conduct e-business. Businesses are eliminating the 'functional silos' in traditional supply chains that are characterized by disconnected processes, stand-alone applications, and disjointed communication channels for information exchange.

Supply chain integration challenges

The principal challenges in repositioning the supply chain for e-business are as follows:

- *Integrating business processes and enabling the inter-operability of applications to provide information visibility in the supply chain.* This provides basic capabilities such as available-to-promise, ie the ability to respond to a query on the availability of a product in the supply chain either as finished goods or planned for production. Consider for example the IBM Technology Group business, a leading OEM supplier to PC manufacturers such as Dell. The IBM supply chain is being repositioned to do e-business so Dell can view the availability of parts in the just-in-time inventory store as well as that planned to be shipped to Dell over the next two weeks. This required IBM to integrate the core fulfilment processes, underlying applications, and to Web-enable access to information.

- *Exchanging information electronically among trading partners in the supply chain.* Supply chains rely on longer-term preferred relationships with suppliers and customers. Consequently, supply chains must be capable of exchanging information among trading partners such as forecasts and planned shipment. A number of businesses, already invested in proprietary messaging and value-added networks such as electronic data interchange (EDI) to facilitate information exchange, are transitioning to more flexible and standards-based messaging, based on XML. The ability to exchange information electronically among trading partners in a supply chain has had the effect of shrinking overall response times and increasing supply chain efficiency.

- *Organizing the supply chain by market segment enables delivery of customized products and services through extended self-service transactions.* Best-in-class supply chains are allowing customers not only to browse information but also to configure products and services, initiate transactions, and monitor the transaction over its life cycle. Such self-service transactions reduce process and transaction costs while improving customer service performance. Supply chains are traditionally product-centric and typically push standard products through the channel using aggressive product mass marketing. Customer-centric supply chains on the other hand allow customers to pull customized products and services through self-service transactions.

Leveraging buy/sell-side e-markets (dynamic supply chain)

Dynamic supply chains are supply chains that use buy-side and sell-side electronic marketplaces as trading partner applications to generate process and transaction efficiencies. The *e-procurement* application is a buyer-centric marketplace that provides supply aggregation, ie an aggregated view across many suppliers and a single interface to all supplier catalogues with the ability to scale to include new suppliers. The *e-store* application is a seller-centric marketplace that provides demand aggregation, ie support for multiple buyers through a unified catalogue with the ability to propagate changes to products, prices, promotions, etc. This is shown in Table 8.3. Associated *e-payment* capabilities can manage and reconcile the financials of these buy and sell operations.

E-procurement applications in practice today are predominantly used for indirect procurement, items not used directly in the production of finished goods, also known as MRO (maintenance, repair, and operations) procurements. The compelling return on investment of such applications is attributable to savings in order processing costs and the reduction of maverick purchases that typically carry 15–27 per cent premiums in purchase price.[2] The e-procurement applications typically support market mechanisms such as RFQ/Quote/Bid.

Production procurement, ie items consumed in production of finished goods, remains a challenge for e-procurement applications. EDI has been used for production procurement

Table 8.3 The e-store

Buy-side	Mechanism	Catalogue Demand/Supply Aggregation	Sell-side
Several buyers procurement systems	Buyer benefits	• Lower search and transaction costs • Broader supply base	Supplier hub
Each working with different subset of suppliers	Seller benefits	• Lower transaction costs • Broader customer base	Working with all buyers and all sellers in market
	Works best	• MRO products • Fragmented supply chain • Preplanned purchase	

in some businesses but these are mainly expensive peer-to-peer links with none of the aggregation economies generally available in e-procurement. The main challenge in production procurement is supporting collaborative processes between buyers and suppliers, to exchange engineering design and production plans and schedules. In some industries such as the automotive industry, suppliers work with the manufacturers to collaboratively design the parts that they will supply. The e-procurement applications can certainly support such processes but will require significantly more capabilities than are being used for MRO procurements. Most businesses are therefore automating production procurement by beginning with smaller suppliers that require less collaboration and inter-action.

E-store applications today provide an electronic storefront with support for large catalogues (> 10,000 items) and self-service configurators for customers to customize products and services. They also provide technical and promotional product information and support the basic e-commerce process of searching a catalogue, negotiating, ordering, and fulfilling the order. The e-store applications in their current format face several business and technical challenges.

The primary business challenge for supply chains to embrace e-store applications is to avoid conflicts with existing distribution and sales channels. Many supply chains are applying a hybrid strategy of using e-stores to generate the sale and letting existing channels fulfil and be credited appropriately (eg automotive e-stores with onward links to dealers). Technically, the e-store applications are currently limited in their ability to support core supply chain sell-side process such as collaborative forecasting, planning, and replenishment process. Another technical challenge in sell-side e-commerce is to integrate the e-store to back-end supply chain planning and execution applications to update the product, price, and promotional information as well as to provide product availability and order status. The sell-side applications also require integration with third party logistics service providers. The ability to sell round the clock with a global reach and with enhanced customer self-service increases the revenue through new product sales, increased sales to existing customers, and sales to new customers. A sell-side e-commerce solution also has the potential to generate cost savings in order processing, back-order administration, sell-side deployment such as product warranty administration, and customer service through reduction in call centres as well as through better order accuracy.

Compressing the supply chain (electronic hubs)

Electronic hubs (e-hubs) are beginning to recast supply chains as collaborative trading networks. Such hubs (see Figure 8.3) can be vertically specialized, consisting of trading partners in a vertical industry (eg plastics), or functionally specialized, to provide supply chain execution services (eg transportation).

Businesses that hold the most power in the supply chain (eg the big three vehicle manufacturers in the automotive industry) strongly influence the overall structure and best practices of supply chains in which they belong. They also influence the behaviour of other businesses in the supply chain particularly when it comes to adopting new ways of doing business (eg the adoption of EDI among tier 1–4 suppliers in the automotive industry). It is not surprising therefore that the 'compression of supply chains', with the advent of the e-hub, is also being led by the so-called power brokers in the supply chains. Recently, both GM and Ford have announced the formation of an e-hub that will compress their multitiered supply chains to provide key procurement and logistics advantages to all players in their supply chain globally.

Supply chains across industries, particularly those that are fragmented and multitiered, will reconfigure to take advantage of business-to-business market efficiencies of the industry vertical e-hubs. Supply chain execution processes such as order management, warehouse management, transportation management, and international trade logistics are

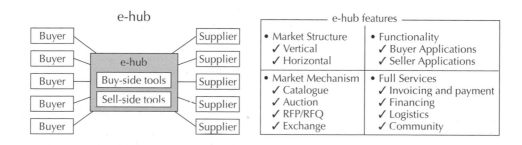

Figure 8.3 E-hubs

prime candidates for transitioning to the e-hub as either shared or outsourced value-added services. It is also possible that certain supply chain execution processes such as transportation management will have their own functionally specialized e-hub. These logistics e-hubs will then provide services to various industry vertical e-hubs to form a network or matrix of e-markets.

Independent software vendors in core e-ValueChain processes such as ERP, SCM and CRM are fast repositioning to provide application services to the emerging network of e-markets. This trend will further enhance the attractiveness of the e-markets by generating supply chain process efficiencies (through better planning and scheduling decision support) in addition to the transaction efficiencies.

Collaborative e-commerce (e-ValueChain)

The e-ValueChain vision is of an ultra-responsive and efficient supply chain through frictionless collaborative e-commerce. The combined effect of having a supply chain seamlessly integrated with collaborative business processes within and between trading partners and taking advantage of the business-to-business efficiencies of e-markets is to create a 'virtual enterprise,' an electronic value chain (e-ValueChain). In the future, it should be possible for e-businesses in an e-market or a network of e-markets to come together as an e-ValueChain to address specific market opportunities that otherwise would not have been possible for any individual e-business. This is what we mean by frictionless collaborative e-commerce.

Realizing the e-ValueChain requires e-markets to have additional capabilities than that conceived today. The e-markets must be 'recombinant, ' ie have the ability to match a market opportunity with a subset of their members based on their business and technical capabilities, formulate the coalition of partners as a supply chain, and spawn the e-ValueChain. It is possible that such an e-ValueChain, a virtual enterprise, will be even legally recognized as a new e-business. The Commonwealth of Pennsylvania, for example, is considering the creation of a virtual industrial park that will register virtual corporations as limited liability corporations (LLCs) to conduct e-commerce.

The e-market challenge

Several e-markets have evolved as various businesses seek to leverage via the Internet to reduce transaction costs, access new channels, and improve efficiencies. We are likely to see as many flavours of e-markets as there are variations of business-to-business e-commerce. A number of e-markets that are transforming the supply chain have been already identified:

- the *e-procurement* buyer-centric e-market;
- the *e-store* seller-centric e-market;
- the *e-hub* that can be either vertically specialized as an industry-specific trading exchange or horizontally specialized as a supply chain execution hub;
- the *e-ValueChain* that can host virtual corporations engaged in collaborative commerce.

Buyer- and seller-centric e-markets are *one-to-many* configurations where one business interacts with many other businesses to either buy or sell goods and services respectively. The e-hub is a *many-to-many* configuration. There are many buyers and sellers. This subsumes one-to-many interaction. The eValueChain is a *one-to-any* configuration where a participant can interact with many other participants either individually or as a coalition of participants constituting a new virtual enterprise.

E-market segmentation

The adoption of e-markets varies from industry to industry. Two factors that affect the applicability of this set of ideas are: fragmentation of the market; and product/process complexity.[3] (See Table 8.4.)

Affiliated e-markets such as the e-procurement/e-store are typically deployed where there is high market fragmentation and relatively low product/process complexity. Buyers and sellers have practically no incentive to adopt e-markets when the market fragmentation as well as the product/process complexity is low. Consequently, in such scenarios a peer-to-peer business-to-business model is more likely to be used.

When the market fragmentation is low but the product/process complexity is high the few participants in the market can use the e-hub as a trading hub. Traditional participants in a supply chain, with low market segmentation, can use this model to conduct supply chain execution processes. On the other hand, when the market fragmentation as well as the product/process complexity is high the e-hub and the e-ValueChain business-to-

Table 8.4 Factors affecting applicability of e-markets

Market Fragmentation	High	e-procurement (buyer-centric)	e-ValueChain (Virtual corporation)
		e-store (seller-centric)	e-hub (exchange)
	Low	business to business direct (peer to peer)	e-hub (trading hub)
		Low	High
		Product/process complexity	

Source: Adapted from AMR 1999

business models are deployed. The e-hub in this case serves as an exchange for goods and services among the many participants – the domain content specific to a vertical will be typically high in these exchanges. The eValueChain manifests itself as a virtual corporation to execute engineer-to-order type of business with high product/process complexity. It is also useful to segment the e-market to understand where the market is today and identify areas of opportunity. The segmentation, shown below, is based on two dimensions – the functional scope and the solution capability of e-markets (see Table 8.5).

The *functional scope* includes design, sourcing, operations, and sales and service activities – basic activities for product and service life cycles. The design function includes all activities associated with the design to manufacturing aspects of the product life cycle. Sourcing function includes determining the source for the materials and acquiring the materials that go into the making of the product. The operations function includes planning and execution of the production and distribution of the products. The sales and service function includes the pre-sales, sales, and post-sales activities.

The solution capability of e-markets includes transaction, content, aggregation and discovery, and community and collaboration. The transaction capability is the ability to execute e-commerce transactions such as catalogue updates, request-for-quotes (RFQ), orders, invoices, and payment. The content capability refers to managing content such as product catalogues, terms and conditions, user profiles, and also provides the ability to configure products. The aggregation and discovery capability features various market mechanisms such as fixed/contract price, auctions, and exchanges. The community and collaboration capability provides support for collaborative business processes and buy-side/sell-side decision support tools.

E-market segmentation based on functional scope and solution capability suggests that today's main focus for e-marketplaces is on content and transaction capabilities for sourcing, sales and service functions. Further, such e-markets support the trading of low-touch and low-margin commodity-type items (eg MRO e-procurement and e-store for office products). This implies that a large segment of the e-market remains largely uncharted and presents a significant opportunity.

Table 8.5 E-market segment opportunities

E-market segments	Functional Scope			
	Design	Operations	Sourcing	Sales and Service
Solution Capability: Collaboration and Community / Aggregation and Discovery / Content / Transaction	Uncharted			Current Focus

The e-market value proposition

The e-markets are gaining momentum in business-to-business e-commerce because of the multidimensional benefits they offer to participants such as buyers, sellers, and market makers. Here are some examples of the business value in e-markets from the individual participant's perspective.

Buyer value proposition

- Streamline procurement processes.
  - Standard parts available to all organizational units within the buyer enterprise thereby reducing parts proliferation.
  - Single purchase order to cover products purchased from multiple suppliers.
  - Single consolidated billing to buyer.
- Reduce transaction costs.
  - Reduced search time for parts across multiple suppliers.
  - Demand aggregation allows pooling of demand from several smaller buyers for preferential treatment from large distributors.
  - All organizational units within an enterprise can benefit from pre-negotiated contractual pricing.
- Access new market opportunities.
  - Value-added search to identify market opportunities, especially important in volatile markets.
- Transcend time and geography boundaries.
  - Conduct business with suppliers located globally.

Seller value proposition

- Provide a new sales channel:
  - The e-markets provide a means of establishing revenue streams outside of the traditional dealer channels without an expensive sales team.
- Improve yield of production processes:
  - For perishable by-products, e-markets provide a quick exposure to a large pool of buyers thereby improving the efficiency of the production process.
- Offload excess or obsolete inventory and excess capacity:
  - Sellers can maintain anonymity as they offload excess or obsolete inventory that they cannot sell through their existing channels.
  - Sellers can offload excess capacity to the highest bidder that would have been gone either unutilized or fetched less than competitive prices.

- Anonymity:
  - Anonymously posted items can prevent the sellers from alienating their existing channel partners. Sellers disclose their identity either offline or after initiating an e-commerce transaction.
  - Anonymity offers advantages to smaller sellers as they can transact business with larger buyers on a level field without undue pressure.

Market maker value proposition

- Time to liquidity:
  - Market makers host and administer e-markets. The seller and buyer value propositions, compelling as they are, should make it possible for market makers to achieve the necessary liquidity in the e-markets quickly.
- Multiple revenue streams:
  - The business model for market makers accommodates several sources of revenue. These include subscription fees from members, usage fee as a percentage of e-commerce transactions (10–20 per cent for aggregators, 5–10 per cent for auctions, and 1–2 per cent for exchanges), mark-up on demand and supply aggregation, advertisement revenue, and revenue from selling business intelligence.
- Operating efficiency:
  - Technology affords market makers to provision automated e-market solutions that are operationally efficient as well as extensible and scalable to accommodate business growth.

Market makers, therefore, can make significant gains in e-markets. The overall gains of the market makers, however, will hinge on the 'leverage' offered by specific e-markets in business-to-business e-commerce. As mentioned before, this leverage is influenced by the market fragmentation and the product/process complexity of the e-marketplace, among other factors.

E-market requirements

The business and technical requirements of an e-market are categorized into information services, e-commerce facilitation, transaction support, and business integration.

Information services

- Content management. Content aggregation across several suppliers and creation of a single unified view help the buyers in searching through the catalogue, which can contain several thousand items. Content engineering is required to organize the rich data on products and services including support for product categorization, support for market and product ontology and schema. Addition of a new supplier's catalogue should be straightforward and easy.

- Industry knowledge and domain expertise. The success of vertical e-markets depends very much on the domain expertise within the industry. Providing access to industry-specific news, event calendar, discussion forums, online experts, etc, will help maintain member loyalty.
- Directory of buyers, suppliers, and third party service providers. An organized way to search through the member directory containing listing of various buyers, suppliers, and third party services is fundamental to help users realize the strength of the e-market.
- Business intelligence. A wealth of knowledge can be gathered by analysing the e-commerce transactions, the search requests, and the RFPs (requests for proposals) and RFQs initiated. This knowledge can be provided to member companies either in summary form (ie industry-wide studies) or specific to the member's own business. Data mining capabilities provided by the e-market can be a source of additional revenue to the market maker.

E-commerce facilitation

- Support anonymity prior to initiating e-commerce transaction. For different reasons, many sellers and buyers would prefer to remain anonymous during the information exchange process and will reveal their identity only after the e-commerce transaction has been initiated. E-markets should support this requirement.
- Support multiple market mechanisms. Depending on product complexity and the nature of supply (inventory, capacity, etc), different market mechanisms may be required for conducting e-commerce. These market mechanisms include fixed price catalogue supporting spot-buying and buying under long-term contracts, auctions and multi-round negotiations.
- RFPs or RFQs. Depending on the specificity of the asset and the terms of sale, market mechanisms other than the catalogue will be required. Table 8.6 shows the additional market mechanisms that an e-market should support.

Transaction support

- Improve trust through pre-registration. As businesses look to conducting commerce through e-markets, one of the risks involved is that of dealing with strangers. This risk introduces inefficiencies within the e-market. Qualifying every member during the registration process reduces this risk. It involves performing credit checks, getting

Table 8.6 Mechanisms an e-market should support

Mechanism	Product/Service Specificity	Terms of Sale Specificity
Fixed Price catalogue	Standard part or service	Price, availability, delivery conditions explicitly stated
Request for Quotation (RFQ)	Standard part or service with or without minor changes	Product/service attributes, price availability, etc, may need negotiation
Request for Proposal (RFP)	Modifications to standard part or service or entirely new design	Product/service design, price, availability, etc, may need negotiation
Request for Information (RFI)	Buyer still formulating product idea or testing concept feasibility	Pre-sale activity which includes delivery of expert judgement, white papers, etc

clearances from member's bank, and conducting other forms of due diligence. The use of business certificates issued to each member by the market maker can further facilitate quick checks by market participants before initiating a transaction.

- **Hold account receivables.** To facilitate e-commerce, several market makers are holding account receivables on behalf of the sellers. This is accomplished through relationships with banks and insurance companies. In many cases the market maker provides escrow services, either their own or through third party escrow agencies. This can be an additional revenue source for the market maker.

- **Provide order status and shipment information.** Currently, most e-markets bring buyers and sellers together to facilitate the transaction but the financial and logistics issues are settled outside by the parties involved. However, as buyers look to place orders for multiple products from multiple suppliers under a single purchase order, they also need information on the order status, shipment details, etc. This requires integration with the back-end systems of suppliers as well as shippers.

- **Support pre-negotiated terms and conditions.** Many businesses are both buyers and sellers in e-markets and so establish policies regarding preferred business partners, access control to their catalogues, etc. E-markets should support these policies so as to build market participants' trust. Policies usually include preferred vendor and buyer lists, restricted access to information for competitors and contractual pricing.

Business integration

- Support long-running transactions via workflow. Most business transactions involve several steps that occur over a period and require participation by several users. For example, the buying process usually includes a user selecting the product or service, the purchasing manager approving the purchase, a purchase order being generated, etc. As e-markets expand their view of the transaction scope, support for long-running transactions, including monitoring and exception handling is required.

- Process and workflow integration. The e-commerce transaction is not only long-running but may also span several organizational boundaries – the buyer's, market maker's, seller's, and other third party service providers' (banks, logistics providers, insurance companies, etc). Although most e-markets currently limit the process scope to only within their own environment, it is not long before integration with back-end systems and processes of buyers and sellers will be a major differentiation. Market makers should develop strategic relationships with providers of ERP systems, supply chain management systems, and support various XML-based industry standards for integration.
- Linkages to other e-markets. By linking with other e-markets, buyers and sellers can have access to a much larger pool of market participants. For example, vertical e-markets could establish relationships with horizontal e-markets for logistics to get instant access to the best shipping rates. Additionally, many businesses are expected to be members of multiple e-markets. Linkages between e-markets can help facilitate transactions that span across e-markets, especially with cross-certified business certificates.

E-CHAIN CHECKLIST

This section provides a checklist to help you decide whether to move your business model to incorporate e-chain ideas, and how you might need to change your organization to do this successfully.

Decisions to be taken

- What are the main operational activities within the supply chain (eg manufacture, stockholding, sale, return of merchandise, service)?
- What are the key decision areas within the supply chain (eg product design, supply volumes, promotions, pricing, partner choice, channel choice, inventories, logistics)?
- Who makes the key decisions?
- When are they best shared or coordinated and when are they best left to internal competition?

Organizational entities and their systems

- What are the organizational entities in the supply chain (eg customers, suppliers, business partners, etc)?

- Do their systems communicate with each other? About what? To what benefit?
- What are the characteristics of data transfer (eg volumes, content, frequency, etc)?
- Are there are lapses or failures in this communication?

Planning and management activities

- What are the main management and planning activities?
- What information is required to support them?
- From which participants in the supply chain does this information come?
- What is the quality of the information currently supplied?
- Can the information be transferred between the systems of different supply chain participants, easily and without too much manual intervention?
- What gaps or delays exist in the information required for planning and management?
- What are the business consequences of these gaps or delays?
- What are the main analysis and reporting requirements generated by supply chain cooperation?

Data management

- What are the main data entities for each of the operational activities and management decision areas?
- What is the current state of the data (eg quality, scope, depth, immediacy)?
- What is the state of information ownership and control, between different pairs of partners?

Specific supply chain data and analysis requirements

- How is data on customers and products matched for different purposes (eg promotions, sales, service, pricing, yield management, etc)?

Marketing issues

- How are changes in the supply chain reflected in ways that suppliers mount campaigns to solicit business from partners further down the supply chain?

Knowledge in different parts of the supply chain

- What are the costs of assembling data from different parts of the supply chain?
- How can these be transformed into knowledge?
- How can this knowledge be transformed into profit (eg by selling more, selling greater variety, reducing interaction costs; enhancing interaction relevance – including customization of products, services and information)?
- Are there non-profit benefits arising from this knowledge?
- How important is coordination of different information and communication flows within the supply chain? Is it really necessary, and what are the costs and benefits thereof?
- Is it possible to identify parts of the flow of finance, materials and services where the best mix of cost, benefits, expectations, advantage can be achieved by integrating information flows?
- Is there a predictable end-state to the evolution of the supply chain, or at least a predictable future state?
- Will this involve different combinations of customer management models than currently in place in the company and its markets?
- Is it possible to identify the business intelligence requirements for this state (eg what will require immediate decision; what will be automated; what will be needed for planning; what exceptions will need to be reported)?
- How will the main measures of effectiveness change?

Supply chain and channel structure

- Is the supply chain structure premised on particular models of customer management?
- If the required model changed would the supply chain be able to adapt?
- How would the information flows within the supply chain have to change as a result?
- Where would be the main changes in information requirements (eg breadth or depth of view of customer further down the chain, location of inventory or risk in the chain, visibility of happenings further up the supply chain)?
- How important is it to the function of the supply chain that there be end-to-end visibility to all participants and end-to-end automated processing for all transactions? Is speed an issue here?
- What are the relationships between the evolving supply chain and evolving marketing and communication channels (eg wireless, the Web, call centre, sales office, retail outlet, mail/logistics)?
- What are the risks of not understanding and managing these relationships?

- What are the legal implications from the ways data will need to flow as models of customer management, distribution and communication channels, and supply chains evolve?

Support

- What should be the role of systems suppliers, in providing information processing capabilities? How will this role change?
- What should be the role of outsourcing? Will it differ in the future?
- What is the role of the IT department in supporting improved supply chain management?
- What techniques and skills are required to manage information and turn it into knowledge? How will these change in the future?
- What processes are required to ensure that the right information is delivered to the right point for action, and then translated into profit? Will these processes change as models, channels and supply chains change?
- What change programmes are required to optimize supply chain intelligence? What new programmes will be required as supply chain and channel structure change?

THE MAIN COMPONENTS OF THE ARCHITECTURE

There are several components that need to be considered in designing the architecture for customer management within a supply chain. In the following section, we consider the basic architecture of a customer management system, and consider how this can be spread over a supply chain. Figure 8.4 gives high-level overview of the arrangement of such systems.

Source systems

Back-office transaction or legacy systems

These are systems which manage the core transactions and store the data that provides the internal view of the customer context. This includes contact details, sales, payments, order status, credit exposure/limit and activity data, such as enquiries, complaints, calls, research data and so on. Traditionally pricing engines, contract and customer data were stored here, but as this data becomes valuable across a relationship it may occur in a common personalization system or party database instead.

	Peer-level partners				
	Access to partner systems and databases				
Higher-level supply chain partners			**Customer management systems**	**Customer contact technologies**	**Lower-level supply chain partners**
			Front-office systems	Web/WAP/kiosk	
	Supplier management systems		Campaign management systems	Telephone, mail, fax	
	Purchasing and ordering systems		Customer administration systems, eg billing	Sales force, counter service	
	Upstream logistics systems, eg goods inwards	Logistics systems shared with partners	Customer database, data warehouse, data marts	Downstream logistics systems	
	Access to supplier systems and databases		Analysis, mining, segmentation systems	***Access to customer systems and databases***	

Figure 8.4 Overview of supply chain customer management systems

Middleware

Middleware interfaces the transaction data to the data warehouse and its views or data-marts. IT architectures which exploit appropriate middleware function to reconcile, move, combine and clean data in batch or online can help manage the serious IT issues imposed by multiple back-office systems, which are frequently exacerbated by mergers and acquisitions.

Knowledge base

Customer knowledge base

Providing a full *customer* 'context', the sum of customers' dealings with you as a company, their previous and current sales and status, the methods by which they prefer to transact with you, what they have told you about how they want to be managed, and about their possible future needs, what you predict their future needs – these are all critical building blocks for CRM of the future. Data warehouses are the starting point for this, but a real-time context is a goal towards which many are rapidly moving. Integrating all touchpoints and channels, including contact centres, account managers and the Web is clearly important here.

External context

This will provide information on the external factors which may be influencing customer behaviour and attitude. Depending on the company, this would include competitive activity, weather, GDP, interest rates, events (eg a World Cup) and so on. These could be held in the data warehouse referred to above, for use by applications that use the views or data marts for data warehouse access.

Business rule tables

It is not an easy task in an organization with disparate systems to define a common set of business rules across channels to ensure that the customer is dealt with in a consistent manner where appropriate (eg offers allowed, trigger proactive communication, deal with call more sympathetically). The new architecture should take into account (1) the customer context (eg lifetime value and specific needs) and (2) a particular behaviour (eg browsing, enquiring, buying, not buying, not enquiring, complaining, paying, not paying, moving, opening new office, marrying, divorcing, wanting technical support). Rules will be many and varied in organizations, especially in large enterprises or organizations selling through intermediaries, and some semblance of order and agreement must be obtained. However, the benefit is consistent treatment of the customer no matter what the business unit, department, office or channel of contact.

Knowledge navigation engine

To support the comments in this chapter on *transparency* and *locus of control moving to the customer*, the architecture needs to consider how customers and partners (and staff) will navigate through the 'knowledge' and context available to find what they need, within defined security rules of course. Again, we have referred to the types of navigation customers and partners might want to make in the first part of this chapter. Considerations would include providing technical support, product selection, tailoring unprompted inbound customer contact, maybe promoting appropriate offers, providing order and complaint status and so on. The advent of the Web as an additional channel provides many benefits for the customer and the organization as we have illustrated earlier. It also enriches the context about the customer or partner, not just in terms of any profile data he or she may give us, but in terms of the screen navigation, product interest and so on. If systems are set up correctly, they can also be an effective provider of context-rich information to the customer, tailored to the context in which we know the customer operates.

Management information, measurement and modelling

These systems are required to provide data for planning (as discussed in this chapter) and measurement. Data mining tools are most often used for segmentation and scoring (propensity modelling), while dynamic management information with drill-down capability can be used to ensure performance is on track against strategic and operational scorecards. This would include measurement information on Web channel usage (eg click stream, telemarketing). Software tools can be deployed to model patterns in the data and investigate alternative future scenarios.

Process assistance systems

An example here are campaign management systems, to aid the set up, management and analysis of integrated media test matrices and campaigns. Other process assistance systems can provide automated support to guide buyers or sellers through a complete workflow.

Front-end applications

These are applications used at the sharp end, in dealing with customers, partners and staff. They will include telemarketing, field force and account management support, Web applications, together with other channel and e-business applications. They must enable consistency of customer management through access to common customer data, product, contract and personalization systems and support.

Changes in trading relationships

The software market, although consolidating in terms of vendors, appears to be changing shape with new Web-based vendors challenging traditional vendors and becoming serious players in several of the areas described above. The middleware vendors play an increasing role in the essential integration of the architecture application content.

How such systems work commercially depends on the trading relationships within the supply chain. For example, in some cases companies further down the supply chain act as commission agents for those further up the supply chain, but the intermediary company does not take title. This is common in designer label retailing, where the manufacturer supplies to retailers on a sale or return basis. This means that consumer sales have to be entered directly into suppliers' systems. Insurance agents do not sell 'the whole product', as the insurer handles the subsequent risk.

The Web is making this once-simple situation more complex. For example, it is now common for financial services companies that both supply and act as agents for other suppliers to have a portal on which combinations of products and services from the company and from its partner suppliers, and even from competitive suppliers, appear. This is to keep the customers on the site, and encourage them to maximize business to the site owner. In financial services this is an e-implementation of 'wealth management' principles. In practice, the same supplier will now more often appear in different places in the value chain at the same time. Therefore, it is imperative that one architecture/systems solution fits all, ie that it is scalable and transferable from supplier to agent situation.

As the research described later in the book shows, one of the major barriers to supply chain data sharing is lack of trust. For this reason, having trading partner agreements with supply chain partners must be deemed a critical success factor. It is not essential that these agreements are underwritten by systems integration, but consideration must be given to the use of common middleware to facilitate business process automation across business partners. This will allow customers to take actions that lead to automated consequences elsewhere in the supply chain.

Notes

[1] Source: Yankee Group, March 1999
[2] Source: National Association of Purchasing Managers Survey, 1999
[3] Adapted from the report on e-commerce, AMR, 1999

9

Customer value management (CVM)

Harvey Thompson, Merlin Stone and Bryan Foss

One of the biggest problems facing CEOs today is how to continue to attract customers and attain growth, often in an environment where products and prices among competitors are moving closer and closer together. Traditional bases for differentiation, such as product features or cost, are becoming less tangible and senior management are forced to look for new ways to be attractive to a target market. Many companies are now using a customer value management (CVM) approach to identify the 'value' that can be delivered, not only by products but by processes and services, then engineering their business capabilities to deliver 'ideal' customer-defined value at each customer interaction.

Due to the rapid introduction of new technologies and resultant rapid changes in customers' perceived 'needs' and 'values', companies are institutionalizing this approach in order to continuously monitor and maintain an alignment between the customer's vision of 'ideal value delivery' and the capabilities of the business to deliver that value. CVM offers a new basis for competition and for growth. The goal of CVM is to deliver optimal value to customers – to align business metrics, improvement programs, capabilities, processes, organization and infrastructure with *customer-defined value*.

DEFINITIONS AND KEY CONCEPTS

CVM is defined[1] as:

> A **methodical approach** for achieving the **strategic**, **profitable** and **competitive** positioning and alignment **of a company's essential capabilities** – its **processes**, organization and infrastructure – and where appropriate of the **value chain of which it forms a part** – to ensure the meeting of **current and future target customers'** highest **priority (current and future) needs** for benefits delivered by the company's products, services, processes and relationships.

Let us explore this definition by focusing on the highlighted words.

Approach and process

A business process is the sequence of activities that usually flows across the different functions of a firm, rather than just within one function, resulting in the delivery of a desired outcome, product or service. When a process runs across functions, it is often compromised as each of the functions that make up the process tend to be optimized to meet the needs of the individual function, rather than those of the whole organization and of the customer. 'Business process management' is a systematic approach by which an organization avoids functional sub-optimization by documenting, standardizing, improving and optimizing its horizontal cross-functional processes. A key concept in process management is the realization that every business process has a customer, who receives the output, product or service that is delivered by the business process – and that the final arbiter in deciding how well the process is performing must be the customer. In today's competitive world, management must ensure that the organization's processes are customer focused and constantly recalibrated against customer needs. CVM ensures that this takes place.

A methodical approach

CVM is a business improvement methodology. However, a methodical CVM approach may be applied in two ways.

First, CVM may be applied to an individual issue, eg to understand and improve delivery of the value/benefits customers receive from an individual business process, product or service. Using a medical analogy, we call this 'topical' application.

Second, CVM may be institutionalized within a firm's management system, as a standard, continuing repeatable business process in its own right – the CVM process. A CVM process can be the engine which fuels major decisions affecting the entire enterprise, such as which processes should be focused upon or what critical business capabilities/competencies are required across the enterprise.

Throughout this chapter, we distinguish between the enterprise-wide business processes to which CVM may be applied topically – and the CVM business process itself.

Strategic

The decision to use CVM is a strategic business decision, not just a marketing approach. When marketers refer to meeting customer needs, they may be considering CVM, but they may also be referring to attunement of a particular aspect of the marketing mix, eg a product, a distribution channel, a marketing communications campaign, to the needs of a particular group of customers – in our terms a topical application of CVM to part of the marketing process. CVM can be used in this way, but the big gains from CVM come when it is applied strategically, to every aspect of how a company manages delivery of value to its customers. A fundamental of CVM is that it goes beyond mere marketing or customer management – it is the total engineering of a company's business processes to ensure that capabilities to perform are in concert with the 'promises' that are being made by marketing and other customer-facing functions. The promises and the business processes and capabilities are in turn aligned and linked to the desired 'outcomes' or 'values' that drive targeted customer behavior and loyalty.

Profitable

The aim of CVM is to help a company achieve higher profitability than it otherwise would. The underlying philosophy of the approach is as follows.

Using CVM, a company can be focused to deliver customer benefits more effectively. This results in an increase in net value – the difference between what customers are prepared to pay and what it costs to service them. Part of the resulting increase in net value can be taken as a benefit by the company (reduced cost or increased revenue from delivering a more appropriate benefit).

Of course, in some cases (eg where a company's position is under attack from competition), CVM can be used to maintain or prevent a decline in profitability.

Competitive

The most successful deployment of CVM is in competitive environments, where other companies (and sometimes other entire value chains) are seeking to win away the company's target customers. CVM ensures that the company invests in the right capabilities and then deploys them to their maximum effectiveness in recruiting, retaining and developing its target customers, in the face of competition.

Alignment of essential capabilities

This refers to how the processes, organization and infrastructure of the company are brought together to make it capable of delivering high-priority, customer-defined value to target markets. Business capabilities are usually expressed as a verb and a noun, eg commit a delivery date, or assign a trained service representative. The delivery of products or services relies upon cross-functional cooperation, or business processes, so the scope of capabilities must cross all aspects of a company's operation — all business functions, all geographical areas, all products and services. But it is possible to start with one business process, one product or one service. Essential capabilities are the few things that must be done for the company to be able to deliver the highest-priority benefits required by customers of the business process being analysed.

Company and value chain

The CVM approach may spread beyond the traditional boundaries of the company, and in the age of e-business, is almost certain to, due to the emerging transparency of the supply chain (see Chapter 8).

In many industries, the tendency towards vertical integration has been impeded by the realization that managing a vertically integrated chain requires expertise in managing every level of that chain within the same culture. This has proved difficult to achieve. However, inter-company information systems have made it easier to optimize and manage a multi-company value chain. Companies working closely with other value chain participants to deliver products/services to (end-user) customers further across the value chain find the CVM approach helps them to understand and optimize the several customer–supplier relationships that extend backwards into suppliers and forwards into end-user customers (particularly where these customers are other businesses).

Current and future target customers

The CVM methodology incorporates a key concept from CRM, namely that success comes from focusing on, understanding and serving targeted customers or groups of customers. This is because a company that serves the needs of a clearly defined target set of customers is more likely to capture the major share of that market segment, leaving competition behind. An important criterion for targeting customers is their actual and potential value to the company. This value is based on what customers pay or might potentially pay for the benefits delivered by the company to them. The aim of the CVM process is to optimize the *value delivered to* customers, to enable more value to be *extracted from* more customers (because it is justified). This does not mean that CVM necessarily leads to an exclusive focus on high-value customers. Different markets have different distributions of potential customer value, and costs of serving higher and lower 'gross value' customers also vary, sometimes leading to different patterns of 'net value' and profitability. For example, applying CVM might lead to the development of improved capabilities for managing large numbers of medium-to-low value individual customers at low cost, for high profit.

As a strategic methodology, CVM also focuses on the future customer as well as the current customer. This always makes a difference in a company's recommended business strategy, but in some cases, where customers are only in the market for a short time, or where customers buy in bursts (perhaps every few years), or where technological, demographic or some other long-term change is bringing new groups of customers into the market, this can make a very big difference.

Of course, choice of target customers is a critical strategic decision, and depends on a company's current and feasible future capabilities. The choice is therefore one of the earliest decisions in the strategic cycle. It can be approached from two dimensions:

Which customers do we wish to target and what are the required capabilities to meet their high-value needs? and/or

What are our capabilities and how can they be leveraged to provide high value and attract customers via a fulfillable promise to meet their needs? Which customer segments could be attracted?

Highest priority current and future needs for benefits

The primary engine of a CVM approach or enterprise process is customers' needs for *benefits.* The CVM process extends beyond classic market research techniques, which typically identify desired product or service attributes as 'customer needs/wants'. Rather than focusing only upon the current attributes of products, services, processes or relationships, which normally only describe the delivery of status quo benefits, a true CVM management system will instead probe the target market's underlying 'values' and will develop a customer-defined vision of 'ideal value delivery' in terms of possible future benefits. CVM provides a structured approach to identify highly actionable target customers' needs, in terms of the 'value' or 'benefits' customers can ideally envisage receiving (and which drive buying behavior and market share). These are then converted to become the 'design point' for new product/service/product attributes which would ideally deliver that customer-defined value.

Customer-defined metrics of success are also identified, to allow prioritization and measurement, in customers' terms, of how well the company's products/service/process deliverables are meeting their needs and providing the underlying values/benefits they desire. Requirements for revision to current deliverables, or development of a new set of customer-defined deliverables, is then translated into a set of business capabilities required to provide these deliverables.

Capability gaps

Current capabilities are assessed against those required, and a prioritized list developed to close the performance gap. Gaps in capabilities, or the absence of the 'ability to' provide exactly what the customer desires, are resolved by identifying and securing the specific infrastructure enablers, which cumulatively provide the required 'ability'.

Enablers

Enablers are dependencies or prerequisites that must be present in the infrastructure to support/enable each essential capability. They can usually be expressed as 'nouns' and include: information, training, skills, resources, practices, management disciplines and certain organizational characteristics (alignment, measurement, culture, etc).

DESIGNING CVM-DRIVEN PROCESSES

Simple overview

The design of a new, CVM-driven business process involves:

- analysing the company's current capabilities;
- comparing it with the capabilities required to meet target customers' high-value needs;
- identifying any gap between desired and current capabilities;
- identifying the enablers required to close the gap;
- closing the gap.

The deliverables

These are customer-defined 'outcomes' from products, services, relationships and processes. This broad set of deliverables is the conventional focus of marketing policy.

However, in CVM, two particular issues are critical. These are: that it is the customers' perception of the deliverables and whether they are perceived to deliver the customer-envisaged value/benefits; and that customers must be involved in shaping the deliverable to meet their needs, whether for 'hard' products, service offerings, customer-facing processes or for customer relationships. This means that the company must have formalized, definable and repeatable processes to ensure customer participation in the definition and development of products and deliverables.

JUSTIFICATION FOR THE CVM APPROACH

The traditional approach

Senior managers have traditionally focused on the ability of a 'business system' to accomplish 'internal' business goals and objectives, with the customer effectively treated as a constraint. The formulation of the business problem was typically in terms of performance issues, such as market share, costs, defects, cycle times, or customer satisfaction (with the outcome of predefined processes). This often led to an improvement approach, such as TQM or benchmarking, where the focus was on gradual improvement to existing processes and functions, with the occasional radical change. This was achieved through a series of tactical and strategic action plans, and with a desired end-state in view (though this was often never reached). Effectively, such an approach answered the question: 'Where do we want to be and how do we get there?'

This is symptomatic of an 'internally focused' company culture and provides an 'inside-out' view of the company – and subsequent business strategy. Often, this approach would be applied within each function, with the effects on other functions' performance and costs overlooked.

However, given today's environment of rapid change and shift of power to the customer, this can easily become a 'going-out-of-business' strategy. From the customer's perspective, each change achieved by such internally focused methodologies might be seen as a 'patch' or a 'fix', while the overall process for managing customer-value delivery not only failed to improve, but might actually have deteriorated, particularly if customer needs continued to change.

A major office equipment supplier

The service function of a European office equipment supplier was held accountable for customer satisfaction. It therefore focused on the benefits that its specific portion of the value chain delivered to customers, in terms of restoring failed equipment to usability again. As a result, the service organization focused on metrics of success such as service engineer response time, time to repair, spare parts availability, satisfaction with service and the like. However, from the customer's perspective the prime problem with the equipment was reliability and serviceability – both factors determined at an earlier stage of the value chain, by product design and manufacturing, and by components sourcing. Japanese competitors, however, designed their equipment for maximum reliability and ease of service, resulting in lower total costs and improved availability to customers. Although it attempted to be customer responsive, by focusing on a single piece of the value chain, the company actually lost share to the Japanese until it re-engineered its total processes for serving customers.

As the above definitions outline, CVM involves a business assessing its capabilities and infrastructure against those required to deliver an 'ideal' level of value, as defined by a targeted market. Target/potential customers and their needs for benefits dominate the assessment and the consequent business transformation that takes place, using a variety of techniques. These techniques may include classic TQM approaches, but given the extremely rapid change driven by rising customer expectations worldwide, this may require a more radical redesign (process re-engineering or business-wide transformation) to attain new, customer-defined performance levels. Put simply, the CVM approach involves answering the question: 'Where do our **customers** want us to be and how do we get there?'

This is characteristic of an 'outside-in' view of the company and results in an externally driven, market-defined strategy. Maintaining this consistent and systematic focus on customers prevents the business from making classic errors. It is all too common for process improvement projects which are not customer driven to lead to outcomes which are lower in cost, but lead to loss of valuable customers. In many cases, excellent management teams, often with good intentions to be 'customer focused', have actually created significant customer dissatisfaction, due to the absence of a methodical CVM approach.

Power and light

In a classic example of good intentions going awry, a now infamous power and light company embarked upon a three- to four-year journey to attain one of the world's most prestigious management awards, the Deming Quality Award. In a relentless march to accomplish this objective, the management team was literally driven by the CEO to plan and execute an intensive quality programme, which included a well-known requirement for customer focus. In an equally classic example of a customer focus 'methodology', the management team itself developed a menu of 'customer needs' that would be targeted for quality improvement. As a power provider, located in a geographic area regularly subjected to foul weather, high winds and rain, power outages appeared to be an opportunity to apply quality disciplines and drive increased customer satisfaction. This was, of course, only one of several targeted areas for improvement, but is an example of how companies often establish an internally derived 'customer vision'.

As a result, over the next two years the average down time that customers experienced (the amount of time incurred between a power failure and its resolution and return of power) was managed and reduced dramatically – from several minutes per event, to only a few seconds per event. The management team celebrated attaining its 'customer focused' metric of success. This type of objective-setting, standardized measurement and attainment tracking, analysis and root cause removal was done for many similar objectives across the company – resulting in the great day of public recognition for the management team. They won the Deming Quality Award... and the CEO subsequently retired.

The new CEO, on assuming the reins of the now famous 'quality' organization, was greeted with a disturbing message from the public regulatory agency. While proceeding down a path to attain one of the world's most prestigious forms of quality management recognition, the company had lost the connection between company investments/results and customer satisfaction. For example, the metric established by the management team to reduce the 'average amount of time per outage event that customers are without power' was a company-defined metric of success, ie an answer to the question: 'Where do *we* want to be and how do *we* get there?' Although rooted in good intentions to provide increased customer value and satisfaction, the metric was not based on *what customers valued,* nor how customers measured or perceived success in delivering that value. In the case of power outages, when a power failure occurs, the customer is reminded of that occurrence by having to reset every digital clock in the household – every bedside alarm, every cooker timer, every VCR digital display, etc. For this power company's customer, the benefit and the measurable metric of improvement was not only the length of each power outage, but the number of outages per month and the subsequent requirement to reset all household clocks. By the customer's metric, performance had not visibly improved on this and other important topics. This resulted in dissatisfaction, complaints to regulatory agencies and the need for the new CEO to take quick and dramatic steps to understand customers and align business metrics, improvement programmes, capabilities and infrastructure investments with customer values.

The power company management team was highly successful in improving its internal capabilities. Unfortunately, it focused on aligning those capabilities with an invalid perception of what its customers valued. However, as the next case study shows, management teams with a much better insight into what their customers 'value' have also missed the mark, by failing to follow through to engineer an alignment of customer-desired 'ideal value delivery' with company processes and infrastructure.

An international hotel chain

Maintaining alignment between the 'promises' made to high-value customers and the actual capabilities of a business (to perform to those promises) is a critical element of CVM. It is not enough to understand the 'values' of the customer and appeal to those values via targeted marketing; the capabilities of a business must also be focused on managing the faultless delivery of the promised 'value'.

The management team of an internationally renowned hotel chain learnt this lesson in a painful way. The senior management team singled out the business traveller, in a correct decision to identify high-value market segments and target them. One can easily imagine the hotel management asking themselves 'What does the business traveller value?' and 'What could *we* do to appeal to that value system, thereby making our chain attractive to and ideally preferred by this strong growth segment?' Management journals and bookstore shelves at the time were full of titles slanted toward the issue of the day: zero defects. Motorola's programme of *Six Sigma*, or 99.99997 per cent defect-free quality, was being heralded as the value system for all right-thinking business people. This became the 'value system' that the hotel chain chose, in order to attract the business traveller segment. Full-page advertisements in major newspapers and periodicals proclaimed 'Guaranteed Defect-Free Stays' for the business traveller who frequented the hotel chain. It became a part of the chain's brand image, as the firm created market awareness of a 'promise' of a specific level of product and service performance.

The authors were told about the following experience by an international corporate executive (certainly a member of the business traveller segment) who, on seeing the advertisements, made reservations at the hotel chain for his next business trip. This customer's account of the resulting experience with the hotel is every CEO's nightmare:

They advertised a guaranteed defect-free stay, but when I arrived they had no record of my reservation. Fortunately, they did have a vacant room and I was given a key and directions to reach the room. On unlocking the door, I reached inside and flipped the switch, but no light, ie defect number two. After fumbling in darkness to turn on a bedside lamp, I saw a cardboard placard in the colours of the hotel chain, sitting on the little round table that all hotels have – the one that is so small you wonder what the purpose of the table could possibly be. In this case, the purpose of the minuscule round table was to hold a sign proclaiming 'Guaranteed Defect-Free Stay'. As I began to unpack my suitcase, I turned on the television. It did not work, ie defect number three.

The business traveller then recounted going downstairs to the lobby and speaking with the hotel manager.

He said he was very sorry and that he hated it when this happened. Apparently it was not the first time. The manager said his company wanted to appeal to the business traveller and had advertised 'guaranteed defect-free' stays. However, there were actually no new capabilities to perform at that level, nor any customer benefits if defects did occur. He said that no new training, personnel programmes nor reservations systems had been deployed, at that point, to generate improved performance.

In short, management's intention to target and attract a high-value customer segment had actually raised the customers' expectations and then created dissatisfaction by not also raising standards of delivery by introducing the required processes, capabilities and infrastructure.

Building the CVM process into a company's business management system ensures that the company keeps refocusing on today's and tomorrow's customers' needs, by methodically managing and preventing gaps such as these from emerging between what it promises, what it delivers, and ultimately what the customer expects. Good intentions by good managers are simply not sufficient. A methodical process is required.

THE MAIN STEPS IN THE CVM PROCESS

Transforming a company using CVM requires a balanced and disciplined approach, to align, link and manage all critical business elements. These are listed and explained below:

- Business direction – vision/mission:
  - target market and segments;
  - customer needs/wants;
  - goals and objectives;
  - deliverables – product, marketing, relationship and service strategy.
- Core capabilities/competencies:
  - business process capabilities;
  - technical competencies.
- Enabling infrastructure:
  - organization structure;
  - human resources;
  - culture;
  - business policies and practices;
  - measurement systems and controls;
  - incentives and rewards;
  - assets and financial resources;
  - IT.

IMPLEMENTING CVM

Business direction

CVM-based transformation requires the development of a customer-defined vision of ideal outcomes from doing business with the company, in terms of the optimum possible value being received as the result of ideal vendor (company) products, services or delivery processes. This involves first specifying carefully who target customers are and will be, and then identifying how they derive value from the company's current product and service offerings, what would be the optimum level of value they could experience, and what are the attributes of the ideal vendor and/or value delivery. This is then translated into a vision for the company which includes the specific capabilities and infrastructure required to deliver the customer-defined high-value outcomes, or, in other words, 'premier fulfilment of customer-defined value'.

For a company to achieve a vision of being 'The Premier Provider of "X" In The Eyes of Our Customers', the vision must be actionable. For this the company must have a clear definition of who the target customers are. This requires segmentation of the marketplace based on factors in concert with the business mission statement and goals. Today, to become or remain competitive, a firm must segment its marketplace on at least two dimensions: current or potential profitability of each customer/segment to the company; and needs-based segmentation, by identifying customers with common needs/wants/values, which drive buying behaviour and are the design points for engineering the required company capabilities and infrastructure.

Without these, clearly defined and communicated to the full management team, a vision to become the premier provider of products/services to customers is not highly actionable, nor focused. However, once the market has been segmented based on profitability and needs/wants, a CVM approach can be fully leveraged to improve the business. An ongoing CVM process may also be implemented to continuously monitor each segment's changing needs (or perceptions regarding company and competitive performance), establish measurable goals and objectives which link to those needs, and develop product/service strategies to fulfil them. That ensures an actionable, customer-focused business vision/direction, which can then be operationalized as described below.

Core competencies and capabilities

This portion of a CVM approach, or process, focuses on *how* the required deliverables are to be achieved. Once a market segment has been targeted and actionable needs/wants/values determined, the company must define the critical things at which it must be competent (or capable of doing). This is best explained by example. Suppose that the CVM process has highlighted that one, high-leverage customer requirement is to 'meet all your commitments made to customers, on time and defect free'. The CVM process then needs to focus on what the company must be **capable of doing** – to capture and meet all commitments.

The capabilities identified might include the abilities to:

- Understand each customer request.
- Develop a valid commitment ('deal'), which means that the business process in question (eg sales or customer service process) must be capable of determining both the company's current abilities (including those of all the company's relevant functions) and those of any third parties involved in the value chain.
- Make a valid commitment, including the commitment of all relevant cross-functional resources.
- Capture and retain commitments, so the company 'knows' about them and can follow through.
- Communicate commitments to all involved in the value chain.
- Coordinate cross-functional resources (in-house and third party) so as to meet the commitment.
- Identify a critical path, checkpoint, and take preventative action to guarantee on-time delivery.
- Ensure quality workmanship.
- Validate the customer's agreement that the commitment has been met.

Suppose that an electronics manufacturer identified that their customers' vision included 'Fix my machine quickly, with no callbacks'. In this situation, the service capabilities involved might be those required to:

- Ensure an inventory of technicians trained on the product line and machine types.
- Identify and capture the machine type, the customer location and the problem with the machine.
- Identify technicians trained on the customer's machine type.
- Identify the closest/next available technician.
- Commit technician to customer.
- Contact and inform the technician.
- Ensure technician has all requirements (eg parts) to restore customer's machine to perfect working order.
- Dispatch technician.
- Assure consistent, high-quality service level.
- Identify service defect root causes and remove them... etc.

In our third example, suppose that a firm's customer's vision includes, 'No matter who I contact, or which medium I utilize, my requirement is handled' (otherwise known as one-stop shopping or seamless service). Here, the businesses capabilities might include the abilities to:

- Provide accessible points of contact in each medium the customer wishes to use.
- Ensure that information flowing in and out through each medium is immediately available, cross-functionally, to staff dealing with customers through other media.
- Ensure that contact staff can access full information on all products, services, processes and the complete customer relationship.
- Ensure that contact staff can deliver cross-functional information, commit action and ensure resolution.

Finally, suppose that the customer vision for a bank includes, 'My bank should use the data it already has regarding me, and complete all application forms with these pre-existing details, leaving me to fill in only new items specific to the application, correct any changes to previously given data and to sign', otherwise known as the 'one-time give' of customer information. Here, the capabilities might be:

- Customer data is captured once, accessed and utilized throughout the bank.
- Customer contact points for any transaction involving forms are able to access full details of a customer's bank relationship.
- Contact points understand which data is required for each application.
- Contact points can transfer existing customer data to the application.

In each case, all of the company's functions, processes and information systems must be evaluated for their ability to do the above (cross-enterprise capabilities assessment), and changes made where gaps are revealed. These changes will be to the infrastructure, which cumulatively result in or enable the needed capabilities.

Enabling infrastructure

Following through on our 'make and meet customer commitments' customer vision example, the enabling infrastructure might be:

- A single source (not necessarily a single database, of course) of data on customers, commitments (deals) and all relevant aspects of each deal, ie: products, configurations, services, processes, available inventory, production and delivery schedules, terms and conditions, prices, etc.
- Data available at appropriate times and places to all involved in making and delivering the commitment.
- Empowered, qualified, trained and briefed front-line and back-office (value chain) employees motivated to meet customer needs, as individuals and as cross-functional teams.
- Process and task management disciplines, eg definable, repeatable, predictable fulfilment processes – including keeping the customer informed of state of deliverables; protocols for identifying and achieving critical path checkpoints; process ownership and improvement methods; closed loop customer feedback, etc.

Following through our electronics 'fix my machine quickly with no call-backs' example, the enablers might include:

- a database of repair technicians and their skills and training;
- a database of common product faults and remedies;
- work availability schedules;
- dispatchers empowered to commit cross-functional resources;
- two-way radios;
- documented, definable, repeatable (and therefore predictable) service processes;
- technician education, personal measurements and incentives linked to process execution;
- process management disciplines, eg TQM, process ownership.

The enabling factors for our 'seamless service' one-stop shopping example might be:

- a strategy which aligns and links company business goals with service objectives;
- empowered, trained, motivated , customer-focused front-line and back-office employees;

- individual and team incentives based on meeting customer needs;
- a single source of customer relationship and company product data with distributed access;
- networked knowledge workers (a network of on-demand expert skills);
- customer goals aligned with company's measures and service standards;
- business process management disciplines (horizontal ownership, documented processes, etc).

The enabling factors for the capabilities to provide customers with 'one-time give' of customer information might be:

- contact point empowerment to act;
- contact staff training to understand application forms and contracts;
- centralized customer information;
- distributed access to customer information (accessible by all contacts);
- definable/repeatable processes for each application type;
- contact point education and incentives linked to process execution;
- post-transaction customer satisfaction surveys;
- contact point compensation linked to customer satisfaction.

CUSTOMER VALUE ANALYSIS

It should be clear by now that customer value is central to a CVM process or project. Customer value is not a new idea – it has been the focus of marketing for many years. However, the CVM approach we have described (which has been used worldwide, cross-industry, to identify and prioritize customer needs and benefits) includes a unique 'customer value analysis' element that significantly differentiates it from earlier approaches.

A CVM customer value analysis begins with examining 'moments of truth', which are events or encounters when customers could experience 'satisfaction' or 'dissatisfaction' when dealing with the company or with a specific process or service in question. However, we have redefined this concept as 'moments of potential value'. If we go beyond understanding what customers wish for or want at each of these moments, and probe the benefit or value they can or could receive, the moment becomes an opportunity to influence customer behaviour and loyalty by providing the optimum possible benefit or value delivery. The value customers receive from a product, service or process interaction is what creates the demand for it and a market.

Moments of truth turn into moments of value depending upon how the company's deliverables fit into the customer's *hierarchy of needs*. We have adapted the classic Maslow's hierarchy of needs and simplified it with research that divides customers' needs into three buyer-behaviour-driver categories, as follows.

First, let's look at needs which, if *not* met, are likely to cause the customer to reduce the volume of business done or, at worst, to defect completely. We call these *'basic expectations'* or *'basic needs'* – and for the company they are 'attrition issues'. These would provide the foundation levels of a Maslow-type analysis or depiction. These are the customer 'must-haves' and are the business equivalents to 'food and shelter'. If not provided, basic needs drive dissatisfaction and will motivate customers to leave. For basic needs, a minimum acceptable level of performance must be understood and provided. However, over-performance of the basics (eg answering the phone in less rings than a competitors) will not attract additional share, and overinvestment in being the best at basic expectations must be avoided.

At the other extreme are *'attractors/differentiators'*. These are needs which if well satisfied will lead a customer to remain, conduct more business with the company and advocate the company to other buyers. These are at the top of a Maslow-type analysis and provide such a high level of benefit or value that they can influence customers to actually change vendors to obtain them. Understanding which needs/values are the attractor behaviour drivers, and the performance gaps between the company and competition, is key. Attractors are the needs that the company should target and invest in the capabilities to provide a 'best of breed' delivery.

In between are *'satisfiers'*. These involve factors which can improve the customer's satisfaction and/or relationship with the company, but whose presence does not cause loyalty, and whose individual absence does not cause attrition. Whereas basic needs and attractors may each individually drive negative and positive buying behaviours, the satisfiers do not.

Note that these categories are fluid, and particular types of needs may change categories over time (eg move from attractor to basic expectation, based on market dynamics and on what is being delivered by competitive or parallel, non-competitive industries). For this reason, businesses may believe they know their customers needs/wants and behavior drivers, but in today's world the hotel customer, for example, is having needs and expectations revised hourly, by receiving high value during similar, parallel moments of truth interactions with other industries such as rental car agencies (Hertz Number One Gold Service) and airline frequent flier reservations (Singapore Airlines, British Airways). Of course, rental car or airline customers are having their expectations reset by interactions with hotels, such as Marriott and Mandarin Oriental.

The aim of the customer value analysis is to identify which combination of customer needs (basic; satisfiers; attractors) provides the company with the strongest competitive advantage (by avoiding or containing attrition, and by maximizing attraction and retention of customers through differentiation). This requires the identification of where customers perceive that performance gaps exist between the company and its peers (competitors and leading companies in parallel industries) and estimation of the changes to customer buying behaviour that will result if these performance gaps are removed. In cases where customer value analysis shows that the company is ahead of its competitors, the analysis would focus on whether the company is over-delivering in areas which do not drive equivalent incremental loyalty or share (basic needs), or whether moving even further ahead would generate additional market share (attractors) considering likely competitive responses. To achieve this, the company's performance must be analysed, using a portfolio approach (each 'customer needs' factor is analysed according to its priority and the company's relative performance).

One of the main decisions to be undertaken by companies which are behind parity with their competitors on either basic expectations (in which case they are likely to be losing customers) or attractors (in which case they will have problems attracting new customers and developing more business with existing customers) is to decide which mix of these two will best meet the company's objectives in terms of overall customer attraction and retention. One strategy might be for the company to focus resources to ensure that minimum, basic needs are being provided for both the current customers/segments and future, targeted market segments – while achieving maximum differentiation with a smaller group of highly profitable current customers and to attract high-value market segments. These investment decisions are critical. Once the decision has been reached as to which set of benefits should be delivered, then the CVM analysis can focus on the deliverables and the processes and capabilities required to deliver them.

SOURCES OF CVM INFORMATION

Our search for customer value information is focused by the drive to achieve success with target customers. The techniques used include:

- Market segmentation – whenever possible using the transaction data of the company together with customer data, to be 'mined' for clustering of customers with like behaviour. These can then be probed to identify common underlying 'values' which account for similar behaviour, and which can be used to develop a customer-defined company vision.
- Market research – in particular, qualitative work to identify and categorize needs and establish their value drivers, supported by quantitative work to provide performance ratings and identify 'gaps' with competition to support investment/resourcing decisions. A critical focus of customer needs research is on 'value' or 'benefits' and then envisaging the ideal delivery of that value.
- Benchmarks of performance delivery to customers – to include within the company (where, for example, some branches might be performing significantly better than others), the industry and across parallel industries; this may also include a literature

search and must take an international perspective. (Remember, your customers' needs and performance perceptions of you are driven by *their* experiences, cross-industry and cross-geography, and are not necessarily limited to you or to comparisons with your direct competitors.)

- Brainstorming and invention – for cross-functional buy-in by all value chain participants to build a joint understanding of the end-user and customer needs, and to develop an envisaged end-state where (cross-value chain) capabilities are optimized for ideal delivery of customer-defined value. It is in this phase that major breakthroughs occur, as the different functions, processes or companies in the value chain begin to understand their collective relationships and impacts upon the final deliverable. In many cases functional representatives (often executives) will proclaim the high benefit of such sessions and reveal that 'this was the first time that we have actually met as a cross-functional team to solve a common issue'. Being able to place the 'voice of the customer' up on to the wall for these sessions appears to be the single most powerful element in 're-engineering' or 'transforming' a diverse organization, or a value chain. A strong 'case for action' is made, in the words of their common customer, and the team rallies (usually for the first time) to fulfil the customer's vision. Additionally, by understanding the reasons why customers have particular needs and the values/benefits that underlie customer 'needs', the group is often able to envisage leveraging unique combinations of capabilities or existing competencies to provide even greater levels of value than the customers were able to foresee or articulate. Again, here is where breakthroughs are envisaged, by highly motivated representatives of the groups who must ultimately implement them.

WHEN TO USE CVM

When should a company use a CVM approach? The answer is: any time a major investment in infrastructure is about to be undertaken. Of course, the reason for the infrastructure change or investment will often, in itself, reveal a need for CVM approaches. For example, when market share or customer satisfaction issues are the catalyst for change, then the need to make such investments or changes customer focused is obvious. However, when the driver of the change is more internally defined (ie reduce cost; reduce defects; downsize; develop an IT strategy; etc), then the need for a highly actionable, customer-focused approach is typically not evident. But when a firm re-engineers a process to 'reduce cost', why should it not also make the new process an attractor which could potentially increase its market share by differentiating on service? While a company is downsizing or making any other revisions to current infrastructure, why not make sure that it is being done in a way that will avoid alienating customers or result in attrition? When developing a five-year IT plan or strategy for a company, a rational approach might be to begin with the *outcomes* envisaged by customers which would make the business an ideal provider, and only then define the capabilities and underlying infrastructure required, including IT, as the basis for the strategy.

The following case studies give examples.

Process re-engineering in petrochemicals

A global petrochemical company was experiencing problems in Asia with its 'order-to-invoice' process. Customer order fulfilment through invoicing was not being performed at a cost and quality level consistent with the company's business objectives, nor with its customer satisfaction goals. The project was initially a process re-engineering exercise. The company had recently identified its core enterprise-wide business processes and had embarked upon a journey to implement horizontal, cross-functional optimization and management. Process owners were appointed for each key process, including 'order to billing'. Cross-functional teams were also commissioned with responsibility to identify and implement process improvements. Re-engineering workshops were begun and new creative ways of doing business were envisaged, along with a myriad of different alternatives and potential courses of action. The question ultimately became, 'But which of these should we actually do? And which align with and fulfil our customers' needs?'

CVM, normally a primary driver of (and preceding) re-engineering design, was in this case brought in after initial visioning workshops, to become the 'arbiter' for working through alternative actions and the 'validator' of the front-line team hypotheses regarding what the customer wanted and needed. The existing, traditional customer satisfaction surveys were found to lack the actionable elements for effective CVM, prompting a fast-path effort to commission 'customer round-tables'. Outside CVM experts, working with front-line staff, then secured (by key market segment for each moment of truth) the customers needs and underlying values. These became the customer-defined design points for the re-engineered 'to be' process. When the re-engineering team took their 20+ final recommendations to the board, each recommendation was anchored in the perspective of the customer, and costs/benefits were presented both in terms of reduced costs to the petrochemical company and also in terms of the potential benefit to customers and the resulting indirect benefits to the company. All recommendations were approved, and the approach became a critical first step not only to re-engineer a process, but also to transform the enterprise to be 'customer focused'.

Customer service strategy for credit card call centre

When a major credit card company wanted to establish new standards of performance for call centres and a strategy to attain the standards, its initial approach was to rely upon benchmarking to identify the 'measurements' of top performing banks and then propose those metrics/measures as standards to the association of member banks. The intent was to attain for the brand an internationally consistent face to the customer, and level of service.

Once project planning began, it became apparent that bank benchmarking would produce a very internally focused view. It would also become very difficult to secure acceptance and buy-in by member banks to a standard set solely according to the performance of other banks. CVM was then introduced by the credit card executive team as a vehicle to resolve these issues.

A customer-defined strategy was developed, by identifying the key targeted customer segments, probing moment of truth interaction between the customers and the credit card call centres and establishing needs, wants, values and desired levels of service required to retain customers (basic needs). For banks wishing to differentiate themselves with, and compete on, service, an attractor level of service was identified. This became the recommended 'service standards' for the association, with each bank encouraged to survey its own customers to identify specific local perceptions regarding priorities and current bank performance level for each standard. This allowed individual banks to identify the optimum 'mix' of needs to focus on for improvement.

Finally, for a complete CVM analysis, the 'how to deliver' the new performance levels was addressed. Primary and secondary benchmarking was conducted to identify firms inside and (more importantly) outside the industry that had distinguished themselves on these service topics. The research identified the specific capabilities and enablers within these best firms, which accounted for their outstanding performance. By incorporating these 'ideal' capabilities and enablers into the CVM study, the credit card company was able to establish an actionable call centre strategy which not only identified what customers wanted from call centres but how to attain that performance via the identified capabilities and infrastructure. The strategy has since been made part of an educational package for members and is currently being used in Asia and the United States to attain a consistent level of customer service and brand image.

Service differentiation by a pharmaceutical company

Faced with increasing competition from other leading producers of ethical pharmaceuticals, including generic products, a leading pharmaceutical company decided to identify differentiators which were not based on the product. Research into its relationships with doctors showed that there were many market segments which wanted an easier and more beneficial sales and service relationship with the company. If this relationship could be delivered, they would be prepared to buy more, albeit at existing prices (which were very profitable). The company then focused on its customer service and sales order entry processes, and on the information and telecommunications systems that supported them. By reconfiguring them to meet the needs of a pilot market segment, they experienced a large increase in sales within only a few months.

Designing a totally new distribution company

A CEO of a major Mexican holding company was concerned that the upcoming approval of the North American Free Trade Agreement would open his market to new competitors from the United States, bringing with them new business capabilities and redefining what it would take for his own companies to remain competitive – and in business. The CEO selected one area of his business holdings for analysis – the construction of a completely new value-added distribution company which would become part of his total value chain and allow his manufacturing companies to differentiate themselves and compete on distribution service. Here, the requirement was not re-engineering but engineering. What would a new business look like? What would be the needs/wants from the most important customer segments? Which would be the critical processes required to meet those needs? What world-class capabilities would be needed to attain parity with industry leaders? What infrastructure would be needed, and what investment required? The CVM framework was used to define the new business, beginning with envisaging moments of truth with key market segments, and ending with the enabling infrastructure to support 'ideal process capabilities'. With this as a blueprint, the company was able to identify and understand the costs associated with building a new company and the related benefits in customers' terms.

Entering a totally new market

A major high technology company, facing the opportunity of a huge new market in China but with limited local infrastructure, needed a framework to identify, prioritize and manage the critical success factors to develop the market. The country management used CVM analysis to identify the 'must haves' for the market and to envisage and assess themselves against the required capabilities and infrastructure. The analysis allowed the company to identify, focus on, size and establish resource plans to provide the key infrastructure elements which would determine the business's success. Also, by using the customer as the focus of their business design, the cross-functional management team was able to reach agreement more quickly on complex issues and make decisions that were responsive to the market.

IT strategy in financial services

When a major financial services company (involved in mutual funds, financial planning, etc) discovered that its IT infrastructure required significant revamping, the CEO commissioned an IT strategy. External experts were brought in to provide the methods/approaches to envisage a new IT architecture and infrastructure for the strategic period. Ultimately, as the analysis was being conducted, questions began to be raised: 'How much is this new IT approach likely to cost?' 'How do we know that this is the correct IT and strategy for our business?' 'How do we know we have the correct vision for our company, much less that this is the right IT required to support that vision?' As a result, the IT strategic planning was altered to include the construct of a new vision of a desired 'end-state' for the company, which the IT strategy should support and enable. A first inclination for the CEO was to 'convene five or six of [the company's] best people' to develop a draft of the vision.

Ultimately, a CVM approach was approved and implemented to secure an outside, customer-defined vision of what the ideal provider of financial services should look like. This, in turn, defined the company's vision of specific processes and capabilities. The IT strategy was then completed by aligning and linking its support elements with the customer-defined vision. In the course of the CVM work, the CEO learnt that some 'needs' of certain segments could not be met by the processes currently in place, nor by the existing mission statement for the company. As a result, additional core strategic processes were added to the enterprise model, for subsequent re-engineering, and the business mission/vision was amended to encompass these important customer wants/needs. The IT strategy represented a major, strategic investment, requiring total commitment by the heads of the lines of business and management board. The CEO secured that commitment by first having the CVM project presented and securing board approval to the customer-defined vision. The subsequent presentation of the IT strategy, linked to the critical capabilities required to fulfil the customer vision, was quickly approved. The voice of the customer had enabled rapid consensus. In a postscript, the company subsequently also used the CVM results to calibrate and drive the re-engineering of key processes to ensure customer focus, and the following year announced new processes for customer access to company products and services, operationalizing the new vision.

Companies move towards the customer value proposition slowly, as they discover that internally focused processes do not deliver for them. The speed at which companies should move towards using a comprehensive CVM process is determined by a variety of factors.

One of these factors is product design or manufacturing technology – a company which consistently stays ahead of its competitors in terms of applying technology may discover that all it needs to do is to continue staying ahead – the success of its products outweighing other deficiencies it might have. From a customer vision point of view, this might occur if customers indicate that their top priority is 'products which perform better, faster, more reliably, etc, than any other currently available products'. This tends to occur when technology is moving very fast – driving evolving customer needs – and the industry is therefore immature. Examples of this include PC software, online services and aircraft manufacture. While the emphasis upon CVM in this chapter has been on identifying and implementing process or enterprise-wide business capabilities to meet customer needs, the concepts also apply to product design – by understanding what customers want and why (the value/benefits desired) during product interactions (moments) and then engineering to those desired 'outcomes'.

Competitive structure is another determining factor. Let us consider two examples. First, in a stable market with common/competitive products, a particular need for CVM occurs when there are major competitors, operating under relatively stable (but not necessarily atrophied) technological conditions, targeting the same customer groups and aiming to build or sustain large market shares. As products and prices come closer together, how does a company differentiate itself in order to attract and retain loyal customers? One powerful answer is to differentiate upon services, or the service element of every customer interaction with the company, its processes and employees. In this situation, companies are likely to fall behind if they do not utilize a CVM-like approach to understand what customers value, beyond product and price, and give it to them – either through engineering of company service capabilities or through leveraging third party members of the extended value chain. Examples of this include utilities, fixed (ie not mobile) telecommunications, automotive, retailing, airlines, etc. All of these markets are somewhat mature, with customer needs and technology moving ahead steadily, and new technologies available to all participants, from third party suppliers. Second, where there is a dynamic structure – rapidly changing customer needs and/or changing, emerging technologies – the CVM approach is particularly likely to produce high dividends. Where customer needs are highly dynamic, they require close monitoring and alignment. The same applies when one or more dynamic, newly emerging technologies can be deployed to create new, unprecedented value delivery. But there is also high risk of market instability. In this environment, CVM can be used in two ways. Firstly, it can be used to monitor and help a company respond to rapidly changing customer needs, values and performance perceptions. Secondly, the CVM equation can be 'worked backwards', by starting with the emerging technology (part of infrastructure possibilities) and the new capabilities that could be enabled, then 'envisaging' unprecedented new deliverables that would redefine the 'value proposition' and the attractors for that marketplace. The Internet is a good example of such emerging technologies. A CVM approach provides a framework to operationalize a strategy to compete on 'customer value' by harnessing and leveraging the e-commerce capabilities of the Internet and related new technologies.

Redefining a newspaper value proposition

This case study looks at using database marketing, the Internet and call centre technology to redefine a newspaper value proposition.

A leading national newspaper researched the needs of its advertisers, who were responsible for well over half of the newspaper's revenues. It identified that the foundation for advertisers' demand for advertising space was not simply the need to deliver messages, but to create and keep more high-value customers. The newspaper identified the types of customer that its advertisers wanted to recruit and reoriented its entire marketing and sales processes, using the latest database marketing analysis and profiling techniques, and a strong Internet presence, to recruit as readers the types of customer its advertisers wanted. Parallel research showed that its own readers would become more loyal if the newspaper delivered relevant advertising messages from readers' favoured suppliers. The result of this customer value orientation was a sustained increase in profitability at the same time as other industry leaders were losing money, and steady growth in circulation while its competitors' circulation figures were falling.

Redefining the motor insurance value delivery process

A start-up insurance company used advanced IT to redefine its value delivery process. It identified that customers would be willing to buy directly over the telephone rather than go through agents, particularly if insurance products could be made cheaper. It created a world-class combination of call centre technology and practice, laser printing and customer database management, to deliver much higher levels of customer service to insurance buyers, more quickly, than had ever been achieved before. The unprecedented 'value delivery' resulted in this new entrant differentiating itself with 'service', and it became the market leader in its product category within five years.

HOW TO GET STARTED IN CVM

In today's and tomorrow's environments of rapidly changing customer needs, wants and perceptions of 'value', accelerated by the application of e-business techniques to relationships between members of the value chain, it is critical that a company continuously monitors and maintains alignment between the customers' vision of 'ideal value delivery' and the actual capabilities of the business to deliver that value. In this chapter, we have highlighted the main components of CVM as the approach to accomplish that alignment and provided some examples of how, when and where to use it. The involvement of an external partner may be required in order to attain the optimum benefits from CVM, whether implementing as a one-time project to address a specific current business issue or implementing as an ongoing CVM process, to become an integral part of the management system. The ongoing process is recommended, in order to: avoid becoming 'one day out of touch with customers' the day after your project is completed; and prevent continued dependency upon your outside partner or consultant-expert.

The critical success requirements for this include:

- a methodical framework to compete on customer-defined value and to institutionalize customer knowledge;
- a reach that matches your company and its value chain, eg national, continental or global (so the needs, behaviours and linkages of *all* customers and suppliers are understood and integrated);
- experience in strategy implementation, not just in strategy development;
- industry knowledge (ideally of your industry and that of your customers);

- experience in organizational design, including cultural transformation and sustained change management programmes;
- demonstrated ability to craft actionable marketing research and link to business engineering;
- experience in business process design, development and implementation;
- understanding of how to conduct and interpret benchmarking exercises (ideally with an image and relationships worldwide, which will open doors with potential benchmarking partners);
- understanding of how IT is deployed at the customer interface and throughout the value chain, to maximize customer value, and experience in deploying it.

Note

[1] Merlin Stone (1996) *Customer Value Management*, IBM/Policy Publications

10

Wireless customer management

Merlin Stone and Edward Ben Nathan

INTRODUCTION

It is clear that the way in which technologies and services are developing, and from emerging applications, that the mobile phone and other wireless devices will revolutionize our thinking about customer management. It is reversing many of the assumptions we have made over the last two to three years about the use of IT in customer management. It is opening new possibilities to customers for obtaining value, and also new risks for companies of investing much and gaining little. In will also enable companies to engage in 'rapid loop closure' – which means that instead of waiting for the normal series of media interactions required to complete a sale, it can all be done via the mobile immediately, whether or not the customer has access to a PC.

It will also open many new opportunities for companies to use mobile technology to differentiate their services and gain a competitive advantage. The rapidly developing technology of mobile phones – particularly the broadening of the applications supported by them – turns them into wonderful instruments of personal liberation for consumers and managers. It also turns them into powerful tools for businesses that want to catch the attention of their customers, suppliers and business partners.

For the marketer, wireless technology allows customers the real possibility of managing their relationships with their suppliers anywhere, anytime. For the customer service function, the new technology is the ultimate in notification, problem avoidance, and complaining. Both functions face enormous potential – and enormous chaos. Many companies are already unable to cope with the volume of unstructured enquiries and complaints stimulated by the Web, and some have closed down e-mail access because of this. What about a world in which customers are in our locations, wandering around our stores, or even on a business customer visit to our location, and decide to give us some feedback or make a sales enquiry? What use will it be if they respond long after they have left? Clearly, the early failure to structure inbound communication and put in place processes to handle it rapidly will multiply problems if extended to the mobile customer.

The other health warning is that although we are used to US technology driving the world via US users being among the most advanced, at least at the time of writing this was not so. Mobile penetration rates in the United States are low. Nor does the UK look too good, with countries such as Finland, France and Italy looking far more innovative in actually implementing mobile-based applications. In France, the smart card culture is firmly established, so moving to the wireless-based smart card for handling micro-payments is not such a big jump.

PERVASIVE WIRELESS DEVICES

Mobile phones are just one kind of wireless device that can be used in customer management. Combined with an appropriate smart card, the mobile phone adds remote functionality to the smart card, enabling the customer to execute all kinds of transactions that would have required insertion of the card into a reader, such as banking, share trading and accrual of loyalty points. Of course, there is no reason why the technology has to be constrained to a smart card, as the storage function can also be carried out by other removable devices (eg a miniature hard disk drive).

Coming from another direction is the personal digital assistant (PDA). With operating systems designed to optimize use of a limited display and battery life, PDAs are already used extensively:

- for scheduling;
- for e-mail/fax;
- for office productivity (word processing, spreadsheet, presentation);
- as address books;
- for games.

Basically, an organizer is a small version of a laptop. Palm versions now usually have handwriting recognition functions that remove the need for a keyboard. However, the display size is much larger than a mobile phone, and they have better software availability. They are used in many applications. For example, they are used by doctors to check patient records, sales staff to carry client details, and in general for access to corporate databases. In some applications, the mobile PDA is expected to dominate, combining the best of mobile and PDA features.

PRINCIPLES OF MOBILE CUSTOMER MANAGEMENT

The mobile phone is essentially a new channel – a channel or medium of communication and a channel of distribution. It is just one part of a wider development called pervasive computing, and probably the first true mass-market embodiment of pervasive computing. As such, it poses many questions to marketers about how it should be used, its cost/benefit profile, the advantage it can confer if used properly, and so on. It is too early for a clear picture to be emerging, so this chapter does not include many other aspects of pervasive computing. Also, we recognize that even with such well-established media as the mail and TV, many companies with strong marketing reputations would consider that they still are not using the medium as well as they could or should. In this section, therefore, we highlight some of the issues which companies need to consider as they move to using the mobile phone as an important and possibly dominant channel in customer communication.

Mobile phones offer a new way of achieving an individual or one-to-one relationship with customers and a unique opportunity to get people's attention. The fact that the mobile is a telephone offers the possibility of creating an interactive conversation with customers. For a supplier, one objective of doing this is to exploit the technology to learn from customers' interactions. The mobile also allows many ways of tailoring the dialogue and avoiding what is little more than an unrelated series of sales pitches.

Being constantly in touch, providing and receiving lots of information is especially advantageous for three groups of people. The first are vagrant bosses. Because of the current fashion for companies to contract out everything but their core businesses and hand as much power as possible to front-line workers, bosses now spend much more time establishing relations with potential business partners than telling their employees what to do. Mobile phones make that relationship building easier. The second group of people is the vast army of people who spend their time either on the road or at clients' offices rather than sitting at their desk. The third group of people is obviously consumers.

In many sectors, companies need to:

- Get to know their customers, and keep renewing their knowledge of customers.
- Stay in touch with the customers, with timely and relevant communications, ranging from promotions to useful information.
- Identify quickly when customers are not being served well and react.
- Identify the customers' needs – often before customers realize them – and fulfil them quickly.

Today's average mobile phone was in origin essentially a dumb device, which helped with only some of the above tasks. It was good for allowing people to talk and send text messages, but not very good at managing the information that makes customers lives go round, except where it was being used as a remote PC connection device. The idea, when it comes to customer management, is to create a single smart wireless device that will allow customers to:

- Check their e-mail.
- Feed data in remotely.
- Use the Internet.
- Plan their schedule, communicate it to others and schedule meetings with others.
- Coordinate their lives with others.
- Locate (or be informed of) the nearest point of service (by receiving messages which use their location as registered on the mobile network). The service could be a parking meter or a pub, or both!
- Express preferences to suppliers.
- Have electronic purse loading and use.
- Use ticketing.
- Use micropayment – make very small payments remotely that are too expensive to make remotely by other means.
- Receive customized sales and service information and alerts from suppliers and content providers.
- Control their household automation.
- Call for help (eg breakdown services) and receive acknowledgement of progress with supplying the help.
- Download music or games (eg for mobile phones merged with MP3 players or with a game chip merged with mobile phone devices).

There are other possibilities, in other words; customers could have a device that is a pervasive mixture of an electronic organizer, a PC, alarm, remote control and a mobile phone.

Of course, there is a real danger that the above is just a wish-list describing the things that can be done by any mobile phone company, manufacturer or computing firm. This is very supplier oriented. The essential question is what customers will want and how companies can improve customer management and develop better mutual value (by providing benefits to customers and/or cost savings to themselves). Benefits to the customer will be in terms of:

- managing within companies;
- managing relationships with business partners, customers, etc;
- increasing competitiveness – through speed, lower cost, higher quality;
- managing family and social lives.

These *benefits* will be derived from the way the *features* of wireless technology (which we consider later) are translated into the *advantages* of:

- contactability;
- acceleration of activity;
- automated, secure identification;
- reduction of cost;
- improving the quality of information on which decisions are made;

and so on.

Some of the most advanced customer relationship management systems already combine transaction processing with the analysis of customer interactions, leading to the optimization of each future interaction via integrated customer touch-points. This is already being achieved by some retailers and direct marketers, who have demonstrated that more personalized customer relationships can help them retain and grow business with existing customers, as well as attract new customers. For many companies, it is service to existing customers that is the key. This is in contrast with the early development of the Web, where business-to-consumer applications often focused on customer recruitment, and more in line with the business-to-business use of the Web, usually more strongly focused on managing existing customers.

Suppliers of various products and services have come to understand that it is possible to get more value from customers by using customer information in every customer interaction via various customer-facing channels. However, delivering this idea in practice is difficult today, even with relatively restricted channels, many of which have time lags built into them. The most important of these is usually the time it takes the customer to get to the channel to communicate his or her need, whether in a sales or service episode, and get response. In its most advanced form (already under planning) we can see the scenario of the future versus the scenario of the present, for example, in the mobile car service cycle (see Table 10.1).

The prospect of instantaneous identification and fulfilment of needs clearly raises opportunities and problems. Customers are already using the telephone to check the news headlines, follow the stock market and read horoscopes. However, many customers want to get further than this. Using their mobiles they can already manage their bank accounts, and soon they will be able to buy virtually anything this way. Companies will be able to keep in touch with their customers always – and provide the right information at the right time to the right customers, wherever they happen to be. When customers are entering a shopping centre, they will be able to dial a number and find out about any special offers. The information will be updated throughout the day. When customers are near to running out of petrol, they will be able to use their mobile and download information about the nearest petrol station. Customers will be able to get access to all sorts of local information, from news and weather to details of the best bargains near the hotel where they are staying, to the location of the next parking space, wherever in the world. What could really add to a relationship and make it even stronger is receiving potential advertising over the telephone

Table 10.1 The mobile car service cycle

	Current Cycle	Future Cycle
Identification of Need	Driver looks at mileage and decides it is time for a service, or car tells driver it is time for a service	Car transmits data about need for service to garages that driver has given permission for quotation Several providers provide quotes and booking times and car collection times (if an option) via mobile
Booking of Service	Driver calls one or more garages to ask for quote, booking and collection and replacement car possibilities, not always getting through Driver calls selected garage to book car in and confirm collection time Driver calls insurer to confirm temporary replacement car insurance	Driver presses option buttons to select supplier and booking time, replacement car and to arrange insurance for replacement car
Service Day	Driver takes car in or it is collected	Driver is reminded of need to drive car in or that collection is imminent Driver takes car in or it is collected
Notification that Car is Ready	If extra work is required, driver is called – possibly not contacted first time Driver calls or is called to say car is ready	Driver is messaged (if requested) to say that service has commenced, is on schedule, etc If extra work is required, driver is messaged with options and agrees or not by pressing button, or sends message requesting clarification Driver is messaged to say car service is complete and asked to confirm collection or delivery time
Car Delivery	Driver collects/receives car	Driver collects/receives car

in return for the chance of getting a bargain. Those advertisements can be adjusted to fit the customer's preferences and demographic profile, and can be sent the time when he or she is in the best place for buying the product. Customers can also be monitored so that companies know how they are responding. The portability of mobile phones turns them into unique instruments of personal liberation. Of course, advertising at such a personal level could be considered an intrusion by certain customers, hence the need for permission marketing.

One of the questions raised by these developments is that of multiple intermediation. Everyone wants to 'own' the relationship with customers – the dealers and retailers, the mobile operators, content providers, software and hardware providers, and so on. This may lead to the rise of 'relationship managers', agents who manage all manner of contacts for customers. There may be a dilemma here – customers are getting wise to the value of their data, and the uses to which it is put, and are increasingly not willing to part with it to build what has often been a very one-sided relationship. Hence the rise of permission marketing. General relationship agents are, of course, well placed to manage this, as they can maximize the value of a given piece of customer data by allowing all kinds of supplier to use it.

Towards 2010, the quantity of information that individuals currently consume and send out is projected to increase, as is the amount of information-related household expenditures. In response to individual needs, further globalization and technical innovations will occur, freeing people from physical constraints such as time, location or distance. The increasing popularity of portable computers over desktops is an indicator of the changing ways in which people like to work. Mobility and flexibility are nowadays seen as key to productive working. As customers have become ever more critical of the service that is provided to them, they are mostly interested in convenience, speed and the quality of the services that are provided to.

One way of achieving the above is to provide customers with a continuously connected real-time environment – a horrible phrase which unfortunately captures the idea of providing the mobile individual with access to the data and applications they require anytime and anywhere. Although being continuously connected is not a condition for mobile provision, it is arguable that users perceive themselves to be so (when they want to be). Visualizing this future – what is possible, and what someone, whether supplier, customer or both, will pay for – will be central to the successful application of the new technology.

In order to prioritize areas where mobile customer management might be used, it is useful to consider how customers' needs are evolving. Here is a checklist to help:

- What are your customers, business partners or suppliers doing at any stage of the sales or service cycle that requires instant or messaged contact – away from the computer?
- How do your customers' needs vary according to the type of customer? For example, is there a difference between business customers (whether the corporate manager, the departmental manager, the worker or the business individual) and consumers? Do they vary by business function? How do the needs of the mobile worker vary from those of the hot-desker and the driver? How do needs vary between different family members – parents, teenagers and young children? What about public sector workers, such as educators, local government staff, health professionals, security and military personnel?
- How do your customers' needs vary according to your existing relationship with them (for example, new customer, existing customer, high-value customer and dissatisfied customer)?

- What are the different scenarios of the value of information to the customer – nice to know, immediate value, catastrophe avoidance, reinforcing contact?
- How does the existence and continued progress of wireless technologies combine with the availability of data models/databases and rapid e-business development tools to facilitate the rapid development of new applications which bring value to customers? On what basis should a company choose which application to develop and why it will be valuable to customers?

THE VALUE MODEL

When a new medium emerges, a central financial question is who will benefit and who will lose from its use. The answer to this question is, of course, that it depends how the medium is used. If we take the Internet, for example, it is clear that some of the major financial beneficiaries have been, among others:

- Telecommunications companies, who have seen use of their fixed telephony systems grow very rapidly due to online time.
- The earlier shareholders of Internet-based companies (whether suppliers of product or services or portal sites), who saw their share value sky-rocket, enabling them to sell (if they did).
- Customers who are able to buy more cheaply or more appropriately or obtain information more easily through the Web. This includes students who are saved many hours of time and travel expense that they used to dedicate to library searches.
- Logistics companies who benefit from the direct delivery business stimulated by the direct order business for physical goods.
- Systems suppliers, who benefit from the business generated by companies.
- User companies who save relatively higher communication costs of other media (eg using Web bookings instead of taking bookings through call centres or face to face).
- User companies who are able to give much better levels of service before and after the sale.
- User companies who have re-engineered their entire business to make it a Web business.
- User companies who used the Web to extend their reach nationally and globally, or to enter new markets, possibly at much lower costs – some of these companies were totally new.
- Intermediaries who are able to present product and service options more effectively to customers and manage relationships more effectively with suppliers.
- Content providers, who have found new markets for their content.

Losers have been slightly less obvious, but include:

- Later generations of shareholders, who bought Internet stocks at high values and saw them depreciate.
- Companies owning communication or distribution channels which have been displaced wholly or partly by the Web.
- Systems companies and clients which were late to adapt their businesses to the Web and lost share to those who gained.
- Intermediaries who fail to adapt to or to exploit these new technologies.
- Many advertising agencies, especially those stuck in the culture of the post-war 30-second TV advertisement and print advertising. They now have interactive agencies.

In general, the losers were losers because of:

- lack of planning;
- poor vision;
- interpretation of technological advance as a solution rather than a medium.

At the core of the gainers and losers is the issue of free provision of the Web. The nearest model for this is, of course, commercial broadcast media, where the medium is paid for by advertisers. Commercially published media are similar, as they are often free or only cover some of their costs by their cover price. However, here, what we see now is the end-product of years of experience of clients discovering which media it pays to advertise in. In the case of the Web – a new medium with limited access by final customers – a close parallel is with the early years of commercial television, when the audience was relatively limited. At the same time, we also have the clear evidence from satellite and cable TV of the willingness of customers to pay a premium for communication channels that meet their needs. The same applies to the mobile phone itself. Although rates are falling rapidly, the basic subscription level for mobiles in most countries implies at least a doubling of the telecommunications expenditure of the average consumer or business individual.

However, in some countries, 'pay as you talk' schemes offer zero rental cost, with a low telephone purchase price only – typically US $60–100. These schemes were originally targeted at telephone users who wanted to control costs, but now some such schemes appear to be targeted at people who are non-users (eg people who buy the telephone for emergencies, or to be contactable, but not to make calls). This opens up a market of pensioners, housewives, children, etc, who could be users of other services. Perhaps advertisers will pay to access these groups, as they do not intend to pay – but now have telephones. For example, there is a scheme in Japan, where people get free calls if they agree to listen to a 30-second advertisement every time they use the phone. Here, we may expect practice to follow that of the Web, where customers can post their e-mail address to receive advertisements, and gain rewards for doing so. Users will also be able to personalize the roster of companies they receive messages from – a good example of transparent marketing.

In the case of the mobile as a medium for customers and suppliers to communicate with each other before and after the sale, there is a big difference. It lies in the enormous diffusion level of the mobile phone that exists at the time when it is becoming a medium rather than just a communication device – which it is in around 80–90 per cent of households in certain countries. However, many of these customers are relatively new customers and use the mobile as a basic communication device, so we must be careful not to overestimate the speed with which the mobile will turn into a communication and distribution channel. At the same time, the widespread use of a relatively primitive technology (SMS text messaging) indicates the acceptability of the medium.

The conclusion here is that some mobile-based customer communication services will be chargeable at a premium (typically those that save customers' time, stress and effort or those that entertain them). Other services (perhaps the 'nice to haves') will need to be funded by third party advertising or out of the other commercial benefits that the supplier using them might derive (eg lower-cost marketing, higher market share).

One of the major benefits of the new services is that they increase customers' commitment to their operator – partly due to the time taken to optimize the new service to the needs of the individual. This means that by offering data, mobile network companies can improve loyalty and lower churn rate. A company with 1 million customers is paying US $90 million each year to replace the subscribers it is losing. Dropping the churn rate to 8 per cent saves US $66 million each year.

Many operators of mobile phone networks are looking to this new phase of development of the mobile phone market to earn the high returns that their enormous initial investments demand. So they will have to be particularly careful not to be drawn into offering services that deliver no revenue while attracting cost. They, as well as all those who use the new services to manage their customers, need to pay attention to the following points:

- Will it save operators money or add cost – overall and for particular activity types and particular customer types?
- Will it change the profile of the cost to serve particular customers or market, versus the revenue derived from them?
- Can customers be charged for particular services, and will they use these services less as a result?
- If operators save money by providing a service via mobiles, should the saving be passed on to customers?
- How can operators stop customers taking free services they might supply while imposing cost (the good and bad customer issue)?

One of the warning signs we should bear in mind is the cost of supporting the mobile worker. Mobile users may need even more support than desktop users, as they are literally moving targets, connecting via different routes from one session to the next. To ensure positive returns to investment in management of mobile workers, it is essential to focus on situations in which a continuously connected environment provides the mobile worker with information needed in real time in ways that the worker can add value (eg by selling more, reducing service cost).

Collapse of privileged service

One of the central ideas of CRM is giving better service to higher-value customers. This idea is premised on an assumption that it costs more to provide better service, and therefore that this better service should be reserved only for higher-value customers. From the customer point of view, in some industries it has seemed that the only way to get half-decent service is to become an important customer (eg the major account of a business-to-business supplier, a high-value frequent flyer, a premier customer of a bank). That is not to say that the expectations have always been delivered, sometimes because a high-value customer has more complex requirements.

This model has been under siege for some time. Even good use of call centres made it possible to give high value to very large numbers of customers, whose value varied widely – this is the basis of the top vanilla model. However, the Web has challenged this model, because it places much of the onus of obtaining good service on to the customer. The customer is responsible for data entry, accurate selection of the required product or service, and even sometimes for checking the level of service delivered (consignment tracking, bank balance checking). However, the relatively restricted availability of the Web (clearly not pervasive as it requires access to a fixed line or, at a premium, a mobile line) means that for many customers it is not the ideal tool for managing the relationship with a supplier. With WAP technology and the network strategies being adopted by mobile network companies, supported by government pressure on PTTs to provide low-cost interconnection, we see a world in which everyone is permanently connected to the Web and (implicitly) their suppliers and customers, via their mobile. Where the service is based on information, customers and suppliers will be able to exchange the most recent information that is relevant to any sales or service exchange, for any customer, with the mobile acting as the customer-validation device.

The penetration, ubiquity and immediacy of the telephone means that certain buying habits will become highly time and location dependent. This will to a certain extent act against (longer-term) relationship management. People will buy from the best value now and here rather than from their trusted brand. The issue will then be to ensure that you (whoever 'you' are) are on the list of people the 'best' consumers consult regarding best buys. These best consumers will expect to be valued for the value they bring to companies – they will not expect to have to earn their way into privilege.

The collapse of privilege is an interesting trend – visible even in the collapse of optional extras on cars. Extra services offered by suppliers are the key to reducing 'churn' – services create 'stickiness', where in this case stickiness means sticking with the relationship. The collapse of privilege means that you have to work ever harder to deliver higher-quality services to the 'best' customers, who are always changing. This can affect companies' approach to long-term relationship management strategy. A key question is whether long-term relationship customers are different from customers who look for the best buy all the time for all needs (usually known as cherry pickers).

Given the complexities of meeting customers' needs in this new world, one issue is whether CRM/e-CRM/mobile-CRM should be outsourced to people who do it best – a similar issue that arose in the early years of telemarketing, and still arises. This is an issue which we will be addressing later in the book. The usual issues will apply here, in particular determining a company's core competence. There will be the usual worries about whether outsourcing suppliers are helping competitors, whether companies can stay at the wave-front on services to the 'best' customers if they do not own the intellectual capital, whether the intellectual property is in the overall approach or just in the specific service. If the latter, competitors can copy it fast, especially if they are using the same outsourcer. However, using a leaky outsourcer may be better than an incompetent insourced department.

Advancing expectations

The latest flight delay information is already available to all customers in some countries, reducing stress for the customer, congestion for the airport owner and capacity usage in the airline call centre as customers call for the latest delay information. Customers can be told of the next pub that stocks their favourite brand of beer, whether their favourite item is on sale in their local supermarket. Service engineers can be informed of other problems on client sites while they are still there. The collapse of time and distance is apparent – and it is available to all customers. This means that companies who based their sales and service model on privilege will have to face the collapse of privilege – and use the mobile to meet the needs of customers who want to be informed all the time. Naturally, the phenomenon that all suppliers have experienced – the inflation of customer expectations – will apply here. One supplier will do the job well, and all other suppliers will be expected to! The ultimate expectation will be not only to be able to send and receive the most up-to-date information all the time, but also to get responses in real time. The disappointment evidenced by customers who fail to get this service from Web sites because of crumbling or non-existent e-mail management systems is very evident.

Competing in time – accelerated version

The more suppliers make it possible for their customers, business and consumer, to exploit the immediacy of information giving and response to their benefit, the less business suppliers who do not exploit immediacy will do. We first saw this in operation in the 1980s with the advent of the big call centre-based suppliers in areas such as financial services. An objective measure of the value of customers' time is what they earn (the economist's notion of the marginal utility of time). However, perception is reality, and many studies have shown that customers' feelings about the value of their time have been advancing faster than the real wage. Busy managers, whether of households or businesses, feel the same way.

The collapse of distance

Similar to the demand for immediacy, but less widespread, is the demand for globality. In the Web world, we got used to the idea that a competitor, albeit on the other side of the world, was only a click away. This is fine for sales situations, but often fails in service situations, when a telephone call is often required to solve an emergency problem. However, the irrelevance of location is becoming a norm in certain businesses (eg software), so the very high premium charged for international mobile calls is clearly under threat by mobile-based Web services that allow good communication with a supplier on the other side of the world.

Value chain implications

One of the most interesting implications of the Web and then the mobile is the addition these technologies make to the transparency of the value chain. This applies in situations where effective management of the value chain depends upon some degree of human intervention (ie wherever normal systems interconnections cannot do the job); and where the human being concerned is not tied to a desk or other location where a computer screen is located

Here, the immediacy of the mobile allows acceleration of business processes. For example, warning of a late delivery can allow the receiver of a consignment to reprioritize work or implement Plan B.

SERVICES BEING OFFERED OR PLANNED

These are changing very rapidly. The interest will be in linking them to earlier histories of diffusion of take-up, whether this is a good guide to the future, possible step changes in patterns, and new categories or service being created. They include:

- personal messaging (business to business, business to consumer, consumer to consumer);
- Web enablement;
- third party content – here the key issue is who will provide it, how they will obtain value from its provision, and how it will be updated;
- authorization/security services – parallel to credit vetting in older channels.

In order to assist the development of mobile-based services, IBM has set up a new team in Europe to help customers to rapidly extend their e-business services to WAP-enabled mobile wireless devices. Requests for WAP solutions and projects have increased dramatically, and the WAP team addresses this demand, helping customers to get started on WAP applications within days.

The sectors affected

The sectors we expect to be affected by these developments include:

- Financial services, where wireless technology is already being used for trading, checking balances and the like, and where we expect it to be used in areas such as claims management and general customer service.
- Travel and transport, where the prime use will be checking schedules, booking, delay alerts, tracking, locating facilities and the like.
- Automotive, where use will be in marketing and sales, in locating new and used cars, managing the service cycle, and as an in-car device for all other purposes.
- Utilities and telecommunications, where billing, switching and servicing will be the prime uses.
- General business to business, where general use for communications within the supply chain will be supplemented by all other uses in this section for managing customers, suppliers and business partners.
- Retail and packaged consumer goods, where use will be as an ordering device, alert for promotions, complaints. The mobile looks like being an excellent way for brand owners to speak to consumers, particularly women and young families. It offers an economic means to talk and listen to consumers with whom suppliers have no direct transactional relationship. These suppliers are used to spending big budgets on marketing, and it looks like the mobile will attract some of it.

MODELS OF CUSTOMER MANAGEMENT

The use of the mobile has the potential to change quite radically the cost/benefit profile of a number of our models of customer management (see Chapter 8). Here are some examples of the change.

In the one-to-one model, the company gathers lots of data about the individual and tries to adapt its entire offer as closely as possible to the individual customer's needs. We expressed scepticism about the long-term future of this model as long as all the information gathering was done by the company and as long as the information processing required to determine the offer was undertaken in batches, with the consequent risk of delaying attunement of the offer. However, we also suggested that if control of this model could be passed to the customer, in terms of specifying requirements, then the benefits rose relative to the costs – both for supplier and customer. The mobile phone is in many ways the ideal transparent marketing tool, not just because it is with the customer all the time, but also because compared to many other technologies it is simple to use, and also its frequency of use allows for rapid learning.

The model most at risk from the mobile, in our view, is classic CRM, in which customer data is used to group customers to allow them to be managed in a limited number of segments with significantly different offers for each segment. This implies that membership of the group is more important in determining customer value and needs than individual variations. This view overlooks the importance of time – in particular the immediacy of need (whether to buy, complain, get more information, etc). The general underinvestment in immediacy is apparent from the comments we made at the beginning of this chapter about companies' inability to handle high inbound volumes of unstructured feedback from customers. We believe the advantage will go to companies that are able to take and process feedback and requests immediately, converting customers' needs for information and offers into immediate replies.

In the personalized communication and targeting model, the offer is similar to all customers, but modified slightly to allow basic personalization, and targeted appropriately. It will retain its strong position as a model because of the relatively small investment in attunement per customer. For really mass-market suppliers, allowing customers to use the mobile to enhance personalization will represent a very cost-effective combination of this model with transparent marketing. 'Your' company via the mobile will be very powerful, even if 'your' only means 'your modularized version'.

In the top vanilla model, a best of breed offer is made to all customers (often combined with CRM for the most valuable segment). 'Vanilla' is used because this is the flavour designed to appeal to as much of the 'desired' market as possible; 'top' because it offers more than most customers require and is better than competitive offers. Its central idea is that instead of a heavily segmented offer applying to each market segment, the top vanilla approach is offered to, say, 90 per cent of the customers the company want to deal with,

with an additionally segmented approach for the other 10 per cent of customers. Offers via the mobile phone can be made to all customers with a very low communication cost. However, the best offers can be made to those customers who are considered to be the best customers. Customers who value and are prepared to pay for additional services and the relationship with the provider can be offered exceptional service. As these higher-value customers may be the same customers targeted by many other companies, it may well be these customers for whom validation is most intense (to identify current or expected future *net* value – including any downside risks). However, as we have already pointed out in our discussion of the collapse of privilege, it is these customers who usually receive the excellent service that is destined for all customers later. As early targets of new services (because they provide the value to suppliers which justifies the new services), they are important to have in your customer base if for no other reason than this. So, it will be for these customers that companies will invest in identifying most quickly when their needs are not being served well and in reacting fast; and identifying their needs and fulfilling them – perhaps even before customers realize they have them.

In the channel partnership model, the company works with channels to create and manage relationships. The Web world has taught us that, contrary to the rather naïve belief that the Web works in favour of removal of intermediaries (disintermediation), in fact most success comes from clever intermediaries, and some companies become intermediaries themselves. One of the reasons for this is that the workload involved in developing a very smart interface with customers is significant, and should perhaps be left to experts, whose whole business depends on successful management of the interface. This is still evidenced by the very poor quality of many Web sites that are run by product and service suppliers compared to the quality of those run by businesses that depend upon attracting people to buy the products and services of others. As long as technology and customer behaviour both continue to evolve as rapidly as they are doing at the moment, we see this situation continuing. Complex partnerships are being established between:

- product and service suppliers – the 'clients' for the service;
- mobile phone system and handset providers;
- mobile operating system providers;
- content providers;
- specialized agents who develop a presence solely or mostly 'on the mobile' as intermediaries;
- systems and software providers, who provide the infrastructure necessary to take the information flowing to and from the handset user into the systems of all the above.

The above are effectively relationship-focused models. We also identified some models at the other end of the buyer-commitment spectrum. They were:

- pure spot-selling – in which the buyer buys on the basis of best value at the time;
- spot-selling within a managed roster – in which the customer spot-buys from a limited roster of companies, so the company focuses on getting on to the customer's roster, and then offering best value;
- spot-selling via an agent, in which it is recognized that agents make choices on behalf of the customer, so the aim is to get on to the agent's roster (if any) and then deliver best value.

We found that these three models answer to the customer's basic need to get best value at the time. Even though they may provide a good basis for launching a relationship, we should not suppose that these models will always be replaced by the relationship model. Indeed, for the customer, the more value that is at stake, the more he or she is likely to search for best value, albeit within a roster (to control the risk). As the number of choices increases, so the potential for the agent also increases. We therefore expect there to be a strong push in this area. For example, while retailers might be trying to tempt customers into their specific stores via mobile messages, some consumers might prefer to subscribe to a service in which they can review all the best offers in a specific product category in their neighbourhood. Such a spot-buying service could realistically only be provided through an agent.

STAGES OF RELATIONSHIP

In Chapter 1, we identified the opportunities for improving customer management using a simple analysis of stages of the relationship, as follows:

1. Targeting – when the customer is targeted as being an appropriate customer for the company, and induced to 'join'.
2. Enquiry management – when the customer is in the process of joining.
3. Welcoming – after the customer has joined, depending on the complexity of the product or service, it is important to ensure that the customer is 'securely on board' (eg he or she knows who to contact if there are problems, knows how to use the product or service).
4. Getting to know – a crucial period, when both sides exchange information with each other. Additional customer needs may become apparent, and the customer's profile of use of the product or service becomes known. More is also learnt about the customer's honesty, ability to pay, etc.
5. Customer development/retention (eg renewal, persistence, loyalty) – the relationship is now being managed securely, with additional needs being identified in time and met where feasible.

6. Customer development (eg up-sell, cross-sell) – the ideal state, though quite a few customers never reach it, and often dip into the next stage or remain in the previous stage for a long time.
7. Problem management: intensive care through service failure – the customer has such severe problems with the service delivered by the company that special attention is needed to ensure that the customer returns safely to account management.
8. Problem management: intensive care through customer changes – the customer has changed and the company does not know it, so continues to manage the customer as if he or she is still the customer he or she once was.
9. Problem management: pre-divorce – if the required attention is not given, the customer is so dissatisfied that divorce is imminent.
10. Problem management: divorce – the customer leaves. However, the leaving may only be partial (eg from certain categories of purchase, or resulting in reduced frequency of purchase).
11. Problem management: win-back – the customer will usually, after a cooling-off period, be ready for 'win-back'.

Wireless technology can help companies at all stages of the customer management cycle. It can help companies and customers do things when they want, better, faster and also cheaper. But it can also create risks of enormous flows of contacts and information, which may be poorly handled, or very expensive to manage properly. The move towards transparent marketing, such as mobile technology, is encouraging, will change how companies manage the stages of their relationships with customers. In particular, the mobile will do two things.

First, it will allow customers to signal which stage they are in – and which they are about to move to. For example, a customer who is dissatisfied with merchandise may be able to signal it in-store direct to a central system far more effectively than through a complaint to a low-level member of staff. This would allow the company to inform the customer that, for example, a product change is on the way, that the item is in stock in another store and (if necessary) can be transferred to the home store by the next day.

Second, it will allow customers a much better tool to provide data to suppliers, enabling the latter to manage the customer's progress through into the ideal state of customer development.

At all stages of the relationship, our research has shown the following factors to be important in ensuring professional management of that stage and transition to a better stage:

● timeliness;
● relevance;
● responsiveness;

- accessibility;
- service recovery;
- access to prior-given information by the supplier at the moment of contact.

The mobile clearly helps with all of these.

FUTURE-PROOFING YOUR CUSTOMER MANAGEMENT

In this final section we suggest a checklist to help you determine what your actions should be.

Research

- Identify how your customers are currently exchanging information with you, in the many different situations they find themselves (eg different locations, stages of the relationship, etc).
- Identify customer requirements for value through information and service, how they are currently met, and what the priorities are of different types of customer.

Analysis

- Identify different ways in which you can provide value.
- Identify how the costs of providing this value might be met by customers, business partners or your own suppliers.

Develop a return on investment model to show who gets returns.

Models of customer management

- Identify which models of customer management are implicit in customers' behaviour towards you.
- Identify what communication flows are required to improve the working of the model.

Customer benefits

Analyse the true value-added to the customer as follows:

- Improve the end-user's business.
- Improve the business of the product/service provider.
- Provide new business services.
- Satisfy business needs more effectively.
- Save time and/or money.
- Communicate with friends and family and manage family affairs.
- Entertain/be entertained.

Customer recruitment

- Promote mobile services with virtual reality models.
- Cooperate with other suppliers – as partners and distributors.

Customer development

- Develop highly personalized services, which are constantly related to the time and the geographical position of the customer.
- Use the ideas of permission-based marketing to overcome customer resistance to taking up more services.
- Offer trials of the next level of services.
- Integrate your services with others in partnership to provide the customer a total solution.

Customer retention

- Ensure that all customer feedback is dealt with swiftly.
- Provide services on all open mobile platforms.
- Use special offers to activate sleeping accounts.
- Consider compensating complaints or irregularities by use of services.
- Set, implement and measure standards of service for information delivery.

Systems

- Accept only systems designed for continuous operation.
- Require open platforms to support seamless integration with enterprise resource planning (ERP).

- Monitor performance and add resources in anticipation of declining service quality.
- Use only open standards, platforms and interfaces.

Data

- Do not flood the customer with information.
- Utilize your data effectively.

Implementation

- Ensure that your processes for customer management are adapted to use this new technology.
- Ensure that the consequent data flows are properly managed.

11

Smart cards

Merlin Stone and Chris Field

OVERVIEW

The main barrier to using smart cards as an essential device for managing consumers has been the absence of card-readers in locations where consumers are managed – in the home, at the workplace, on the Web, in the store, etc. This barrier is now being removed by:

- The rapid diffusion of digital TV. Most households of interest to consumer marketers will have a digital TV set-top box by the end of 2001, with a second smart card slot. Software to support different applications can be downloaded directly by the TV operator. This opens up a vista of mass-market advertisers being able to address most of their customers directly, in a personalized fashion, including the delivery of personalized coupons in digital form, collapsing the costs of the redemption process and significantly reducing the opportunities for fraud.
- The introduction of smart cards by credit card companies, with strong incentives for retailers to install readers in the form of lower commission charges, funded by the reduction of costs in handling fraud and by the greater reliability of smart card readers and the cards themselves.
- The appearance of kiosks in a variety of locations, funded by suppliers of services and products made available through them, whether in post offices, transport sites (ticketing, parking, etc) or retail stores.
- The take-up by governments all over the world of smart card technology as the key to consumer access/permissions for public facilities and services.

- The introduction of Bluetooth technology, allowing short-range communication between digital devices. This means that even if there is no smart card reader, a consumer who inserts a smart card into another device (eg a dual-slot mobile, a personal organizer) will be able to communicate with other devices (eg point-of-sale terminals, vending machines). At home, even a single card reader (eg digital TV) could be used as a device to distribute and receive smart card data to other devices, (eg PCs, mobile phone).
- The possibility that most cars will be fitted with a variety of 'telematics' devices, some shared with devices outside the car (eg dealer systems, mobile phones, parking systems) access to which will be controlled by a smart card.

Some of this is distant, but much of it is very near. However, marketers' obsession with a single, centralized, real-time updated view of customers, the Internet or mobile telephony have caused them to overlook this opportunity. This is particularly surprising in view of the fact that the smart card could be the integrator they need, especially for these new areas of marketing endeavour.

This has already been realized by retailers such as Boots in the UK. It is not widely known that the key reason for Boots using a smart card in their loyalty scheme is that most customers regularly shop at several Boots shops, ie they do not have a 'home store' in which the points database can be held for redemption purposes, as with the Tesco and Sainsbury schemes. A smart card offered the most secure and lowest-cost way of allowing points to be stored on the card which can be read at different stores, without having to update a central database immediately. This shows that if a smart card is used together with one or more customer databases (as it normally will be – whether the databases are within one company or in several companies), it can provide the ideal combination of immediate identification and access to the most recent data, wherever it is presented.

An additional, and for some companies a really major benefit, is that smart card technology offers significant opportunities for reduction in fraud and the costs of managing it. This applies to fraud by customers, staff and intermediaries, eg dealers. This fraud occurs not only with credit, charge and store cards, but also with customer loyalty schemes, coupon redemptions, service data and sales data. Although major advances in fraud detection have taken place in the last few years, fraud is still running at high levels and is the main reason for the credit card switch to smart cards.

Smart cards are now commonplace, thanks to mobile telephony, incorporation in various credit, charge and loyalty cards, personnel identification systems and digital television. The resulting volumes of cards and readers being produced have accelerated technological developments. This means that smart cards are now relatively cheap, sophisticated pieces of equipment able to handle a multitude of functions, including electronic purse (able to handle crediting, storage and payment of cash), loyalty scheme management, storage and updating of personal identification information and dynamic data relating to the customer, and so on. Smart cards with displays are even in use.

This chapter, therefore, suggests that when companies who deal with millions of customers through many channels for many interactions break through their obsession with the Internet and mobile telephony, they will realize that under their nose is a sensible technology for managing customers. Key points are that:

- This technology has been under their nose for some time.
- Acceptance of this technology is exploding because of credit card, digital TV and government use.
- It allows lower-cost, more customer-friendly and higher-quality methods of improving relationships with customers – whether independently or in cooperation with other companies.

THE IMPACT OF CRM

CRM has become one of the most powerful fashions on the business circuit. Yet evidence is emerging that many companies are having trouble in this area. They are acquiring expensive systems, costing millions or even tens of millions of pounds, but then experiencing severe problems in implementation. One of the major stumbling blocks to successful implementation is customer data. The idea of the single view of the customer, so attractive in theory, is very hard to achieve in practice. Most big companies have many sources of customer data. For example, it's not unusual for a financial services company to have a separate customer database for every product, and possibly even one for every contact channel. Airlines may have separate databases for business flyers, holiday fliers, responders to marketing campaigns, and complainers. The data is not only spread around many systems. It's usually of very varied quality, and it's not easy to make the different data sources consistent, and to improve the quality of the data.

So is the dream of a single, centralized view of the customer – said to be essential for the customer to experience consistent treatment by all parts of the company – unrealistic? Not really, but it's certainly sensible to be sceptical about dreams of achieving it at one stroke.

An alternative vision of CRM is one in which some of the data about customers – their basic details, recent purchasing history, responses to promotions, recent transactions with the various channels that they use in their dealings with a supplier – is held by the customer. With smart cards on the brink of mass-market distribution being driven by sound business sense, government initiatives and customer demand, there is the possibility of dramatic improvement in how companies can achieve improved customer management through the customer holding at least some of their data. So this chapter explores some aspects of how smart cards are being used, and how they are planned to be used, in improving customer management.

DEFINITION

Smart card technology for customer management is defined as technology that allows a single card to be used for a variety of applications. These include:

- Customer loyalty. This may be by one company or several, either working closely together as part of a shared loyalty scheme or working more loosely together by using the card's ability to host several applications.
- More accurate customer identification for marketing purposes (for example, more precise targeting and tailoring of offers).
- More accurate customer identification for validation purposes (for example, fraud prevention). This includes identification as the customer appears in several channels, particularly in the real world (eg in-store) and virtual worlds (eg the Internet, digital TV and mobiles).
- Local storage of customer data, particularly when the customer may interact with the company in many different places and/or through many different channels, and there are problems with ensuring that relevant customer data is available at all these points to optimize the transaction.

Smart cards offer ways of allowing customers to be managed or allowing customers to manage their relationships with companies so that both sides can get the best out of the relationships. The usual benefits of CRM can be delivered through integrating the use of smart cards into a wider CRM approach. Businesses that understand their customers can build long-term relationships with them and attract new ones. The more information a business has about its customers in terms of their behaviour and shopping patterns, the easier it is to target marketing activity in a way that addresses their needs and ultimately, boosts profitability.

AUTOMATION OF DATA CAPTURE

Many companies are still having problems with the automation of data capture from the customer. Although the use of call centres and e-commerce has allowed many companies to identify the customer, and update their customer service history, most industries still require the customer to provide information which is then entered into computers at the point of sale or service. This leads to higher costs due to inefficiencies and errors in data collection, and detracts from the provision of state-of-the-art customer service. Two emerging technologies are particularly suited to automating the capture of customer data at point of service: smart cards and wireless technologies.

Smart cards have the capability to provide 'wallet compatible' front-end to back-end CRM and ERP systems. When integrated into the merchant point-of-sale (POS) system, smart card readers provide the capability for merchants to improve customer service while simultaneously helping to track customer buying habits and to implement loyalty programmes. The same system could potentially be used to simplify expense reporting by tying POS payment points to corporate customers' ERP systems.

Potential applications include cards for storing customer profile, purchase, service history and to upgrade information for real-life 'objects' such as car and home. Consumers benefit by expedited service at dealers and other third party vendors and by being able to maintain purchase and service history on a portable smart card. Merchants benefit by being able to provide faster and more efficient customer service.

In practically every retail environment where sales and service are provided, dealers can use smart cards and wireless technologies to store and retrieve customer profiles, service history, warranties and similar information instantly when the customer comes into their establishment. In an increasingly competitive environment where technology is increasingly a key differentiator, wireless, smart card and other hand-held technologies can provide a major competitive advantage.

CONTROLLING FRAUD

No payment method is immune from fraud. However, the ease with which magnetic stripe cards can be copied has opened up exposure – not just to payment cards but also to loyalty cards. Multi-user magnetic stripe schemes are also relatively vulnerable, as all parties need to agree procedures, and it is much harder to have claims validated by a central database. Smart cards are more difficult to copy, and more security is continually being built into them as they become a central focus of the fraud control effort in a variety of applications. The need for better fraud control is evident not only in companies dealing with consumers, but also in government agencies dealing with the public, particularly where entitlement and validation of identity are issues.

Although smart cards are no guarantee against fraud, they do help to prevent it. The fraud problem is particularly serious for online merchants, though some types of e-commerce sites carry a higher risk than others:

- Downloadable software may cost several hundred dollars, but if the fraud is not detected when the transaction is being made, the fraudster can have downloaded the product and disappeared before the merchant is ever aware of the problem.
- Adult and instant entertainment sites are also susceptible. Adult sites also get a high rate of chargebacks from participants who claim to their wives or partners when the statement comes that they never signed up for the service, that it must have been some big mistake.

- Information sites are also likely to receive some 'hit-and-run' crooks.
- High-cost items, such as computers, airline tickets, and diamonds, are prime targets for thieves.

USING SMART CARDS IN MARKETING

For many years companies have wondered why smart cards that allow multiple uses have found relatively little application in marketing, sales, service and other customer-facing disciplines. For some time, all that there was to show for this globally were a few national schemes and local schemes, combining a variety of promotional and stored value uses.

However, the situation is changing, for a number of reasons. Many cities in the world now have smart card schemes, covering transport and a variety of other services. Mobile telephony and digital TV have caused an explosion in the demand for smart cards. Some of the most successful loyalty schemes use smart cards. Finally, the use of smart cards in credit and debit cards is imminent. Governments are also adopting smart cards as a more secure way of managing services and payments. Finally, the Internet world is starting to adopt smart card technology as the basis for security.

Infrastructure cost has been the major inhibitor to adoption thus far. It is not clear whether smart card readers are going to be included in devices in pervasive use – PCs, PDAs, mobile phones (other than the SIM card of course). Many companies are waiting/hoping for someone else to jump first so that they can then piggyback on their infrastructure. Many companies see loyalty/CRM as an add-on 'nice to have' feature rather than the core application. There is usually more talk than action. CRM does not have such a great payback as many claim – other applications may yield better returns. Call centre applications are critical for clients, and later it will be multi-channel integration and data mining. A more important area is the identification/security token – particularly for secure Internet access – given the high level of fraud. Readers are the critical part of the infrastructure. If customers cannot use the cards they will fall into disuse. If there are widespread outlets, it reinforces the consumer's choice of card.

When used properly, the smart card provides a good, secure approach to recognition, promotional targeting and instant redemption, as in the Boots Advantage scheme. Also, if several partners get together, then service can be much enhanced, eg airlines partnering with hotels to recognize mutual customers. In general, smart cards offer a more flexible platform for loyalty applications, allowing a combination of loyalty and ancillary applications – for example travel, loyalty, club access and electronic ticketing. But the value proposition to both supplier and customer must be clear, and this has been a problem with other CRM approaches. That is why combining CRM with low-value transactions and promotions and communications is a good idea. Enablers, such as smart cards, come later. It is critical this time around for companies promoting such approaches to be seen as adding value, not pursing a particular enabling technology.

In terms of fraud control, smart cards offer ways of executing payment more securely. A smart card's portability is a strong advantage. A single card can carry all a customer's digital credentials and, when interface specifications to PCs or mobiles are agreed, will be able to use any digital device to transact. But until the infrastructure is available, and there is secure deployment of digital certificates and common standards, this will not happen.

So, the smart card mist is beginning to clear – but only just. Many companies that were sceptical about various smart cards are taking a second look. At the same time, many are sceptical, and the phrase 'waiting to see who will jump' recurs again and again in the research carried out for this project. This research shows why there are reasons to look again at the multi-company side of things. In particular, it shows that there are many situations where, while a single application may not be cost-effective, a multiple application, covering customer loyalty or other promotions, e-purse and other applications may be appropriate.

How to make smart card schemes work

Consumer acceptance is not merely a question of ensuring that there is a large number of cards and card-accepting terminals in a particular town or region. Each consumer has a different pattern of behaviour, and critical mass has to be achieved for each consumer. The major areas of uncertainty in evaluating or using smart card technology in customer relationship management are customer need, real cost, security, customer perception (will they think you will put prices up to pay for it?), lack of a sponsor (is it IT, marketing or what?). These need to be resolved. There is a need for alliances rather than tension between the interests of the various participants. The key sponsors of schemes are generally very large retailers, financial institutions, and/or very large services organizations. It is also feasible, but difficult, for a technology-provider to act as the main driver. Schemes are too complex to implement all at once. It is essential that the first phase contain enough promise to interest all relevant parties, but be sufficiently open-ended that additional functions and additional parties can be added later, with relative ease.

KEY CHANGES

Several major changes in the business and social environment have triggered the need for this second look. Some of them are quite controversial, with the evidence required to prove them not being available for public scrutiny, eg single-company mass-market schemes. In other cases, the forces are overt and well documented. Let us examine these forces.

Single-company mass-market loyalty schemes

In the last few years there has been a strong focus on CRM systems where business cases are based not on making things easier or better value for customers, but allowing companies to sell more to customers. This has led to many investments in CRM systems and approaches failing to meet their objectives. The same could be said to be true of single-use loyalty schemes. After a surge of interest in the global marketing community in the 1990s, marketers (and of course finance directors) are now looking more closely at these schemes. The economics of such schemes are in theory simple. The idea is that the cost of setting up and running such a scheme is offset by additional profit. This profit comes from five main sources:

- Additional sales of the company's existing products to existing customers.
- Customers switching all or part of their relevant purchasers to the company because of the attractiveness of the scheme. This switching may come from other companies with similar schemes, or companies with no schemes.
- Sales of new products and services, particularly ones that yield higher margins than the existing product range. Financial services are the main contender here, with most retailers with loyalty schemes entering into partnership with major financial services providers. Other important areas include utilities, Internet provision and telecommunications.
- Greater ease of marketing, setting up and running home delivery operations, although this has turned out to be loss-making for most companies.
- List rental (within the terms of data protection legislation).

Obviously, whether the revenue outweighs the cost depends upon:

- whether customers can be influenced in the above ways, ie will they increase or switch their spend?
- the margin resulting from this;
- whether the same result could have been achieved more cheaply, and in particular without a loyalty scheme.

Here are some examples:

- Dixons managed to build an Internet business (Freeserve) without a loyalty scheme.
- Safeway withdrew its loyalty scheme because it was rewarding customers for doing what they would have done anyway.
- Asda, Waitrose and Tesco continue to gain share (and achieve profit through the first three of the five sources listed above) by focusing on classic retail policy.

However, while the success of Sainsbury's scheme is in the balance, as the company itself is being turned round, other companies such as Tesco, Boots and Sainsbury's Homebase are achieving successes with single-company schemes. Probably the most successful of these is the Boots scheme, as their products have higher profit margins, while their stronger market share and brand gives a much stronger ability to influence customers. Their products are generally more discretionary, so customers can be influenced to buy.

Emergence of multi-user schemes

Slowly but surely, we are seeing the emergence of local schemes, eg shopping centre schemes, which support the objectives of many companies. This keeps the set-up and running costs low, as the more partners share in the scheme, the lower the costs to any one partner. As we shall see, however, the emergence of really big users who will be carrying much of the infrastructural cost means that radical new promotional opportunities are about to open up.

Threats to the classic store card

As credit and debit cards continue to improve their distribution, customers who were formerly restricted to store credit and charge cards for easy payment methods have effectively put pressure on companies who did not accept these more general forms of payment by taking business away from them. In the UK, the two most notable cases of this are Marks & Spencer and John Lewis. Once stores accept more general methods of payment, the use of their own store card starts to decline. Stores have generally been poor at creating service benefits for these cards. One of the reasons for this is that it is hard to discriminate between customers in stores, and some companies consider it unethical to do so. The result is that without a loyalty card, such stores' knowledge of their customers is deteriorating. Surprisingly, these stores are ones with higher margins and which sell products which are discretionary in their nature, fulfilling two of the key conditions for the success of a loyalty programme.

Real-time access to data at all customer contact points

With many magnetic-stripe-based loyalty schemes, if the user company wants to allow the customer to credit and redeem points at any point of physical contact (stores, customer service counters), there must be an interface with the company's database, or else the company is exposed to fraud. Ensuring that the customer database is available at any point of contact is feasible but expensive. The ability of a magnetic stripe card to cope with this is limited. Retailers have developed compromises (eg the 'home store' concept). A smart card can contain more data, and with higher levels of security possible, the ability to redeem points as cash or merchandise in any location can be offered more confidently. As Visa and Mastercard move to a smart card system, the ability to read smart cards will exist in most stores, and this will break one of the critical barriers to the deployment of smart cards in loyalty schemes (see later). However, for really mass-market retailers, the card's cost will be the main problem (reader costs are relatively small). This makes it more likely that retailers interested in customer loyalty and promotions through card techniques will look for a shared use card.

Mass-market product suppliers

After years in which mass-market product suppliers have teetered on the edge of using anything beyond the classic media advertising supported by in-store promotions and the occasional piece of direct mail, we are now starting to see some serious contenders emerge for the next generation of marketing. Interestingly, the idea of managing direct relationships with customers for these products is alive and well both in domains where the retailer is closer to customer data through their own loyalty scheme, and in situations where retailer loyalty schemes are not used. The main problem is that the margin available per customer for a single product is not enough to justify direct contact. That is why the only major consumer non-durable suppliers seriously active in this area either run direct activities over all their products (eg Procter and Gamble) or else combine in consortia (eg the Unilever, Cadbury, Kimberly Clark consortium, Jigsaw). The mechanism they use at the moment is questionnaire-based direct mail, bearing relevant coupons. Some are starting to experiment with mobile telephony, as the cost of delivery for a coupon is very low. However, this requires either questionnaire activity to obtain mobile phone numbers, or else cooperation with a mobile phone company (see the example of such a scheme mentioned below). As acknowledgement of fulfilment is required for promotional schemes such as these to work, it is likely that the only way forward in which this could involve smart cards is through a multi-user scheme involving at least one retailer. This might allow accumulation of additional points for the products of particular manufacturers, stored on the card. These could then be redeemed at the retailer.

After the dot.com debacle

The year 2000 was the one in which the truth about the Internet dawned on many marketers. They realized that if there is no clear way forward to increased profitability using the Internet, there is little justification for using it as a main business model. However, in 2000 it was also realized that the Internet is an excellent device for combining with other marketing and service approaches for real companies. In other words, 2000 was the year of the 'bricks and clicks' companies. In most cases, customers are continuing to buy from shops. However, they are using the Internet to gather information about the products that are available. They are using it to set up relationships with big brands. They are enrolling in promotional schemes. Note that in both cases the initiative can lie with the customer. However, it can be prompted. Just as Boots' retail kiosks ask customers to insert their card to receive relevant promotional offers, so could the PC, mobile phone or digital TV box. The offers could then be redeemed at a retailer. As has been shown by the first mobile phone pilots and initial experiments with Internet coupons, using digital coupons with tight deadlines for use is usually more successful than when they have long deadlines. The cannibalization of existing business is less likely too. If a consumer is told to go out and buy this weekend, when the normal purchasing frequency is every month, there is less probability of cannibalization.

The pieces of the jigsaw have not yet come together, of course. One of the major missing pieces is the standardization of interfaces between a smart card and various digital devices (PC, mobile phone, digital TV). But it is sensible to envisage a situation in which a customer uses a combination of the Internet, PC or mobile or digital TV, and marketing smart card to manage relationships with product suppliers and retailers to mutual benefit. Once again, this will require a number of companies to come together to share the cost. But at the moment, the extremely high acquisition costs involved in many Internet channels and their (normal) separation from other channels means that the current situation must be described as primitive compared to what is possible. The reliance of the marketing industry on technology of 30 years or more ago to attract and retain customers is evidence of two things. First, It takes a long time for a new technology to find its place in the market. Second, once the technology has found its place it lasts a very long time, because everyone gets used to it (consumers and suppliers), and standardization takes place, allowing more applications to be built around it.

Of course, the Internet is a new area for fraud. A key problem is the inability to truly identify the customer who is online. The smart card offers this possibility, and is at the centre of developments in fraud reduction. This will be very valuable in the area of consumer-to-consumer transactions (eg auctioning of personal effects).

Adoption of smart cards for debit and credit cards

Magnetic stripe technology has been with us for decades, but slowly the world is turning to smart cards. Within two to three years, there will be widespread distribution of smart card readers in stores and ATMs all over the world. Banks have been slow to move on this because of the enormous investment tied up in magnetic stripe card-readers. This is entirely natural. The smart card represents for banks a small increase in security in exchange for a big investment. However, one of the problems is that they see the bank card as standalone, rather than being combined with other uses, or indeed with other cards. For example, at the moment a bank card relies on three additional sources of security:

- the PIN number;
- identification of abnormal transactions by rapid analysis;
- notification if the card has been lost or stolen.

If a card stores more data securely, then, for example, additional matching questions can be asked about recent transactions on the card. Rapid matching of personal characteristics can also be achieved. A smart card can store digitally the details of a fingerprint or the iris and these details can be matched with the data collected by the appropriate scanning device. This approach is already being used in highly secure establishments, though primitive fingerprint recognition is already in use as a security control for personal organizers.

Digital TV

As with other new technologies, digital TV is creeping up slowly on us, but the pace is accelerating. Within a few years, in some countries, over half of households will have this technology. In most cases, the group with the highest take-up will also be the group with the strongest propensity to buy brands and respond to promotions. In the UK, digital TV tuners all have a smart card slot, though the first applications have yet to emerge. One application area will be gaming. In the UK, Sky's target was to have 40 per cent of Sky Digital viewers playing games at least once a month within two months of launch from January 2001. Datamonitor estimates that 78 million people in West Europe will be playing games on interactive TV by 2004, compared with 122 million on mobile phones. But the business models for this are not yet developed. There is evidence that interactive TV and set-top boxes may replace ISPs for many applications, not just in the UK but also in Germany.[1] Forrester, Ovum and PWC reports all agree. But this ties customers to home, so how will they be recognized, rewarded, etc? A smart card per user, with the ability to use in various channels, seems the obvious answer.

THE E-PURSE – THE GOVERNMENT ANGLE

Although fraud reduction can be a major benefit of a smart card, an opposite benefit is the possibility of carrying money without identity. This is important in situations where customers prefer anonymity. Despite this, much of the focus of multi-user smart card development has been on associating the e-purse (where anonymity is possible) with loyalty applications. One of the main reasons for this is the reduced risk to cash security of electronic transfer of money. Of course, while in most countries most adults have credit or debit cards, this is by no means true of younger people. This is one of the reasons why campus cards have proved so attractive. Governments have another interest in the e-purse – the avoidance of social exclusion, particularly among those who do not have or cannot obtain credit cards or those who prefer cash payment. Finally, governments are starting to use smart cards as a way of securely managing groups of citizens so as to avoid high administration costs (eg the UK government's plan to use it for training allowances).

One of the most important uses of smart cards has been the area of parking and vehicle movement. In public transport, where the need for a simple system to handle large and small payments (eg season ticket payments as well as single/return fares) has led to the use of smart cards in many transport networks. In some cases, the consumer has been prepared to pay for the card because of the sheer ease of use in a busy station. In other cases, introduction has been supported by discounted travel offers. We expect this use to continue to grow, as governments throughout the world put increased emphasis on restricting access and parking entitlement in major cities. Interestingly, it is not necessarily in the richest countries that smart cards have been most attractive. In developing countries, the advantages of a cash substitute have been very appealing to city authorities. Cash handling costs and fraud are reduced. For example, the UK government is committed to using smart cards in transport, because they offer smoother, more flexible and more efficient passenger travel, providing the user with maximum flexibility when travelling across the country using a variety of transport modes and operators. The government will be inviting proposals from consortia for smart ticketing trial that can operate across public transport operators and modes. This will help develop best-practice guidance and test emerging standards for the design of smart card systems.

Smart cards – the catalyst for intelligent mobility

No one needs reminding of the relentless growth of traffic in developed economies: governmental organizations around the world are actively seeking and implementing measures to influence and control its inexorable growth. Developing and fostering use of public transport is a key component of any solution, but a truly sustainable change in travel behaviour – particularly the change from car to public transport – is only possible if the traveller is given a better alternative. Turning the car driver into a confirmed public transport passenger requires an integrated transport network with services that match individual needs.

Integrated intelligent client device

Independent transport and traffic studies have shown that availability of one common electronic ticket across an entire public network makes it more attractive to potential users. Integrating transport network ticketing, and then intelligently controlling and manipulating its component services, relies on innovative use of IT, and a sophisticated client device is an essential ingredient in any such solution. The smart card – particularly in its contactless form – provides that one electronic ticket, catalyzing the integration of transport services and satisfying the (often conflicting) demands of traveller and operator. The miniature computer inside the smart card, with its built-in security, means that different transport businesses (and indeed civic and other services) can come together in complete trust of the shared payment medium of the smart card. They can then devote their time and ingenuity to exploiting its potential rather than worrying about safeguarding the integrity of transactions. In its simplest form, the smart card ticket is an electronic memory device: each time it is used for a journey, the ticket cost is deducted from value stored on the card. This reduces the need to carry money for tickets, and to collect cash from machines, helping minimize fraud and revenue loss. Paper-based tickets, in contrast, remain vulnerable. They can be copied, allowing multiple travel on one ticket: adding a magnetic stripe carrying journey information to paper tickets can help reduce fraud, but smart cards – particularly those incorporating embedded processing – are significantly more secure. Contactless smart cards are ideal for transport applications using automated ticket inspection – the short, fast transaction interchanges maximize ease and convenience for the traveller, and improve the operation of the service by reducing boarding times.

Carrots and sticks

Improving the public transport networks relies partly on intelligent manipulation of transport services, implementing incentives and barriers to influence travelling behaviour, and examining and analysing the impact of these measures. This has to be based on accurate and robust mobility data – before you can improve mobility, you have to understand how people move. The smart travel application – whether delivered as a standalone ticket, an application on a city card or a card that is resident in, say, a mobile phone – is the catalyst for this next major step. First and foremost, the smart card provides the fundamental security that allows the personal data essential for tracking behaviour to be securely stored on the card. Then, it provides the multi-application environment that allows an individual's mobility-related activities, and therefore needs, to be accurately monitored and assessed. Cross-analysis of multiple databases is essential for an accurate assessment of the impact of changes in policy on behaviour. Smart cards are a key enabler: they provide a common client device that allows access to, for example, train and bus service databases, on- and off-street car parking databases, as well as many major services in the town such as library and leisure facilities. Thanks to the common factor, the smart card, this data can be mined to answer questions such as: when and where do travellers go, how do they get there, and how long does it takes them? Collected and analysed data can then be used to conceive and implement intelligent mobility, and innovative and flexible ticketing and pricing strategies. Flexible tariffs can be linked to journey profiles -- the offer of cheap park-and-ride at the weekend if a bus has been used at least three times during the week, for example. And information to help the consumer plan and utilize services more effectively can be delivered via the mobile phone or palmtop. Implementing schemes like these requires not only a range of technologies, but also a systems integration capability and a broad grasp of the issues involved. The involvement of Schlumberger in this sector meets these criteria. Its activities span the provision of car parking and ticketing terminals and cards, to the communications, servers and software required for the back-office systems. A number of recent projects demonstrate aspects of planning for intelligent mobility.

MOBILE TELEPHONY

There is a great question mark over mobile telephony. While subscription mobile phones themselves are now nearly all based on smart cards, these are proprietary and do not lend themselves to extension to marketing and service use. Indeed, from the mobile phone companies' point of view, anything that reduced the to and fro of data between customer and supplier is bad news, as it reduces charges. Often, this is exactly what smart cards do, by storing more data locally. Only when smart cards themselves lead to additional data exchanges will mobile companies find extended uses interesting. In addition, the emergence of Bluetooth technology means that in many situations the SIM card (and its later developments) may act as a substitute for an external smart card, as the mobile phone itself will be able to transmit any validation or crediting data. Smart cards may play a part where the mobile device cannot be used, eg on airliners, etc, to allow charging to the phone account to take place. It may also be used as a 'secondary' security on handsets for mobile commerce.

Meanwhile, shopping via the mobile may be opening up new vistas. For example, at the Lakeside shopping centre, 150 retailers (three quarters of the total) are participating in a project for sending text messages to the phones of shoppers signed up for this service. They receive hourly messages, eg 'Free coffee at Costa Coffee', '10 per cent discount on purchases over £50 at Dixons'. Teenagers are the prime target as they are time-rich, cash-poor, like using mobiles and keen to try novel ideas. They can also collect 'ZagPoints' each time they respond to a message, and receive 500 points for signing up. Each point is worth 1p and can be redeemed for mobile pre-paid vouchers. Reebok offered a free pair of £50 trainers to the first 15 customers presenting the relevant ZagMe message at the store. Teenagers are likely to tell others about such a service. The users of the service disclose a few basic demographic details such as age and gender. Time-limited messages are more likely to succeed, as they generate a sense of excitement (eg 'Free doughnuts with coffee for the next half-hour'). The power of text message was shown this summer at Ibiza, where daily bulletins alerted clubbers to the whereabouts of the next rave. Text messaging is growing dramatically – with 500 million messages in October 2000 compared with 14 million June 1999.

Wireless technology itself is moving rapidly. Ericsson is currently piloting a wireless wallet, due to be on the market by 2002, which will be able to connect to smart cards in the wallet, and make secure transactions, on-line and off-line. Bluetooth technology will eventually allow smart cards themselves to transmit and receive. In Singapore, Gemplus has provided smart card technology for the world's first commercial launch of a mobile phone e-purse reload service by MobileOne (M1) and Network for Electronic Transfers (NETS) in Singapore. The CashCard, an e-purse smart card, is widely used by motorists and other consumers in Singapore to pay for road tolls and other small value purchases. The new service gives users more flexibility and convenience in reloading their CashCards as and when they need to. All they require is a dual-slot mobile phone, a smart ATM card and a PIN number. Besides reloading, customers can use the service to check the balance in their CashCards and to view a history of previous card transactions. Future applications include a service that will enable M1 customers to pay their bills using their mobile phones. More details on this service will be announced later. Gemplus worked with NETS, M1 and Motorola to define the application design and develop the service based on agreed specifications.

RETAILERS

The benefit retailers would expect to get from deploying smart cards in customer management is that they would expect to raise spend among the 20 per cent group that already contribute to profit. Branding possibilities of the card are also of interest.

UK Internet banking pioneer Egg and its partner, Boots the Chemist, have developed an end-to-end multi-application smart card solution – the first such smart co-branding offering in the UK – the new 'Advantage Card Powered by Egg', a combined credit and loyalty card. The new combined payment and loyalty cards are based on the EMV smart card, certified by Europay, MasterCard, and Visa. It enables the issuer to strike a precise balance between security, retailer and customer convenience, and operating overheads. It incorporates an exceptionally powerful processor – supporting high transaction speeds and high levels of security – and the capacity to host multiple applications, enabling new partnerships between banks and the retail community. It also provides additional post-issuance flexibility, through the ability to activate the PIN to reflect local market changes. The sum of all these features is a platform which offers card issuers and their retail partners highly cost-effective performance, and the flexibility to adapt as local requirements change.

The roll-out of EMV cards by the banks is seen by many retailers as a necessary condition for their adoption of smart cards. EMV dictates that all cards be smart by 2003. It is being introduced to schools too. If the cards are adopted by the high street banks or credit card companies (especially Mastercard, Visa, Switch, Barclays Connect), retailers will implement them quickly. For some time retailers have had offers to include these readers for very low cost from technology suppliers (less than £10 per single unit plus fitting). Most new loyalty schemes are likely to be smart card based. Whether a retailer chooses a smart card will be less to do with the price of the readers and more to do with the individual production cost of the cards. Retailers may be looking at anywhere from 5–15 million cards, so if a magnetic stripe card were half or a quarter of the price of a smart card, or had a very substantially longer shelf-life or mean time between failures, these would have to be considerations. A main reservation about the cards is how easy they are to forge or duplicate. (If a card has a financial value rather than purely being an identifier of an individual consumer then retailers have reservations about using them in an offline environment without the ability to validate that the card is genuine and has not been replicated.)

From the marketer's perspective, a determining question about whether to go smart card or not will also have to do with how many colours of printing there can be on the physical card, whether it can be embossed/overprinted and whether it can be lacquered/varnished. Retailers are particularly concerned about the brand impact of getting customers to carry a card with their name on around with them it, and making sure that it correctly reflects the corporate identity. Smart cards can also be used more easily to get around systems differentials that experience with multi-channel retailing. It is effectively a multi-channel means of 'tracking', influencing and rewarding the customer, for loyalty schemes as well as tactical promotions.

The more a card can store, the more it can be used in any channel, to allocate and redeem rewards. More advanced retailers are looking to reward recency and frequency as well as spend. It is also a means of building third party offers and rewards into existing schemes. Online dependency with stores is removed, and the smart card also delivers communication cost reductions. The smart card gives improved multi-channel/single view of the customer and therefore improved targeting of offers by channel, etc. For many retailers, the prime advantage is that it provides a way for underaged customers to buy online. Smart cards also allow ways for pensions and healthcare credits to be spent. For retailers that sell via the Internet and via touch-screen kiosks, the most likely application is as a personal identifier. If the technology gets into people's homes (for example, if the features that BT already builds into some telephone handsets start to be activated), then retailers will consider extending these features to the Internet.

Other retail application areas include door entry systems, staff time and attendance recording, and possibly application for people who use touch-screen ordering kiosks in stores. Also included is the possibility of using the cards as an economic method of passing product/price data to hand-held terminal/portable data capture application users who do field-based stock counting and on-shelf price checks. Given that the readers can be slotted into symbol terminals, etc, at very low cost, this may be particularly practical and relatively low cost. Because of the large numbers of staff employed and the need for security (some retailers mention that up to 50 per cent of shop theft involves members of staff, either directly or in collusion with fraudulent outsiders), staff use is an obvious area of application.

This also applies to other companies where staff security is important. In IBM UK all staff are being issued with smart cards for all internal IBM purchases, transport, etc. It is possible that a few far-sighted employers might extend the use of such staff cards to include personal benefits, in conjunction with partners. It seems that work-site marketing has not been tried properly as an approach. This would involve more work-site selling (eg meeting employers' needs for ID cards).

If the banks move to using smart cards in order to reduce fraud, this might mean a national retailer processing around 50–200 million transactions a year in this way. Using the cards for employee applications like time and attendance, a retailer might require about 25,000–60,000 cards and 1,000–2,000 readers (eg 2 per store). Most retailers say that fraud is a significant issue, because shrinkage eats directly into overall profit. Rejected card transactions relate to a relatively small slice of overall losses, but are nonetheless an area of focus and concern. There is scope to increase overall profit by about half of one percent if this could be tackled cheaply and effectively. Fraud is a concern rather than a major issue. Smart cards can reduce it.

The primary nature of many retail businesses is high street retailing, and with millions visiting stores each week, the major driver of increased footfall is actually television advertising, the promotions and signage in the window. As e-commerce business grows, CRM will play an increasingly important role. Looking five years ahead (with increased sales via the Web and digital TV) CRM could be a key strategic marketing tactic. For many retailers targeted promotion via the Internet and through more conventional rented lists of names for mailings are important – plus the use of EPOS till-based mechanics to drive up spend per transaction and to stimulate repeat business. This multi-channel approach means that a card which is usable in all channels is going to be a great asset. For some retailers, customer service and satisfaction is a key objective. CRM is an issue, but has yet to be clearly adopted by the business. At the moment smart cards are an option for this. Decision whether to go down that route has yet to be taken. Set-up costs are the main barrier to smart cards.

The major areas of uncertainty in evaluating or using smart card technology in customer relationship management by retailers includes the level of penetration of the technology among UK households. The key variable is usage by customers in the target market (eg do they tend to pay by cash, do they resist loyalty mechanics?).

Companies that retailers see as leading in smart card applications are high technology companies across computing, audio-visual, etc, the major players in the mobile communications market (eg Vodafone, BT). This is because the socio-demographic profile of their customer base includes a lot of socially advantaged, technology-friendly people, who broadly fit into the category of 'early adopters', who enjoy exploring new technologies and charting the way for the rest of us.

Supermarkets will lead the introduction of smart cards if they are to happen in the UK, because their level of plastic card usage is the highest anyway and their depreciation cycle for EPOS technology is the shortest. As they process vast numbers of transactions through their tills, typically the technology gets refreshed every 12–18 months, meaning that they are best placed to adopt new ideas quickly. Some retailers are very aware than smart cards have particular uses in healthcare and government. This is because they can hold lots of personal history in a compact, accessible format that could save many lives and help avoid fraud, so they are watching these types of applications for learning about the true potential of the technology.

Hotels are likely to be interested if smart cards allow private purse transactions on a shared card. Most hotels expect to host all their data about frequent business users on a central database, copied to the local site, so this function would not be important. One of the barriers is the lack of availability of smart card readers on PCs and other terminals – when these are available it will help with validation. The lack of consumer reason to carry the card is important. Leaders are seen to be public transport operations. Petrol retailers are mostly adopting a wait and see attitude, except, of course, for Shell.

CONCLUSION

After a difficult start, smart card usage is going through the roof. The wireless telephony revolution is responsible for the current surge, with bank and government usage likely to be responsible for the next two surges. The emergence of mobile telephony and the Internet as major channels of communication to the mass market means that many companies will take up smart cards as means of identification that work securely with minimal fraud in all channels, as hardware interfaces are developed. Different companies will combine different applications in different ways – credit/debit card, e-purse, loyalty, tactical promotions, customer-record management. Which particular type of smart card succeeds is going to be a matter of how flexible the providers are to meet the many different needs that are emerging.

However, industry has generally a rather poor record in applying CRM technology, with a few star exceptions. What does this imply for smart cards? Table 11.1 suggests the CRM opportunity, with opportunities for smart cards identified. However, as with all CRM approaches, making profitable use of smart cards is going to take a different approach from that adopted by most companies to date.

Table 11.1 CRM opportunity for smart cards

CRM Focus	Opportunity for Smart Card Deployment
Integrated targeted marketing, to ensure that customers who have been designated for particular actions are correctly targeted, especially at moment when they present themselves, that their responses are handled correctly and recorded correctly	X
Customer identification at all transaction points, to allow relevant additional offers to make to customers. This includes service counters (especially integration with POS systems) and individual locations within outlets (eg particular shelves, locations within airports, on planes). It also includes where transaction point is PC or digital TV box	X
Security, to ensure that 'good' customers can be served with ever increasing efficiency and speed in all channels while protecting them and the bank from fraud and other criminal activity	X
Personalization, to allow transactions to be handled as relevantly as possible at point of contact with customer	X
E-banking, to encourage customers to transact and interact by most cost-effective, most customizable channel	X
E-insurance, to allow customers to be profiled efficiently, to receive a quote for cover, and to secure cover quickly	X
E-wealth management, to allow customers to manage their investment portfolios from any location using most advanced support tools possible (eg forecasting, at minimum costs)	X
Customer knowledge management, to ensure that knowledge about customers and about what works in managing them is transferred to where it can be profitably acted upon	X
Data protection and privacy, particularly to give customers control over what data is stored, allowing them to review it in any context in which data is supplied	X
Customer document management, so that the information from complex 'cases' is managed efficiently, and matched to appropriate customers	X
Wireless transmission of case data (eg auto accident)	X
Information systems support for mobile staff (eg sales, service, professionals – consultants, doctors, etc) and for third party agents, including sales commission validation	X
Regulatory compliance, especially where this involves ensuring that person seeking information is approved to receive it	X
Portable data store for citizen, especially to control entitlement or to ensure consistency of treatment when given by multiple agencies	X
Integrated, multi-sense contact centres, to ensure that customers are handled relevantly, by best channel, at lowest cost, including credit-checking and other validation (eg for loans, quotation, transaction management, insurance claims)	
Customer profitability analysis, to ensure that marketing efforts are focused on serving 'best' customers, and on turning less profitable into more profitable customers	
Data mining, to allow complex patterns of transaction, response and claims/default data to be analysed to support tactical and strategic customer management policy making	
Supply chain integration, including forecasting, so customer needs can be matched with supply contract management, and in case of retailers or others with physical facilities for managing customers, integrating physical and virtual channels, space planning, merchandising and integration with POS systems	

Most of the approaches to CRM that we have seen have been based on carefully worked-out business cases full of flawed assumptions about the extent to which customers will agree to be managed by large companies. Once provided with technologies that allow them to take control, customers tend to 'run away' with them, discovering new applications, or using them with very different frequencies from that envisaged by corporate planners. Mobile phones are perhaps the best example of this. Given this, it may be time to reappraise the future of such a customer-friendly technology as the smart card, particularly when customers so often complain about failure to recognize them and/or their needs.

Notes

[1] Mercer study quoted in *The Financial Times*, 14 November 2000

Part 3

Implementation

12

Global customer management

Merlin Stone, Bryan Foss, Rich Harvey, Brian J Scheld and Richard Whitaker

This chapter investigates some of the problems large companies have in transferring customer management knowledge, expertise and processes between countries. Customer management consists of a range of business practices, ranging from fully-fledged customer relationship management to its contributing disciplines such as direct mail, telemarketing, customer database management, campaign management and e-business. Many global companies have initiated new activities in the last few years, often in individual countries. Some of these companies are now looking to consolidate their gains and ensure that good practice in one country or division is transferred across the business.

The research and analysis for this chapter was sponsored by UPS, the world's leading supplier of logistics services. UPS has, of course, benefited considerably from the development of e-commerce, as it has encouraged supply to/from everywhere. However, UPS is concerned to ensure that its customers' rapidly developing operations conform as closely as possible to best practice in customer management. As a company with global operations, it is also concerned to improve its own practice in customer management across the world. The study was carried out using the following:

- An e-mail questionnaire sent to 50 members of the Customer Management Group, an IBM-sponsored group of large companies that are interested in improving how they manage their customers. The members are all middle/senior managers who are accountable for some aspect of customer management, whether on the marketing, service or systems side. The companies are all nationally recognized brands. Only 11 responses were received, as the deadlines that were imposed were very tough due to the need to slot in the work with other priorities.

- Additional informal discussions during the period of the research with around 20 individual companies and 7 conference presentations in South East Asia, Australia and New Zealand, with 3 individual companies and 10 conference presentations in Europe. These discussions took place in the context of material developed by Professor Stone on the subject of implementing customer management strategies.
- Discussions with leading customers and suppliers during recent trips to the United States.
- A review of some of the recent literature on customer management in global companies.
- Data supplied by IBM's Travel & Transportation Industry Solutions Unit and by UPS.

This chapter first analyses some of the hot issues in global customer management. It then reviews the detailed findings of the research, with case studies of two industries: travel and transport; and financial services.

ISSUES IN GLOBAL CUSTOMER MANAGEMENT

CRM – a graveyard for marketing?

We have already expressed a strong scepticism about the blind acceptance of some of the ideas promoted under the guise of CRM. We stress that there are many other models of customer management, many of them classic, some of them working much more profitably than CRM, and the newer e-business-based models actually helping customers get excellent value by cherry-picking, spot-buying and resisting relationships.

Nevertheless, CRM became a global fashion in 1999. However, as the more cynical among us suspected, the popularity of this fashion (which in its most naïve form translated CRM into 'CRM system') is already starting to evoke yawns among senior management as they see the problems caused. A study in October 1999 by the Meta group has confirmed this. The study confirms that many CRM initiatives in the world's largest companies are at 'serious risk of failure'. The Meta Group, in conjunction with its research affiliate, IMT Strategies, interviewed 50 end-users including Eastman Kodak, Nortel Networks and Sprint. Although 80 per cent of companies polled said they have at least one CRM application up and running, they are failing to benefit fully from them. For example, they are not using data warehouses for in-depth analysis. Few of them are using applications that allow proper collaboration with customers. While many companies are employing customer-facing applications such as call centres and Web sites integrated with front, back and mobile offices, Meta estimates the world's largest companies will have to spend as much as US

$250 million over the next two to three years to achieve tangible returns on CRM investments.

In a press release, Mark Huey, Meta Group senior research analyst, said: 'It's often very easy for companies to justify expenditure when there are obvious, short-term returns on investment. But getting it right in the long term, getting that 360-degree view of your company and its dealings with customers, is harder.' The report advises companies rolling out CRM projects to 'take dramatic action to optimise their systems around the customer, or their customer relationship investments will not pay off'.

The report quoted Toby Detter, customer service programme director at Shell, which has implemented a large-scale CRM project: 'We haven't had problems with the data mining side of CRM, but it depends on what you're trying to do. The challenging part of CRM is changing the mindsets of people in established companies and the way they approach CRM. That takes time.'

These problems are confirmed by Sistrum, The European Centre for CRM Issues. With over 200 members from across Europe, Sistrum offers a fast track for managers involved in sales, marketing, service or customer management systems to learn from experts, keep abreast of current issues and benefit from the experiences of other organizations. In October, Sistrum announced an initiative to help CRM project managers. This was an exclusive network for those involved in active pan-European or global CRM projects. The Sistrum group is very well known for its incisive work on the implementation of sales and marketing automation projects (and for its conclusions on the high failure rates in these areas). Wendy Hewson, previously Research Director at Sistrum (now with the newly formed Hewson Group), said:

> This year we expect companies in Europe to spend some £835 million on marketing, sales and customer service systems rising to over £3.1 billion in 2001. But we, together with other leading analysts in the US and Europe, estimate that between 50–60 per cent of all CRM projects launched this year will fail, and international projects are high on the risk list. The Global CRM Project Group is being launched at the request of many Sistrum members. It will be an intimate network for people involved in international CRM projects. In the largely uncharted territory of international CRM systems, you need to be able to call on other people's expertise and experience.

Any model of customer management requires a balanced approach, covering strategies, people, systems, processes, data, measurement, and the like. Improving customer management globally is an even greater task – yet some companies are working on it, and some are succeeding. One of the reasons why global capability is important is that e-business has given immense impetus to the global capability of customer management.

Global commerce, global CRM and the death of distance

One of the current dominant influences on management thinking is the idea that 'competition is only a click away'. Although this simplifies the nature of competition, there is no doubt that what Frances Cairncross calls 'the death of distance'[1] is a reality for many managers. The telecommunications and IT revolution that we are still experiencing means that distance is now only a minor factor in the cost of communicating, and becoming less and less important as more communication moves off conventional voice into data. This makes location less relevant to business success. Businesses need less and less to be located near the markets they serve, provided that the logistics network is in place to deliver all the products, services and information required to ensure smooth transition through the value chain. Size is also less relevant. Once, only larger companies could afford the complex IT, telecommunications and logistics infrastructures required to service global markets. Now these are all available, cheaply, to almost any company. These infrastructure developments – which have accelerated since Cairncross wrote her book – mean that any kind of customer can be served anywhere in the world, customizing the offerings of the world to their needs. It is no longer necessary to be an important customer. Friction is disappearing from markets, as economists would say. Nearly all customers can access price and availability information at any time in any place. This creates much more transparency in markets. All the same, it is not always evident – to individual suppliers or customers – how to exploit these developments. However smartly this new capitalism works, customers need to learn how to use it, and companies need to learn how to spread the capability throughout their global network. This chapter shows that despite all the advances in IT and telecommunications, big companies are well aware that, at least in the customer management area, there is a wide gap between best and worst practice between their operations in different countries, and that improving practice still depends crucially on people.

This, of course, puts some companies at risk, because they cannot rely on their competition being equally slow. It is increasingly possible to refuse to serve a market 100 per cent locally – the people (and their skills), the processes, systems, data and so on can be located in best practices countries, while local operations do the bare minimum.

Global knowledge and information management

A critical part of improving customer management performance across the globe seems to be having some kind of approach to transferring knowledge and skills. However, it is clear that there are two very different approaches. One is to formalize and codify knowledge (in this case about how to manage customers) and transfer it through global systems and processes. The other is to recruit very skilled people and assign them to the creation of improved customer management in a particular country or region. There is no golden rule here, and much depends upon the nature of the product and service. There is evidence, for example, that where the relationship with customers is very ideas-based (eg in management consultancy), the latter approach is likely to be more profitable, but where the relationship with customers is highly automated and functional, the more formal approach is likely to be more profitable.[2]

In either case, it is clear that knowledge of customers is a critical component of improving customer management. Only one of the companies in our survey had anything like a global approach to customer knowledge. This was embodied in their approach to systems, data, analysis and measurement. Others are struggling towards it. One reason for this is that many companies have simply not realized the importance of business intelligence. As John McKean's research shows,[3] the really serious problem is that not enough senior managers understand business intelligence – how it works, what it delivers to their company, and indeed what individual business intelligence items mean. The criticality of this has been accentuated in the UK recently. Here at least three major companies (who must remain nameless because we have business relationships with them) have suffered a significant downturn in performance because they ignored information that was already flowing through their organization. In all cases their middle and lower-level staff understood this information – but who wants to be a shot messenger? Here, our recommendation is very clear – a *critical* component of globalization of customer management is business intelligence. However, merely having a business intelligence 'black box' in the systems department is not enough to create an 'intelligent business'! An intelligent business has senior management processes for using business intelligence – however bad or good the news it may bring, and however much the suggestions it produces diverge from the company's conventional wisdom.

Changing systems

Just as we are beginning to settle down to the idea that the Web – as we know it – is revolutionizing customer management in ways that we are learning to predict, along comes another revolution – the mobile phone as the location of customer management activity. The signs are already clear that it will have an effect that varies greatly by country – this is the subject of another chapter. However, let us consider why it poses both a problem and an opportunity for global customer management programmes.

Teenagers, among the most avid users of mobile phones, already ask why they need to be in a particular room to receive a phone call. However, many business customers already know that they do not need to be physically connected to anything in order to carry out any transaction, receive any information, or keep in touch with customers, suppliers or colleagues. They share the vision of the mobile phone companies, in which each individual is in communication with whatever he or she wants to communicate with, with permanent or temporary connection according to that individual's wishes, but at relatively low cost. That means that the customer is often connected via a mobile phone to a computer, not a person (except in cases where the computer cannot do the job).

The mobile phone vision is supported by the widening gap between mobile access and Web access in most countries. This gap is widening very rapidly in those countries where the Web had the slowest uptake (eg in South East Asia). In the United States, on the other hand, the relatively poor development of mobile standards and networks has caused the country to fall behind.

The interesting thing about the use of the new e-enabled mobile technology is that it provides excellent service at low cost to *all* customers, not just to a few premium customers. In fact, our vision of 'top vanilla'[4] is fast becoming a reality in some industries. The vision is clear – everyone ought to be able to interact freely with company systems (subject to appropriate validation and security), reducing staff-based costs and exploiting the changing complexity/cost profile of the different electronic media (see Figure 12. 1). We call this the 'collapse of privilege'. This could be for anything from buying a product or service to viewing status. The new technology allows customers to manage their relationships with companies anytime, anywhere, at very low cost. Because customers will not need to be privileged customers to manage suppliers in this way, they will be able to maintain relationships with several suppliers. Switching will become easier, and companies will have to focus on ensuring that all their validated customers can get the best information, irrespective of the volume of business done. Also, because the cost to the company will be low, companies will not need to worry too much about the value of each customer.

This vision is in effect part of the vision of what IBM calls 'pervasive computing', which extends well beyond the mobile into virtually every part of our lives. Note that the word

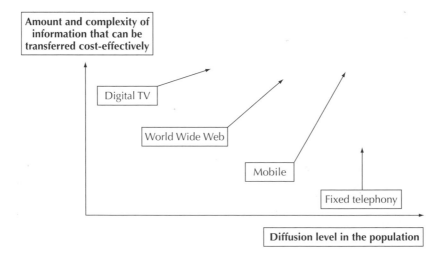

Figure 12.1 Changing technology profiles

'pervasive' is used – definitely not 'invasive' – as a central idea here is that the customer can turn devices off! However, it still implies enormous advances in the ability of customers to access their suppliers and vice versa. Today, in many respects, the mobile phone is the most secure device of all, as it contains a powerful microprocessor and significant storage capacity, enabling the use of much smarter customer validation techniques than a credit card. However, who knows what tomorrow's devices will bring?

Of course, it is the development of mobile means of sending and receiving information, rather than just mobile phones, which is bringing the reality of individual customer management to the fore. There will be even more of a need to ensure that the preferences and requirements of customers are managed and targeted in the right way as the more things become this close to the individual, the more the potential for infringing on the customer's privacy.

Changing customer management

If this vision is to become a reality, what must change in customer management? We see the following as the key areas of change.

The supply chain

In many situations, this is 'sticky' (ie slow, complex, opaque). Transferring data along the supply chain and managing the eventual relationships with customers is difficult even using established technology. Companies will need to adopt a different vision of how they interact with customers; free up data within their supply chain to make it available to customers; and free up their supply chain to make it possible for customers to influence the chain itself.

The customer management model

Companies will need to reconsider the nature of their customer management model. If it is based on privileged service to privileged customers, and if that privilege is based on access to and influence of the supply chain, the position is vulnerable, as other companies will be able to make what was privileged access available to all validated customers.

It may seem that companies that have very frequent transactions with their customers (eg banks, airlines and retailers) may be the first to benefit from this technology. However, frequency of transaction may not be the issue, if value of transaction is high enough. A used-car buyer can request mobile notification of when an appropriate vehicle comes into stock, or can review the stock availability of a nearby dealer. A new-car buyer can request mobile notification of delivery status. A customer waiting for completion of annual maintenance can receive notification of a problem and request for authorization of additional work, or that the car is ready for collection or delivery.

Content management

As customers are able to access or receive the latest information from companies, so they will need to combine information from company and other sources. For example, knowing the latest share price or transaction balance is one thing – doing something about it is another. If a flight is seriously delayed, what are the hotel or other dependencies and options? There is also a problem with internal content consistency – even today, customers have problems because the different channels of access offered by companies provide differently timed views of the company situation.

At the moment, access via mobile is becoming as cheap as landline access, but data transfer is relatively slow, which is why most product and service suppliers are focusing on services that can be made available through simple SMS text messaging or mobile e-mail. But the forecasts are that this will have changed radically within two or three years, with higher speed transfers and immediate connections. So the recommendation is the old one – be there or be square. However, as we know from earlier changes to marketing technology (direct mail, telemarketing, the Internet), being there today is important. This is mainly because of the need to learn how to do it, so that when it becomes the main medium for customer access (perhaps in three or four years' time), you know how to do it!

There is another tougher implication – resource switching. Each change in marketing technology implies a switch in resources. It is our view that the big switch – but only over the very long term – will be away from call centres. Call centres are currently excellent for customers. They often find it the most convenient way by far to contact large companies – quicker and less complicated than logging on to the Web. In Germany, which of the five major European countries is one of the most advanced in Web use, increasing investments in major call centres are taking place, similar to those made in the United States and the UK over the last few years. Today, most customers have a clear preference for call centres as the only practical way of accessing large companies, particularly given the slowness of many companies to respond to e-mails. A few companies who use call centres are finding that the centres are drowned by calls from customers who give no value during the call (eg status inquiries) or at all (because they are low-value customers anyway). Cost to serve is an important issue in customer management, and is likely to become the prime justification for investment in mobile-based methods of customer service in the future. Each new or modified channel of communication can add cost. The key questions companies should ask are:

- Does it bring in more margin (eg increase revenue without a commensurate increase in other costs) – whether directly or via improved customer service/branding?

- Does it reduce costs in other communication channels (or cause channel conflict and cannibalization of business)?
- How long does it take to achieve the required changes?

In the next few years the need for call centres will not go away, and the strong trend will be towards integration of Web and call centre channels. This is especially the case in areas like travel and financial services, where many purchase decisions are complicated and relatively high value/high impact. For example, many companies have been caught out with insufficient call centre agents because they thought that their Web site would deflect callers away from the call centre. In fact, Web sites usually make callers more knowledgeable when they telephone the call centre, and this leads to more complex dialogues. However, this example also shows the need for companies to examine carefully the total cost to serve across all channels.

Perhaps the toughest implication of all for companies is the possibility that they will discover how badly they communicate with their customers, by making it hard for them to get the right information at the right time. The new technology will allow customers to set (and reset) their communication parameters with large companies.

Finally, it is worth considering the implications of these developments for IT and telecommunications suppliers and the impact it will have on clients. Their clients look to IT and telecommunications suppliers to help them with their globalization of customer management capabilities. The battle between the mobile and PC-based access for and to customers is fast becoming one of the most interesting competitive battles we have seen for years.

To the cynic from the telecommunications industry, the way PCs have developed over the last few years can be seen as a conspiracy of profligacy – profligacy in use of memory, storage, and transmission capacity – hence the worldwide wait. Consumers have accepted this because most PCs are used in environments where this does not matter, and nice enhancements provided by the latest version of operating system software and the newest, fastest processors can be obtained relatively cheaply by upgrading every two to three years. On the other hand, telecommunications suppliers, particularly mobile suppliers, tend to be very parsimonious with bandwidth and processing because it is not available in limitless amounts. The operating system that most suits mobiles in their new roles as a customer access tool is therefore not one which is a derivative of a desktop PC system, but one developed specifically for small devices. An example of this is that used by the members of the Symbian consortium, which includes all the main manufactures of mobiles and mobile systems and two out of the three leading manufacturers of palmtop devices. Technology companies based in the United States, where mobile growth has been stunted, risk being caught out by these developments. Companies seriously interested in optimizing global customer contact management are already using the operating systems (if that is what they could be described as) provided by mobile phone suppliers, and services provided by specialist multiple e-channel information suppliers such as MicroStrategy. From the corporate point of view, this is good news, because dominant suppliers are always bad news for customer service.

THE SURVEY RESPONDENTS

The respondents came from the following sectors:

- banking;
- wholesale financial services/reinsurance;
- petrochemical;
- physical distribution;
- energy;
- IT;
- motor car (automobile) manufacture;
- software supplier;
- travel/financial services;
- conglomerate business to business (construction, IT, telecommunications);
- animal feeds.

THE SURVEY RESPONSES – CASE BY CASE

Because the sample of respondents was not meant to be a valid sample but a poll of companies, the results are presented qualitatively. First, we present a selection of the cases. We have not simply repeated each case. Rather, we have singled out the best-practice company, and then provided summaries of key aspects of certain others. This is followed by an overview of key topics raised.

Travel and financial services supplier – best practice

This company is a truly global brand, and one of the principal supports to its branding is the level of service it delivers to corporate and individual customers. It has a very mature customer management process compared to the other respondents in this survey. The company has been a well-established multinational for decades. It is a very mature user of sales force management and direct marketing models (telephone and mail) to improve its business performance, and has a comprehensive set of processes and measures to support it. The company also uses internal and external benchmarking. It has a well-defined model of customer management, following classic principles of customer acquisition, retention and development. It monitors success and failure in customer management across countries explicitly. The approach to analysis is standardized across countries, and measurement is managed through a complex matrix and scorecard monitoring system. Global strategies, priorities and standards are very much to the fore, particularly recently.

Many of the company's processes and standards are established internationally, and many support departments are internationally centralized. Regional offices support implementation. Good practice is rewarded through a bonus system. Failure to comply with standards means that no bonus is given. Reward and recognition schemes operate nationally and globally. Codification and documentation of processes are strong in IT, finance, HR and operations – less so in marketing. An in-house project management methodology is used.

Any outsourcing is to global rather than local partners – ensuring the transferability of any outsourcing arrangement. Any 'one-off' arrangements that may be needed in particular national markets are phased out. The company only uses one marketing communications agency throughout the world.

The choice facing it on a country-to-country basis is whether to deploy the model fully in each country in which it operates. Its global marketing strategy is matched to each country through a formal optimization process. One of the main determinants of whether to deploy the model fully in a particular country is the local availability of skills. However, the company overcomes problems as far as possible by strong encouragement of international movement of staff and global advertising of vacant positions. However, it acknowledges that it still has much progress to make in training.

Its most difficult challenge is in the former Eastern Bloc countries where service cultures have been non-existent until recently. In most other countries, because of the long-standing presence of Western multinationals, the service culture is well understood and staff are trainable.

Language, time zones and the state of the telecommunications and postal infrastructure of course moderate the speed of transfer of new approaches. The language of management is English and most staff are expected to have English as a mother tongue or second language. Local cultures have a substantial impact, as do issues of costs and profitability. Every policy change is determined as far as possible according to return on investment. So, if in a particular country there are not enough customers with whom the appropriate return on investment can be made by the introduction of a new approach, the approach will not be introduced.

The company uses Lotus Notes in most of its locations worldwide, and conference calling meetings are common. The company also has an intranet, and more and more user tools are Web-enabled. Its databases are standardized globally and analysed centrally.

Software supplier – early stages

This company has already featured in some of our other survey work, and normally rates very highly in terms of its professionalism of management of customers of its core businesses, although occasionally it faces problems when it needs to develop new ways of doing business for new product markets.

It is a supplier of 'heavyweight' software to large companies all over the world. It has grown very rapidly over the last few years and its model of customer management is less mature. This company represents the very earliest stage of customer management practice transfer – one in which it is just realizing that there may be benefits from a more formal approach. As it sells mainly to large corporations, its model of customer management is largely based on client management and personal relationships. Some of its customers are resellers of its software, but salespeople manage them also. Because it is at an early stage of globalization, different subsidiaries in different countries have different approaches to customer management and different skills. Transfer of good practice is informal. However, its approach to customer management is slowly becoming more explicit. A working group is currently evaluating how to improve good practice in customer management.

The issue for this company is whether its informal model of customer management, which works very well in times of success, will work equally well in times when problems start to arrive. Until recently, its market was very product-led, but now the successful implementation of major projects using the kind of software the company supplies has become a major issue, so it will be interesting to see how this company fares under these new conditions.

Energy products company – emerging good practice

This company is one of the top global companies in the world, in terms of size and assets. It has had a global customer management initiative in place for some time and is making steady progress with it. As most of its customers are business customers, the focus of this programme is on application of the principles of account management, combined with targeting based on current and future customer value, supported by enhanced communications (intranet, extranet) and marketing technology (customer databases, call centres, etc). The incremental benefit of the approach is formally measured. Many of its problems in implementing this programme is the product-based division of the company, so that customers are subject to disparate contacts from different parts, but a combination of account management principles and cross-divisional systems and processes are helping the company overcome these problems.

The company recognize that the transfer of good practice depends greatly on people and their skills rather than enforced processes, and a 'pull' rather than a 'push' approach characterizes its efforts. Its intranet is central in best practice transfer, particularly in the area of database marketing, where skill levels are highly variable between countries. In general (although not always) the flow of ideas and good practice is from countries where the customer management approach is more mature, but special efforts are made to incorporate examples of good practice from countries which are on the whole on the receiving end of practice transfer.

Monitoring and measuring customer management practices is an area of focus for the company, but it recognizes that it has much progress to make in this area, particularly in the area of retention management and future customer value. Award schemes and internal communications focus on supporting identification and transfer of good practice. Formal knowledge management techniques, often supported electronically, are used to support the diffusion effort, but use of these techniques is still at a very early stage. Interactive/CD-based training supports skills development, and individuals are accredited with specific customer management skills. Coaching and mentoring are also used. One area of particular interest to this company is how to manage customers across borders from one physical call centre – how to retain the feel of the local sales office when the call is in fact being answered in another country.

Country cultures do make a difference to practice transfer. For example, in some countries the very clear preference of clients for face-to-face contact (eg in Southern Europe) means that the company is not moving forward so fast in telemarketing in these countries as it is in other countries. As it happens, this preference for face-to-face contact is often in countries where labour costs are relatively low. Over time, the company expects the move to telemarketing and Internet purchasing to accelerate in these countries too.

Skills shortages (both within the company and with local suppliers) are an important barrier to progress, so the company has a series of templates, and the tendency is to implement the simple ones first.

Motor (auto) manufacturer – culture and dealers are problematic

Like most motor companies, this company sells worldwide via motor dealers, so many of its problems in improving customer management across the globe depend on its success in persuading or motivating dealers to work with it to develop good practice. This requires not only good process, but also good people, so recruitment of staff for managing dealers is a key element in success. At the same time, as dealers are not owned, they want to develop their own approaches to customer management. Cultural differences are very large. For example, Asian and Arabic cultures have a very strong service orientation, but based on people, not data and systems. Therefore, it is hard to implement an approach biased towards the use of data and systems.

Like many automotive companies, the management culture is very product and sales oriented, not customer focused, so a cultural change is under way as staff with stronger customer orientation are being recruited throughout the world.

Web technology is seen as critical to ensure the diffusion of data, processes and good practices, as many operations are in countries where the rest of the infrastructure for customer management is seen as weak.

Physical distribution company – people are key

This company does most of its business in one country but has significant operations in other countries. It is currently in the early stages of reshaping its entire business to focus on customer management – both of its own clients and its role in the management of customers of its clients. It has recognized that its success depends upon some degree of formalization of its customer management process and its embodiment in people, processes and systems. Its start point has been to focus on identifying the current state of customer management, using QCi's CMAT to benchmark itself against good practice (as have the previous two case studies). Its intranet provides important support to its management of major corporate clients, but practice from this area has yet to be diffused into other parts of the business. Formal knowledge management techniques are used, but on a limited basis. It uses the idea of centre of excellence to develop strategies, processes and systems and then roll them out to other parts of the business.

Financial services provider – adding value through knowledge

This company works at the wholesale level of the financial services industry, so its clients are financial services providers all over the world who supply business and consumer customers. Its model of customer management is to use knowledge ('global expertise' and 'global best practice') to add value to the core services that it provides. This knowledge is given free to clients who provide it with business. This approach helps its clients to develop better-quality business, improving this company's own profitability. The key issue faced by this company is the scarcity of skills in the area. Diffusion of best practice is in the end a people-intense process, although as far as possible electronic (intranets, extranets, knowledge databases) and physical publication approaches are used to support it. Geographically, the flow of knowledge is outward from the United States and the UK, which are seen as markets where practices in this company's sector of financial services are strongest, towards continental Europe and Asia Pacific. The ability of clients to take advantage of this depends strongly on their people and the state of the business infrastructure in their country.

Bank – early stages

This company is in the early stages of the development of a customer management approach across Europe. It is working with managers from several countries to develop a model of customer management that suits the particular services this company offers. Consultants support this process. The initial focus is on the development of skills among the country marketing managers, so that they can adapt the general principles of customer management being articulated by the headquarters group responsible for the process to the needs of their own countries. The need to achieve this is driven by an aggressive business plan. Transfer processes are relatively weak and are therefore being created through common formats for planning and an internationally managed business development process. An intranet has just been launched and is expected to be a key platform for knowledge transfer. Common performance measures will be introduced to facilitate measurement and transfer of good practice.

THE SURVEY RESPONSES – TOPIC OVERVIEW

Awareness of the customer management issue

All the respondents were aware that transferring the skills, knowledge and practices of customer management, in whatever forms their company desired, was a significant issue, and one to which most had no simple solution. Only the respondent with the most mature strategies, models and processes seemed to have a reasonable transfer process. In many cases, attempts are being made to develop a transfer programme, but the process of creating and implementing the programme was fraught with difficulties, many of which are identified below.

Lack of local awareness of benefits

Some companies seem to be caught in a vicious circle. If local staff do not understand the principles and practices of customer management, they find it hard to understand the benefits. In some cases, this problem may only be resolvable by staff transfer. However, local scepticism about the benefits may be justified if the company has not worked out what the benefits are and demonstrated them clearly in its more mature operations.

Global programmes

Some companies claim to have global programmes, but many of these should not be considered as much more than 'dishing out tasks'. Each local unit is given the job of trying out a particular approach, often with poor support and knowledge transfer, and then asked to report back some time (perhaps a year) later. Such programmes usually achieve little. Once again, companies with mature customer management models and strategies are more likely to be able to conduct such a programme and achieve the desired results.

Recognition of requirement of explicit transfer

All the companies were aware that transfer would not happen by itself, but rather required an explicit effort and top–down sponsorship and allocation of resources to achieve the transfer.

Effect of global systems

Having a global approach to customer management systems of whatever kind (call centres, data warehouse models, campaign management, profitability analysis, interconnection standards) clearly helps the transfer approach. Although local systems initiatives might enable particular operating units to make progress, this can cause a nearly random effect, much more dependent on the skills, understanding and motivations of local management.

Preference for own systems, processes

This is clearly a barrier to transfer, and this is confirmed by our consulting and more general research experience. Senior managers in all functions in operating units have a strong preference for developing their own approaches – for some it is a sign (and a benefit) of their seniority. Such managers like to be able to deal independently with local suppliers (even if they are just local divisions of the same multinational supplier that is serving the company as a whole). This situation can sometimes be overcome by involving local managers in international initiatives, but there still remains a tendency to proliferate local approaches.

Some companies solve this problem by a tough, highly centralized approach, but this can result in a negative impact on local business and local managerial attrition, unless there is a clear involvement and progression path for local managers into the international management approach and cadre (a key incentive).

Awareness that particular marketing strategies are not the determining factor

Some companies understood that the particular marketing strategy being followed at the time did not necessarily imply particular customer management approaches – as these may need to be determined for the local market conditions. They understood that what they were trying to develop was a capability that would be usable for different customer management strategies (eg rapid recruitment of new customers, management of existing customers).

Skills transfer strategy

A properly planned and thoroughly executed skills transfer strategy is rare. In many cases, companies attempt to achieve this through the transfer of one or two key individuals. International training programmes are rare, and exist only in companies with mature models of customer management and internationally planned customer management strategies.

Understanding importance of measures across countries/divisions

The same comment applies here as above. In many cases companies are unhappy with the measures of customer management that they use even in their most advanced operations. In particular, the balance between volume (customers acquired and managed, interactions (eg calls handled) and quality/value is a constant issue, also between isolated measures (eg lead generation) and overall objectives.

Use of internal benchmarks

Some companies regard these as very valuable. Being honest about the starting point in customer management in any country is critical. To help companies identify their precise starting point on the journey, and to measure their progress, we developed a CMAT software package, which allows companies to identify where they are, benchmark themselves against similar companies, and measure their progress. Of course, throughout the world, skills are in short supply, and the initial findings of audits across countries, within companies, confirms this. One of the major weaknesses CMAT identifies in companies is the quality of their analysis and planning of customer management. Companies have in general poor knowledge of where they are, and use their data on customers poorly to extract conclusions about which they are likely to obtain more value out of, keep, etc.

Cultural issues

One company commented that African and Asian cultures do CRM very well, but they did not call it that, and they did not understand the importance of recording data for future use. This was 'CRM in the head'. This situation, which is confirmed by our consulting experience, poses particular problems for customer management systems and processes. However, pilot projects, which demonstrate the value of such data when it is made available through systems to a wider team, usually may prove to be the way to solve this problem.

Senior management skills, motivation

This was seen as critical by some companies, and is closely related to the issues raised above concerning development of local approaches. For a multinational, one of the main benefits it can offer local managers is the promise of further promotion. It can be argued that so long as this is independent of the local managers' record in implementing the required approach, the latter will not be implemented.

Conflict with ideas of delegation of authority/devolution

One respondent raised this as a serious issue. Fashions in management have led to a swinging of the pendulum in this area, and even today we can see companies in the same sector operating on completely different models. Perhaps it is the oscillation itself that is the dangerous phenomenon.

Reliance on internal networking

Some companies recognized that their culture was one in which internal networking was the most effective (and perhaps the only effective) process for transferring knowledge and skills. This is not necessarily a bad thing, and some companies took the view that it should therefore be used rather than combated.

Importance of IT support to the transfer process

Several respondents mentioned this and it is a finding confirmed by our other work. The lack of such IT support is evident in some companies, where people doing an identical job in different countries have no way to benefit from relevant experience. In some cases, an intranet is in place, but poorly structured and chaotically used – users often never discover relevant ideas because they do not know where to find them.

Consistency of customer management maturity across the global enterprise

These findings are consistent with our other customer management research, in that those companies that do well in a few areas of best practice, are often no better than average in other areas. However, in this survey a few more mature implementers are achieving higher average capabilities in support of their best practice areas.

THE TRAVEL AND TRANSPORT SECTOR

In this section, we investigate two related but very different sub sectors of this industry –package and document collection and delivery (UPS' sector) and passenger air travel.

Package and document collection and delivery

UPS, as the world's largest carrier of packages and documents, has been active in pushing out the frontiers of global customer management. One of the strong factors in its favour here has been the relative lack of intermediation – although agencies are still used in a number of emerging countries. This ensures that all customer management procedures can be implemented through line management processes rather than the influencing and motivational approaches required to ensure that agencies manage customers in the desired manner. For UPS, the challenge has been to ensure that the quality of customer management continues to advance through the use of technology, while containing costs so as to ensure that UPS's competitive marketing position remains strong.

In the age of e-commerce, this has become even more important. On many Web sites of suppliers of merchandise, customers can now choose the carrier of the merchandise simply by clicking on the logo of the preferred carrier. Many customers will do this on the basis of price. In the United States, this has given UPS a competitive advantage over its main direct competitors and allows it to compete effectively with the US postal service.[5] Customers who choose UPS can now also track their consignment through the Web. In fact, over half of the tracking enquiries made through the Web by customers are via these 'partner' Web sites. This is an interesting example of partnership CRM at work – UPS is now able to influence customers who are 'intermediated' via the product suppliers.

For UPS, one of the keys to the globalization of its well-established but continuously developing customer management model is the availability of advanced telecommunications infrastructure. Customers (shippers or receivers) anywhere in the world wanting to track their consignment need to have the device required to receive the data. UPS's own technology ensures that the data about the consignment gets immediately to UPS's systems. The latest version of its Delivery Information Acquisition Device (DIAD) transmits information as soon as it is scanned in. With the mobile telephony developments mentioned earlier in this paper, customers who need it will get nearly instant notification of delivery.

All this, of course, refers to the operational process of customer management. In terms of installing and developing the process of customer management, the issues faced by UPS are very much those highlighted among our research respondents. The model of customer management in its most mature market is evolving very rapidly because of the impact of e-business throughout the supply chain (see Chapter 8). The new development is that receiving customers can now specify UPS more easily – or not. Therefore UPS must extend its brand strength from business customers to any customer who could be receiving – and therefore choosing – UPS on the Web. Meanwhile, in emerging economies, UPS is still installing a more conventional call-centre-based infrastructure of customer management, knowing that this will have a shorter life than in more mature economies because it will be overtaken by e-business methods of customer management.

In terms of our models of customer management, UPS follows a policy of top vanilla for most customers, with a strong CRM/major account offer for large commercial customers. Top vanilla standards have to advance rapidly under the impact of e-business. But e-business also makes it easier for major account customers to have relationships with multiple carriers, so the standards of service and costs offered to these customers need to be extremely competitive.

Airlines

Air travel is one of the most heavily intermediated industries in the world. The parties involved in making sure that the passenger gets from A to B include at least two airports, ground handling companies, travel agents, airline catering companies, global distribution systems, lounge provision companies and so on. This makes the consistent delivery of a customer management model quite difficult. For example, business travellers often complain that the criteria for lounge admission are never fully understood by lounge staff, particularly in 'remote' stations. The airline industry is also overpopulated – there are still too many companies chasing business. One way round this has been the formation of alliances – which itself adds more intermediation, as one airline becomes an intermediary for another's passengers. Of course, multiple intermediation creates multiple sets of customers within the value chain, making development and maintenance of a model of customer management even more difficult. Finally, the advent of low-cost airlines, the dramatic improvement in transparency of pricing achieved through Web-based travel agents, and the emergence of seat-auctioning have all given customers much greater choice.

IBM's 1999 World Airlines Benchmark report[6] indicates that these pressures are pulling airlines in two conflicting directions. Based on interviews with senior airline executives, it shows that airlines are struggling to balance their top priorities of improving customer service, loyalty and market share with optimizing yield, unit costs, route structure, capacity offered and network match to demand. They see alliance participation as a clear key to this.

In future, we therefore expect two models of customer management to remain dominant in this industry. The classic CRM model of managing frequent flyers will continue to yield high rewards, and these will become greater as airlines continue to develop alliances and rationalize capacity, so that the benefits of being a very frequent flyer within a particular alliance will grow. At the other end, the low-cost airlines will continue to develop their top vanilla offer, and it will become increasingly e-business based simply because of the lower costs and better customer service offered by the e-channel. Somewhere in the middle will be high-value leisure customers – often neglected by airlines because of their invisibility and by the failure of most airlines to include a strong family offer to their frequent flyers. This segment is growing very fast (it includes the baby boomers passing through their periods of frequent business flying and now travelling with their families, spending the money they have accumulated during the post-war years of growth and asset development). Here, we expect the emergence of schemes more similar to retail personalized loyalty schemes with relatively small incentives and some service benefits.

Of course, e-business will assist dramatically the globalization of all models, as IBM's 1999 European Customer Relationship Management Audit for the Travel Industry shows.[7] At the moment, airlines are largely reliant on their very good operational systems to manage information about customers. However, the information they manage is limited. Information about different aspects of the customer relationship is often split between different systems (eg lost property, complaints and promotional enquiries). So we expect that further development of customer databases, Web-based solutions and the use of middleware will help to ensure availability of all customer data to all authorized staff anywhere in the world may remedy this situation. As alliances develop, the weaknesses of inter-operating between their systems will become exposed. Not all alliance members have access to crucial ticketing data, enabling them to make changes smoothly.

One of the main problem areas for airlines will be the call centre. As competition intensifies, the relatively high-cost nature of transactions through the call centre will be exposed. Some airlines are very proud of the proportion of their business that they are now booking direct, but they have discovered that much of the new business booked through call centres is turning out to be of suspect profitability. Consider two bookings. A business flyer requests a booking from A to B at a specified date and time and flight class, being prepared to pay whatever the fare is. The deal may be done in 2–3 minutes, and possibly several thousand dollars has been earned by the airline. A leisure traveller calls to make a booking, from Country Y to Country Z, for the cheapest possible price, with investigating of many time and date options. The result: each call takes 10–15 minutes and may yield a few hundred dollars of revenue or no booking at all. It is these latter customers that need to be moved to the Web, and global e-commerce seems to be the way to move.

INSURANCE AND FINANCIAL SERVICES

The merger and takeover frenzy

The insurance industry has been characterized by a frenzy of global takeovers and mergers. As we move into the new millennium, we see an industry dominated by a few global players, plus a number of regional participants. In many markets very few companies now operate independently of the global players.

The first steps after a merger usually involve the creation of a common, simplified and reduced cost infrastructure, covering all the 'overhead' and shared functions such as treasury, personnel, and IT. This is usually accompanied by rationalization of brands (AXA is perhaps the most aggressive example of this). In the most successful companies, this first stage tends to be followed by a series of well-defined global projects, such as the following:

- CRM strategy and prioritized execution plans;
- common standards for shared developments (eg data models and interchange formats);
- single view of customer and partnerships (by country, or globally if relevant);
- reduction to a preferred supplier list and bulk purchasing arrangements;
- call centre enhancement and rationalization;
- e-business introduction and development;
- standardization of campaign management processes and systems, for both direct and intermediary customers;

- data analysis – customer scoring and segmentation, sales analysis, product and customer profitability analysis, either on a shared data warehouse or common data model structure;
- product improvement, risk pricing and rating;
- claims and fraud analysis and improvement – smarter determination of current and future good and bad customers.

Not all these initiatives are successful, and only in the best companies can these be described as truly global programmes, with sharing of information, common development of knowledge, and rapid transfer of good practice. However, given the proven gains that can be achieved by such projects within countries, we expect that the companies that take the strongest line on globalization of these initiatives will in the end emerge as the most profitable.

One area of strong focus after many mergers or acquisitions is identification of common business processes and infrastructures that can be merged or at least shared (eg in IT and communications, common hardware, reuse of tools, sharing call centres), to reduce costs and complexity. This is usually done without changing the different business models that operated independently prior to the merger. It may be that the initial focus apparent in some companies on securing a common customer is not appropriate, given the demonstrated gains that can be made from infrastructure and process commonality.

Perhaps the most widely referenced example of mergers undertaken mainly for a customer centric purpose is Citi Groups bringing together of Citibank and Travelers. Conseco is another US financial services conglomerate that has grown quite rapidly through acquisition. It faces issues of business organization, process and data integration each time it absorbs a new acquisition. These companies and other companies are discovering that achieving one 'operational' view of the customer is much more difficult than was first thought. Other companies following the same direction are AIG and the major European headquartered companies Zurich, Allianz, ING and Fortis. The race is on to achieve a holistic view of the customer in a industry fraught with 'silos' – business units operating with different data sets, processes, systems and customer management models, all focused on the same or overlapping sets of customers. However, some of these companies have decided that integrating without prioritizing is dangerous, and are now prioritizing their integration efforts.

Another issue that companies are facing after merger/acquisition is the branding issue. This is very important to multinationals because while there are significant economies of scale in global branding, there is also a risk that customers will see reduced rather than increased value. AXA, Zurich and Allianz specifically have faced this as they have merged their Equitable, Farmers and Fireman's Fund brands into their more worldwide-known parent companies. Each of these companies is in a different stage of branding and brand acceptance.

One consequence of mergers is that putting together diverse brands also means putting together a diverse customer base, which is more difficult to understand and manage as a whole than they were when managed by separate companies. Because of the size and number of many of the resulting databases the customer management implementation focus has often become blurred and energies diverted to technical (eg database and data) rather than customer issues. There is still a divide between the life, general, health and new product divisions of most insurance companies. Not surprisingly, most customers fail to see the benefit of being served by one company across these areas, because there is no clear joint proposition or benefit. The differing cultures of merging organizations have caused great difficulties for global programmes. In some cases, there has been a clash between short-term results and project orientation and longer-term relationship orientation, and mergers have often created setbacks for continuity and the customer management implementation process. In the worst case, the customer management programme has been destroyed, sometimes because it was at too early a stage to have identified the business benefits clearly or to have become a well-grounded deployment programme in the organization.

When a merger or acquisition is announced it normally gives rise to cost-reduction commitments to the stock market. The race is then on to achieve these by the next results announcement. There is a tendency to slash costs through layoffs, channel reduction (fewer agents, consolidation of call centres), product reduction (allowing usage of fewer administrative systems, therefore lower operating costs, etc). However, the impact of these changes is often to drive customers away. This often increases attrition among those customers who bought from and stayed with the company due to the products and/or channels that are now being slashed. In very few cases do companies devote the time and resource first to merge their customer data to understand common customers, cross-product holdings and even estimate customer value *before* taking action to reduce products and channels. Having shown cost reductions, a company needs to demonstrate to shareholders that it is more valuable as a single company than as two. This is the 'value add' phase that some major European insurers and financial services are now in, but some others are struggling with it! At this stage the focus moves to common standards, shared value through reuse of (data, infrastructure, processes, etc). As the customers of each company/country may be entirely separate, there is often little direct value in sharing customer data, only the indirect value of learning and shared development cost.

Meanwhile, new entrants using the best of new technology have challenged the merging companies to respond. New entrants are finding the insurance model a particularly easy one to approach via the Internet (eg Quotesmith.com in the United States, Mysis in Europe). The visibility of price and the simplification of questions are making the shift to commodity purchase inevitable with the absence of any real value being offered to customers who stay or buy more from traditional insurers.

To meet this challenge and improve profits, a number of companies are now embarking on global initiatives to create and implement a model of customer management which helps them increase market share while reducing costs. Some global players have global/international customers, but others have different customers in each market/country. Where this happens the local market companies usually own the budgets for customer management projects (and other major marketing initiatives) and need to form a corporate board to agree on standards for prioritization and reuse, as central management power and the global use common systems are usually diminished.

This corporate board (or similar group) can assist programme design and execution by developing and promoting standards and/or processes that relate to areas such as: a common programme management capability and project method; and understanding of the interdependencies of projects carried out in different areas (eg customer research, skills development, Web deployment, warehousing, contact centre development). This avoids the projects simply being 'handed out'; rather the board members take on the lead role for different initiatives dependant upon the match with their own prioritized business objectives.

The central group can also help as follows:

- It can assess (or help different country operations assess) the CRM 'maturity' in each country, and the improvements in maturity and ROI resulting from each prioritized local project, or reuse of developments from other projects.
- It can set common systems standards where appropriate (eg a common data model and interchange standards on which applications are developed or integrated).
- It can conduct global negotiations with suppliers, as a global licensing arrangement can often be achieved for the equivalent price of a small number of major country implementations.

Where these issues are not tackled, the company is likely to have a lower ability to execute their CRM projects on an international basis. Projects are likely to result in smaller benefits through lack of scalability or integration with projects that are interdependent.

In the insurance and financial services industries, following the wave of mergers and takeovers, several companies are developing and deploying these capabilities right now, usually in close cooperation with one or more international suppliers (to ensure consistent availability of services and support in their many markets). Our research indicates that those companies who do not see the importance of or cannot develop these capabilities will be operating sub-optimally.

The global insurance players seem to have strategies which are too similar, and which do not sufficiently take into account their differing abilities to execute those strategies, with differing customer bases. Some of our clients have expressed the view that consultants appear to reuse 'standard CRM visions', without an understanding of the achievements and learning experiences of the company, or of the company's ability to develop new capabilities from that base.

GLOBALIZING DIFFERENT MODELS OF CUSTOMER MANAGEMENT

Chapter 8 describes a number of models of customer management (one to one; transparent marketing; classic CRM; personalized communication and targeting; top vanilla; pure spot-selling; spot-selling within a managed roster; spot-selling via an agent; channel partnership).

However, when it comes to globalization, an additional set of factors comes into play. This relates to issues such as:

- Is the model clearly articulated so that managers from different countries can understand it?
- Are the reasons for adopting it understood?
- Are the skills, processes and infrastructure required for successful implementation of each model understood?
- How well does each model fit with the different cultures in which the company operates?
- How easy is it to codify the management requirements for successful implementation of each model?
- How widely available are the skills required to implement each model? Are they available in the company's key markets?
- Does a model require a particular quality or breadth of infrastructure in each country? Is the infrastructure actually available?
- If partners are required to implement the model, do they exist in each country?

From our research, it is clear that there is a big difference in the transferability of models (see Figure 12.2). Although our best practice company uses the classic CRM model, it has been doing so for decades. It has had time to articulate the model fully, and develop the systems, processes and skills required to deliver it successfully in each market in which it operates. But many later entrants into its market have preferred the top vanilla model – excellent service to all customers in the company's target segment. This model requires much less analysis, less complex skills, and so on. Although the call centre systems usually associated with this approach are complex and expensive, they are readily available from a number of suppliers in many economies.

Meanwhile, the fully Web-based models such as auctioning and spot-buying seem most easy of all to diffuse. They depend for customer validation on the services of credit referencing and similar agencies, so wherever these are present, the company can set up business. If access is through the Web, little channel development is required – merely enough advertising to stimulate initial use. With logistics services available globally, there is little in the way of problems for companies to deliver products to people anywhere in the world.

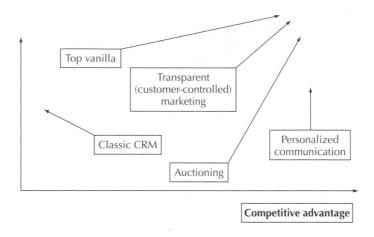

Figure 12.2 Ease of internationalization of some models of customer management

DEVELOPING A GLOBAL PERSPECTIVE

Knowledge management

One of the major issues in the transfer of knowledge related to customer management across country boundaries is that the formal structures set up to transfer knowledge are often based on the history of an organization, rather than the current customer management focus. For example, intranets are often set up by product group or by internal project. Therefore, the fora set up for CRM often become the theory and thought leadership behind the programme and are not considered as practical and business related. These groups are often led or managed by marketing or IT as 'nice to haves' rather than essentials. This is also reflected in the types of interactive fora that are generated. Without a clear model for customer management and organizational roles allocated to focus on customer management, the focus of managing knowledge is unlikely to be the customer.

Global versus local in a project

A customer management programme can be managed across borders. However, most global organizations have markets and customer bases which are so diverse in nature that the local organizations will relate very differently to a customer management programme. In some countries a company will be in a market-leading position, in others a follower. Some markets may be highly deregulated, others not. Some countries have extremely complex and demanding customer bases and the company may struggle to keep above water as a player. All these naturally result in different requirements for internal 'selling', skills and technology. If this is assessed and the programme roll-out planned effectively, and where possibly countries or communities with similar requirements brought together to share examples and experiences and debate the rate of change, the programme is more likely to work.

Implementation

The key in structuring a global project is to find the balance between perfection and delivery! Some companies have developed planning paralysis, because they do not believe they know enough about the customer base or their proposition in order to move ahead, so they decide to gather and analyse more data. Others are not planning enough and assuming too much, and are therefore not applying the right measures and milestones to assess their real success with customers. The central measure of success is customer response and the development of increased value to and from customers. Obsession with theory does not help here!

Notes

[1] For more on this, see Cairncross, F (1997) *The Death of Distance*, Harvard Business School Press, Boston, MA

[2] For more on this, see Gamble, P, Stone, M and Woodcock, N (1999) *Up Close & Personal, Customer Relationship Marketing @ Work,* Chapter 9, Customer Knowledge Management, Kogan Page, London

[3] See McKean, J (1999) *The Information Masters*, Wiley, Chichester

[4] See Stone, M, Woodcock, N, Foss, B and Machtynger, L, (1998) Segment or succeed – the new 'top vanilla' culture in financial services marketing, *Journal of Financial Services Marketing*, **2** (2), pp 107–21; and Gamble, P, Stone, M and Woodcock, N, as above, Chapter 5, Segmentation and the Top Vanilla Offer

[5] For more on this, see Field, D (1999) FedEx not ready to abandon shipping, *USA Today*, 20 October, p 38

[6] See www.ibm.com/solutions/travel

[7] See www.ibm.com/solutions/travel

13

Customer management through people

Merlin Stone, Neil Woodcock, Roy Sheridan, Michael Starkey, Liz Machtynger and John Mullaly

INTRODUCTION

One of the most difficult questions facing all companies interested in improving their customer management is: 'I've decided what customer management strategy to put in place. I've decided which model(s) of customer management to use. I've bought my systems. I've decided on my implementation programme. Now, where on earth do I get the people to manage it all?'

This is the wrong question. Leaving the people area until last is not a good idea. Indeed, companies that succeed in implementing new approaches to customer management tend to appoint much of the team first, and leave the team to develop plans. This follows the excellent principle of not expecting people to implement plans that they had no hand in shaping.

Of course, it is not possible to appoint a complete team before deciding what to do, as the decisions about what to do, and where and when to do it, affect decisions about the nature and size of the customer management team. Indeed, it is this 'chicken and egg' interdependence between appointing the team and developing and implementing a customer management plan that causes such stress in many companies trying to improve their customer management.

Customer management research suggests a very high correlation between having the right people and people programmes in place, with achieving results for your customers and company. It is perhaps not surprising that some successful managers extol the mantra 'the customer comes second', meaning that where there is internal focus on employees they in turn will be able to understand customer needs and manage relationships effectively.

THE PEOPLE ASPECTS OF CUSTOMER MANAGEMENT

Until the time comes (if it ever does) when customer relationships will be managed entirely by computers talking and listening to computers, managing people and managing customer relationships will be closely related. Research using the scores from QCi's CMAT (see Chapter 1) indicates clearly that good performance in people aspects of customer management is highly correlated with good customer management performance, and with business performance. Let's have a look at a selection of the scores in the People section of CMAT in more detail. They are shown, with our comments, in Table 13.1.

But if it's 'a people thing', what are you supposed to do to manage your people so that your CRM initiatives deliver better results? At the risk of oversimplifying, this chapter summarizes some of the key ideas that you should consider. First, however, let's remind ourselves that, as our briefing on global implementation of customer management programmes showed, the people issue is an international one.

We used an experimental research technique to try to shed more light on some of these issues. The technique involved respondents calling up a toll-free line and keying in responses using the telephone keypad. A company called Viewscast supplied the technology. It provides this approach for companies wishing to get opinions or responses quickly. The respondents (just under 100) were recruited from one of the author's e-mail contact lists, and subsequent viral recruitment. The respondents were one third users, two third suppliers, mostly full function agencies or outsourcing suppliers. Nearly half the respondents had direct marketing as their main job, and about a third had customer service as their main job. Of the users, about a third were mainly business to business, the rest mainly business to consumer.

In the first set of questions, we used questions derived from CMAT. Respondents were asked to give their answers on a scale of 1–5, where not at all = 1 and completely = 5. About 80 responses were received to each question. We believe that scores of below 3 indicate severe problem areas, and that an average of 3.5–4 would be satisfactory. The averages with comments are shown in Table 13.2, arranged from lowest score upwards.

The survey, which is of course self-assessment and in our experience therefore prone to optimistic feedback, confirms that while senior management aspects of customer management seem to be dealt with quite well, most of the basics are neglected.

Table 13.1 CMAT people scores

Topic	Score	Comment
Creating the organization Organization support for implementing strategies Does the organizational structure facilitate the smooth transition from the creation of new customer strategies and approaches to their implementation?	41	There are often barriers between different parts of the organization, and these obstruct everything from customer-focused planning to coherent delivery of the proposition to customers
Customer management ownership Is customer management owned as a MAIN job role by a senior manager within your organization?	43	Despite leadership (see below), companies are still reluctant to put a job on the line!
Senior management leadership Do senior management give clear, visible leadership in achieving excellence in customer management?	57	Better news – the message is getting home!
Identification of customer management staff roles Have all the staff roles (including non-traditional customer management roles) and associated competencies that impact on customer management been identified and aligned with customer management objectives?	34	This needs more attention, as those whose roles are not traditionally associated with customer management often have an important affect on customers (eg invoicing, credit collection)
Management role in coaching Do operational-level managers understand their role in encouraging and coaching good customer management behaviour?	45	This tends to be higher in call centre environments where development of customer value is included in performance criteria
Managing your people Job descriptions Have customer management competencies been clearly defined in all relevant job descriptions?	44	This is a basic building block, and although not a bad score, should be higher
Competencies gap analysis Has a competencies gap analysis been carried out based on current staff in all customer management roles?	36	This shows that companies are not following through from definition to implementation
Training plan Is a customer management training plan in place that addresses the competencies gap analysis?	38	Same comment as above
Training resources Have appropriate, specific training resources (money) been allocated in the area of customer management?	40	A similar score to training plan, not surprisingly. Without this, not much will change
Objectives cascade Do you have a clear cascade of objectives from overall corporate level through the organizational structure to individual customer management people?	30	This is a significant weakness. It means that even if there is leadership, it won't be translated into measures or action
Links with people's performance contracts Are there explicit links between people's personal pay/career progression and their customer management objectives?	22	This is very poor. If customer management is important, then it needs to be reflected here

Table 13.1 *continued*

Topic	Score	Comment
Contact strategies and customer-facing staff Are customer-facing staff clear about the customer management strategies in place for different types of customers and prospects?	25	This is a technical factor, but absolutely essential, as without it customer-facing staff may handle customers wrongly
Coaching in customer management Are successful people in customer management used to coach and mentor others?	40	This is such an important part of general people management practice that it should be higher
Employee loyalty Are customer-facing people happy at work and is there an overall positive attitude to work, colleagues and the objectives of the business?	57	Good news – managing customers is not a bad job!

Table 13.2 Telephone survey – Results 1

Are staff encouraged to experience your competitors as customers?	2.0
Are staff encouraged to experience your organization as customers?	2.6
How easy is it to structure your organization so as to ensure focus on customer management?	2.7
How often do you carry out methodical surveys to assess whether staff have a positive attitude to work, colleagues and the objectives of the business?	2.8
Do all customer contact points (including third parties) have access to up-to-date information about your proposition to customers?	2.9
How often do you test that customer-facing staff understand your proposition or offer to customers?	2.9
To what extent is there full and open cooperation between all parts of your organization in the resolution of customer complaints?	3.1
Are all senior managers encouraged to have regular contact with a broad range of customers?	3.1
To what extent do you have a no-blame culture that encourages staff to record complaints as a positive means of improving customer service?	3.2
Do senior management give clear visible leadership in achieving excellence in customer management?	3.4
Is customer management owned as a main job role by a senior manager in your organization?	3.7

This was followed by some questions about ease of recruiting and retaining customer management staff (see Table 13.3). Respondents who said that the question did not apply to them were excluded. The range of responses allowed was very difficult = 1 to very easy = 5. Again, scores of below 3 indicate severe problems, while an average of 3.5–4 would be satisfactory.

Table 13.3 Telephone survey – Results 2

How easy is it to recruit good managers in customer data analysis?	2.3
How easy is it to recruit good managers in direct marketing?	2.5
How easy is it to recruit good customer-facing staff?	2.7
How easy is it to retain good customer-facing staff?	2.8
How easy is it to retain good managers and supervisors?	3.0
How easy is it to recruit good managers in customer service?	3.2

STRUCTURING THE ORGANIZATION FOR CUSTOMER MANAGEMENT

Where should customer management be located?

While we have pretty solid models of how customer management should work in a direct-only environment (eg mail order), these models cannot be simply imposed on a company with a 'real' business. Because customer management cuts across many other dimensions of marketing (and indeed business) management, there will always be arguments about the status and accountability of customer management versus other lines of authority in a business. This is no different from the arguments about the relative positions of product, channel or area. There is one simple rule – if a particular dimension (such as product or customer) is absolutely critical for competitive success, then this dimension must be relative in importance in the organizational hierarchy. But where several dimensions are considered to be equally important, then it seems that the best approach is to have them equally important organizationally, reporting to the chief marketing officer or marketing director (provided that the latter is responsible for marketing, sales and service). Quite frankly, if a company is unable to determine the relative importance of theses different dimensions, and leaves it to fighting between managers responsible for these dimensions, then structural decisions will not solve the problem. However, customer management is likely to thrive if the following two conditions are met.

First, there is clear criteria for success with products, areas, channels or customers allocated to different managers. Second, where a good conflict resolution process exists (based not just on estimated profit – often hard to determine – but also on the aim to achieve balance and compromise).

Organizational dotted lines thrive in the world of successful customer management!

Here are some examples of ways that companies are using to deal with and overcome structural problems:

- Segment teams. Some organizations have set up customer segment teams containing all elements of the marketing sales and service competencies (eg the 'young family' team).

- Time-boxed. A few organizations are now setting up the concept of continual 'programme management' around customer management solutions launches. No element of the programme takes longer than three months or it's out! This forces more creative thinking across teams to shorten timescales.
- Cross-functional. One organization sets up cross-functional mini teams tackling specific issues (eg 'retention in first year') including 'unlikely suspects' (eg delivery drivers).
- Linked measures. Organizations that are successful manage to link measures across marketing, database, sales and service processes, and measure individuals accordingly.
- Overview of the customer. A single view of customer data established across the areas dealing with customers, including past and planned communications, tends to promote more proactive and cooperative behaviour around the customer.

Our research shows that an increasing number of senior managers now own one or more aspects of customer management. The role of the senior customer management 'champion' varies across organizations from IT director to customer services director or marketing director. This tends to indicate the focus of the programme within the organization.

In the best examples, a company director or similar owns the customer experience, and develops and owns the business case for the implementation. This is then implemented through 'steering groups' or teams combining marketing, IT, service, sales and HR. This can mean taking every company decision on investment or cost cutting through the 'customer check' – eg how could it impact on the customer experience. However, few organizations have the strength to sustain this strategy and many breakages occur due to senior management changes.

IMPLEMENTING CUSTOMER MANAGEMENT

Large organizations have to make some difficult changes to the traditional structures and ways of working in order to achieve what they want to in customer management. This is made difficult because organizations have often been sliced into departments or areas of competence that directly impede a positive experience for customers – this has to be changed. Core measures and reward systems tend to promote customer acquisition activity and distract from sustained relationship building with the customer base – these have to be changed. Senior leadership is critical to the drive and continuity of the strategy. All those involved have to see how they have an impact on successful delivery of customer management – and should be rewarded accordingly. Partners will necessarily play a key role; as such they need to be managed and measured in line with the strategy. How is all this to be achieved?

Our research shows that just a few critical factors explain why customer management programmes succeed or fail.

- Restructuring current teams to create the right environment can be extremely difficult: old frames of reference constantly creep in. For an established company, a team that understands the history of the company and the pockets of people that really make a difference to customers should drive the change.

- Strong programme management is absolutely critical. Many customer management programmes have been rebadged as project management or IT programme management to enable this. This is business programme management and requires senior business management responsibility, with a strong HR component. If this fails, companies end up with great project plans, strong processes and systems but the people leave or are disenfranchised.

- The management role needs to change. New metrics and competencies are required. Many managers find it hard to adjust, and benefit from sharing their experiences with their peers in other parts of the company and in other companies.

- Using consultants too much can create dependency in critical areas or lack of buy-in from the 'troops'. In some areas it is critical to gain expert input and an external view. These include strategy formulation, programme design, quality management, IT architecture/design, analysis/profiling, system supplier/product selection, database construction. In some areas, external help is needed to plug resource gaps temporarily, particularly IT implementation, service/contact centre. However, it is always important to be clear why external suppliers are being asked to take over essentially internal roles, and to manage the input well.

- Keeping people is probably the most difficult thing once the organization has developed them. There seems to be a 70–80 per cent loss rate of senior programme managers in this area after two years. There is enormous demand for them. The pay and other rewards they receive often fail to match the stress involved.

- Customer management cannot be owned by the IT or marketing department alone. Companies in the United States, the Netherlands, Scandinavia, Australia and South Africa have realized this and the realization is now spreading to the rest of the developed world. So good customer management programme managers are getting even harder to find as the competition for them is becoming more international. However, the balance between creativity and structure in the change programme varies. For example, Germans tend to go for a more structured approach.

- There is a need for more focus on working with partners to provide sound customer management propositions and to implement customer management. This should take into account the culture of the organization and the fit of people working together. Exchanging staff with suppliers and other business partners can advance programmes greatly.

- Knowledge management is at the heart of customer management. People developing and sharing knowledge about customers, how they behave, how they react to the company's proposition, what works and what does not – these are all critical elements of a customer management programme, and require the appropriate infrastructure, measures and technology to support them.

- It is important to link pay and rewards to customer management where possible. For example, if a data model has been built to support retention activity and the retention activity based on the model works well, has the database team been rewarded for its success?
- It is important to define certain key roles and accountabilities in the customer management programme and how they need to change, then keep them under review, although this is hard at the beginning of the programme. Key responsibilities that must be allocated include those for customer acquisition, retention, development and for the cost-effectiveness of customer management.
- Building teams around customer groups is a good way to motivate people. One company built a centre team around acquisition sales and service for regions of the customer base and watched the conversion rates soar by 12 per cent.
- Achievement/recognition is often the area that has the greatest impact. It is not all about money. The best example of this is an organization that gains key customer input on individuals' performance and creates monthly, quarterly and annual communications around these. Based on this feedback, individuals and teams are provided with additional development roles.
- The emotional aspect of the customer management programme should not be forgotten. The ideal (though difficult) objective is to change feelings in the hearts of customers and staff. There is a fine line between motivation and emotion. If you can create more positive customer emotions, and the impact of this emotional change is demonstrated to staff, this can have a really positive effect on how staff think and work. It can also reduce some of the stress and conflict that customer management programmes can lead to if conflict with other policy areas is not resolved. Being part of something that is different in the marketplace and is recognized as being successful also promotes a buzz. When a company succeed in creating this kind of emotion, it is immediately obvious in the tone and content of e-mails from customers, for example. It is just as important to recognize that negative customer emotions can have a serious effect on customer-facing staff. For this reason some companies create 'mentoring' networks for those dealing with very difficult complaints or claims processes.

THE CRM TEAM AND ITS MANAGEMENT

CRM missionaries make poor programme managers. They are usually so committed to CRM and its core ideas of customer focus that they do not pursue a balanced approach to developing a company's CRM capability. They may be impatient – not recognizing that it is hard to simultaneously develop a new customer management capability and start to use it.

Missionaries tend to alienate senior managers in charge of areas such as products, marketing communications, operations, channels of distribution and IT. A good programme manager builds a team including managers from these other centres of power, and insists on a steering group of senior management from the same centres. Good programme managers always involve at the earliest possible stage managers and staff from the customer service function, who usually have to cope with the increased frequency and complexity of customer contact that normally results from CRM programmes. Finally, attention should be paid to the balance between individuals in the team – a good mix of line managers (who know how to manage achievement), technical experts (eg data quality, analysis), classic marketing management, and project management skills is required.

Customer management leadership

Senior managers often give lip-service to ideas of CRM, but the way they are managed forces them to compromise customer management objectives when faced with pressure in other performance areas, rather than allowing a degree of balance. Commitment that is both genuine and long term is critical. If it is absent, the jackals will pounce, and the CRM programme will fail.

Programme planning

One of our best clients developed a two-year programme plan covering all the functions and business units involved. It was not just a systems implementation programme. It included training, analysis, pilot projects and so on. Implementation was prioritized, not just on the basis of financial returns, but taking into account feasibilities and learning curves, as well as potential recruitment difficulties.

Objectives and strategy

Often, an unrealistic (in terms of timing and/or results) business case for CRM investment is agreed by the board, and then the task is 'thrown over the wall' to a manager appointed to head the CRM effort. A team is quickly appointed and money is spent like water in building a CRM infrastructure, with no clear basis for deploying it. This is the wrong way around. A general case can be made for improving customer management, and the team should then determine which aspects need improving, how and how fast, and what objectives and strategy would be appropriate. A global company that did it the wrong way around found that the whole initiative produced no results except expenditure, because a centralized view of objectives, strategies and timing did not match what could be achieved in most business units.

Classic HR management

This includes recruitment, selection, communication, training and motivation. CRM programmes – if and when they work – require many people to behave differently, and work with different colleagues. They need to understand the world they are moving towards and then to function within it. So a structured programme is required – including work on job definition, assessment of competence, appraisal, coaching and mentoring and culture change. Organizational design is key. The organization required to run CRM is not the same as the organization to set it up. Performance criteria need to be changed. New kinds of measurement are needed (eg retention, customer value). Getting staff to experience the company as a customer are helpful ways of creating a customer-focused culture.

Supplier management

Often, suppliers are viewed just as providers of specific services. But suppliers can be an integral part of the team, working on customer management in areas such as analysis and planning, actually managing customers, supplying supporting data and systems, and of course measuring the results. The highest-scoring company in our CMAT work so far fired its advertising agency because the agency found it difficult to work within the company customer management strategy. CMAT has a section on supplier management, and interestingly it is part of the people management section, because the two are so closely related.

KEY ISSUES

A company's customer management history will partly determine the attitudes of staff and the skills they have. If a company has only just started using customer management, or if it is slowly increasing its use of customer management techniques, there will be a variety of attitudes towards customer management. Attitudes will also differ if customer management is seen as having a basically tactical role to play, as opposed to being the fundamental basis for a company's competitive strategies.

People's attitudes are also be affected by the state of development of customer management processes. These may be quite rudimentary monitoring and control procedures, perhaps aimed at ensuring that customer marketing campaigns yield some profit, sales or information. As a company gets more sophisticated in its use of customer management, it may develop sophisticated management systems for ensuring that objectives are achieved. The company may use scheduling processes and systems, for example to ensure that campaigns do not overlap, and to ensure that markets are covered by the right campaigns.

Working in customer management is exciting and rewarding, but there is a shortage of good staff. Keeping good staff is as difficult as in any area of marketing. This is not just a question of pay. Many do not leave for money (though some do). They may leave because they are looking for a company where customer management is more accepted (where they will not have what they see as basic credibility battles to fight). They may leave because they find a particular application of customer management rather routine. They may want more challenge and excitement. They may be looking for more or less management responsibility, more or less opportunity to work with the experts.

The skills required can be better understood if we examine the jobs involved in customer management. There is no ideal customer management organization. But there are a number of kinds of post which seem to occur in most customer management organizations. Here are some examples.

The customer management leader

This person is the leader of the customer management organization. He or she is likely to report either to a more general senior marketing manager (sometimes head of the marketing communications or marketing services organization) or, more rarely, to a non-marketing person. In some organizations, there is no customer management manager, and customer management specialists are quite junior, reporting in to marketing middle management. Their role tends to be confined to analysing customers and the impact the company has on them. The highest level of seniority is achieved in the largest companies and/or those with the most commitment to customer management. The lowest level is achieved in smaller companies and/or those with least commitment.

The direct marketing specialist

This is the most frequently occurring customer management type. He or she is often recruited from an agency or another company for their technical skills. Sometimes, however, this specialist is taken from elsewhere in the organization and thrown in at the deep end with a small injection of technical training. He or she is typically the one on whom the burden of developing campaigns and making them work devolves. It is these people who require the broadest mix of management and technical skills. Paradoxically, it is just these people who are often regarded as quite junior. They are underinvested in from a training perspective. Worst of all, they are not managed in a manner which encourages them to develop the mix of skills they require.

The systems specialist

In smaller companies, much of the systems work is contracted to external suppliers. Here, there are unlikely to be any systems specialists dedicated to customer management. However, in larger companies committed to their own customer marketing database, there may be many in-house systems specialists involved in customer management. They often arrive at this job from being assigned to it by the manager of their particular systems department. Some will be only temporarily involved: in setting up and running in the company's marketing system. But in a large company, a permanent team will be needed to support and continue the development of the marketing system. Our experience is that such people need to develop additional areas of skill.

They need to develop new technical skill areas, such as direct marketing. But it also helps if they also develop more general marketing skills. This is because they will increasingly be asked to help integrate the work of customer management with the mainstream marketing approach of the company. This means, for example, drawing off customer data from more general marketing systems, and feeding back data gathered from campaigns into marketing systems. It may mean devising decision support systems that can be used in all marketing contexts (eg management reporting systems).

The statistician

In the early stages of use of customer management, as with systems, most statistical expertise is hired in. This may be as part of a package deal with a direct marketing agency, which will undertake to carry out (or use specialist suppliers to carry out) the statistical analyses which are so central to customer management. However, at this stage, these analyses are likely to be relatively unsophisticated. They involve fairly simple comparisons between the results of different tests, different selections within a campaign, and so on.

Then the company gets more sophisticated in its use of data – particularly if it develops its own customer marketing database. It begins to see the potential of using more advanced statistical techniques to analyse its customers and group them into categories likely to be more responsive to different kinds of offer. When this stage is reached, the strategic advantage gained from successful analyses of this kind makes companies realize that they are dealing with a highly sensitive competitive issue. This makes them worried about using external suppliers. Also, the depth of the analysis required means that there are real gains in having internal experts. They know the company, its customers, its strategies and its data.

Good business statisticians are rare birds. They do not usually require great skills in statistical manipulation. This is often done by sophisticated computer packages which can even tell them what is worth analysing. A good customer management statistician must have insight and creativity, but not be a statistical purist. Such a person must be prepared to live by the fundamental rule of customer management – what works, works. Most customer management statistics are 'dirty statistics'. These do not observe the nice theoretical rules of pure statistics, designed to provide scientific degrees of certainty in making predictions, rather than find patterns which can be shown to continue (or not!) by testing. So, statisticians recruited into customer management for their technical skills must be trained in marketing and customer management. They must also be involved in some campaigns, so they can see the practical context in which their analyses are being put to use.

The wider organization

Although the in-depth training requirement may be within the customer management department, most of those requiring training will be outside the customer management department. They will be staff involved in marketing and sales who need to deploy customer management to achieve their objectives. These are the users or internal customers. The workload may be allocated between the specialists and the users in many ways. At one extreme, the users may do most of the work, and the specialists may provide the infrastructure (eg the customer database, campaign selection and scheduling approaches). In this case, users become 'doers'. At the other, the users may brief the specialists, who act on their behalf with all the suppliers. In this case, they are 'internal customers'. Your company may be at any position along this continuum.

Either way, users will need some training. Where users are 'doers', they will need much of the training that a customer management specialist requires. Where users are 'internal customers', they will need a limited amount of training. This should cover how customer management works, what it can do for them, and what they need to do to ensure that the specialists can do a good job on their behalf (eg brief them well, give them clear deadlines, and stick to their own side of the bargain).

Senior marketing management

Senior marketing management are important. They control the financial resources that allow companies to recruit staff, invest in systems and pay agencies. If a company has committed to customer management as a strategic move, which is going to make a big difference to its overall marketing approach, then senior management must receive training. They must receive enough for them to understand what they are taking on. If not, their understanding of customer management may be based on their experience in other companies, what they have read in the trade press, presentations on seminars, and so forth. They may need to develop additional skills in managing marketing. Particular requirements here are likely to include:

- understanding customer management performance measures (eg campaign statistics – market measures and financial results);
- understanding how to relate resource allocation decisions to performance results;
- recruiting, motivating and appraising customer management staff;
- for companies developing internal customer databases, managing systems investment, working closely with the information systems department.

This training for senior management is particularly likely to be needed if a company's marketing management has come from a different marketing culture. It may have come from the consumer brand culture, where marketing communications is driven strongly by sales promotion and published and broadcast advertising. It may have come from technical product marketing – where marketing is driven strongly by product specification, sales management and after-sales support.

Customer service staff

These already exist in large numbers in most organizations, often working in call centres or customer-facing branches. The introduction of customer management introduces new data and disciplines for them to work to. All too often these staff are neglected in the planning stage of introducing customer management, so that at the point where customers are actually managed, achievement is much less than planned.

KEY SKILL REQUIREMENTS IN CUSTOMER MANAGEMENT

Skills requirements are many. Few companies would claim that they had all the skills they required, in the quantities they require them. Developing and keeping the right mix and level of skills is a constant battle. The phrase 'two steps forward, one step back' rings very true here. As soon as a company recruits and/or trains to the right levels, strategic needs may change, or key staff may leave to join other companies. This section discusses the ideal mix of skills, and what a company can do to move towards the ideal, while recognising that the ideal will never be reached.

Core competencies

Setting out and understanding the core competencies you need for customer management is critical. Some examples of new competencies that organizations have to develop are:

- understanding customers – customer analysis and research;
- customer strategy design;
- contact strategy design and management;
- understanding business impact – profitability, building a business case;
- managing customers/relationships – key account management;
- managing, coaching and developing people;
- managing and interpreting customer information;
- innovating for and with customers (in teams);
- researching the market;
- customer programme design and management;
- customer proposition/product design;
- customer product rating/pricing;
- Web site content design and management;
- Web community design and management;
- customer process and service level design.

Management, personal and technical skills

In training, we usually distinguish between three fundamentally different types of skill, as follows:

- Management skills – the type of skill required to manage or work with teams of people in order to achieve a particular goal.
- Personal skills – the type of skill required for an individual to function well, as an individual, in a variety of contexts. These contexts include the family and friends, and peers, subordinates and superiors at work. Many personal skills are important contributors to management skills.
- Technical skills – those relating to the individual's specialism. In customer management, these include customer management itself, statistical skills, and computing skills.

The dividing line between these type of skills is not always neat. For example, in some areas, a personal skill may also be a technical skill if it is an essential requirement for the job. The personal skills of self-presentation are also part of the technical skills of a major account salesman, for example.

The distinction between these types of skill is very important. For example, when a company gets started in customer management, it tends to import technical skills (direct marketing, data management, data exploitation and systems), because it is devoid of them. Its early training emphasis tends to be on technical skills. As the company begins to take customer management more seriously and integrate it with its overall marketing approach, the size and significance of customer management projects grows. A much higher level of personal and management skills is required. The personal skills particularly needed include the ability to manage one's time, present concepts to others, and influence and negotiate with them. The management skills required include the ability to implement complex campaigns, using a mix of department staff, other members of the company, and a variety of external suppliers.

What then are the key skill requirements? In our view, they are the following.

Fundamental marketing skills

You might be surprised by the number of people working in customer management whose level of knowledge of marketing and of certain customer management disciplines is weak. If they are specialists who have been drawn from an agency (and before that were fresh graduates), they will have had little chance to develop broader marketing skills.

What kind of general marketing skills would we like in our customer management staff? Here is our shortlist:

- Customer orientation: the ability to see things from the customer's point of view. In customer management, it is all too easy to get carried away with the technicalities of the approach. Staff should be able to stand back from their work – a letter, a planned telephone call, a brochure or a catalogue – and see it as the target customer would see it. They should then be able to ask themselves, dispassionately, the question 'What customer benefits are highlighted?' and be honest in answering.
- Understanding of different basic approaches to marketing – brand managed, sales-force-driven, retailing and the like, how they work and why they work. This is an important part of basic development. This is because the work of customer management often involves either supporting or substituting for one or other of these approaches.
- Understanding of the basic marketing approach. This covers identifying customers and their needs (conceptually and analytically) and determining ways to meet them profitably through the deployment of the marketing mix (product portfolio, price, promotion, distribution channels). This understanding is critical for integration of the customer management approach with your company's approach.

Many customer management specialists may have worked in a supplier company that specialized in one area of customer management (eg direct mail and telemarketing). If so, they may know little about other specialisms, if none of the accounts on which they worked used them.

Personal skills

Personal disciplines are usually at a premium in customer management, two skills in particular. The first is communication – the amount of teamwork required to develop and launch customer management campaigns means that those involved need to be good communicators. This is not just for formal presentations, but also in the sense of keeping the team informed (staff and suppliers). The second is team-working (for the same reason that communication skills are required)

Data and database skills

Customer management is probably the most quantitative form of marketing. Direct marketers need to understand how customer databases are built and maintained. They must know what sort of data is required as the basis for successful customer management, how to analyse data to find out which approaches work, and so forth. They do not necessarily need to be able to carry out the analyses themselves, as these are often contracted out to third parties. But they must understand the basics of data analysis in order to make sense of the results. They also need to understand the structure of marketing databases and how the system in which they are housed affects how they can be used. If they are to be given online access to your company's marketing database, then they also need the skills to operate the system.

Are the same skills always required?

Although the broad management skills requirements are common across most industries, different types and sizes of companies need different mixes of customer management skills. The major differences are likely to be as follows.

Smaller companies

These are unlikely to be able to afford many or any dedicated customer management staff. Staff responsible for customer management activity will have as their main task the orchestration of external suppliers (often small companies themselves) to achieve effective campaigns at low cost. The skills of supplier management are likely to be at a premium (clear concise briefing, communication, monitoring and control, etc), as are the 'efficient' personal skills (eg time management, diarying). At the same time, the staff concerned will need to be closely involved with the development of overall marketing policy, and probably be expected to contribute to it, rather than taking it as given. In such situations, the marketing all-rounder who is a personally effective worker is likely to be at a premium.

Larger companies

These can afford and do need specialists. Their tasks are likely to be more precisely allocated as part of an overall marketing plan. As specialists of various kinds, they will be 'pitting their wits' against their opposite numbers in competitive companies, to gain an advantage over them. This degree of precision in job definition implies that these staff will be working as members of a large in-house team. The team needs to be communicated with, listened to and influenced, rather than told what to do. Even the external suppliers may not be appointed directly, but as part of a wider corporate – even international – policy. So in this case, the skills mix needs to be richer in the areas of team-working, as well as there being depth in the particular specialism concerned.

Consumer marketers

Companies marketing mainly to consumers need to have skills relating to the more 'mass-market' media – mail, inbound telemarketing, published and broadcast media, Web-marketing – as these are likely to be used more intensively. They also need to understand the kinds of consumer data available from third parties, and the kinds of analysis that can be carried out on such data to segment the market.

Business-to-business companies

These will need mass-market skills if they are marketing to small businesses (whether as final or trade customers). However, if their market is mainly larger organizations, they will need specific strengths in the areas of telemarketing (especially telephone account management), Web management, and using customer management in support of sales staff or large agents. In the last case, they will need to be very strong in the skills of 'working with'. These include communicating, influencing, negotiation, functioning as part of a team. Sales forces are rightfully suspicious of new approaches to marketing which involve addressing people they see as 'their' customers.

Long-term relationship marketers

Companies marketing to customers who maintain a long-term relationship with the company (or have potential for so doing), eg if the purchase is frequent, or if there are additional products and services which can be sold after the 'main sale', require the skills of database marketing. This is because they will probably find the development of an in-house customer database cost-effective.

Operations-intense companies

Companies with 'real' operations facilities, whether service or 'hard' product (eg manufacturing, transport, product retailing) operate with more constraints in terms of their flexibility to customer needs (eg inventory, capacity) than companies without such facilities (eg personal or financial services). Although this distinction is not hard and fast, customer management staff in the former type of company need to plan further ahead and remain closely in touch with the situation in inventory or capacity. There may be less flexibility in product design here. The latter type of company can often create products specifically for customer management campaigns. In the former type of company, direct marketers may need very good communication and influencing skills, in order to work successfully with those responsible for product specification and delivery.

Hybrid skills

As projects combine people from different parts of the organization in order to increase cooperation and likely success of customer management projects, individuals are more likely to gain skills in multiple areas (eg IT and marketing) and can be valued and rewarded for doing so. Their jobs are more likely to change substantially as they move departments internally, are recruited externally or change from client-side to supplier-side, and back. A number of professional bodies now have development programmes for people who have another primary profession. Together these changes tend to develop more hybrid skills in people.

Company heritage

This is important. For example, a strong engineering heritage means that customer management staff marketers will need to work closely with engineering-driven product management. They will need to educate them into the idea of marketing customer benefits rather than selling features, and of designing products to fit markets rather than finding markets for pre-designed products.

A sales-force-driven company will need to be educated away from thinking of customer management as just a lead-generating device, rather than as a way of managing markets. The idea of a salesperson working to customer management disciplines will not be easily accepted. These disciplines include:

- total accountability for the cost-effectiveness of each call;
- high visibility of this accountability;

- measurement of sales force effectiveness against other potential media for contacting and doing business with customers;
- structured calling programmes following clear contact strategies, often in combination with other media.

In this situation, the customer management staff may need to work on a long slow campaign to educate and motivate sales management.

After the investment?

If you spend good money on recruiting and training good marketing staff, do not forget that this is only the beginning. You must make sure that you follow all the principles of good management and work hard to keep them. Giving good training and user support will help. But here are some ideas as to how you can keep them in today's competitive labour market:

- Reward them for achievement. Build evaluation into their appraisal, and reward success by increased remuneration and promotion.
- Allow them to work towards success steadily, by giving small projects to work on initially, then build them to being able to handle larger projects.
- Manage their workload. Don't expect staff to succeed if you give them very high workloads in some months and compensate for this by low workloads in others. Don't expect them to succeed either if you continually give them short notice of new approaches to customer management. They'll find it very difficult to manage under these conditions.
- Allow them to contribute their expertise to strategy development. Accept and develop their ideas, and give credit for them.
- Give them the opportunity to express their feelings about how they are being managed and what they are learning, through work and training. Use formal anonymous questionnaires and act on the findings.

14

Programme planning, team selection and management

Merlin Stone, Liz Machtynger, Neil Woodcock and Michael Starkey

INTRODUCTION

One of the more difficult issues to resolve in CRM implementation is how the CRM change programme should be constructed and led. To implement anything other than tactical approaches, the programme sponsor must be senior, visible and totally supportive. The sponsor of any large programme must be a senior person with cross-functional responsibility. Normally this person should have a board-level role and needs:

- executive team authority;
- access to a significant budget;
- to be a great communicator/motivator;
- to have considerable experience in customer management;
- to have clear measure against which to benchmark progress.

Sadly, the reality is often that the board-level person does not really own the project and is just a sponsor in name only. Sometimes this is due to the fact that the board-level person is not experienced in CRM, or does not really believe it is his or her responsibility. This lack of commitment leads to common problems such as:

- limited project visibility;
- non-attendance at key meetings;

- being slow to respond to emerging blocks to the project;
- loss of momentum in the project;
- demotivation of the project team.

The champion of any programme should be a senior manager. This is not the project manager, of course, but a programme champion who is there to chair the steering group and become involved in steering direction and helping to solve key 'blocks' to project success. Sometimes this is the 'sponsor'. There are two common pitfalls. First, this person does not allocate enough time to ensure that the project is progressing along the lines of the points in this checklist. Second, the project is just skin-deep for the 'champion'. He or she does not really champion it and the project team feels that he or she does not really understand the issues.

A programme manager should be appointed to be responsible for delivery. The qualities the person requires are:

- experience;
- understanding of the business;
- vision;
- not being locked into legacy thinking;
- strength – he or she will not be dominated by 'concept touting' consultants.

The programme manager should work closely with the work-stream leaders and with the project manager to ensure the project is on-track. Key functions and responsibilities of the programme manager ought to include:

- communication to ensure that the organization is fully 'engaged' in the process;
- quality control to ensure that the output is well thought through;
- managing commitment, ensuring that users, or non-core project people, involved in some work-streams provide appropriate commitment to the project.

The programme manager may have to import some key skills, but the priority should be to train current employees. New people coming in may have a different culture that alienates staff who must do the actual implementation.

Often the programme manager will appoint an independent consultant adviser, with experience of managing similar projects, to work with him or her. Most companies will require some independent expert help to guide them through an implementation, but be mindful of the impact on having an alien culture of 'consultants' or system integrators being seen to 'own' the project. The external team should clearly be led internally. If the programme manager is external, as is often the case because of the skills and knowledge required, it is important to make sure that he or she quickly becomes part of the team and that his or her 'culture' and work behaviour fit with the organization's.

WORK PLANNING

The team must have the authority to ensure that individuals in suppliers or functions not under their direct 'control' make time for and contribute to the project in the ways required. The programme manager should develop a clear outline of work to be done and output required, and provide realistic guidelines as to how much time it will take. If the programme team members are unclear about the time commitment required, this will become frustrating for the others involved. The programme manager should monitor the quality of the work, focusing on the most important tasks or those being carried out by 'at risk' teams (those with less obvious commitment). Where the work is clearly rushed as the deadline approaches, the resulting output may not be well thought through. The programme manager should counsel the project team leaders to ensure that their issues and worries are resolved and also be able to change people involved in the project if required. If the scope of the project implies significant potential change, the programme team must have the authority to implement organizational change.

The steering group should be chaired by the champion, as above, and attended by managers from each of the functions impacted by the strategy (often IT, marketing, sales, service, finance, HR, analysis and research). The programme managers should also attend along with the project manager. Others may be asked to attend depending on the work carried out and the stage in the project. A common problem is that the business functions nominate lightweights – the people with time on their hands. The members miss meetings and do not read project status reports. They are 'named' members only and people in their function or department. quickly pick this up and become unresponsive to meeting and work requests from the project team.

Failure is more likely when core or non-core team workers have hidden issues/worries (some genuine, some not, but all perceived) concerning the project which go 'unlistened to' and unresolved. This will impact on the quality of their output and the mutterings within the organization may grow into significant barriers to change. Setting up an informal network designed to raise early issues to the programme manager is a key success factor here. There may be very valid reasons why the project plan may need to change.

COMMUNICATION

Communication is key in projects which involve organizational change. People are used to ways of working, want to protect their and their staff's future security and position in the organization. At a more mundane but nevertheless critical level, they may have personal issues against members of the project team and will always be looking for the project to fail. The programme manager needs to win the hearts and minds of the organization. This requires an internal marketing campaign using appropriate, relevant and timely messages that people will accept. Aims and objectives, likely benefits, or key messages are usually not repeated often enough. As in any marketing, or propaganda activity, the repetition of a message is central to the message being understood and remembered.

One of the key change roles will be that of senior sponsor and champion. This person needs to have powerful influencing skills, and must make them available to the programme manager. The programme manager needs to clearly relate the underlying programme's positioning and the organization's reaction to it carefully, and discuss the communication role of these senior champions.

Communication during the programme, in different ways, with different messages, is vital. This is usually forgotten. People who are in other ways really expert at customer management often ignore the importance of internal communication to users and influencers. In one key account management process, we identified pan-European user-influencers within the organization and involved them in the implementation process. They returned to their local organizations and trained/advocated the approach to their immediate account teams and peers, who then came on the training. This networked the implementation into the organization very successfully.

Attention should be paid to:

- the type of person who needs to be communicated to;
- the type of messages they need to hear;
- the contact strategy applicable: looking in particular at media (face to face, telephone, e-mail, newsletter, posters, etc);
- the frequency (eg daily updates, weekly, monthly, at key trigger points).

Different types of content will require delivery to different people in different ways at different frequencies with different messages. Key targets include:

- business unit managers;
- personnel/HR managers;
- finance managers;
- marketing and sales personnel;
- operations personnel;
- stakeholders (including partners and customers).

It is important to select key influencers at grass-roots level and work with them to turn them into advocates. Winning advocates is yet another key programme management point. The project team should determine who in the 'user' organization are key influencers of others. They should be brought into the project and encouraged to provide input. It is important to demonstrate that their contribution is valued and that is being listened to. Another possibility is also to get them involved in user-testing of the process or system, and designing the training so that they feel as emotionally involved in its success as the project team.

ENCOURAGING CHANGE

People are naturally resistant to change, but many will be prepared to change if they are encouraged and reminded. An implementation plan needs to:

- Consider ways to reduce the constant pull back by old world behaviour 'magnet', for example, making existing processes, systems obsolete, or managers requesting to see regular 'output' of new ways of working.
- Consider ways to pull (carrot-led) to new world desired behaviour, for example, recognizing 'new-style working' in coaching and appraisal systems, and making appropriate comments or giving appropriate rewards, providing real benefit to all in using the new system, ensuring that senior and line managers 'live the vision', reinforcing it through their behaviours.
- Consider ways to push (stick-led), for example, identifying 'old-style working' in coaching and appraisal sessions and taking appropriate action, using charts and targets that rank people's 'new system' behaviours and performance, making sure that senior people insist on the new way of doing things.

The usual practice is to rely on pull (carrot-led) tactics, but this is often done in an insular and not holistic way.

It is important to try and ensure that there are real benefits for all users that save them time, really help them achieve their targets, and add some other value to what they do. This may change the scope of the programme a little. For example, in a sales management systems project, this meant building in additional functionality ('what if?' management information reporting) to encourage the sales managers to use the system and encourage their teams to use it. If there are no obvious benefits that users can buy into, then the change required of them will be harder to enforce. If the users have a choice, they will naturally revert back to the old way of working. This is not because they are being obstreperous or deliberately malevolent, but because it is human nature.

Changes need to be introduced carefully in a multifaceted way. Training has an important role to play, of course, but implementation does not end there. Coaching on site normally has a large influence on the success of change programmes. This reinforces training concepts, and helps individuals apply them in the real world. This can be supported by:

- management reinforcing the concept through behaviours and attitude;
- peer influence;
- building into performance contracts;
- changing personal targets and objectives to reflect the need for the desired behaviours;
- maybe changing remuneration structures to encourage behaviours;

- providing short-term incentives;
- changing appraisals to look for the hard and softer aspects of the change required;
- online training reference courses;
- online coaching consulting.

We have already mentioned coaching. Coaching is an essential part of the change process. Here are some examples of its deployment:

- An organization that found out that a group of its call centre people had over 90 per cent success rates in retention developed a programme to transfer this group's successes through call observation, using the key people in other teams and gaining customer feedback – this improved overall retention by 5 per cent overall.
- An organization that had developed targeting models in one business unit transferred some of the team to a completely different business unit to coach the team in the second unit on how they had achieved success in targeting.
- Most successful organizations have a policy of coaching less experienced team members in direct customer contact methods.
- Some companies extend this coaching practice across company boundaries to partners.

The role of staff and customer research

It is very helpful to carry out research into employee attitude and behaviour (just as with customers) during the implementation programme. This helps you:

- identify weak areas;
- determine training and support needs;
- improve results.

Research should also be carried out to understand change in customers' attitude and behaviour as a result of the programme, and the two sets of research should be compared. A similar approach can be applied to other stakeholders – intermediaries, suppliers, sponsors, shareholders – helping a company identify whether problems are likely to emerge later.

SUPPLIER MANAGEMENT

There are many kinds of suppliers used in customer management programmes, and then in the departments or units set up to manage customers. They include:

- data management/data providers;
- software (applications and middleware);
- hardware;
- integrator;
- strategy consultant;
- proposition delivery (eg provides an additional service to customers);
- data management agency;
- Web agency;
- creative agency;
- brand/above the line/PR agency;
- research agency;
- delivery (eg delivers the product);
- call centre/telemarketing agencies (eg provides sales or servicing);
- sales force;
- fulfilment houses;
- customer management agencies;
- list suppliers and brokers;
- computer bureaux;
- print creative providers/print production;
- premium providers.

These suppliers not only work with the client, but also with each other. It is therefore important to bring them together at an early stage of your work with them (and then at intervals during the period they are working together). You should get them to identify any management problems that have emerged and possible solutions. Many inter-supplier problems are caused by overcentralization of communication, so that all communication must pass through the client. In practice, it is best if suppliers work closely with each other according to a tight programme or brief from the client. This is much better than their having to rely on the client being at the centre of a network of communication.

Selection of suppliers is an important first step. Obviously, there are many criteria by which you can select suppliers. They include:

- Creativity. Do they provide that extra spark, but one which is consistent with your brief? For agencies, this may depend on the quality of the creative brief as well as on the quality of creative staff. You should always sign off the creative brief yourself.
- Quality. Is their work of a consistently high standard?
- Reliability. Can you rely on them to perform well every time?
- Ability to observe deadlines. Do they meet all their deadlines? If there are problems, do they tell you quickly enough, or try to hide them?

- Ability to understand your needs.
- Openness. Are they honest with you?
- Ability to take criticism and bounce back with better solutions.
- Price. Do they give good value for money? This does not mean being cheap. Can they account properly for the money you invest in them?
- Ability to work with others (yourself as client, and with other suppliers). Do they enter into the team spirit, and not try to look good at others' expense? Do they accept problems as team problems?
- Ability to add value to your efforts. Do they execute the brief blindly, or do they help achieve more by identifying weaknesses in the brief and remedying them?
- Ability to share investment, responsibility or risk.
- Ability to integrate and/or subcontract.
- Ability to commit required skills and senior management attention.
- Ability to resolve issues when they arise.

Increasingly, large clients put the emphasis on management quality rather than creativity. Customer management relies greatly for its effectiveness on 'managerial' factors. It is good management that translates strategy into action. In selecting suppliers, it is worth paying close attention to managerial factors such as:

- their management processes;
- the management experience of staff;
- budgetary and costing processes;
- ethics – whether they avoid expanding projects at your expense;
- their clients' experiences (eg do they deliver on time, of the right quality, within budget?).

Once a supplier is on board and working with the client campaigns, the following 'good management' rules should be applied:

- Always give clear instructions. These should cover what is to be achieved, by when, by whom and at what cost.
- Explain the criteria by which suppliers will be judged – overall and on each job.
- Measure progress against target service levels and communicate results of this measurement constantly through clear feedback. Evaluating and appointing partners should be a continuing process based on these measures.
- Reward good performance – by recognition, renewal of contracts, additional work.
- Punish bad performance, by querying or refusing invoices, negotiating lower fees, or asking other suppliers to bid for the work.

- Draw up objectives and service levels for each of these suppliers who play an important role in the delivery to the customer.

Managing the strategic relationship with suppliers

Many client companies are moving towards an arrangement with suppliers whereby the latter receive an annually negotiated fee for their consultancy, account management and planning, and creative work. All other costs are charged at cost, with no mark-up, and only when agreed.

In this situation, achievement of cost-effectiveness depends heavily on fee/mark-up negotiations and on close vetting of *content* of work, as competitive tendering is foregone or only weak.

Benchmarking methods can be used to improve the situation, particularly when using external experts with access to other sources of cost information. Competitive tendering can be introduced even within this framework. But using a restricted circle of suppliers for competitive tendering can lead to collusion and work-sharing by suppliers. Rationalizing the number of suppliers helps achieve strategic coherence, but can lead to this cosy circle emerging. On the other hand, repeated competitive tendering among suppliers may demoralize them. It is also very demanding of clients and their time.

Here is a suggestion on how to handle this situation:

- Decide which areas are to be opened to increased competition, whether on a period, project or campaign basis, whether on a complete or part-area basis. Previous justification for strategic commitment should be re-evaluated, as should arguments for a single supplier. This might lead to distinction between core areas (where a single supplier is essential) and peripheral areas, where freer competition could prevail.
- Where strategic commitment is maintained, fee, cost and mark-up control should be enforced, but periodic tendering and negotiation should cover these elements up front, on a competitive basis (eg every two to three years).
- For specific projects or campaigns within well-established supplier–client relationships, a request-for-tender approach should be used. This would be part of the brief, but also ask for cost details and options. Supplier accountability for a consultative, quality, approach should be clear, ie accountability for output, not input.
- Relationship contracts should include the installation of quality and cost-control procedures (including progress reporting).
- Keep the supplier network reasonably wide. Separate between strategic large agencies, second-tier agencies and fast-track agencies. It should be clear that favoured suppliers will need to pitch against others, who will be given some business to maintain interest. It is sometimes worth (eg if a problem of shortage of suppliers has been identified) helping to develop smaller agencies so they can compete.

- For specific marketing campaigns, the estimated and out-turn costs of every campaign should be published as part of the cost-control process. Benchmarks should be developed from these, and budget-setting should be based on analysis of these costs.

THE CHANGE IMPLIED BY CUSTOMER MANAGEMENT

Customer management means change. Management of change is a key capability. Here are some examples:

- Business units traditionally aligned to selling product, now have to realign to focus on customers.
- Marketing focuses on retaining, developing and acquiring the right customers.
- Sales becomes relationship oriented.
- Service becomes multifunctional and more proactive.
- Products become solutions or propositions.
- Pricing policy is more focused on customers rather than one-off product sales.
- IT becomes embedded in change programmes rather than a separate, distant function.
- Information about the effect on customers of any of the company's activities becomes an important new ingredient in many decision-making processes.
- Measures – whether marketing, finance, operational, logistics – add a customer dimension.

All this means a real need for strong and sustained management, and a lot of trust and support from the organization!

Measurement

'What you cannot measure you cannot manage' applies very strongly to customer management. It is through new sets of measures that staff will understand whether they are making progress.

However, most companies have large numbers of measures in place, many of them long-standing, which can get in the way of customer management progress. For example:

- For call centre staff, the total focus on time on call can distract from a broader relationship and development.
- For sales staff, the focus on acquisition can result in acquisition with little focus on what happens to those customers acquired.
- For marketing, the focus on acquisition cost can drive towards acquisition of the wrong customers.
- For service staff, the focus on service efficiency (speed or cost of processing) can drive towards the prioritization of the wrong things and customer dissatisfaction.

The lack of linkage between these measures and the overall goals of the company can lead to inconsistent treatment of customers – eg when costs need to be cut, they are cut across the whole of marketing activity rather than specific activity for certain customers. It is therefore important to undertake a separate measurement project, evaluating how existing measures work and how they need to change at different stages of the customer management cycle, from targeting to win-back, to allow the company to meet its overall customer management objectives.

Knowledge management

Some organizations attach a value to customer knowledge, and to the people (human capital) who have this knowledge and the expertise to use it. Knowledge management in customer management requires a briefing of its own. For the purposes of this briefing, you should consider whether you are able to answer the following questions:

- Have you outlined the areas of expertise around the customer (competence)?
- Do you know who the experts are?
- Do you create forums for people to bring these areas of expertise together?
- Do you make the most of intranets/extranets to transfer/exchange and apply knowledge?
- Do you create forums to develop knowledge of the changing circumstances of your customer base/technologies/environment, etc?
- Do you promote and reward good ideas?
- Do you transfer your ideas and expertise to customer propositions (eg content on the Internet)?
- Are you forced to relearn through loss of customer management knowledge and prior experience?

Knowledge management often falls to the bottom of the list as a 'nice to have', but leading companies such as Virgin, BP and Skandia base their strategies on knowledge creation and management.

THE FIVE KEY ELEMENTS OF SUCCESS

We have identified five key elements required for success in CRM, as follows:

- Customer management strategy – which customers are to be managed, for what products or services, through which channels.
- Customer management models – how these customers are to be managed (eg through classic segmented CRM or through a top vanilla best-service-for-all approach).
- Infrastructure – systems, data, operational customer management capabilities (eg call centres).

- People – who is to develop the new capability, who is to manage it, and how.
- Programmes – how new customer management capabilities are to be installed.

One of the most common errors general managers make is to confuse particular areas. The worst error is to confuse the organization required to *implement* CRM with the organization required to *manage* CRM – although continuous change tends to blur any boundaries here. We describe this as confusing 'getting there' with 'being there'. The former is a combination of strategic and programme management. It involves determining what kind of capability is required to manage customers and changing the organization's capability in the area of CRM. The latter is best described as a functional task, one of using a newly developed or modified capability to manage customers differently. However, both tasks involve managing teams of people to do things, so neither should be given to managers who are poor people managers. A common mistake is to give the one or other (or worst of all) both tasks to a 'CRM advocate', someone who is a 'true believer in CRM'. Because, as we shall see, the customer management dimension usually cuts across other dimensions of the customer-serving organization (eg products, channels), such a person usually alienates senior managers responsible for these other dimensions. The net result is usually either a failed CRM programme or a customer management capability that can never be properly used because it has lost a battle for authority that should never have been started.

Our research indicates that companies are more likely to succeed in improving their customer management if they adopt an approach similar to that described in Table 14.1. It is obviously highly simplified, but makes the distinction between programme management and using the new capability very clear. Obviously, if a company wishes to deploy its capability before it is completely ready, then Tasks 2 and 3 will overlap.

KEY POINTS

If this chapter is to leave you with just a few points, they should be these:

- Ensure senior management ownership and active leadership of people management in customer management.
- Create cross-functional working around customers/groups where possible and focus on smooth customer experience across functions.
- Ensure that a people motivation and development programme is in place – based around measurement and reward, team-based approach, recognition programmes including the customer.
- Focus on promoting trust and sharing in the organization.

Table 14.1 Customer management programme approach

Overall Task	Detailed Task	People Requirement
1. Strategy and Planning	• Review approach to customer management, including current strategies and models • Determine requirement for any change, and urgency, size and general scope of change • Develop business case and obtain approval	• Generally best done through combination of routine corporate strategy process, perhaps combined with special task force consisting of cross-section of involved functions/departments, marketing/ customer service suppliers, and possibly consultants • May require in-depth assessment of current approach – what the company does (eg using CMAT), what the results have been (eg net value and persistence of customer base – perhaps using data warehousing and data mining techniques), and what customer feel about it (using market research techniques) • Probably best to have board-level sponsor(s) and steering group
2. Detailed Programme Planning and Implementation	Programme details planned and implemented	• Programme manager appointed to work with senior sponsors to appoint team, allocate tasks, recruit suppliers, etc. Included in this list of appointments is customer management leader • Organizational sub-project determines structure, size, accountability and outline budgets of customer management department • Steering group composition may change to reflect functions most affected by change
3. Capability in Use	Programme manager hands over capability to be used by customer management leader	• Customer management leader implements new approach to customer management • Starts by appointing team and suppliers • May be relatively high level of outsourcing of some operational tasks until full capability developed, as company may require that capability comes into use before complete (indeed programme management approach would suggest this)

- Recognize the importance of coaching, using those who are good at customer management activity.
- Link individual measures to customer management performance (retention, development and acquisition of customers) and to the ROI measure.
- Promote knowledge sharing and creation programmes.
- Understand the core areas of competence and develop and recruit around these.
- Set up service-level agreements/game plans for partners/suppliers relating to customer performance, and monitor them closely.

15

Campaign management systems and processes

Merlin Stone, Tess Harris and Bryan Foss

TRENDS

Over the last 15–20 years, there have been significant changes in the nature of marketing, customer management and marketing communications activity. This applies particularly to distribution channel management and to all marketing communications disciplines: advertising, PR, direct marketing, sales promotion, conferences, exhibitions and road-shows, etc.

The main trends are these:

- use of multiple channels of distribution and customer contact;
- uncertainty over which models of customer management are right for particular markets;
- broadcast/published media proliferation;
- changes in telecommunications and systems support;
- tighter targeting;
- more 'across the line' campaigns, ie involving several (above and below the line) media;
- customization/perzonalization;
- greater availability of skills;
- more outsourcing of activity;
- greater risks of lost knowledge;
- increased consumer response propensities.

Use of multiple channels of distribution

In the last two decades, most marketers have realized that customers do not wish to be confined to particular channels by suppliers, on the basis of supplier-oriented or prescriptive criteria, such as: only being able to buy certain products through certain channels; or being categorized according to particular characteristics (eg businesses of particular sizes, types or locations; consumers with particular asset values, incomes or locations).

Typical restrictions include:

- Consumers can only buy retail or over the telephone.
- Small business customers can only buy over the telephone or through dealers.
- Major account customers can only buy from a direct sales force.

Companies that try to regulate markets in this way have often lost share as competition and market dynamics increase. However, multi-channel or 'hybrid' marketing leads to greater complexity in planning and implementing marketing and marketing communications. Without careful planning, it can also get out of control – particularly through the introduction of additional costs and channel contention.

Uncertainty over models of customer management

There has been much discussion and experimentation to establish, for example:

- whether customers prefer to buy within relationships or to buy best value for money at the time;
- the extent to which customers are happy to give information about themselves;
- whether if a company invests in managing customers as individuals, it will gain a return.

Concepts such as 'one to one' marketing and CRM are still being tested by companies with excellent reputations for marketing. Many companies have realized that one model does not apply to all customers. Managing marketing using more than one model involves even greater complexity than in the days of single model, single channel marketing.

Broadcast/published media proliferation

The constant need of clients for ways to address specific groups of customers was one of the reasons for the proliferation of media available for this purpose. Enabled by advances in communications and publishing technology, companies have available a much wider selection of media to address customers. This has been most readily observable in consumer and trade press, radio, and cable/satellite broadcasting, and of course in the static or declining coverage of the old 'mass' media (terrestrial analogue broadcast TV, newspapers). However the new media of Web, digital TV and mobile can be used as broadcast or targeted media in different situations. Each medium has its own targeting and timing requirements, and is likely to require changes to be made to final content. Purchasing and deployment have also become more complex – hence the rise of specialist media buying and creative agencies. The result – each campaign has many more options and executions.

Changes in telecommunications, systems and data support

Similarly, direct marketing has been stimulated by rapid improvements in various areas, such as:

- Telecommunications hardware, software and network services now provide much more sophisticated support for inbound and outbound telemarketing, enabling companies to achieve better coverage and higher success rates, more cost-effectively.
- In many cases, direct response TV has been combined with inbound telemarketing and advanced direct mail to produce total customer management solutions which substitute dramatically for retail marketing. The latest examples include the success of new entrants in the credit card and short-term savings markets.
- Printing technology continues to improve, with the latest ranges of digital colour error-correcting laser printers becoming affordable for in-house production. Use of billing and routine administrative communications to carry varied copy is expected to increase dramatically. This will produce great variety and potential personalization of copy and image.
- Data supply (internal and external) has also improved, allowing established companies and new entrants to target customers more accurately. This in turn leads to greater variety of copy than in the days when virtually all mailings were 'mass market'.

Tighter targeting

This is a corollary of the above. A campaign with given objectives and coverage (in terms of number of customers) tends now to have much greater variety and personalization of messages and creative.

More 'across the line' campaigns, ie involving several media

Increasing ability to target applies not just to customers, but also to media. Therefore, we tend increasingly to choose specific media for specific tasks for specific customers. For example, we might use TV to raise awareness, change perceptions or motivate, mail to drive a specific and perhaps personalized message home to selected customers, and tele-marketing to handle response, with Internet providing a channel of influence and response.

Customization/personalization

Implicit in much of the above, we are now able to use better data, systems and more targeted media to produce an offer much more precisely targeted to small groups of customers, personalized through the use of their details (previously given information, past transactions). This in turn leads to more varied copy.

Greater availability of skills

All the above would not be possible if we did not have the staff to plan and manage the activity. For example, in the UK the CIM, CAM, IPR, IDM, the DMA and institutions of further and higher education have made great efforts to promote careers in marketing and marketing communications and ensure widespread availability of training. This means that generally – though not in all areas or necessarily in the quantity required – we can usually find staff to carry out the more complex communication activity we need to meet out objectives.

More outsourcing of activity

Many of the above skills serve marketing communicators better from external agencies, where they can continue to specialize in specific aspects of marketing communications. Media buying probably offers the best examples of this, closely followed by specialist creative and data analysis agencies. The need to specialize has, of course, been driven by increasing complexity. However, this also means that to achieve their objectives, companies now need to use a wider range of agency types or skills, on any one campaign, possibly increasing coordination problems.

With the greater variety of skills required, it often makes less sense to have them in-house, as a specific skill may only be used occasionally. The skill level of the individual will tend to fall, along with his or her cost-effectiveness. However, the greater use of external skills can create divisions between projects which would otherwise thrive from improved coordination.

Greater risks of lost knowledge

As campaigns become more complex and as staff move between companies, the risk of lost knowledge (what is happening now, what worked in the past in our company and with our customers) increases. However, best practices and additional skills can be imported from other companies, industries and service providers with greater staff movement. The benefits of system-based approaches to customer knowledge management and managing communications have become very clear – customer information is not lost and is accessible to whoever is managing the customer. In many companies, when a member of staff leaves, or is even sick, work slows down because it takes time to transfer knowledge or even identify current status and regain momentum.

Increased consumer response propensities

In sectors where targeting has become more precise, companies are experiencing higher response rates. This is not surprising, as all that it means is that consumers are getting more appropriate messages and responding to them more often. However, they also have higher-quality expectations (eg they do not expect the telephone response line to be engaged, or to have to wait so long for an e-mail or letter of confirmation). What this means is that media integration needs to be planned more carefully, to ensure capacity is available at the right time.

Increased competitive activity

Of course, marketing tasks have also been changing rapidly. The key reasons for this include:

- Easier competitive entry – improved marketing technology, data, media availability and skills means that companies can now attack new markets more easily.
- Privatization – many markets formerly monopolized by governments or public sector corporations are now in the private sector or at least subject to competition – telecommunications, postal activities, energy, rail and air travel.
- Deregulation – many industries and markets formerly severely restricted by regulation have been liberated, allowing all companies to compete for all customers and/or all need areas. Financial services is perhaps the best example.
- Value chain break-up – in many cases of privatization and deregulation, driven by EU directives, the approach taken is to break up established value chains. In the UK, rail, telecommunications and energy are the prime examples of this. This has created a

customer-facing part of the value chain that is free to buy and sell capacity from other parts of the value chain, typically over the whole market. In some cases, this value chain break-up has been stimulated by poor performance of incumbents (eg short-term savings, in which retailers have combined with banks to attack the market).

In nearly all cases, marketing skills, processes, technological support and the like have been transferred between companies, resulting in very sophisticated attacks by new entrants upon incumbents. Incumbents have found that their existing marketing communications processes have simply not stood up to this challenge, unless defended by a near monopoly.

Accountability

The increasing complexity of marketing communications has generated problems in this area. Marketing communications spend is increasingly fragmented, and more often crosses the line with other functions (eg inbound telemarketing as part of customer service, marketing databases and campaign operations as part of IT). Marketing communications spend has become more widely based and difficult to control. Meanwhile, the general instability and complexity of the marketing communications environment means that it can be harder to see what has worked, particularly if detailed records of what was done to whom, when, with what effect, have not been kept.

The move towards e-commerce

Still at its earliest stages, it is clear that Web-based and other electronic means of communication are further changing the way marketing communicators are working. However, the immediacy with which a consumer can view companies' offers and respond to them over the Web is in sad contrast to the slowness with which companies can move in responding to current market challenges. This is because most companies are using what are effectively manual methods to generate and update initiatives and material that are eventually destined for the Web. Companies are beginning to realize that this is a source of serious competitiveness weakness that is visible to all.

GENERAL BUSINESS ISSUES

In addition to the above market developments, there are also some specific general business issues that affect campaign management.

Impact of company size

The very largest companies have particularly sophisticated campaign requirements. These are driven by:

- the number of customers they hope to manage relationships with and communicate with;
- the frequency of direct interaction;
- the broad range of channels and value chain partnerships in place or being developed.

Size has a particular effect when it comes to:

- Managing very large integrated marketing activities, across a number of channels and through many communication campaigns. To achieve the required quality and return through such campaigns, they need to be very smartly managed. With the competitive pace often accelerating, larger companies will find it increasingly difficult to achieve their objectives without taking a strong line on marketing process automation and management
- Retaining knowledge. Large companies' knowledge of what they are doing in marketing and marketing communications at any one time is spread across a very large number of people, within the company and in external suppliers. Failure to deploy this knowledge results in lost opportunities. Failure to maintain and share it leads to bad decisions and poor implementation.
- Performance management. With complex sets of marketing and marketing communications activities, it is often not only hard to see what is going on at any one time and ensure that it is being progressed according to plan. It is also hard to see what is working and has worked.
- Downstream dependence. Very large companies often have a large number of staff in direct contact with customers – downstream of those generating customer management policies. In many cases, the dependence of these customer-facing staff on higher level decisions/work/plans is not recognized by those who generate the material which customers see. The result is that these downstream staff are often poorly briefed on what customers have seen and on what customers want to discuss with them. A consequence of this is worse customer service and lower sales. This applies at every contact point with customers. Poor knowledge by customer-facing staff may lead to customer attrition because of general dissatisfaction with service.

Impact of new competition

In many sectors (eg financial services, utilities, telecommunications, travel), new competitors, using different business models, and working to very short marketing decision cycles, are posing problems for incumbents. New competition often comes from sectors (eg retail) where marketing practices are very different, and in particular where there are established processes for rapid campaign management. These new competitors are often very attuned to EDI between suppliers and themselves, and are already examining ways that this can be applied to agency relationships, as well as to improve internal communications. Their stricter budgeting disciplines mean that they are more likely to tie such approaches to financial systems. These capabilities may or may not be appropriate in their newly entered market but can potentially change the rules of the game for existing players.

Impact of remote working

The general increase in remote working has led to a situation where office costs can be saved while quality is maintained or even improved, because access to systems to progress projects does not depend upon physical presence in the 'home' office. The world of integrated marketing and communications has, perhaps surprisingly, largely resisted such trends.

The requirement for new-style agencies

Resistance to change to new ways of working may be as strong in the supplier world as within the client world. Separation often exists between traditional and new media skills and methods, across agencies or even within an agency. Some agencies clearly make money from their clients' inability to project manage their communications, and simply absorb the chaos behind their walls. However, with marketing communications agencies focusing increasingly on the Internet, some have realized that these particular physicians must heal themselves, and move to more integrated approaches and more effective electronic ways of working.

GENERAL IMPLICATIONS OF THE DEVELOPMENTS

Companies need to manage their increasingly complex and integrated marketing, sales, channel and marketing communications programmes:

- in a more integrated fashion, exploiting the most effective combinations and treatments;
- properly communicated to all involved in the process;
- faster and more timely to customer needs and market change;
- with more consistent output quality – to avoid the delays of rework;

- not necessarily cheaper, but with more effective use of marketing spend, as marketing communications will be one of the most important weapons in attracting and keeping customers.

To do this, they will need systems and processes that deliver the following benefits:

- ease of extracting relevant management overviews and reports, and consequent ability of senior marketing management to view current status, progress and results against strategies;
- ability to handle increased volumes/complexity of work through current resource levels while maintaining quality, cost and target dates;
- maintenance of quality, reduced error-rate, control of risk of rework or exposures;
- improved satisfaction of marketing staff through reduction of lack of structure in decision making and project management, and possible reduced staff turnover due to improved perception of professionalism and development;
- improved customer service through access to past, current and planned communications, offers and responses;
- improved satisfaction of customer-facing staff, eg in call centres;
- improved supplier relationships and value-add;
- reduced loss of knowledge, direction or momentum through staff turnover;
- ability to repeat or clone successful campaigns more easily;
- ability to mount or update campaigns more quickly;
- enhanced learning about what works and what does not work;
- reduced need to pay agencies for project management work;
- ability to respond faster to competitive challenges and mount attacks quicker;
- lower costs of creation, delivery and administration;
- distributed access – allowing travel avoidance, working from multiple sites, cooperative working with agencies and others, home working, and international working.

THE RESEARCH

Research topic coverage

The research into campaign management processes for this chapter was conducted via e-mail on a non-random basis. The questionnaire was designed for rapid completion by e-mail. It took about 30 minutes to complete. It was sent to a selection of our contacts – managers who are responsible for or who heavily influence decisions in this topic area. We received responses from 16 companies, some via agencies or other suppliers. The topics below were covered:

- business sector;
- organizational structure for managing marketing communications;
- number of offices, branches, stores, call centres, etc, where contact is made with customers (eg face to face, by telephone) and where marketing material is used;
- number of staff who might be in contact with customers in these locations;
- number of marketing communications staff;
- total number of agencies used across all marketing communications;
- approximate annual marketing communications spend (all media);
- number of major campaigns each year (not sub-campaigns or treatments);
- change in number of campaigns;
- change in complexity of campaigns;
- work processes;
- IT usage in work process;
- systems skills;
- staffing pressures;
- relationships with marketing communications agencies;
- communication with agencies;
- roles of agencies in campaigns;
- current state of communications between marketing communications staff;
- past process/systems projects;
- current plans to modify or acquire campaign management support systems;
- current plans to modify campaign management processes;
- barriers to change;
- expected annual cost of software;
- budget responsibility for changes to systems support;
- most likely choice;
- systems approaches to supporting marketing communications;
- content expected;
- user characteristics in a support system improved support;
- advantages of improved systems support;
- benefits from improved systems support;
- types of supplier of system support that respondents might turn to;
- particular companies that respondents might turn to;
- other products which might be used.

FINDINGS – OVERVIEW

The respondents were from the sectors shown in Table 15.1.

Table 15.1 Survey respondents

Travel and leisure	2
Transport	2
Retail and mail order	2
Financial services	4 (2 non-UK)
Industrial engineering and electronics	3
IT and telecomms	2

The key findings were as follows:

- Companies are running more campaigns.
- Campaigns are getting more complex.
- There is a large variation in process clarity and formalization of campaign development.
- There is relatively low level of IT support for automation and management of campaigns but people are actively looking to introduce IT support and process change. One or two respondents are in the middle of developing or implementing a new system.
- There is increasing pressure on quality, measurement and the return on campaign investment. Headcount reduction is not a priority, instead getting more out of existing headcount, faster, without reducing quality, is the key priority.
- Companies tend to have more strategic, longer-term relationships with agencies.
- The budget responsibility for IT to support marketing campaigns is at marketing director or even MD level.
- The key functions required for new campaign systems are project planning, selection management, campaign/results tracking and campaign team communication.
- There is a low level of expectation around being able to store video and audio along with documents and graphics.
- The ease of navigation and intuitiveness are more important considerations than other specific functional areas.
- The key potential benefit areas are seen as sharing of information, standardization of processes, improved quality of work, improved retention of learning and increased staff productivity.

DETAILED FINDINGS

Table 15.2 shows that although most of the respondents managed marketing communications from a single site, a good number did this from multiple sites.

Table 15.3 shows that most companies are managing customers from multiple locations, with two respondents being giant in this respect.

Table 15.2 Organization of marketing communications

Company Offices in UK or in Home Country	Number of Survey Respondents
1	9
2–4	3
5+	3

Table 15.3 Number of places where contact is made with customers and marketing communications material is used

1–5	6
6–10	0
11–50	5
51–100	3
101–250	0
251–500	2
500+	

Table 15.4 shows that the companies with most staff in contact with customers also tended to be those with a larger number of locations of contact, though not necessarily with more offices for managing marketing communications.

Table 15.5 shows that the numbers of marketing communication staff involved was quite large.

Table 15.6 shows that although most companies use only a few agencies, half use six or more.

Table 15.7 shows that although some of the respondents had low annual expenditures, most have significant budgets.

Table 15.8 examines the number of major campaigns per year. The definition was deliberately left subjective, as defining what exactly is a campaign (as opposed to a treatment) can be a problem. Even 20 or more major campaigns a year represents a significant coordination problem.

Table 15.9 shows that only two companies reported fewer campaigns, while nine reported more campaigns.

Table 15.4 Number of staff in contact with customers in above locations

Fewer than 100	4
101–500	3
501–1000	1
1001–5000	3
5001–10000	2
10001+	3

Table 15.5 Number of marketing communications staff

1–5	4
6–10	3
11–15	0
16–25	4
26+	5

Table 15.6 Total number of agencies used

1–5	8
6–10	5
11–15	0
16–20	1
20–25	1
26+	1

Table 15.7 Approximate marketing communciations spend per year (all media)

<£5 million	6
£5–10 million	2
£11–20 million	1
£21–50 million	3
£51–100 million	1
£101 million+	2

Table 15.8 Number of major campaigns per year

0<10	6
11–20	1
21–40	6
41–60	2
61–80	0
81–100	0
101+	1

Table 15.9 Change in number of campaigns

More than 20% less than last year	0
11–20% less than last year	0
1–10% less than last year	2
About the same as last year	5
1–10% more than last year	3
11–20% more than last year	2
More than 20% more than last year	4

Table 15.10 is a stark reminder of the increasing complexity of the job, probably due to the increasing pressure on effectiveness of existing and additional campaigns.

Table 15.11 is pleasing, in that at least a few companies have a comprehensive process. At the other extreme, several companies have a long way to go.

Table 15.12 shows the fairly basic state of communication in most companies, but some pleasing progress has been made by a few. These were not mutually exclusive, so the total is more than 16 (one company which chose option 3 also marked option 8, and another company marked options 4 and 10).

Table 15.13 shows a little confusion generated by the questionnaire concerning systems skills. These were meant to be incremental options, one company marked options 2, 3 and 4, two marked 2 and 3 and one 3 and 4. However, the conclusion is that workgroup software could make a development contribution to several respondents.

Table 15.14 examines staffing pressures. The responses showed a strong focus on quality and ROI are key.

Table 15.15 examined communications between clients and agencies, and shows the potential for the agency extranet, as the strategic relationship is dominant.

Table 15.16 showed the parlous state of communication with agencies.

Table 15.17 examines how the workload is split between client and agency. It shows the workload to be roughly evenly split, with a strong need for close co-working.

Table 15.18 examines communication between marketing communications staff. It shows a big improvement over the years, and is probably due to the fact that most of these companies have some kind of campaign scheduling system in place. They have also understood the importance of internal communications to achieve integration or manage campaign complexity. However, perhaps the alternatives suggested were too stark and finer gradations of opinions should have been allowed.

Table 15.19 considers how companies have fared in the past with systems projects. It looks positive, but again the alternatives offered may have been too stark.

Table 15.10 Change in complexity of campaigns

Complexity falling	0
About the same	2
More complex	14

Table 15.11 Work processes

No structured and well-documented process	1
Developing such a process	3
Has process, but only parts of communications cycle	4
Has process, but only certain communications disciplines	2
Has process – covers all cycle	6

Table 15.12 IT usage in work process

Standalone support	0
Above, plus e-mails	4
As above, but share some files on server, but no structured process for version control, and some key files not shared on server	5
Most files kept on a common server, but no structured access, updating, sign-off process	2
Most files kept on a common server, and structured	2
As above and process includes one or two suppliers	1
As above and includes all suppliers	0
Intranet on which some of process managed	1
Intranet on which most of process managed	1
Extranet linking us with agencies	2
Extranet links us with agencies and used to manage most of process	0

Table 15.13 Systems skills

Most staff have problems operating a PC	0
Most staff use basic WP and spreadsheet confidently	3
Most staff use e-mail confidently	10
Most staff use workgroup software confidently	8

Table 15.14 Staffing pressures

Reduce headcount	2
Increase productivity significantly	6
Improve the quality of campaigns	8
Increase ROI from campaigns	10
Not under above pressures	1

Table 15.15 Relationships with marketing communications agencies

Agencies for each campaign	0
Few agencies which work longer term	5
Increased proportion of work by agencies	1
Few agencies on a strategic basis, but asks others to carry out specific campaign tasks	10

Table 15.16 Communication with agencies

Fax, courier, meetings and telephone calls	1
Some e-mail	10
E-mail taking over, with meetings where critical agreements are required	4
E-mail main form of communication	1

Table 15.17 Role of agencies in campaigns

Company does all planning and measurement and some execution	6
Company does all planning and measurement and agencies do execution	3
Agencies do some planning and all execution	5
Agencies do most planning and all execution	2
Outsource marketing communications almost completely to agencies	0

Table 15.18 Communications between marketing communications staff

Not well informed of work of colleagues	3
Well informed	12

Table 15.19 Past process/systems projects

Long history of failed projects	1
A few failed projects, some successes	7
Mostly successes	8
Nothing but success in this area	0

Table 15:20 shows the strong emphasis on support systems.

Table 15.21 shows that processes are also under the microscope.

Table 15.22 examines barriers to change, and indicates reasonable potential for trying out new approaches, with proof points.

Table 15.23 shows budgetary responsibility for software decisions. Interestingly, the managing director scores oscillated between 5 and 1. The marketing director was mostly either the budget holder or signer-off.

Table 15.24 examines the type of features required. There is a strong requirement for database interface, tracking and basic project management functions.

Table 15.20 Plans for support systems

Definitely not planning to acquire or modify	0
No clear policy	6
Definitely planning	10

Table 15.21 Plans to modify processes

Definitely not	1
No clear policy	2
Definitely planning	12

Table 15.22 Barriers to change

Marketing systems not important	0
Very conservative approach taken	5
Likes to try new approaches	4
Likes to pilot and/or test	4
Applies strict cost-benefit principles	4

Table 15.23 Budget responsibility for changes to systems support

0 = we do not have this role, 1 = not involved, 2 = consulted but not budget holder, 3 = key influencer but not budget holder, 4 = budget holder but not final sign-off, 5 = sign-off

Relationship marketing director/manager	1.7
Advertising/marketing communications director/manager	2.3
MD	2.6
Direct marketing director/manager	2.6
Finance director	2.7
Marketing director/senior marketing manager	3.3

Table 15.24 Systems supporting marketing communications

1 = not at all important, 2 = indifferent, 3 = important and 4 = very important

Results tracking	3.8
Campaign tracking	3.6
Project planning and follow-up	3.4
Selection management (working with database)	3.4
Direct interface with customer database	3.4
Final results analysis	3.4
Deadlines approaching, due and overdue	3.3
Communications between all parties	3.2
Campaign change notification	3.1
Media planning	2.7
Sign-offs – required and achieved	2.7
Market/sector planning	2.6
Ability to set up user groups and keep informed	2.6
Archive	2.6
Help functions	2.4
Training functions	2.4
Search capabilities (topic, text, image, sound, video)	2.3
Direct interface with accounting systems	2.3
Media buying	2.1
Push basis of communication (to be explained)	2.0
Chat room	1.5

Table 15.25 examines the content that the system is expected to manage. It has similar results to Table 15. 24, except that Web pages are important.

Table 15.26 examines characteristics required by users. It shows the importance of simplicity and accessibility.

Table 15.27 examines the advantages of improved systems support. Standardization, communication and ease of use seem to come to the fore here.

Table 15.28 examines the benefits from improved systems support. Although the respondents emphasized that cost-cutting was not their key objective, getting more out of existing resources is a key theme here, as is quality and knowledge.

RESEARCH CONCLUSIONS

A fairly clear picture emerges of they way many companies are thinking about developing their management of marketing communications, and the systems and processes they require to do it. The key messages are that integration with the customer database, project management, internal communication, and knowledge management are important to companies, with e-commerce starting to raise its head.

THE IMPACT OF 'E'

Different marketing communications mix

Still in its earliest stages, it is clear that Web-based and other electronic means of communication are further changing the way that marketing communicators work. The familiar, traditional marketing communications mix employed by marketers to reach and speak to customers is undergoing a rapid transformation in the online marketing world.

Table 15.25 Content expected

1 = not at all important, 2 = indifferent, 3 = important and 4 = very important	
Numerical databases (eg customers, costs)	3.4
Diagrams (eg campaign flow charts)	3.3
Web pages	3.3
Spreadsheets	3.0
Text, eg briefs, reports	2.9
Call centre decision trees and scripts	2.9
Static digitized images (eg of print, stills)	2.5
Sounds (eg radio commercials, call centre conversations)	2.0
Video (eg TV or cinema commercials)	2.0

Table 15.26 User characteristics

1 = not at all important, 2 = indifferent, 3 = important and 4 = very important	
Ease of navigation	3.7
Security firewall	3.4
Accessibility from variety of locations	3.3
Intuitiveness	3.2
Ease of error recovery	3.1
Accessibility from other applications	3.1
Accessibility through World Wide Web, with tight security	3.1
Total synchronicity – even with multiple users of same content	3.1
Clear ownership and version control structure	3.1
Use of familiar terms/concepts	3.0
Storage of frequently used entities – circulation groups, searches, etc.	2.9
Opening of several different items at the same time	2.9
Distribution list maintenance	2.9
Ease of return to indexed positions	2.8
Ability to annotate and transmit/store annotation	2.7
Tracking of access frequency	2.6
User programmability	2.5
Access audit – by whom, when, etc	2.4
Personalization of screen, reference	2.2
Link with purchasing and other operational systems	2.1

Table 15.27 Advantages of improved systems support

1 = not at all important, 2 = indifferent, 3 = important and 4 = very important	
Sharing of information	3.7
Standardization of project templates	3.4
Standardization of process	3.4
Ease of measuring	3.3
Ability to modify past campaigns for rerunning	3.2
Ease of reporting	3.2
Thinking and creating time maximized	3.1
Ease of reviewing	3.1
Ease of approving	3.0
Real-time management and tracking – on-time, every time	2.9
Version control	2.9
Geographical independence	2.9
Chasing re/checking and worrying time minimized	2.9
Ease of discussing	2.9
Project and action step ownership made possible and visible	2.8
Virtual teaming	2.8
More confident referral for approval	2.8
Automated administration	2.7
Easier, more secure delegation	2.7
Ease of archiving and retrieval	2.7

Table 15.28 Benefits from improved systems support

1 = not at all important to your company, 2 = indifferent, 3 = important and 4 = very important	
Improved access to and retention of knowledge and information	3.4
Maximizing staff productivity	3.4
Ability to work in a more structured/higher-quality fashion	3.4
Lower costs of creation, delivery and administration	3.4
Time saving	3.3
Strategic rigour	3.2
Retention of intellectual capital	3.2
Reduced likelihood of information loss due to error, staff turnover	3.2
Reduced error rate	3.2
Final customer/agent satisfaction/quality	3.2
Immunity to staff turnover (except system training)	3.1
Reduction of chaos	3.1
Reduced effort	2.9
Distributed access	2.9
Improved supplier relationships	2.9
Improved staff retention (if required) due to reduced stress	2.8
Travel avoidance	2.6
International working	2.4
Home working	2.1

Until the World Wide Web arrived, marketers had a well-defined range of techniques and implementation tools to choose from in formulating their marketing communications plans. The creativity and content of the messages were determined according to the capacity and constraints of the chosen medium and the desired behavioural response. Measuring the effectiveness of marketing communications was subject to tried and tested research methodologies and metrics. Typically, the traditional mix would comprise some or all of the following elements:

- advertising above-the-line in TV, radio, press, posters and other ambient media;
- personal selling through sales forces or in store;
- point of sale/purchase (POS/POP) merchandising;
- sales promotion;
- direct marketing, in particular direct mail and telemarketing;
- PR.

While today's e-marketers have a broadly similar range of communication methods, the tools, the media, the messages, the metrics and the processes are brand new, as shown in Table 15.29.

Table 15.29 The impact of e-business

From	To
Above-the-line advertising	Graphical and banner advertising on portals, other Web sites or in e-mail newsletters
Personal selling	Onsite virtual sales representatives (VSR) – using AI and other 'intelligent' techniques to assess a Web site visitor's needs and respond in a near-human manner Affiliate marketing – using other sites to 'sell' and drive traffic to the marketer's site Interactive, customer-driven Web site functionality – such as 'Call Me' buttons to request a callback from a sales person, onsite FAQs or collaborative filtering algorithms that will 'guess' what a visitor is looking for on the site and make a cross-sell or up-sell suggestion
POS/POP	Static and dynamically generated product images, identified through an external or internal site search engine, or delivered from an online catalogue – allowing the capability to display targeted products or special offers, in real time or according to predetermined mathematical rules
Sales promotion	Electronic coupons and incentives – offered through e-mail newsletters, portals and affiliate Web sites or to stimulate an instant purchasing decision onsite, eg at the registration page
Direct marketing	Personalized e-mail newsletters Listings on search engines, such as AltaVista, or directories, such as Yahoo!, that offer marketers the means to target customers through the use of keywords and Web page optimization and/or paid-for rankings in results' pages
PR	Postings in discussion forums and user/newsgroups Electronic real-time news releases Digital press kits, easily downloaded from a site

Electronic messages

Creativity in the online media differs markedly from the traditional communications environment. The major difference is the significant role played by text. Evidence from click-through rates (CTR) shows that text performs better than graphics in online advertising, whether on a banner ad, linked from an affiliate site or in an e-mail newsletter.

Research suggests that online users pay more attention to text and tend to ignore images. This is supported by the results of the Poynter-Stanford Online News Eyetrack Study (1999–2000), where users' eye movements were tracked and analysed while they were reading online newspaper sites.

One reason is the textual legacy of the Internet's origins. Another is that the Internet is commonly considered a 'lean-forward' medium – as compared with the 'lean-back' medium of TV. People viewing Web sites are in an active *reading* mode and consequently the words are more important than the pictures. Moreover, until broadband becomes widespread, many Web site owners must deliberately minimize graphics to avoid long download times and some Internet users turn off graphics on their PCs – thereby reinforcing the expectation of words rather than pictures in Web-based communications. Conversely, TV viewers are actively looking at pictures and consequently graphics (supported by audio signals) are more important to conveying advertising messages than words.

Where graphics are used in banner advertising, some of the traditional creative rules still apply, for example, careful consideration must be given to:

- size;
- placement;
- message content – intrigue and sex remain powerful attractants;
- branding;
- targeting;
- use of colour, fonts and type styles.

But there are new facets to this type of advertising:

- Banners should be (and can be) frequently rotated/changed – for instance, if a visitor doesn't click through after three servings, the banner isn't working and should be removed.
- Small sizes (memory and dimensions) work better than large.
- Animation helps improve CTR (provided it's not overdone).
- Colour contrasts between the banner and the Web page can have a dramatic impact on CTRs.

Measurement and metrics

Online marketing has spawned a new measurement industry and associated metrics. These supplement traditional business measurement tools and metrics, but heighten the challenge faced by marketers in determining the value of corporate Web sites and the success of online marketing campaigns.

Along with familiar terms such as RFM (recency, frequency, monetary value) measures, marketers must employ a new arsenal, including the prime Internet measures of:

- hit – a single entry in a server log file generated when a visitor 'requests' text, a graphic, or audio file on a Web site page;
- impression – one display of a banner ad served to a Web site visitor;
- page view – a request to view a single Web page (which may constitute several hits);
- unique user – an identified person or computer who visits a Web site (this visitor may make multiple visits to the site over time);

- clickstream – the path with page links taken through the site pages by the user;
- CT (click-through) – the act of linking from one Web page to another;
- CTR (click-through rate) – a measure of the effectiveness of online advertising, usually expressed in percentages, ie 1 per cent CTR means that only 1 in 100 impressions of a displayed banner was sufficiently attractive to warrant a click-through by a viewer;
- CPM (cost per thousand) – cost per 1,000 banner impressions displayed;
- CPA (cost per acquisition) – cost of acquiring a customer (or sometimes a qualified prospect);
- site stickiness – the ability of a site to hold a visitor's attention.

Web sites in addition produce very large amounts of digital data about users that cannot be evaluated using conventional statistical tools. For example, visitors and customers can be monitored and tracked through:

- IP addresses – ie the number assigned to the computer or the browser when online;
- Internet domain names – eg of the service provider or college/company server;
- time/date/duration of visit to a site;
- the browser used by the visitor – ie usually MS Explorer or Netscape;
- the site from which the visitor clicked through;
- cookies – ie text files deposited on the visitor's computer as a result of an earlier visit to the site which can help onsite personalization and identification of repeat customer visits.

The data derived from these measures can be correlated with other marketing communications activities to assess the effectiveness of, for instance:

- e-mail newsletters;
- search engine optimization;
- banner advertising;
- electronic coupons;
- onsite personalization;
- retention and loyalty campaigns;
- customer management processes.

Conclusion

E-marketing communication has changed efficiency and effectiveness. The Internet and Web-based e-marketing activities provide highly cost-effective means for marketers to communicate with prospective and existing customers. Production costs of online banner ads are considerably lower than conventional advertising tools. Moreover, if a banner is not working it can be replaced or refreshed quickly, with a lower penalty than in a non-Web medium. VSRs, FAQs, collaborative filtering and other interactive tools can reduce the cost of human intervention in the customer decision-making/sales process and speed the customer's trajectory through a Web site – helping minimize the propensity of buyers to abandon their purchases before checkout, for instance. E-mail marketing, an increasingly popular way of building one-to-one relationships with customers and prospects, can be created, executed and measured in-house at much lower cost than traditional direct mail. E-mail newsletters deliver targeted messages that can be tailored to an individual reader at marginal cost. E-mail lists can generate incremental revenue as they may have an asset value to other advertisers – generally these are more responsive than traditional mailing lists and fetch a much higher per-name value as a result. PR material costs (eg of press releases, press kits, image production and distribution) can be lowered through the use of digital tools.

Put simply, the Web means that marketers can do more things, more cost-effectively, with greater targeting. However, as recent experience has shown, bricks and clicks work best together, not in opposition. Big brands can drive customers to the Web, and back to the call centre or the store. In business to business, the security of a big brand allows a company to set up a business-to-business exchange and/or encourage buyers to buy on the Web. Relatively few purely digital brands have been able to exploit the cost-effectiveness of the Web to achieve long-term returns for shareholders.

Part 4

Sector studies

16

Travel industry CRM

Merlin Stone, Alison Bond, Jonathan Miller, David Selby,
Doug Morrison and John Mullaly

INTRODUCTION

Much of the focus of travel industry CRM has been on frequent flyers (and Chapter 17 explores frequent flyer schemes further) but this chapter will show that there are other aspects of travel industry CRM! However, it is true that managing frequent flyers involves addressing some important issues that are shared with other industries, but which combined turn out to be quite difficult to manage. These issues include:

Managing high-value individuals

Frequent flyers are normally high-value individuals in many market segments, particularly other travel-related services (other transport forms, hotel, car hire), other communications services (eg telecommunications, package delivery, postal services), financial services, automotive and the like.

Managing corporate individuals

Most frequent flyers are what we call corporate individuals – they work for large companies, and have varying degrees of discretion about their choices (relevance telecommunications, etc). The others are smaller business travellers, and of interest to companies selling services (particularly communications) to smaller businesses.

Managing customers for a limited duration

They are of value for a defined period. They arise from a much larger group of flyers in general, and return to them. Anticipating which flyers are going to become frequent flyers and which are not, and differentiating service in favour of the former, is becoming a key aspect of marketing, as is achieving a transition back to normal flyer status.

Locational variety

They transact with airlines in many different locations – nationally and internationally, and expect a consistent level of service.

International variety

They are international customers. This is related to variety of location, but refers to place of residence and culture rather than where they transact and use.

Loyalty management

Airlines were among the earliest users of individual customer loyalty schemes, and have long-established databases of behaviour, although they do not necessarily manage them well.

Data support requirements

The data to support and complete these transactions needs to be delivered to and recovered from all over the world, and requires 'industrial strength' computing and communications technology to achieve this.

Data depth

Meeting customer requirements properly involves capturing and holding data on a variety of issues – eg preferences (booking – channels, payment methods, seat location, payment methods, etc), propensities (to hire cars, stay in hotels, respond to communications, etc).

Agent issues

Customers mostly book through agents – whether they are corporate or private flyers. They are not known to the airline at point of booking, unless, for example, they declare membership of a frequent flyer scheme.

Value chain issues

The nature of the value chain involved in marketing and providing the service creates immense scope for outsourcing of different parts of the service provision process. This places special demands on systems for managing customers as they pass through the process, experiencing different service episodes during the overall transaction period (eg from booking to return), particularly if certain categories of customer are to be selected for different treatment.

Cooperation and joint ventures

While outsourcing is common (often to competitors), the need for an integrated approach also creates a demand for cooperation. Managing the resulting cooperative value chain involves cooperating in the collection and use of customer data hire, plus access to joint databases of customers.

Customer dependence

Airlines are almost the ultimate case of a service industry, in which the customer becomes almost totally dependent on the quality of service for the whole period during which the service is being consumed – there is no parachute. This period is an intense burst, repeated several times a month or more, and preceded and followed by other interactions – booking, confirmation, complaints management. However, the quality of service delivered by an airline cannot be controlled entirely by the airline. For example, when the airline uses a non-home port, typically most of the staff are contract staff. Customer service also depends upon other airlines, airport authorities, air traffic control and, perhaps most of all, upon other passengers.

General service management

Airline travel is also like other service industries – its product is perishable and non-replaceable; there are quality assurance problems; the service is very dependent on staff, and so on.

Although this list of factors may make airlines seem a case apart, the above characteristics are shared with other industries, though not in the same combination. Other industries are interested in the airline experience, particularly because of the issue of managing high-value individuals. Leading airlines and travel-related companies are often cited as examples by managers in other industries. Another reason is that many marketing and IT decision makers are themselves frequent flyers, and use their experience as a benchmark (not necessarily positive!) for their own policies.

THE TRAVEL INDUSTRY CONTEXT

The bulk of the material for this chapter is drawn from the three major world airline markets, which can be loosely categorized as follows:

- The United States, where travel in all its forms is largely deregulated, and where competitive forces have therefore had fairly free play for a number of years. The much greater competitiveness also means that customers who wish to fly as cheaply as possible have much more choice, so that trends towards flying in economy class, which in Europe and Asia can be partly restrained by yield management techniques (releasing restricted volumes of seats for lower-class fares), work much less well. However, all markets felt the impact of declining yield in the recession, despite the perception of relatively expensive fares for some routes in terms of yield (cents/mile) versus transatlantic travel. Equally, the quality of service can remain very low and seemingly unaffected by heightened competition in recession.
- Western Europe, where deregulation is happening now. The European and in particular the British experience is central, for – as with so many industries – the British market is more advanced in deregulation than other European countries. This applies to air, rail and bus travel. Also, because of its geographical position, the UK is more reliant on air, sea and now rail travel for international access.
- The Asia Pacific region – a complex mix of protected national airlines, but, because of the diffused geographical structure of the region, operating in largely competitive markets.

The changing scene

Travel is income-elastic, and air travel is highly income-elastic, with domestic and international air travel growing at more than twice the rate of economic growth in most countries – although it is assumed that there must be inherent limits to this growth. The European travel scene is certainly changing rapidly. In the UK, Eurostar and Le Shuttle have made a dramatic difference to the cost and speed of cross-Channel travel. Eurostar already reduced airlines' shares of the London–Paris route by 20 per cent (much less than the 80 per cent share taken by the Paris–Lyon and Tokyo–Osaka high speed trains, both about three hour journeys). Business travellers with time pressures don't only look for the shortest journey time, InterCity trains also provide them with the ability to make greater use of the working time during the trip itself. Le Shuttle has taken nearly half the cross-Channel ferry market. Cut-price airlines are operating successfully using minimal marketing, focusing simply on the bare product, the price and easy booking. Many of the 26 new private rail operating companies have been bought for or are being bid for by other transport businesses, such as Stagecoach, which has already had great success in transforming what seemed to be tired old transport companies through a new approach to operations and marketing. Companies such as GNER compete on the London–Edinburgh route with British Airways, British Midland and the low-cost EasyJet. All over the world, low-cost airlines are springing up.

EasyJet was launched in October 1995 by Greek shipping magnate Stelios Haji Ioannou. It aimed to replicate the US success of similar airlines. Its marketing strategy focuses on very low pricing. Costs have been minimized. Over 70 per cent of seats are sold via the Internet. Passengers pay by credit card, receive a booking number, and turn up and fly. EasyJet uses highly efficient information management processes – for example, all external correspondence is scanned in and e-mailed to the appropriate person. The economics are simple, and shown in Table 16.1.

The resulting price is often around a third of scheduled airlines. Prices rise closer to departure dates, rather than the opposite. Of course, the risk was attached to the launch advertising cost, which accounted for 25 per cent of EasyJet's initial capital. Since that time other low-cost airlines have launched, including standalone subsidiaries of major airlines (eg GO, from British Airways – later offered for sale).

Price versus premium, leisure versus business

In all markets, the long-term outlook is for a range of suppliers, ranging from the cut-price to premium suppliers whose focus is on making travel seem less like getting from origin to destination, and committed to the idea of adding value to the basic experience. As travel is

Table 16.1 Economics of low-cost airlines

Category of Saving	Amount Saved
No travel agents	10% to 20% of costs
No tickets	£1 per passenger
Flying from Luton rather than Heathrow	£10 per passenger
No meals	£5 per passenger
Simple computing and accounting	£3.50 per passenger

highly income-elastic, more and more people will travel more frequently, making room for both premium and low-cost suppliers. Of course, yields will continue to fluctuate with recessions and with temporary adjustments of capacity to demand. But competition to provide high levels of service to business travellers will continue, eg BA's individual-cabin-based First Class, its arrival lounges and Business Class beds, Virgin's seamless Business Class travel experience.

It is critical for travel operators to decide whether their prime basis for competition is price or quality, simply because consumers in all sectors do not react very well to confusion. The uncertainty about which basis to use is reflected in rapid changes in strategy among newer (and sometimes older) players. Pricing strategy is key, but loyalty marketing is coming to the fore.

Technology in flight

It is not so long since many airlines were looking to differentiate their service – especially to higher-value customers – by the in-flight experience. The lack of success in this area, due to technical problems, has turned this dream into something of a nightmare. However, most airlines have been through this nightmare and are developing a steadier approach.

In-flight entertainment (IFE)

IFE was once billed to be the great differentiator between competitive airlines, between classes within an airline, and between airlines and other forms of transport. However, problems with IFE and communications systems have been severe – particularly in the area of interactivity. Carriers such as BA, Virgin Atlantic, Northwest Airlines and United had to work hard to make the systems they bought actually work. But the suppliers of these systems now need more in-service systems to help iron out problems, leading to the risk of IFE maintenance interfering with maintenance of the plane – not a happy scenario. Also, airline marketers committed the sin of believing suppliers and ignored their engineers' warnings. However, all airlines still believe in the dream of interactivity – which allows flyers to control IFE services rather than just experience them.

The recent increase in complexity of IFE systems and the virtual lack of technical standardization has made it hard to build and maintain robust IFE products. For example, on the Boeing 777, the aircraft design incorporates 4 million lines of software code, of which 2.5 million are for IFE. The main victims have been carriers that bought earliest.

Interactive services are being led by video-on-demand (VOD) – which allows passengers to watch any movie they wish whenever they wish, with normal VCR functions such as freeze, restart and rewind. Research still shows passengers give high-quality films top priority. After VOD the most popular choice is computer games, eg Nintendo. These are very popular and entertain children small and large, but they find it hard to match what is available on home computers. However, in-flight experience will have to mirror consumers' home entertainment experiences. Business travellers want either to work, eat, interact or sleep, and now much emphasis is being placed on in-flight Internet and telephone usage and computer recharging, with live sporting and news coverage also important.

Virgin Atlantic's IFE is highly appealing to the leisure traveller, despite the lack of games which near the PlayStation standard; the ability to present a consistent service provides a high degree of reduced stress to leisure travellers, particularly those travelling with their family. This reduction of stress is key in the leisure sector – most people view travelling alone as a business traveller as a reasonably comfortable experience, but stress levels increase hugely travelling with one's family. Virgin understand this and reduce such stress by providing good IFE service in all cabins and other complementary services.

Regionalization

In the US market, air transport has been likened to bus transport: it is part of everyday life for most business people, and the choice of carrier is dominated by schedule and (for some) price, though the greater intensity of competition ensures that prices are much lower per mile than elsewhere in the world, making price less of an issue in choice. Of late, American and United have introduced a greater pitch in economy, and power sockets for laptops to plug into. They and Northwest have also introduced more baggage carry-on facilities. It is very clear that a low-cost 'bus'-type service is no longer enough to distinguish a company in this marketplace. Business travellers demand value differentiators.

In the United States, regional airports are of much greater importance than in the rest of the world. The development of hub and spoke operations all over the United States has allowed internal flyers to reach a much greater variety of destinations without having to transit at a major international hub. Regional air travel is increasing very fast. Hub by-pass and similar traffic is growing at 12–15 per cent per year compared to the 3 per cent of transcontinental traffic using major hubs.

This greater variety of access points to air travel poses a problem for CRM, in particular for service differentiation at point of contact. A frequent flyer might pass through the hub dominated by a major international airline rather infrequently (ie only when flying inter-nationally). Therefore, if an airline wishes to use recognition, lounge services and similar techniques to manage frequent travellers, it must make sure that these are implemented in a much greater number of airports. However, the economics of this are problematic. The automation of the ticketing process and the emergence of lounge service providers may make this easier. In fact, the break-up of the service value chain (see below) provides many opportunities as well as threats for the management of the frequent traveller.

Today, these regional flights are provided by a very large number of small regional airlines. But the number is falling. Of course, some regional airlines are also international carriers, or linked with them through franchising or code-sharing, allowing passengers to accumulate frequent flyer miles.

In Europe (and particularly in the UK), traffic at regional airports is growing very fast, partly driven by the increased national demand for tourist travel and therefore the increased viability of a less centralized approach. Flag-carrying airlines which tend to dominate the slots at the major international airports are facing competition from lower-cost airlines linking up with other national carriers to prove much more cost-effective options which include a transfer. The One World and Star Alliances are gradually including more and more members – regional and international. This means that the frequent flyer in certain locations now has many more options as to how to get from A to B. But it also means that a new player has emerged in the market – the regional airport itself, which has its own interest in generating traffic.

There are strong general factors that favour these regional airports, such as:

- high income elasticity of travel, combined with good medium-term income forecasts;
- increasing propensity to travel of the 'post-war bulge', partly due to experience as frequent business travellers (currently growing at an annual rate of 4 per cent);
- incorporation of air travel as a key promotional benefit in many consumer and business marketing schemes;
- strengthening economic situation of ethnic minorities in certain locations with a high propensity to visit their families overseas;
- general expectation that airports form an attractive part of the whole journey, due to improved worldwide airport quality, in design and retail aspects.

In the UK, there are many general factors that now favour regional airports outside the UK's South East over the London or South Eastern airports. These include:

- Lower costs than in South East England.
- Limitations to airport capacity in South East England.
- Worsening surface communications to/from South East England (with the exception of rail links, which are generally improving over the long term, eg the developing Gatwick, Heathrow and Stansted Express airport links around London, now likely to be supplemented by the cross-rail link direct to the City of London).
- High additional travel and parking costs for customers travelling from outside London.
- In addition to the objective reasons for local travel there may additionally be a natural affinity to travel locally, or expressed another way, a natural aversion to London-based travel. This could be complemented by those who feel that small is beautiful – which for many frequent travellers converts into quick entrance and exit from the airport.

- The general neglect of regional airport marketing by the main protagonists.
- The development of freight centres and out-of-London locations.
- The fact that Heathrow Terminal 5 and Gatwick second runway decisions have been delayed, while the Manchester regional airport has recently added another runway and terminal space.
- Improving services which 'hub' regional flights through nearby major airports, including Amsterdam (KLM), Paris (Air France) and others.

Of course, each regional airport also has parallel weaknesses (eg a shared weakness is the general lack of ability to maintain schedules during fog – a consistent and efficient service is a strong requirement of business travellers). But as low-cost air travel becomes more common, it will be increasingly difficult for surface routes to compete, with the main constraint being the availability of jet travel.

If in broad terms the above view of the opportunity for airport marketing is accepted (and the marketing experience of Luton would confirm this), then successful marketing of regional airports is not going to be a question of 'finding things to do'. It will be more a question of professional development of the most cost-effective strategies and pursuit of these strategies with aggression, commitment and speed. This will also result in the creation of a 'countervailing power' to the power of the consolidating package tour companies and the major airlines (premium and low cost). Tour operators, regional travel operators and airlines could work with regional airports to generate traffic in the same way as a manufacturer would support a local store opening or seasonal event. Increasingly, it will be the role of the regional airport to 'deliver' the demand for air travel to airlines, tour operators, and freight companies. The eventual aim of regional operators is to get travel operators to bid for the region's travellers via the airport, rather than the airport having to solicit travel operators to get them to transport people and freight. This positioning of regional airports will, of course, be helped by deregulation.

The same arguments will apply to regional airlines. The targeting of specific local communities (eg particular industries, ethnic groups) will become the basis for building resistance to the loyalty marketing efforts of national airlines and airports.

However, national airlines will respond strongly to this threat, as they mostly have a strong network of regional offices, customer and trade databases which cover most current and future frequent travellers, and (in some cases) sales force coverage. But, as in most other industries, their difficulty will come through the problems national companies have in dividing their competitive focus between regional and international competitors.

UK airports are also the fastest-growing retail areas in the UK. The relevance, and changing role of airports is demonstrated by this phenomena.

DELIVERING SERVICE INTERNATIONALLY

Managing the high-value customer for travel services over an international network poses specific problems. This is for a number of reasons.

First, there is a growing awareness of the big differences that exist on both sides of the market – customers' behaviour and expectations and suppliers' performance. Even within countries, customers are very different – just ask a frequent business traveller about the difference in the behaviour of service staff between London and Manchester, Milan and Naples, Berlin and Munich, Paris and Marseilles! Add the inter-country differences and you really do have a pot-pourri of behaviour. Here are some examples:

- In one country (UK?) looking people in the eye is encouraged, in another (Italy?) it may be considered rude.
- In one country, people use very roundabout language (France?), in another they are direct to the point of abruptness (Germany, Israel?).
- In one country, people prefer to use first names (United States?), in another no names at all (France?).
- In one country, the time taken to deliver a service may be less important than how the customer is cared for during waiting than in others.
- In one country (UK?), airline passengers trust their luggage to the baggage handling system, while in another (Italy?) passengers try to maximize the amount taken on board, and are happy to sit with their feet on it rather than put it in the hold, relying on a shouting match with stewardesses to achieve their goal. Elsewhere (some parts of the United States), passengers will wrap their luggage in cling film to prevent it being tampered with by baggage handlers.
- In the United States people carry on the maximum amount of baggage allowed, this is due to the pace of life, and the distrust in the baggage handling service which universally exists.
- In one country, customers don't mind standing in the rain and cold waiting for service (UK?), in another they do (France – even Disneyland?).
- In one country (UK?), customers like attentive service, while in another (Australia), customers prefer laid-back service.
- Most importantly, in some countries the idea that a customer has rights is much more firmly established than in others – in the minds of both customers and suppliers! The very idea of filling in a customer questionnaire may be seen as fulfilment of a hidden agenda.
- Privacy is a key issue. IBM and other majors have recently appointed Customer Privacy Officers.

Customers resident in one country will bring their service expectations to other countries. If they buy or use a particular product or service in several countries, they may expect some consistency of standards (eg people from countries where bartering is a way of life expect to haggle in other countries where that is not the custom).

Developments in telecommunications and delivery services have made it easier for service to be provided from one location to many countries. For example, some companies, including airlines, now use a European call centre to deal with service queries, with native speakers of different languages operating from one location.

Developments in broadcast media – particularly cable and satellite services – mean that many consumers can be reached with international service messages (branding, service access). But these media also generate international service expectations. For example, service promises for courier companies establish a benchmark by which local offices are judged. This applies not just to time guarantees, but also to image and customer care issues.

Note that these developments affect relations with internal and trade customers as much as final customers. In many cases, the boundary between these categories of customers is blurred – particularly in international trade, where the use of third party distributors and service providers is the normal route to market.

What is international service?

International service is just one step in the evolution of service. We use the definitions of service in Table 16.2 (see over).

Airlines' international service

For the international traveller – particularly for the most frequent traveller, who may be 'in the silver tube' as often as 200 times a year – there is no doubt that service differentiation has been the key to the battle for custom. There is also no doubt that the honours for international service success have gone to those airlines that have decided *which* customers they want to deliver top-class international service to. While BA has done well by focusing on the needs of the older frequent business traveller (eg in the arrival lounge – which is now being matched by others, including Virgin, Air Canada and AA), Virgin has also succeeded by focusing on the in-flight requirements of the new generation of travellers.

This success demonstrates a more general point: success tends to go to companies that decide who their best customers are, and concentrate on recruiting them, retaining them and giving them the best service. In an international service environment, this is often harder. Customer databases and other relevant information systems and the associated relationship management policies are often organized nationally, making it hard to identify

Table 16.2 Definitions of service

Service Type	National	Multinational	International
To Whom?	Customers who experience service in one country only, from company supplying only in that country	Customers who experience service in one country only, from company supplying in several countries	Customers who experience service in more than one country
Examples	Many customers of small firms Many consumer services (eg retail, financial services, utilities), though this is changing	Customers of multinational consumer goods companies	Users of international travel and communications – telecomms, air travel, hotels, car hire, courier, freight Users of services of several different national subsidiaries Customers who are multinational businesses and buy from their suppliers' local subsidiary
Main Competitive Issues	Identify service needs of local customers Monitor competitors' service standards Deliver better service than local competitors Monitor risk of entry from new companies and other industries and countries, and likely changes to service standards	As for national, plus... Develop competitive advantage by transferring (where appropriate) best practice from other countries and (where possible) by exploiting economies of large-scale provision (eg purchasing, inventory management) Overcome inertia often imposed by local employment laws and practices	As for multinational, plus... Identify international service needs of customers Monitor international competitors' service standards Deliver better service than international competitors Strive hard to achieve consistency (difficult when managing different culture, often remotely)
Focus of Service Delivery	Full range of techniques – systems, standards, recruitment and training, etc – used to attune delivery to customer needs	As for national, plus... Head office may focus more on whether methodology being followed and whether right infrastructure exists	Very strong focus on how people from different cultures handle people from different cultures Measurement focuses on customers' perceptions of differences in delivery between countries

best customers, let alone manage them. However, in the airline industry – international by nature – systems and policies have been designed to cope with the international user. The frequent flyer/loyalty scheme is of course the key. Here, it is interesting to note that the US approach focusing mainly on reward has not been imitated by the leading European contender, BA, which has focused more on service differentiation. However, because facilities-based differentiation (lounges, privileged check-in) can be constrained by airport provision, there is still a strong focus on in-flight service provision (eg via staff behaviour, use of customer information). Of course, in some countries (eg Germany), rewarding customers for flying frequently is limited by legislation, and this should put the focus even more strongly on service differentiation. One of the big issues for airline loyalty schemes is the change from an earn culture, where what is really required is a spot-early and reward culture. Loyalty is a two-way street, not something a customer should be compelled to demonstrate before reward takes place.

Hotel chains

These companies have been working hard to provide excellent international standards to their best customers. The best chains have achieved high standards by 'sticking to their knitting', and focusing on the needs of the international market. This consists of not only the individual international traveller, but also multinational businesses that require guaranteed standards (availability, quality, etc) at negotiated rates. Their links with airlines and car-hire companies have helped them in the area of frequent users, via cross-referencing of customer databases. Another development in the US hotel market is that the product has been compartmentalized, similar to the airlines introducing a forth class. The rooming industry has generated new property themes to appeal to different perceived segments. It transpires there are plenty of overlaps, but that is not a major issue. (One example is Marriott, where properties are ranked as follows: Marriott Hotels and resorts; Renaissance Hotels and resorts; Residents Inn Spring Hill suites; Towne Place Suites; Fairfield.)

Car-hire companies

This represents one of the great successes of international service systems. Operating through a variety of ownership structures, the major US-based car-hire providers such as Hertz, Avis and Alamo have used systems, procedures, staff recruitment and training to define standards that the international traveller can rely on wherever he or she hires a car. Of course, this service has a cost, reflected in the premium paid for the top international brands. But once again, the frequent user (personal or corporate) is concerned to obtain good service and value for money, not the lowest price. It is no surprise that these US providers have invested heavily in branding, to ensure that potential customers feel certain that they will get the promised level of service.

Interestingly, the principle of focus on best customers has been used by companies like Eurodollar, which specializes in the fleet hire market, to carve their way into a market formerly dominated by Hertz and Avis. The service package provided by Eurodollar focuses strongly on value for money and information systems, providing customers with the benefit of improved management of hire costs. Alamo has focused on retaining high-value customers (based on past rental), using information systems which provide information on customer value to office staff, enabling them to offer improved service to these customers. Hertz has now introduced an Elite service, which appears to be targeted at high-worth customers.

Consumer credit and charge cards companies

Much of the international service focus of credit and charge card suppliers has been on the international business traveller, but the focus is now moving to the leisure traveller – the true mass market. For although consumers travel abroad much less frequently than their business counterparts (typically once or twice a year in Northern European states rather than between 10 and 100 times per year for the business traveller), the numbers are much larger. (Note that in the United States the sheer size of the domestic leisure market makes international travel a relative rarity.)

The most basic international service proposition is that large numbers of outlets should accept the card, and that it should be usable in enough cash machines. For new credit cards, delivery of this is largely down to partnerships with existing merchant services providers. Beyond this, the service provided is largely an emergency one, sometimes associated with the insurance provided with the card. In some cases, this is best delivered by a local representative, who may be a national of the tourist's country, or at least someone speaking the language fluently and thoroughly versed in the issuing country's culture. Here, the companies whose initial focus was on corporate charge cards (eg American Express) may have a competitive advantage. Until recently, this was outweighed by issues such as value for money when the card is used domestically, but the use by American Express of a very attractive loyalty scheme may tilt the balance in favour of such a card for the more frequent leisure traveller.

Do you need the same standards everywhere?

The above example notwithstanding, the answer to this is clearly no. Each country and customer type should be treated like a different market segment, as far as is possible.

International travellers expect the same standards of treatment in the air, at the hotel or at the car-hire branch, so for these services, achievement of standard levels is important. However, travellers are not completely unaware of cultural differences. International travellers are on the whole a fairly sophisticated breed. They are aware that service depends upon people. They probably do not expect a company to deliver the same standard of service in Moscow and London.

Most service market research shows that on the main dimensions of service (time, quality, etc) customers can differentiate between the following levels of service.

Desired

What customers would really like to experience. The best level of relevant experience that the customer has received often determines this. 'Relevant' is used because it may not be the same type of service that the customer takes the benchmark from. The benchmark may be taken from a company which the customer uses frequently. For example, the level of service received from a retailer may determine desired level of service from a utility. This is called the parallel industry phenomenon.

Expected

What customers expect, given their knowledge of local conditions and their experience of service in local and other conditions. Here, the expectation may be based on experience with a local company from a parallel industry, or even in a 'parallel country' – a country perceived by the customer to be at a similar level of development (eg in terms of economy, competition, service practice).

Minimum acceptable

What they expect from the company, given the local constraints (eg staffing, laws) they think it operates under. This is, if you like, the realist's view. Service below this level may lead to loss of business – if the customer has a choice!

Remember, it is your *target* customers' views that are key – you are not trying to meet the desired levels of service of all customers. Research is an absolutely vital input to setting service standards. In setting these standards, you may find it useful to complete the matrix shown in Table 16.3.

Don't forget that what you aim to achieve is part of your branding, and what your branding should be is determined by the needs and expectations of your customers. The ultimate branding choice that you have to make is whether you are offering: 'Best of British' or American, etc; or 'When in Rome'.

Table 16.3 Matrix of service standards

	Minimum Acceptable	Expected	Desired
Standard relative to best local/parallel country competitor for your target market			
Standard relative to best international competitor			

Our recommendation is that if your research shows that your service standards are generally better than those that prevail in the country concerned, start with the 'Best of' approach, as you'll find it easier to get your staff behind the idea. But note that 'Best of' doesn't necessarily mean 'Copy of'.

Management processes

So far, we have discussed international service standards in general terms, without specifying what we mean by 'standards'. There are several ways of interpreting the term, as follows.

Detailed performance standards

These are standards which specify precise performance parameters (eg time to answer the phone, time to reach the customer or complete a service, customer satisfaction ratings). These standards are usually required where a high proportion of your target customers are international customers who buy centrally and expect the same service standard anywhere in the world. These standards may be determined through research, and may occasionally be built into customer contracts.

Framework of standards

A framework stipulates that in each country, standards will be set for certain named performance parameters, but the standard set will vary according to local conditions. This is appropriate where your service is being delivered under very different conditions, and where customers will expect these conditions to lead to variations in service achievement.

General principles

This is the most 'relaxed' approach, where an international headquarters lays down certain principles of service, but the performance parameters and target levels are set locally. This would be appropriate where local conditions vary so much that even identifying service parameters centrally would be inappropriate.

In general, as a company moves more towards true international service delivery, and as its customers become more internationalized, so it moves from setting general principles to setting detailed operating standards.

The evolution to international service

Many companies start by providing national service. The move to multinational and/or international service is normally evolutionary, and determined by the extension of the company's activities into other national markets. But for some companies, the move is necessarily very quick (eg a new international courier company). To facilitate this move, international distribution techniques are used. Local agencies (franchised or full third party distribution), working to internationally set standards but within local cultures and employment laws and practices, often provide the best route to international service provision, and is a key reason for the success of many US-based fast-food chains, such as McDonald's.

Cloning is a new variation on this theme. This technique, where a company in some respects takes on the identity of another, is increasingly used in the airline industry. Here, it may take the form of route code-sharing, but also use of other systems, branding livery and training. BA is using this technique to raise the service standards of the various companies tied to it via shareholdings or partnerships. Smaller airlines with larger business partners may also use this technique to absorb some of the risk of taking on staff in other countries.

Transferring success

There is no doubt that successful practices can be transferred. The route to successful transfer is the classical service management route of focusing on standards, procedures, systems and – most important of all – people (recruitment, training and motivation), while making allowance for local cultures, laws and economics. The transfer does seem to be relatively one way, with a few stunning exceptions. That one way is from the United States (and increasingly from the UK) to continental Europe and the developing world. In particular, in Europe, restrictions on direct marketing practice inhibit companies from following up service individually by writing to their customers to solicit feedback, to support redefinition of service requirements.

However, setting and managing service standards are not enough – the total service concept must be kept under review. Remember that the most threatening international service concept is usually part of a total business concept designed to be rolled out across the world. Successfully rolled-out international standards are determined by the culture of the country of the parent company, and of course the specific culture of the parent company itself. This company culture will include:

- attitude to customers;
- procedures and systems for managing them;
- attitude to and procedures for motivating staff and measuring success.

Rolling out an international service approach therefore depends upon successful cultural transfer. This usually requires managers to be trained 'back at base' or 'missionary managers' to be sent out to establish strong service practices in the 'outposts'. The latter approach, though more expensive, is often the only feasible route, particularly if the cultural gap is very wide. Training 'back at base' is all too often forgotten. Worse, it may simply be an attempt to achieve the impossible – a virtual head transplant! Many companies forget that this is impossible with current medical science!

THE TREND TOWARDS CORPORATE TRAVEL MANAGEMENT

Given the very high costs of travel for some companies, travel management companies have developed to 'neutralize' travel suppliers' marketing policies and save companies money when it comes to business travel by tracking spend and negotiating deals. Well established in the United States and Europe, they are now extending their influence to Asia. The three biggest companies are American Express International, Carlson Wagonlit Travel and Rosenbluth International. Travel management companies claim they can save a company up to 30 percent on its overall travel bill, as well as carrying out day-to-day booking and administration tasks.

BREAKING UP THE AIRLINE FREQUENT FLIER VALUE CHAIN

As with most service industries, the myth that direct control over the whole value chain is the best way of providing service is beginning to be exploded. The airline value chain never was anywhere near 100 per cent integrated. As we have seen above, travel agents and airports have always been major independent agents. But the process has a long way to go. New entrants have focused on providing directly only those elements of the value chain that they feel differentiate their service from others – the rest is outsourced. Table 16.4 gives an indication of some of the relationship management outsourcing possibilities open to airlines for their frequent flyers.

CONCLUSION

This chapter has identified a number of very strong competitive pressures on travel service suppliers, including multiplication of low-cost offers, stronger competition amongst high-value providers, greater variety in airport offers, stronger international service standards, and tougher management of travel costs. It is not surprising to find that airlines (and other service providers) have increasingly turned to frequent user programmes to retain their customers.

Table 16.4 Relationship management outsourcing opportunity areas

Value Task	Outsourcing Opportunity	Strengths of Outsourcing	Weaknesses of Outsourcing
Outbound promotions using media – advertising, direct mail, telemarketing Response management and fulfilment	Airline develops strategy and brief, leave implementation to promotional agencies	Used specialist expertise rather than airline generalists Usually much tighter control over costs and performance parameters Better results measurement	Possible proliferation of agencies Poor management on client side can lead to high costs and poor results Branding rules may not be observed, unless very tightly controlled Easier for conflicting mailings to take place, particularly if multiple agencies Possibilities of poor data transfer, unless very tightly controlled Loss of strategic advantage if agencies fired and then work for competitors
Customer recruitment	Work with business partners (eg other value chain participants, business partners – eg hotels, car hire, financial services, telephony, loyalty scheme partners, eg retailers) to develop joint customer recruitment strategy	Much lower costs of recruitment More knowledge of customers at time of recruitment, enabling airline to discriminate better between true present or future frequent flyers and the rest	Requires very tight agreement about rules and rights – who has right to promote to customers Possible drowning of own messages amongst those of partners Possible brand compromise
Customer data management	Use computer bureau to manage data Systems company/ software to analyse and predict customer behaviour	Good for batch processing of data Obtain best analytical expertise	Possible (though much rarer today) problems in managing data (delivering to, receiving from) at point of customer contact
Loyalty scheme design and management	Develop and then contract to third party, or join pre-existing affinity scheme	Scheme management requires special expertise, which some third party suppliers now have	Difficulty of integrating external scheme management with internal data flows (especially transactions, customer service)
Booking Ticketing Check-in Luggage handling Boarding	Leave entirely to third parties	Cost savings (though these are diminished the more the process is automated)	If not tightly linked to operational systems, eg yield management systems, possibly worsening of financial and service performance
Lounge	Already rented, but use of common lounge viable. Can be separated from frequent flyer benefits by payment	Good for airlines with low presence at a particular airport Saves costs	Poor branding Poor control of which customers use lounge (major benefit of lounge is customer selection)

Table 16.4 *continued*

Value Task	Outsourcing Opportunity	Strengths of Outsourcing	Weaknesses of Outsourcing
Merchandise sales (duty free, promotional)	Promotional merchandise can be contracted out to fulfilment house In-flight duty free can be rack-jobbed	Better control of flows and costs	None
Traffic control	Already third party	Safety	Reliance on skills and standards of operators from all over the world
Aircraft design and ownership, including IFE	Design already largely third party, but with strong customer involvement, especially in IFE and seat design Ownership – can be entirely third party through leasing Franchising	Saves costs Economies of scale Allows exploitation of lower-cost options while minimizing investment	Weaker differentiation
General customer service – in flight, ground Complaints management	Staff can be contracted rather than employed	Lower costs	Standards will fall unless training, monitoring and control are strong

17

The use of CRM by airlines

Merlin Stone, Dania Spier, John Mullaly, Jonathan Miller, Doug Morrison and David Selby

This chapter concentrates on CRM in the airline business, investigating further some of the issues raised in Chapter 16.

INTRODUCTION

In some ways, frequent flyer schemes have attracted too much attention from the marketing world. The marketing of successful airlines focuses mainly on:

- Product – having the right routes at the right times.
- Capacity planning – having enough capacity on these routes.
- Yield management – releasing the capacity to the highest bidders as the time of departure of the flight approaches.
- Customer service – ensuring that *all* customers experience good levels of service, irrespective of the class they are flying in and their relationship with the airline.
- Branding – creating and sustaining an image of reliability, quality and service, occasionally with a 'cultural' twist. Branding is, of course, not simply a question of advertising – it depends heavily on every visible attribute of the airline and every customer experience.

CRM is only one way of managing frequent flyers. Frequent flyers have certain service expectations, tend to fly in certain classes, and on certain routes. So frequent flyers can be managed by redesign of classes, rescheduling, and redesigning overall service levels. However, CRM has come to the fore as an additional weapon in the marketer's armoury. Frequent flyer schemes, invented by the American airlines, have developed into sophisticated processes for managing those customers who have the highest value for airlines – typically the frequent business flyer.

The importance of the frequent flyer

Frequent flyers provide a high proportion of most airlines' income (the proportion is, of course, determined by the definition of frequency), and an even higher proportion of the profit. But flyers do not suddenly become frequent. Frequent flyers are mostly business flyers, and most start by occasional flying. Then they move into a job that requires more frequent flying. The task of the airline is then to ensure that it gives them good service and develops and retains their loyalty. At the same time, the airline needs to treat 'low flyers' reasonably well, because one day they may become true frequent flyers. Also, as the customer starts flying less often, he or she is more likely to be better off and start leisure flying, so the airline would still like to retain this person's business, even if the now less frequent flyer cannot be accorded all the service privileges he or she was formerly.

The needs of the frequent flyer

Most airlines have carried out studies of frequent flyers and/or business travellers, and their findings match well with those of market research organizations. The typical hierarchy of needs of the business flyer reads as below (though the ordering varies slightly with frequency and type of flying and age).

Reputation and recommendation

Reputation, branding and reliability are closely associated. For unfamiliar routes, recommendation from peers is important.

Safety record

Certain airlines have a very strong reputation, while others are seen as slightly questionable. Sometimes this is associated with perceptions of the airline's national culture.

Choice of airport

This is becoming more important.

Lounge access and segregation

These are important particularly for the more frequent flyers, on longer-haul flights, where the flyer is not travelling hand-baggage only and therefore likely to have checked in earlier. The comfort of the lounge itself is often not as important as the achievement of segregation from tourist travellers. This also applies to the choice of flight itself, as a flight with very few business travellers and a large number of tourist travellers is seen as very different from one with the proportions reversed, particularly in smaller aircraft, where it is harder to achieve total segregation.

Direct flight

The shorter the time abroad, the more likely this is to be important. However, in many cases, indirect flying is associated with a one-off travel pattern. There are signs that flyers from regional airports which are developing guaranteed transfers at certain hubs (eg Stansted Amsterdam) are getting used to the idea that it is more convenient to fly from a local airport and change than go to a major airport for a direct flight.

Convenient times and connections

These are particularly important for shorter flights, as frequent flyers often do day trips for flights of less than two hours, and require an early flight out and a mid-evening flight back. Where a transfer is necessary, the connection time is key.

Ease of check-in

This is particularly important at major airports, where business travellers hate standing in queues with large numbers of tourists at any part of the processing cycle.

Advance check-in

For short flights, business flyers want to be able to turn up a short while before the flight to a guaranteed seat.

Guaranteed booking

As a corollary of the above, they also do not want to lose their seat.

Safe, fast baggage handling

This is still a major issue for business flyers, who usually see waiting for baggage as the most stressful part of a flight, particularly into a major national airport, where they may have to wait some time, while someone is waiting to pick them up. This is a source of advantage to regional airports, which usually achieve quicker processing.

A comfortable seat

A key issue where premium seats have carried all other benefits except larger more comfortable seats.

In-flight entertainment

Less important than most factors, but becoming more important on long haul. Business class travellers are coming to expect enhanced IFE without charge.

Cuisine

This is still important, especially on longer flights.

National carrier

This is becoming less important in many places, as leading international carriers establish stronger branding.

Previous experience

This is more important for older frequent flyers.

Frequent flyer benefits

This is of mixed importance – research shows that the market segments into those who are avid collectors, and those who are largely indifferent.

Special offers

Special offers are not very important, but may be important if the flyer is taking his or her family on a trip.

Cheap fares

These are important mainly for younger flyers, but may be important to people from small businesses. However, the latter are often either passing on the cost to their customers, or like to fly in higher-class cabins because of the implied status.

Of course, not all customers want all of these features all the time. This is why most airlines are now investing in the systems and analysis to enable them to differentiate their offer according to what each group of customers wants, and where possible to tailor offers to individual needs.

The typical relationship

Let's see how the relationship between the airline and the frequent flyer develops, and some of the issues it involves (see Table 17.1).

Here, we combine our standard definition of relationship phases (see Chapter 1) with life cycle analysis. Although there is no necessary relationship between the two, for products and services which the customer uses for a relatively short period (a few years on average), there must be some relationship. This contrasts with retailing and financial services, where the need is normally lifetime. However, as flying throughout a lifetime becomes more common, airlines will have to consider how a customer re-enters earlier phases of the relationship as behaviour changes (eg with the switch from mainly business to mainly leisure flying).

Table 17.1 Policy options for airlines during the customer relationship cycle

Phase Name and Typical Flying Behaviour	Definition	Customer Behaviour, Perceptions and Issues	Recommendations and Issues for Airline
Targeting Frequency may be very low. Pattern may be random, but more likely to involve repeated routes. Some may be existing flyers who have not joined scheme	Two categories: 1) Customers who have just started flying with a frequency that interests the airline – perhaps even just before this stage. But profile already fits (job, company, age, gender, etc) 2) Existing flyers who have not yet joined	For new flyers, individual customer identifies travel agent who can serve needs. May find way to direct booking. Seeks information about which airline(s) best meet product (routes, schedules) and service needs. New corporate customer will be strongly influenced by secretary, appointed agency and peers, but will seek information in similar way to individual. Some customers will be totally indifferent and treat each decision as independent and based on product and price. Affinity customers will seek out airline that gives relevant affinity benefits (eg those already collecting). Existing flyers may have interest awakened because of change in flying pattern (more frequent flying of relevant routes), or because frequency rises enough to increase saliency of schemes	Get these flyers to identify to airline (eg hand raising) that they are moving into category of interest to airline. Create incentives for customer to contact airline. Make sure that customer knows how to contact airline and incentives for so doing. Initiate individual dialogue – provide relevant information (eg about how to get best out of airline and how to enrol for loyalty scheme). If possible, gather data about likely future value. Corporate sales teams should identify likely candidates. Where possible, corporate sales, agency, charge card and other partnership/data arrangements should be used to identify existing flyers who are not members but qualify

Table 17.1 *continued*

Phase Name and Typical Flying Behaviour	Definition	Customer Behaviour, Perceptions and Issues	Recommendations and Issues for Airline
Enquiry management and recruitment Flying frequency likely to be increasing slowly for most, fast for a few. Most of the sectors are likely to be local or regional. This is also likely to apply to existing flyers, some of whose interest will have been awakened by increasing frequency	Customer contacts airline or airline contacts customer. Qualification criteria may be applied. Customer is recruited as scheme member. Contact details given and additional data is collected	Customer wants to know full details of how to join scheme and then to be guided through joining process. In particular, expects to be asked for information about likely decisions and preferences, as this is increasingly being asked for by other loyalty and promotional schemes. If customer has partner who also flies, customer might expect joint membership to be possible, with accumulating privileges (as per retail schemes)	Need to gather enough data at this stage to profile likely future value. Require absolute clarity about company name and address and, for small businesses, type of business. Recruitment process should be quick and professional, with quick delivery of 'signs' of membership (card, tags, timetable, etc)
Welcoming Takes place immediately after recruitment, so flying frequency should not have changed	Customer feels securely 'on board' in the scheme, ie knows how the scheme works, the benefits it brings, how to contact the airline for different purposes, how to declare membership, how to claim points/miles apparently not allocated, etc	Customer may expect to be treated differently as soon as has joined scheme, and may be disappointed if does not experience some change. If customer contacts the airline for any reason, will also expect some recognition of newness of membership and need to 'learn' the script for dealing with the airline. Customer expects to be able to contact the airline easily, and gets frustrated if contact is hard to make, or if dissatisfied with contact. Will benchmark contact against similar organizations and other airlines. May give business to airlines who are easier to contact. If books through agent, agent's perception of airline may rub off on customer. This can happen at earlier phases)	Welcoming is a critical phase, during which many things can go wrong. But new member is usually of low current and high future value, while best treatment is reserved for those of high current value. Issue is therefore to find way of encouraging development of value and making customer feel that reward is not too far off. Also needs to follow principle that occasional reward is often more powerful than consistent reward (eg occasional upgrade). So need to consider a quick early reward for a new member, together with clear message that such rewards will be more frequent but not automatic if value rises
Getting to know Frequency and distance has started to grow and firm pattern is becoming established. At this stage it is likely to be more medium distance and some longer haul	This is the stage at which the airline gets to know the customer, in terms of a much clearer pattern of usage and needs emerging	The customer develops the sense of being a regular flyer, and feels the airline ought to be understanding his or her needs. But he or she may also feel that there are no clear signs of any tailoring of messages – or indeed even asking relevant questions. The last time data was given was when the customer joined the scheme. The customer expects expression of preferences and interests to be followed by the airline making relevant promotional offers	The customer gives data through flying, responding, complaining and complimenting, but is the airline really using it to understand the customer and meet his or her needs?

Table 17.1 *continued*

Phase Name and Typical Behaviour	Definition	Customer behaviour, Perceptions and Issues	Recommendations and Issues for Airline
Customer development: retention and loyalty The customer's pattern of flying is now well developed. The upward trend in his or her flying frequency will stand out clearly, while customers whose flying frequency tends to fluctuate will also be identifiable Customers who are likely to remain at lower levels will also be clearly identifiable	At this phase, the customer has matured, and has well-established habits and preferences, with each airline having a given place in the portfolio. It is now relatively easy to predict the balance of lifetime value	The customer wants a smooth, no surprise relationship with the airline. He or she expects to be kept informed of all relevant changes to the airline's policy towards customers, and expects to be exposed only to relevant promotions. If customer's pattern of travel fluctuates, he or she becomes very annoyed if demotion takes place, particularly if he or she expects to be flying more frequently later on. Withdrawal of lounge privileges is a particularly sensitive issue for some customers, who expect a period of grace. Some will respond to this by increasing their loyalty	At this stage, attrition is likely to take place only if the customer flies less or switches flying to routes which are less well served by the airline, as brand preferences are well established. However, defined market segments will be vulnerable to being picked off by precise attack, so the airline needs to mine its database frequently to identify whether unexpected attrition is taking place in particular groups of customers
Customer development: up-sell and cross-sell As flyers' business life develops, they develop a pattern of flying more frequently or on different routes, buying additional products and services, eg car hire, hotels, financial services. Increased income will also affect their leisure travel patterns	This is the stage at which customers are increasing their purchasing of travel-related products. This stage may coincide with the retention stage, or take place in the middle of it	As well as the points covered in the retention stage, these customers expect to be kept very well informed of additional relevant products and services. Many expect to be given incentives to steer their additional business to the airline or its business partners	Identifying which customers have the propensity to use more travel-related services (including new flying patterns) Develop plans to offer additional services to these customers, including tactical cross-selling actions

Table 17.1 *continued*

Phase Name and Typical Flying Behaviour	Definition	Customer Behaviour, Perceptions and Issues	Recommendations and Issues for Airline
Managing problems: intensive care This may occur at any phase of the relationship, but is more likely at the beginning, while customers are learning how to manage the relationship, the end, when frequent flyer privileges are withdrawn, or after more than one serious service problem	Customers who have had a serious problem in their relationship with the airline	Disappointed expectations are likely to be the most serious phenomenon here, particularly for airlines with very strong service brands This applies not only to the cause of the problem, but also to the resolution or service recovery process	Identifying customers who are in this phase before it is too late Determining and implementing an action plan before it is too late Discriminating between this group and persistent complainers and potential fraudsters
Managing problems: pre-divorce **As above**	The issue has not been successfully resolved, and the customer is about to switch as much as possible of his or her flying to competitive airlines, or may already have started the process	Customer has decided what to do, but may just be influenced not to by a really excellent service recovery process	As above, but now need to implement with much greater attention to detail and speed
Managing problems: divorce As above	The customer is flying as much as possible with competitive airlines	It is too late to influence the customer, and may not be worth while doing so, particularly if he or she is near the end of the life cycle of flying	Damage limitation, to ensure that this customer does not actively dissuade current and future frequent flyers from using the airline Service recovery must still be carried out
Win-back As above	Customer has frequently experienced the service and product of another airline and found them wanting	Customer is ready to try the airline again	Identifying new flying pattern, and separating these customers from new frequent flyers

History of frequent flyer programmes (FFPs)

The first loyalty programmes were introduced by hotels and demonstrated that travellers were receptive to long-term promotional activities. Rewarding loyalty was not a new concept for airlines. In the early 1970s Southern Airlines introduced a scheme awarding 'Sweetheart Stamps' to repeat passengers. True FFPs originated in the early 1980s in the US market – then and now the most competitive. Deregulation of the industry followed the 1978 Civil Aviation Deregulation Act, which effectively allowed carriers more freedom in pursuing promotional activities. This deregulation and the subsequent heightening of competition is the most often quoted reason for this development.

FFPs rewarded loyal passengers for patronage of a particular carrier by free flights and acknowledgement of status. Free travel is a natural bonus. Travel is a great motivator, second only to money. It is an asset airlines have in abundance. Once the aeroplane has left the ground, an empty seat cannot be sold. Load factors vary, but rarely hit 100 per cent, so using this spare capacity to promote customer retention seems sensible. However, if underlying demand is weak, using spare seats as the foundation for a promotional programme can cannibalize this demand and also lead to lower yield (average price per seat sold), so simply off-loading spare capacity in this way is dangerous. The key is to target this to customers most likely to respond in a way that the airline want, ie not by reducing bookings. American Airlines recognized that the data compiled about individual passengers and their travel habits could be used to improve targeting of promotional campaigns. Data was used to identify the most frequent travellers, who would then receive better treatment, thereby creating a stronger relationship between flyer and carrier.

In most airline schemes, demand for redemption normally follows normal demand. Customers choice of destination is not influenced much by the scheme – so to prevent cannibalization, redemption normally has to be limited to times when spare capacity is highest (ie times when customers do not normally want to fly).

From the American Airlines scheme was born the term 'mileage', meaning the number of miles of free flying the flyer would be credited with. The award system had to be structured so rewards were attainable, but it also aimed to focus benefits on the true frequent traveller. A further objective was to compensate people for inconveniences caused by the hub and spoke system. Despite American Airlines' assessment that their scheme offered a distinct and sustainable competitive advantage due to its unique positioning, within two months TWA, Braniff, United and Continental Airlines had all launched their own versions. The multiple birth of the FFP had occurred.

Development of FFPs

Today there are over 100 FFPs worldwide with extensive partnerships between airlines and also with other travel or non-travel-related goods and services providers, particularly hotel chains, car rental companies and credit card providers. The more frequently a person travels, the higher the number of FFP memberships held. The United States has the largest population of frequent flyers. The long membership guides distributed to customers to explain how to participate in the programme indicate the complexity of today's programmes. Information for frequent flyers is also supplied by various publications including a devoted magazine, *Inside Flyer*, complete with its own Web site (www.insideflyer.com).

FFPs were created to keep customers loyal, due to the accepted wisdom that the cost of acquiring new customers far exceeded the revenues gained from retained customers. Initially, they accorded with some of the best principles of marketing. However, they then proliferated to the point where all major airlines either had their own programme or were part of a joint one. This meant that the FFP rapidly became part of the expected core offer and the only airlines penalized were secondary carriers who did not have the resources or extensive network to support a frequent flyer programme. The FFP has moved from being a marketing concept to promote customer loyalty to an unavoidable cost of doing business.

Evolution of the FFP

Most FFPs now offer many additional benefits apart from free travel and upgrades, but the central feature of most is still more miles for more flying. Travelling in higher classes, such as business class, club class, first class, is encouraged through greater bonuses, and decisions to omit economy class travel from the scheme. Some airlines have segregated the customer base to differentiate rewards according to the value of the individual to the airline. One of the most appreciated benefits is use of an airport lounge, and enhanced service before, during and after the flight.

The British Airways Executive Club is a prime example of such a tiered system, with blue, silver, gold and (invitation only) premier categories awarded offering distinct benefits sets. Inclusion of non-airline partners has extended the breadth and penetration of the programmes. The extent of collection and redemption opportunities has increased, to include hotel chains, car rental companies, long-distance phone calls and credit card companies. An interesting recent change to the BA programme is the decision to award limited mileage benefits to reduced and special fare passengers, perhaps a sign that the airline now recognizes that this segment of its Executive Club membership cannot be completely overlooked.

Effects of FFPs

FFPs operate on the basis that rewarding loyalty results in greater customer retention and therefore greater profitability, yielding additional revenues which outweigh the costs. In this respect, they conform to the best principles of CRM. Earlier reports of the success of FFPs vary. A survey of airline marketing concluded that FFPs boost carrier business by 20–35 per cent. However, as all airlines had FFPs, this implied either that the programmes stimulated much more travel, or that FFPs were an astonishingly effective part of the marketing mix, or that marketing staff overestimated their effectiveness. In practice, it was probably the case that particular promotions within FFPs did achieve good results, and also that the FFP was a more effective way of spending marketing budgets than other ways the airlines had used (untargeted advertising campaigns, supporting the brand or promoting route/price offers).

Initially, FFPs did change travel patterns. The 'corporate mileage junkie' was born. This individual relentlessly pursues extra mileage points by taking unnecessary detours or longer routes. This was advantageous in the United States where the main carriers had switched to a hub and spoke system to increase operating efficiency. Two-for-one offers also received unexpected interest, indicating how travel plans were altered in the search for these benefits. It could be argued that the development by corporations of more stringent control over corporate travel is a response to the effectiveness of FFPs.

Although many frequent flyers are members of programmes, in general surveys show that they rank FFPs after scheduling, punctuality, modernity of fleet, extra comfort and efficiency of check-in. However, though the FFP may not be the prime motivator, the lack of a FFP is a prime deterrent. Some industry experts now believe that airline competition may soon return to more traditional criteria. Though airlines have not paid less attention to their core service offer, FFPs dominate promotional activities. It is difficult to change this without angering many valuable customers and risking their loss. Alternative promotional methods to non-frequent flyers have been considered. This might be a direction airlines may explore in the future.

HOW FFPS WORK

Originally, frequent flyer schemes were just continuity promotional programmes – 'use me more and you'll get free flights'. However, today the game has become much more sophisticated. Broadly, the aim of airline CRM is to identify groups of customers (ideally already on the airline's customer database) who behave consistently enough for them to be monitored and managed. This leads to a focused marketing communications policy (mainly mailing and telemarketing policy) and service differentiation (greater privileges to more frequent flyers). Given the appropriate incentive programme, frequent flyers can be tracked. This is important, because most tickets are not bought directly from airlines, but from travel agents.

The frequent flyer behaviour airlines want to manage

The following section describes some of the key issues arising in this area.

Managing the small business

This includes identifying how many small businesses there are, and then which ones travel, why and how often, whether travel is a substitute for other communication, who they travel to, etc.

Managing the corporate business

Many of the above issues appear, but here we have the presence of corporate travel policy (perhaps fixed by negotiation with a corporate buyer), the approach taken by the booker (in-house agent, secretary) and the behaviour of individuals – as they go through their life cycle (eg more flying until they reach a certain level of seniority, after which their staff start to fly to them, and they fly to more 'senior' locations: flying to overseas HQ from a subsidiary, rather than flying around the subsidiaries).

Managing changes in travelling patterns

As a business grows and diversifies, so its travel patterns change. The best example of this is the large accountancy-based consultancy companies, whose staff are now travelling all over the world on consultancy assignments – usually more frequent, shorter trips than when they concentrated on audit work, which often meant longer stays.

The behaviour that airlines are interested in includes:

- travel frequency – and how it is changing (rising, falling, fluctuating);
- destinations – in particular the mix of national, short-haul and long-haul;
- travel class booked;
- channel used – agent, direct line and the Internet.

How frequent flyers are grouped

Most airlines operate relatively unsophisticated segmentation systems to manage their customers. Typically there are one or two tiers of true frequent flyers, a tier of customers who hold some kind of loyalty card, and the rest. The problem for airlines is that true frequent flyers graduate through the basic level, although at greatly varying speeds. For example, in Europe it is not unusual for a frequent flyer to graduate to very frequent flyer status in just two years. The issue for the airline is how early to offer the service privileges that will make it more likely for the customer to book with them. This decision is conditioned by the accuracy with which a future frequent flyer can be identified from his or her early behaviour.

The more structured the airline is in its approach, the harder it has to work to place customers in the right category. Customers placed in the wrong category either get very angry (if the category is too low) or cost too much to service (because the category is too high). Managers running FFPs are under pressure from their financial directors to extract maximum benefit from minimum cost, and in some cases to continually rejustify the programme.

How airlines manage customers

An additional problem for airlines is the diffusion of marketing responsibility over several groups. Typically, an airline has the following groups involved in marketing and sales.

General sales team

A team ensuring that sales on all routes deliver the right yield – not just the number of seats sold but the average price. In larger airlines, there will be separate sales teams at main locations, responsible for promoting routes connected to that location.

Corporate sales team

This team sells to corporate accounts. This involves negotiating overall deals, perhaps working with in-house travel agents, finding out whether the product or service suits the customer, and distributing privilege cards so that managers get automatic entry to the FFP. The larger the airline, the greater the number of corporate accounts covered.

Yield management

This controls the number and prices of each category of ticket that is released for each flight. This involves using sophisticated forecasting systems and current booking trends to obtain the maximum revenue for each flight, irrespective of the relationship between the airline and the customers on that flight.

Trade sales team

This team will liaise with travel agents and tour operators.

FFP team

This will recruit and manage members.

Product/brand managers

These will develop product identity and maximize immediate and longer-term sales of their particular products. This also involves trying to identify future customer needs (routes, quality, etc).

Marketing communications

Staff are required to maintain the brand and ensure that customers are constantly reminded of routes, prices, etc, including special offers.

Partnership marketing

This is required where the airline makes money from promoting partnership services and products, eg hotels, car hire, travel-related merchandise – or any merchandise. These staff should work closely with many of the above players to ensure partner needs are taken into account in their decisions.

Responsibility for achieving sales success is therefore diffused, and so is the measurement of accountability. Corporate politics are played, whereby one group tries to use another to generate revenue, while avoiding cost.

There is also the problem of where to contact the customer. True frequent flyers are often abroad, and may have more than one base. The ideal is to capture their main domicile on the database, and make communication (eg of frequent flyer points) so valuable to the customer that he or she always keeps the airline updated on address. But of course this does not solve the problem that the customer will still be exposed to many different offers and promotions according to where he or she is travelling.

In very large airlines, the activities of the groups listed above are often poorly coordinated. This leads to individual frequent flyers receiving large numbers of mailings, irrespective of whether their route flying pattern makes them eligible for particular promotions. Also, corporate sales teams may not know exactly how many frequent flyers are members of a large corporation, and what their flying value is.

The problems of the broad distribution of customer management responsibility are exacerbated by two facts about most companies' customer database systems. These systems either do not hold all the data about customers that is needed to manage them; or they make it difficult for the different marketing and sales managers to access the customer information they need in order to make decisions (eg promotional response or usage of partnership services of flyers in a particular corporation).

Competitive emulation

A problem faced by airline CRM departments it is that most of the benefits that they give to customers can be rapidly emulated by their competitors. The key to success therefore is the targeting of these benefits on true frequent flyers and those about to become so. This requires a smart customer database and data mining operations which identify those who are on the way up, and those who are on the way down.

Offer complexity

In order to get frequent flyers to take up the different partner offers, it is crucial for customers to be aware of them. Given the plethora of offers, customers need to be reminded of them not only by mailings, but by a variety of other devices including in-flight magazines and point of sales (check-in, hotel desk, etc). Despite all this, there is some evidence that customer awareness is quite low.

Tracking

Tracking will always be a problem for airlines. Although most airlines have achieved high declaration rates (ie card members declaring their card at time of booking), many customers complain that they declared their card and were not credited with the flight. This means that either it was not registered on the customer database as being a flight by them, or there has been a problem in the system which credits points. Keeping track of members of frequent flyer schemes is also a problem. Frequent flyers tend to be corporate high-flyers and move around and up a lot in companies. Unless the customer agrees to be communicated with at home, there can be quite a problem updating data about them. But if they are communicated with at home, then collecting corporate data about them can be a problem.

Affinity rather than loyalty

Many customers who take the airline frequent flyer card are actually not true frequent flyers, but affinity customers – those who want some link with the airline because they fly occasionally and want to collect the rewards for doing so, particularly if the airline participates in a wider loyalty scheme. The figure can be as high as 50 per cent, which is in line with the number of customers taking retail loyalty cards who are not really frequent visitors. This puts at a premium the database and marketing skills of separating the two kinds of flyer.

Understanding the frequent flyer

Even airlines considered as quite smart when it comes to database management are not very good at integrating market research with the database. So the sampling frame for the research may be taken from somewhere else. The worst practice is that although airline frequent flyers are usually more than willing to give data about themselves, their preferences and attitudes, together with their name, market research agencies believe somehow that getting attributable data in this way is unethical. The rules of the Market Research Society in the UK militate against this anyway.

Private versus corporate benefits

One problem FFP's face, which may become more pressing in the future, is that corporations, which generally finance the business traveller, are becoming cognizant of the benefits accruing to individuals. They may feel the benefits should belong to them, and are keen to reduce the effect of the individual's propensity to prioritize his or her own gain over the company's gain. The distortion caused to travel policies has resulted in a degree of corporate backlash, particularly in the United States where companies are demanding that benefits should go to them. However, some companies still feel that the rewards are good compensation to employees for the time they have to spend away from home. Some airlines allow for this in the design of their programmes, by having a corporate account that is also credited with miles or points. Others do it by having corporate agreements that give cheaper flights if miles are not given. Today, therefore, user companies' objectives need to be integrated into a programme to ensure success.

SYSTEMS THAT SUPPORT FFPS

Most airlines have developed solid systems for managing FFPs. They have in general built on their heritage of big mainframe systems accessible worldwide and interfacing with the consortium-based booking systems. Without these systems, an airline could do no business. This systems frame of mind delivers solid performance. So wherever the frequent flyer is in the world, keying in the card number (or swiping it) will be enough to call up the flyer's details on screen, allowing allocation of seats by preference, and allowing staff to see the status of the flyer.

Airlines do not like to experiment with new systems concepts, and when they try, they burn their fingers (see comments on IFE in Chapter 16). Even the Graphical User Interface is regarded as inferior compared to an old-style character-based screen with an operator skilled in keying in short codes. The number of options are simply too many to be displayed in successions of browse lists: an international airline has millions of products – every date, time, origin, destination, class is a different product. Many airlines are now redeveloping their customer database systems for managing their frequent flyers, but we expect them to continue with their conservative tradition.

Because of this 'go anywhere, know anywhere' approach, the systems that support frequent flyer programmes must be 'industrial strength'. This means that they have to be very reliable. It also means that analysis functions need to be separated from processing functions, as otherwise customer management may be put at risk by analysis taking place. This is one of the reasons why a number of airlines are now considering separating the customer database functions into a data warehouse and a customer management database. Here, the former is used for assembling, cleaning and analysing data, while the latter is used to provide data to the point at which the customer is being managed (eg the airline booking system).

Specific systems requirements for managing frequent flyers are outlined in Table 17.2.

Table 17.2 Focus of systems support in managing frequent flyers

Requirement	Focus
Face-to-face contact	Usually operate through booking and check-in systems. Current focus is on reducing costs by automating this as much as possible and dispensing with paper, although some countries require paper back-up. This automation works best with frequent flyers, who are easiest to train to use the systems (because of their frequency of use)
Call centre	For telesales and customer service queries
Complaints and compliment management	Ensures that all non-sales contacts are managed professionally and meet a promise about response time given in the first contact
Customer satisfaction monitor	Usually based on in-flight questionnaires and/or regular mailings
Yield and value management	Based on releasing capacity at lower prices – requires good forecasting input. Yield management is usually based upon the value of the individual ticket, not that of the customer, and this can cause high-value customers to be refused places on specific flights, even if they have tickets
Data warehouse	To pull together all the data required to analyse and manage customers strategically and operationally
Data mining	To analyse the data in the data warehouse, including the development of predictive models and customer segments
Operational data mining	Deploying and improving sophisticated embedded models which utilize multi-channel data to continually monitor (24 × 7) customer state, make recommendations and give early warnings, also providing the statistical support for promotion targeting
Loyalty management	To accumulate points/miles and manage promotion/demotion
Marketing communications	To manage marketing promotions and interface with the various agencies involved in the process

THE ROLE OF SERVICE DIFFERENTIATION

The aim of many airlines is to individualize service – on the ground and in the air. Many airlines now take extracts from the customer database so that the customer's preferences are known to the cabin crew. But increasingly, the focus is moving to the business flyers' communication requirements. In-flight phones and faxes are available, though expensive. However, as many frequent flyers now have portable computers with modems and are intense users of e-mail, some airlines are providing Internet access. This is relatively cost-effective, and much more so than telephone or fax, as the e-mails can be prepared offline and then sent in a burst. Here, the emphasis will be on ensuring high bandwidth capacity for those frequent flyers whose e-mail system allows high-speed transmission rather than the slow speed available on many landlines. The trail is being blazed by mobile operators, who are already offering high-speed access unconstrained by landlines. This access is also available in lounges.

IFE systems, which have been very problematic because of the complex electronics required, will eventually develop in the same direction. True frequent flyers, flying two to three times a week, and spending an average of two to three hours on the plane and another one to two hours in lounges, could be spending as much time accessing remote communications from airline territory as they do from home.

Individualizing service is not just about communications. The eventual idea is to tailor service in the lounges and in the air – initially to groups of customers and finally to the individual customer. For basic issues, such as seating, smoking and food preferences, the data is already held on most airline frequent flyer databases. Name recognition of very frequent flyers who are flying business or first class is also important. But as IFE becomes more sophisticated, it will be possible to provide customers with access to preferred programmes. Meanwhile, we expect to see selection of magazines to be influenced by reader preferences.

Little real progress has been made in these areas, as companies struggle to master the basics of service. It is the service that is costing more as FFPs mature, while marketing costs tend to diminish as recruitment is no longer the key issue, and retention is mainly through service. The main service cost is, of course, the cost of the lounges, which research for all airlines shows to be one of the principal reasons for scheme membership. The other main service cost is service communication. The more frequent and the more loyal the flyer, the more often he or she expects to communicate with and be communicated with by the airline.

The longer the flight, the more important service is – hence the development of arrival lounges for long-haul top-tier arrivals. For shorter haul, as the flyer is in the place for a limited time, mileage rewards can be relatively much more influential in choice. But this may also be so because regular long-haul flyers accumulate so many miles that they cease to become an important factor in the decision. They may even be top-tier customers for several airlines, so mileage accrues anyway. Indeed, some frequent flyers are very astute managers of their scheme memberships for precisely this reason.

Monitoring customer service for frequent flyers

Delivering the relationship to frequent flyers is one thing – monitoring the relationship is another. The problem of identifying the frequent flyer is normally overcome by membership of the loyalty scheme. But frequent flyers are not always forthcoming in their views about the quality of the relationship actually delivered to them. This problem is compounded if an airline does not have its own frequent flyer scheme.

How airlines value their frequent flyers

Most airlines with mature customer databases define customer value by revenue rather than profit, sometimes overlaid with frequency. Likely lifetime value is not usually used, although this should be the most important criterion for recruiting customers into a closer relationship. Loyalty is usually defined using recent revenues. In-flight questionnaires and other market research data are used to track propensity to recommend and the importance of the frequent flyer scheme. Note that as these schemes are usually integral to airline marketing, it is very hard to answer the question: what would happen to revenues without the scheme?

Lifestyle and other non-flying data tends to be useful to support promotions of non-core products (eg wine) but data on flying is the key data for improving customer lifetime value.

Retention management is practised by some airlines (eg telephoning very frequent flyers when they are about to be demoted). However, in general, the experience is that customers who drop down a tier have either changed their travel pattern so that they are no longer likely to qualify, or have decided to give their business to another airline. Some customers do respond to a call before demotion by a burst of travel.

Customer loyalty

Loyalty – for airlines as for most other products and services – is often defined as share of revenue but is actually a state of mind, and airlines do try to focus on changing and sustaining a particular state of mind, and creating and sustaining a relationship. However, the relationship most customers have with airlines is not necessarily the warm, golf-club mutual type. It can be more like the relationship with a bank – the customer feels that it's worth having a good relationship because he or she is dependent on the bank at certain crucial times. However, there is also a desire to be marked out as privileged, and different. The classic story told in this case is of a frequent flyer whose usual seat on a regular flight was occupied, and who remonstrated with the occupant, only to find this card trumped by one of a higher grade!

Irrespective of how the loyalty is created, airlines are very keen to create advocacy, and try to involve their frequent flyers in the business, to humanize the relationship as much as possible. This is why airlines are careful to ensure that promotions of other products and services are seen by customers as relevant, because otherwise they will disturb the customer's sense of logic.

A particular problem, faced by all relationship marketers marketing to households, is that many apparently infrequent flyers have partners who are very frequent flyers, who fly with them and expect to be treated like them. A related problem is how to identify and manage frequent flyers when they fly with their family on holiday.

Partnership products and services

Airlines are deriving an increasing proportion of their profit from partnership arrangements. Very frequent flyers are very closely correlated with very high-value customers – at the very most no more than 1 in 20 of the working population. Airlines are therefore keen to develop this latent value of their databases. In order to sell the use of their database to business partners, they need to identify which customers – and which types of customer – have the highest propensities to cross-buy. In particular, the aim is to identify customers with the highest future value, and this means identifying customers with a high propensity to cross-buy as soon as they become frequent flyers. Typically, around one fifth of flyers move from infrequent flying to very frequent flying in two to three years, and they do this in their late twenties. Propensity modelling based on data mining and other techniques now enables airlines to forecast exactly which flyers are likely to become very frequent and which are most likely to cross-buy.

The obvious target for cross-selling is travel-related services, particularly car hire and hotel accommodation. However, many flyers have their own arrangements for these services, either through a travel agent or their employer, and propensities to cross-buy can be surprisingly low and unstable. Achieving very high levels depends not only on having enough customers willing to cross-buy, but also on having the right partners. With car hire dominated globally by just a few companies, it's not difficult to succeed in this area. But hotels are a different matter, as there must be enough partner hotels in the right locations in the right countries. So although up to a half of flyers stay in a hotel, the take-up of partner offers is usually very low, usually 1 or 2 per cent. In many cases, the airlines' ignorance of their customers' corporate policy is responsible for this, and in some cases this is due to the classic divide between airline corporate sales teams and the marketing departments running FFPs. Where this interface works, then corporate sales teams can sell partnership deals to corporate buyers.

Perhaps surprisingly, it is offers such as financial services (insurance, credit cards), mobile telecommunications and wine that are very profitable, because these do not depend upon a particular journey. Once known responders are identified, targeting can be very precise, resulting in high profits for the airline and the business partner. The margins available on these mailings are high enough to tolerate quite low response rates, but some campaigns have yielded sales rates of 5 per cent on volume mailings.

The other aspect of flyer behaviour that is becoming increasingly important for airlines to understand is redemption behaviour for frequent flyer points/miles. Information that flyers have redeemed at all is important, because it reveals a propensity to take up promotional offers. But just as important is the type of redemption – (eg merchandise, other travel products) as this reveals the kind of partnership offer these customers are likely to respond to. Unfortunately, some airlines do not coordinate the management of their frequent flyer database with the management of redemption data, so this link is lost. One area of some interest to airlines are the 'gamblers' or game players: those who respond to competition-based promotions. These customers are known to be easy to motivate. They will do the minimum to get a free offer. The key is to find the low-value offer which will turn them on.

CONCLUSION

The travel industry is characterized by rapid change – in customer behaviour, technology and competitive structures – against a background of frequent and sometimes random government intervention. However, the secret of success in customer management seems to be to follow a long-term and consistent policy about which customers are to be managed, and to deploy that policy supported by tried and tested technology.

18

CRM in retailing

Merlin Stone and Chris Field

INTRODUCTION

Management of multi-branch or network businesses face one of today's toughest marketing challenges, namely, how to manage customers profitably and with high customer service standards, when they may turn up at any contact point – branch, telephone, airport, etc.

Let's define the problem. The types of business that face this problem have a large number of points of contact with customers. Examples include: retail outlets (eg for products, such as groceries, or services, such as finance); and network access points, whether in consumers' homes connected to the company's own network, (eg power, water and telecommunications), in service delivery locations (eg a transport network – air, sea, rail, etc), or in location-independent sites (eg call handling centres, or a mailing clearing house).

A particular consumer could be in contact via any of the contact channels the business makes available. A few years ago, when ideas of customer service and customer marketing were in their infancy, that customer might have been subject to the same (possibly low) standard of service and marketing as prevailed for all consumers. This was due to the 'retail culture' or 'utility mindset', which held that every shopper or subscriber (the term 'customer' came into use later!) should be treated equally. This pervaded all policies affecting customers, including:

- IT;
- staff motivation and training;
- physical design of contact location;
- customer service (eg call and queue management);
- marketing communications;
- pricing;
- product or service design;
- access management.

Today, we are more aware of the benefits of keeping our best customers and the costs of losing them. We know it is worthwhile investing to attract high-value customers, if we've got the right proposition for them. We also know that sometimes we should focus attention not just on high-value customers – some of whom may be quite fickle when it comes to brand loyalty – but on middle-value customers who show signs of a propensity to be loyal to our proposition.

So, if we want customers to stay with us, we need to be able to:

- Recognize which customers offer us the best potential.
- Keep them informed of what we are doing for them, and persuade them to continue to keep in touch with us and buy from us.
- Give them the type and level of customer service which is appropriate for them (and possibly not for other customers).
- Reward them for staying with us.

Otherwise, our competitors might seek to attract them away by doing the same thing.

That's all very well in theory, but if we translate these ideas into the world of mass-market retailing or services, we face a number of problems. Some examples are given in Table 18.1.

FOCUSING ON CUSTOMERS YOU WANT

One way to cope with these pressures is to focus marketing, customer service and their associated systems on customers who are likely to yield the most long-term value to the company. This, of course, depends upon:

- how much they are likely to spend;
- the profit margin the company makes on what they buy;
- how likely they are to stay loyal.

Table 18.1 Problems and their effects

Problem	Effects on Customer Management
Need to reduce transaction costs due to competitive price pressures	Focus on speed of transaction rather than effectiveness Less opportunity for customers to give data about themselves which can be used to improve company's offer to them Less opportunity for company to inform customer about products and services Possible 'clinical' approach to handling customers
High staff turnover	Staff disloyalty, and consequent failure to internalize idea of holding on to customers Lack of knowledge of customers and their needs Loss of customer information
Low staff skills	Poor ability to deliver customer service Lack of understanding of requirement
IT systems designed to manage transactions, not customers	No 'single view' of customers, history of their relationship with company, needs, etc Difficulties in cross-selling
Pressures on capacity management, asset utilization, or inventory turnover, causing focus on throughput efficiency rather than customer service	Staff and systems focus on efficiency of transaction, and on processing as many customers as possible per unit of capacity

Whether this is right depends upon whether focusing in this way incurs costs that outweigh the benefits. Some aspects of this can be left to staff, who even in mass-market retail or customer service environments can often recognize loyal customers. But their ability to reinforce the relationship is constrained by the procedures of their company (including tight financial controls). So the UK epidemic of customer loyalty schemes can be seen as management's attempt to create a recognition and reward mechanism that can be managed within mass-market norms of efficiency but delivers some of the customer service benefits of personal treatment.

Many current loyalty schemes fail to live up to their name. Although they require significant marketing and systems investment and – more importantly – create customer expectations about the long-term nature of the relationship with the company, many schemes are poorly planned, researched and evaluated and inadequately or never tested.

Put simply, in many cases, management wants what we call 'half a pound of loyalty', and approaches their marketing suppliers to put together, under very tight time pressure, a scheme which looks respectable. In doing so, management is influenced by their own experiences of loyalty schemes of which they are members (typically airline or charge/credit card – neither of which is the best model for their own consumers), or 'consultants' tales' about what works. Our view is that while management should try to talk to any of their peers who are running such schemes and who are also prepared to be honest about what they have achieved, this will is not enough. In the end, the only sensible approach is to research, design and test an approach that is right for your company's own customers. Deciding to manage customer loyalty is as significant a decision as using a major new advertising medium or distribution channel, and no professional marketer would think about doing these without research and testing.

THE 'CLUB' PHILOSOPHY

In the UK, customer clubs as normally defined are very rare. It is probable that this is because other methods of managing important or high-value groups of customers dominate. There are a number of reasons for this:

- The vibrant strength of the UK direct marketing industry, which has imported the best US direct marketing practice.
- A very relaxed legislative environment.
- Two major media owners – the Royal Mail and BT – which have invested millions of pounds in developing UK direct marketing practice and infrastructure.
- A generally quite advanced marketing community, within an economy where marketing is a relatively respectable and highly paid activity. This represents a turn-around from the two or three decades ago, where marketing was considered a lower-status profession.

The net result of this is that consumers are constantly being offered incentives to show affinity. In very few cases are consumers asked to pay for membership so as to obtain affinity benefits. In most cases, they are asked to transact more frequently.

One of the laboratories for customer facing systems is the high-street retailer. For it is here that what were formerly seen as systems for managing transactions are slowly changing into systems for managing customers. In many high-street retail outlets, at least 50 per cent of customers, and sometimes up to 80 per cent of the value of transactions, are being processed through loyalty schemes, the scope of which continues to grow. Let us review what UK retailers have been doing.

HIGH-STREET RETAILING

For any retail store, the first rule is to generate traffic of spending customers. So any specific targeting strategy is bound to be coloured by this need. This means that initial targeting can be quite crude. For many grocery food retailers, the most important target group is ABC1s, but their clientele are actually quite representative of the population – indeed they must be if a retailer is to achieve dominance. The relationship with customers is based primarily on location and on the retailer's brand – and what the latter implies for product quality, reliability, availability and price. For the major grocery retailers, reliability, quality at a reasonable price, range and availability are key. This is because customers need to know what they're going to get – particularly as far as the product is concerned.

There is also an interesting battle for customer demography in the grocery business. Of course, given parity on merchandise range, price and availability (which on the whole is true), location is the dominant influence on purchasing patterns. This in turn depends strongly on work and travel patterns. The commuting buyer, for example, often drops into a store on the way back from work, to pick up provisions for the same evening. This is particularly true for singles and childless couples. In a major metropolis, where more commuting is by public transport, this pattern will favour the high-street store. In other areas, the out-of-town store may benefit.

As competition using CRM techniques hots up, customers are becoming more choosy and demanding, and retailers will have to respond. However, strong customer service – an essential part of good retail practice – is the cutting edge of retailing, and a card is only one part of this. The stronger the underlying service, the more deeply established loyalty is, and the less the need for a card. The weaker the market and the weaker the retail proposition, the greater the need for a card.

All major retailers are aware that the more value the company supply within the relationship, the more customers will be prepared to be managed within it, ie give information, respond to promotions. With very high margins on financial services, one of the clear goals of some retailers is to make sure that this information includes the vital data needed to target financial services products, thereby saving on the very high promotional costs. Purchasing data itself gives a very strong clue to family income and structure. Added to the data given on store card application forms, this creates a financial service marketer's dream.

But all retailers know that they need to find ways of getting customers to express their needs more clearly. Interestingly, as with shopping questionnaires designed to compile databases, retailers have found that in simple questionnaires with tick boxes, consumers will give lots of information, often for the smallest of incentives – the prize draw is king !

At the other end of the spectrum are the problems retailers have in managing relationships. The obvious area for problems is the product – not having the right product in stock or even in the range. This is followed by scanning and queuing problems – retailers are keen to give service guarantees here, but have found them hard to sustain. Retailers track their performance by measures such as queue lengths, product sampling and mystery shopping. We expect that these measures, applied generically at the moment, will start to focus on the needs of the loyal shopper or card holder. Loyal customers fill their baskets or trolleys fuller, and will only remain loyal if they find that they can get through the till reasonably quickly – hence the use of self-scanning. But the more retailers trust their customers, the more the opportunity for fraud. When one retailer experienced teething troubles with its new loyalty card, it had to promise retrospective crediting of receipts. Security cameras identified that customers in car parks picked up receipts and brought them in for crediting!

Of course, in the end, the key financial performance measure is share of basket of existing customers – customers visiting more often, buying more, and buying more expensively. They will only do this if satisfied with the offer – location, product range and price, layout, service. This is where the costs and benefits of retailing occurs. Costs of managing customers will always be an issue in retailing, so any additional costs (like CRM technology and delivery) have to be justified by improved volume or substitution for other costs. It is the latter which is the key, because it takes some time to determine the effect of loyalty and similar schemes and therefore whether other forms of marketing can safely be reduced in scale. Given the intense competitive pressures, retailers are naturally not keen to experiment at the expense of the bottom line. However, this same competitive pressure has also caused management to fear being left behind their competitors, particularly publicly and under the beady eyes of stock market analysts. Loyalty schemes are very public, they fall into the category of 'every home should have one'. When analysts finally learn to interpret the statistics from loyalty schemes, they might even start asking for them!

TECHNOLOGY AND DATA

Management of scanning is one of the keys to customer service and to the management of loyal customers. However, as in other service environments, true 100 per cent self-service is not far away. In petrol stations and for airline tickets, payment by inserting credit or debit cards already exists, and of course the more the Internet is used, the more we shall see payment with no human intervention. However, the very physicality of supermarket shopping raises problems – the purchase is not of a single item but tens of items. Supermarkets are therefore actively involved in development of radio transmitting tags.

All retailers know that they must focus their IT more on managing individual customers, whether through IT or product and service offer. The latter has already started to change to meet the needs of key target groups of customers and retain them, whether through economy ranges for price sensitive customers and baby changing rooms or through up-market merchandise range innovations, or Internet access.

As retailers start to accumulate more data, they will start to understand the purchasing pattern of individual customers. Of course, this does not mean that they will always try to manage them as individuals. The obvious area where this will happen is in promotional couponing, where customers will receive coupons matched to their purchasing behaviour. Remembering that the key aim of retail marketing is to get customers into the store more often and to spend more, most efforts will be concentrated on this, rather than on fine-tuned analysis. Retailers have always been able – if they wanted – from analysis of till receipts, to see what items are purchased together on a single visit. Now they are able to see which items customers buy whether or not on a single visit. Does this give much extra marketing strength? The answer to this is: only if the company has been able to mobilize itself to create joint promotions for associated products, and then monitor the effectiveness of these promotions. Relationship data gives the company the additional possibility of persuading specific customers to come into the store and buy the associated items (eg via a promotional coupon). But the value of this versus good POS display or promotions mentioned in in-store leaflets and small catalogues (minilogues) is not always clear.

STRATEGIES FOR MANAGING LOYAL RETAIL CUSTOMERS

Normal retail pressures militate against long-term customer management strategies using data. Most marketing staff are absorbed in the details of day-to-day operational marketing. However, the longer-term perspective provided by loyalty programmes is starting to change this culture. Nevertheless, most European retailers with loyalty schemes are still at the formative stage, where they have just starting learning about their individual customers and how they can be influenced. A more mature approach to retention management can be expected over the next few years.

Before this happens, specific product promotions will occupy retailers for some time, as these produce immediately observable results that can be translated into bottom line profit. Many retailers with strong brands have discovered that fairly crude untargeted mailing to broadly active customers produces such good results that there is no need for finer tuning. A good example of this are card-holder open days. However, for weaker brands, tightness of targeting and tailoring of offer can make up to some extent for weak branding. The same point applies to specialist catalogues – general catalogues targeted at card holders produce such good results that the additional cost (extra print, lower volumes) of specialist catalogues is rarely worth it.

Market research has a very strong place alongside card-based data. It makes it much clearer who target customers are, and allows the retailer to probe in depth their needs and perceptions – for product, outlets and customer service. In this respect CRM and customer service go hand in hand. All retailers monitor customer service in a variety of ways, including mystery shopping, and for some it's built into staff performance targets. Qualitative research also guides retailers on how it can be improved. When there is a loyalty scheme, use of it is also an indicator of customer satisfaction.

Customers in a retail loyalty relationship expect more from a store than if they were not in a relationship. They know more about what is happening in store. About 90 per cent of customer service is having right product on shelf at right time (size, weight, length, etc). If a retailer can do this, the rest is unimportant. If anything goes wrong, loyal customers are far more articulate than normal customers. A particularly risky area for retail loyalty schemes is the members' magazine. Going out of stock on a featured item – especially if it is on special offer – is the ultimate sin.

Loyal customers would describe their chosen retailer in the following terms:

- 'I like shopping at X.'
- 'It has what I want when I want it, at the right price.'
- 'It has pleasant people.'
- 'It's a pleasant place.'

However, all customers are individuals, and do not like to be considered as part of a group. There is a delicate balance between being singled out in the store (which they don't want) and being recognized (which they do) – hence the phrase 'I'm one of your best customers'.

Put simply, for a retailer, CRM is about visit-buy-visit-buy, again and again and again. Its aim is to get customers into the store, where the relationship is really built. This can be done by giving them additional information and benefits. Because retail buying is an important past of shoppers' activity, shoppers will create a portfolio of retailers and shop very stably within the portfolio. Loyalty card statistics show very slow turnover of shoppers and immense stability in buying patterns for this reason. However, as card schemes are now on offer in many stores, new customers who are going to have a high lifetime value are likely to join the card scheme early. This means that they need to be properly welcomed into the scheme.

Most retail loyalty schemes suffer from the '50 per cent rule' – 25 per cent or so are inactive, and another 25 per cent or so are active rarely, usually only when there is a big price promotion. Also, there is a rapid decay rate down to the 50 per cent active – in other words, most customers who belong to the 50 per cent inactive arrive there within a year or so. Therefore, an active archiving policy is important, to ensure that money is not wasted on mailings and promotions. Loyalty schemes are expected to pay for themselves several times over, because they add to the complexity of POS and systems, in a business where the rules are 'keep it simple' and 'retail is detail' – but the detail is usually applied to getting the stock moving efficiently off the shelves.

However, the strong financial focus of retailers can help maintain consistency in a loyalty scheme. In general, there is regular tracking of customer profitability, penetration of the scheme, reward liability or discount cost, versus target and budget. The importance of this tracking depends on the success of the scheme. With most successful schemes involving up to 50 per cent of turnover, this means that if the scheme is underperforming, the retailer's entire bottom line is affected. Share of spend is tracked through shopping panels, and this gives a very clear indicator of the success of a scheme.

The complexity of loyalty schemes requires particularly close cooperation between marketing and IT departments – and this has not always been the case, leading to implementation problems or to problems in analysing and making use of the data. As it becomes more important in retail marketing, there seems to be a trend whereby IT staff are learning about marketing, and performing better, but marketing staff are still scared of IT, leading them to defensive reactions. IT staff in retailing are much closer to customers than in other industries, and they like being creative with customer-facing IT.

One area in which retailers will definitely have to improve is the helpline, where the standards have been set by big direct marketing and mail order organizations. Well-motivated staff and expensive answering machines are no substitute for big call centres and trained telemarketers. Yet with several million articulate loyal customers to manage, the volume of calls to retailers that needs to be managed within a relationship is rising rapidly.

Customer contact systems and call centres

As increasing numbers of companies initiate direct contact with named customers, the need to deploy smarter technology to help them do so has surged. Nearly every major company that deals with large numbers of customers has now invested in a call centre, or has contracted its inbound telephone call management to one or other of the leading tele-marketing agencies. This has led to customers experiencing much better standards of call handling (although it is still far from perfect), and has increased their expectations correspondingly. Even retailers, who have long rather avoided the issue of handling customer calls anywhere but in their branches, deploy call centres as an essential part of their systems for managing loyal customers.

Customer feedback management has also been escalated to new levels of importance. Many retailers have invested in advanced computer software for logging and managing 'unsolicited customer feedback', of which complaints normally constitute less than 50 per cent – the rest being requests for information and help. If there needs to be differentiation between customers (eg club members and others) it is important that the operator handling the issue has access to both the individual's club data (eg purchasing history, preferences) as well as current and past contacts (complaints, etc).

There are five principal reasons for introducing a special scheme and associated systems for managing customer loyalty:

- To help you to *recognize and welcome* customers – particularly those who you most want to remain loyal to you.
- To facilitate the *collection of information* from these customers, enabling you to determine which products and services are best for them, sold through which channels, etc.
- To enable you to *communicate* with and *motivate* these customers.
- To enable you to *reward* them for their loyalty.
- To enable you to *provide special, differentiated service* to these customers – if this is likely to improve loyalty cost-effectively.

In other words, loyalty schemes provide you with a range of powerful capabilities. But they are only capabilities, which are only worth anything if you can translate them into revenue cost-effectively. The need for each of these capabilities, and whether each can be exploited in practice, depends entirely on the nature of the business and its customers.

Recognition and welcome

This is key for businesses which transact wholly or partially through agents (airlines, motor manufacturers), but less important for companies which have direct contact with customers, such as utilities. But recognition is expensive. It means building a customer database, and providing customers with a device (eg a card) to ensure that they are recognizable to the company in every transaction. The level of recognition required depends on the product. For example, for a repeat buyer of a single product (such as petrol) with no after-sales component, the recognition required may only be that needed to credit reward points. For more complex products, recognition and welcoming may need to extend to having available a complete history of transactions with the customer, including responses to past promotions. Without this, we may end up trying to sell something to the customer that we have already sold to them, or trying to sell to them before we have resolved a serious outstanding service problem.

Collection of information

Once customers have agreed to be recognized (by joining the loyalty scheme), you are likely to want more information about them, and they are likely to be ready to give it to you. But you need to collect it and hold it to support the other capabilities. This involves not only setting up a database, but also a permanent commitment to gathering, cleaning, entering, storing and updating the information and making it available during the contact cycle with customers. The key decision here is to decide how much information you can use profitably. This in turn will depend upon how you propose to manage the loyalty scheme. Do you expect to be providing customers with a series of highly focused offers and considerable service differentiation, or do you expect to give virtually identical treatment to all members? If the former, you'll need a lot more information than in the latter situation. In practice, the decision about how much information to collect is a compromise between the desire for completeness and the costs and practicality of storing the information and making it available for marketing and customer service purposes. The greater the detail you collect, the more you should expect to exploit it, but also the more you will have to invest in systems and campaigns to enable you to do so.

Communication and motivation

This is where many mass-market loyalty schemes go badly wrong. If you are a retailer and your average customer visits your store, say, more than once a week, spending sums in tens rather than hundreds of pounds, and if you have very large numbers of customers, the most cost-effective way of communicating with them is unlikely to be via direct marketing. In-store merchandizing, and possibly a store magazine which they collect from the till, will be much more cost-effective. It is no use expecting to use your loyalty scheme as your main method of telling customers what you have in store, or even to try to get them to come in more often – they should be coming in often enough already. The only exception to this is for store-types where visits are typically infrequent, eg once a month, when incentives can make customers come in more often and spend more. The main value of retail schemes is to ensure that when customers do come, they maximize their expenditure with you. Your reward level will therefore have to be pitched very carefully so as to conserve your margin, as it is effectively a loyalty discount.

Perhaps paradoxically, as many commentators say that loyalty schemes must be long term, schemes can and do work well over short periods – even as little as three to six months, if their main aim is to preserve shopping habits. The major multiple grocers have used this approach, often driven by leaflet drops, as a spoiling device (eg to combat a local competitive store opening). However, even they have concluded that these schemes have the best results when they last. They also reinforce branding, because they thank the customer.

So, high-traffic, mass-market retailers are not ideal candidates for direct mail-based loyalty schemes, because it's simply too expensive to mail to so many people when they come to you anyway. Building a database of such customers may help you to identify profitable prospects, but your best approach to them is through mass media. Direct marketing in such circumstances will rarely do more than just 'wash its face', and is therefore not justified. It works best, therefore, when people come in less frequently but spend more than a typical grocery purchase. Then, it can work to stimulate loyal customers into coming in more often, and spending with you instead of your competitors. In services marketing, airlines and the various hotel loyalty schemes (often combined with credit cards) direct marketing is designed to do just that. However, it is clear that to date, few have achieved long-term success as a services loyalty management scheme.

Reward versus special, differentiated service

Customers do expect reward for loyalty, and the more loyalty schemes we throw at customers, the more rewards they'll want. This leads to 'commoditization' of loyalty – the consumers equivalent of the suppliers' 'half a pound of loyalty'. Customers are being conditioned to think, 'If I give you loyalty, you'll give me a reward'. Yet reward is often not the most important motivator in long-term loyalty – recognition, welcoming and service differentiation are much more powerful long-term factors. Reward should therefore only be used when these more powerful factors are not available. In mass-market retailing, their scope is limited (eg special open evenings), but as we move away from the very high volume end, the scope for them increases. In upmarket fashion retailing, for example, frequent customers who are under time pressure may be able to telephone in and ask for selections to be put aside for them to view. Note, however, that this takes place anyway outside the context of loyalty schemes (eg at Jaeger) – having a scheme helps formalize it and increases the effectiveness of deployment of the practice.

Making it work in practice

Joining the bandwagon of customer loyalty for mass-market consumers requires significant investment in database building and management, POS change and direct marketing, to produce a true 'continuity programme'. These are long-term, strategically planned loyalty campaigns that are a central part of overall marketing strategy. The few that work have become a model to the many that aspire to do so. But the demand for such schemes is growing inexorably, as more and more companies seek to blend the best of merchandising and product management with customer management.

As the focus of so much retail customer management is the point of sale, and because of the increasing frequency of POS card use, the banks have woken up to the possibilities of capturing market share by offering their retail customers the services required for loyalty scheme management. Major credit card operators are gaining new accounts by their offer of free research, database, data capture, direct marketing, data analysis and segmentation. So far, all that has been missing from this offer is managing in-depth customer data and reward accumulation.

As we enter the age of the smart card – still a little too expensive for most retail POS operations – retailers will be keen to exploit its possibilities for loyalty management, and finance houses will be keen to see them blend this with credit and payment management. However, the data and reward pooling that could (and should?) occur will probably lead to the dividing up of the market into competing consortia. If this emerges, we expect each consortium will be composed of largely non-conflicting and dominant service and product retailers (an airline, a hotel chain or a package tour company, a grocery retailer, a DIY retailer, a pub chain, a surface transport operator, a utility, a telecommunications company, a cinema chain and so on). Obviously, key players here will be the broad-based leisure and retail businesses that span one or more of these sectors or have partnership agreements which span them.

Tables 18.2 and 18.3 summarize the implications of using credit and loyalty cards in customer management.

Table 18.2 Issuing retail cards

This table deals with **issuing**, ie the fact of having issued cards to named customers.

Information ie what the issuer will know as a result of issue of cards	• Identification of individual customers, ie name, address and other information gathered at time of issue. This may include basic information on preferences, use patterns, etc, gathered as result of completion of application questionnaire by customer. If card is a payment card, details will also include financial qualifiers, bank details, etc. Data may also include eg which competitive stores are visited, which other cards held. • Implicit information on loyalty (for store credit and loyalty cards) – fact that customer has applied indicates intention to visit and spend. • Profile of customer base, possibly enhanced through third party data applied to customer records (eg profiling system), and consequent ability to identify segments and named individuals who belong to each segment, and also target similar customers for recruitment. • Catchment areas better understood.
Marketing policy ie what the issuer can do as a result of issue of cards	• If card is a payment card, is a more secure method of payment than cash or cheque, as well as ability to combine it with incentives for buying and for using the card. • Incremental revenue generation – eg a loyalty or payment card can yield data vending opportunities to defray a large part of the cost of running the scheme; eg credit card commissions can pay for whole scheme – for some airlines they have been the main source of profit. • Contact customers as individuals at known address, and motivate them to visit and buy (especially valuable if customers visit infrequently), and then target segments composed of these individually, usually much more cost-effectively than any other medium except for store-located promotions. • Run promotional schemes which carry over from campaign to campaign, providing longer-term as well as shorter-term value to customer. • Credit rewards to named customers, who can then redeem them against own or partner products or services. • Target segments precisely for any activity, and address those segments, and related exclusion of customers from promotions if it is believed they are unlikely to respond. • Recognize customers when they present card in outlets, and provide them with special/differentiated services/offers at point of sale. • Store information about customer preferences, so as to provide the above. • Build relationship with customers, as previous contacts can be recalled, customer service issues identified, etc. • Use card as a branded symbol of the relationship, and build value into that relationship by using card as the key to partnership deals.

Table 18.2 *continued*

Problems and limitations	• Cost of issue, especially if smart card route chosen, and if indiscriminate issue takes place regardless of likely usage.
	• Cost of maintenance of customer on database, again higher relative to revenue if indiscriminate issue takes place.
	• Point of sale issuing takes time, although does not require complex technology (validation of customer can take place in central fulfilment operation).
	• Card loss and theft (particularly for credit cards) and fraudulent points accumulation (sometimes with connivance of retail staff, particularly if not company employees).
	• 'Card overload' – too many cards on market, and customer edits some out of portfolio.
	• Devaluation of card and of overall brand if benefits are not as promised or as expected (especially likely if product/service profit margins are low and promotional costs therefore have to be very low, or if poor partnership deals struck).

Table 18.3 Using retail cards

This table deals with **use**, ie fact that customer responds to card-based promotions by visiting the outlet and/or uses card at time of purchase.

Information ie what the issuer will know as a result of issue and use of cards	• Gather information on visiting and buying behaviour of individual customers and segments (frequency and recency of visits and purchases, amount and category of purchase).
	• Develop profiles of typical customers' purchasing behaviour, and relate to basic customer data.
	• Develop profiles of customers' needs.
	• For credit cards, easy and secure collection of payment.
	• Better understanding of catchment area variations for different products and services, different times of day, week and year, etc.
	• Better understanding of range of buying habits of customers.
Marketing policy ie what the issuer can do as a result of issue and use of cards	• Service and merchandise planning, to ensure that outlets are open at times when customers want, stock the products and services they want, etc.
	• Track take-up of promotions, so future promotions can be targeted at those likely to respond, and those unlikely to respond can be excluded from promotions.
	• Track take-up of partner offers, and so identify what other partners would be appropriate.
	• Introduce tiered levels of qualification/bonus, to provide greater incentive for use.
	• Promote greater use of credit card.
	• Identify much more precisely the returns on promotions – eg what kind of customer responded, how much their purchasing pattern changed as a result, and therefore assess the value of different promotions and of promotions against other elements of the marketing mix.
	• Identify lapsed and declining users and target them for attempts to revive their use.
	• Provide differentiated service to regular customers spending on particular types of product or service.
	• Cross-selling, especially if associations found between purchase patterns of different products.

Table 18.3 *continued*

Problems and limitations	● Database cost of storing and updating visit and purchasing data and bonus points, and costs of analysis (but should save market research budget, which can be confined more and more to qualitative work). ● Cost of POS technology to take payment and credit points, and associated staff training. ● Management costs of continuing to run scheme (but should be outweighed by saving promotional management costs for variety and number of schemes replaced). ● Helpline costs for answering customer queries about payments, point credits, etc (but often helpline is good basis for relationship). ● Liability of outstanding bonus points (can be limited by requiring use by certain date or issuing vouchers with expiry date).

A low-risk way to use cards to manage customers is the co-branded or affinity card. Both sides can do well from such schemes, but in some cases the reward required to get customers to switch all their transactions into one card may be too high for the single host retailer – hence the advantage of the consortium idea. These schemes can be more in the bankers' interests than those of their partners – Trojan horses for the banks to get more customers and profit. However, for some retailers they are the ideal, self-funding starting point for a more comprehensive approach to managing customers directly – whether or not in the form of loyalty schemes.

WHAT IS WORKING?

Quite frankly, those who know the answer to this question are very circumspect about what they say publicly, and rightfully so, because a really successful loyalty scheme is the key to competitive advantage. We believe that for a scheme to be considered successful, it must produce increased volume, increased traffic, increased average transaction value, increased frequency of visit and increased loyalty (measured in buying behaviour: a higher share of loyal customers' business; and in emotional terms, an increased affinity of consumers to the brand). It must also serve as the basis for selling additional products and services (eg telecommunications, energy, financial services) and ideally also serve as a launch platform for an Internet business.

Given the costs of setting up such schemes, you can be fairly sure that if a company has been running a scheme with unchanged essentials for more than two years, it must be working in some respect. Few companies would spend the required time, effort and budget unless it were delivering. Retail finance directors are not forgiving of compromising their margin!

It can't work without staff

The key to successful management of a retail loyalty scheme is good people (managers, suppliers and staff), careful planning, well-briefed customer service centres, hotlines, clear information at the point of sale, and literature which is consumer-friendly.

If staff are not behind the loyalty programme, there will be problems. Staff have to sell the scheme to the customers, so they must be knowledgeable and positive about the programme and their role in it, and communicate the scheme and its benefits to consumers. This requires proper training of the classic retail kind, with sessions, workbooks, videos, etc. The idea of customer value can be understood by shop staff – after all, they are also valuable customers themselves. This is vital if staff are not to see the scheme as 'getting in the way of doing business'. Of course, nothing succeeds like success, so communicating success is important. This applies to key performance indicators of the scheme.

Of course, staff who themselves do not feel loyal are unlikely to be good advocates of loyalty to customers, so staff retention is an important part of customer retention. They not only know the company and customers better, but feel differently about them. Ideally, therefore, it should not be necessary to provide an additional incentive for recruiting customers into the loyalty scheme – indeed, such an incentive can lead to over-recruitment.

So, as long as customer service is delivered by staff and not by machine, for a scheme to work at the interface with customers, it has to work for staff at that interface. It must make sense to them, staff must see its advantages in helping them produce satisfied customers who buy more, and it must be easy for them to promote and operate (communication and training are key here). And of course it must not be possible for them or customers to abuse it – a pitfall of several schemes. Finally, just as for the marketing effort as a whole, the scheme must form a central part of staff's proposition to customers, and not just an incidental to offer customers if they happen to be in the mood.

19

Automotive CRM

*Merlin Stone, Alla Main, Harvey Thompson, Mark Cerasale,
John Griffiths, Bill Sullivan, Paul Weston and Dave Cox*

INTRODUCTION

Automotive companies are extensive users of CRM. They have invested heavily in customer databases. They have been intense users of response advertising, particularly press and lately direct response TV. Motor shows have become important generators of leads. Yet still there is a strong suspicion in the automotive industry that CRM has much more potential than it has so far realized. We think this suspicion is correct. This chapter summarizes our researches and consulting experiences in this area, and indicates where we think the main opportunities lie. First, we identify some general trends in the automotive market that – from our knowledge of how similar factors work in other sectors – we know are going to make a big difference to how CRM techniques are deployed.

General product trends

That the automotive market car park continues to grow – with fluctuating but generally increasing flows of new vehicles into it – is no secret. Nor is the increased reliability of cars, and the consequent threat to an until now steadily growing and profitable after-market revenue. A strange mixture of consolidation and fragmentation is also apparent. The number of major players continues to decline slowly, while worldwide manufacture, joint sourcing agreements (parts, engines, bodies and in some cases entire vehicles) continue to reduce variety. But category variety continues to surprise. The uniformity of the 'company car' is in sharp contrast to the introduction of new categories:

- sports utility – initially based on classic off-road Jeep/Land Rover-type designs but becoming more saloon-like by the year;
- multi-purpose (in some cases originally based on van designs) – this category, like sports utility, has clearly separated into large, medium and small variants;
- the revival of old categories (sports cars/roadsters – MGF, BMW Z3, the new Beetle);
- micro-town cars (Seat Arosa, VW Lupo).
- fashion cars (Swatch).

The strengths of these trends vary by country, although of course the internationalization of the automotive industry means that most models will be offered in most countries. However, they suggest that instead of the classic two-car family being 'one large, one small', it is increasingly common for it to be 'one large, one larger', with the second vehicle being dedicated to the school run and being either a SUV or a MPV.

Demographic trends

Demographic trends are of course significant, and with the post-war bulge now passing through into retirement an explosion in demand for high-quality, medium to small cars seems imminent. The upper income section of this demographic group may behave differently from their predecessors. Asset rich, we can expect them to display the financial conservatism which took some of them to the situation they will be in soon – a secure asset-rich retirement but with a need to watch current expenditure because of their expected long life! So while we can expect them to buy reasonably highly featured versions of their chosen cars, they will certainly be looking for value for money in purchase and economy in running costs and servicing, and so will be attracted by the many reliable, economical medium to small cars appearing in this segment.

Retired buyers will increase as a proportion of buyers in all countries, because older people are living longer and retaining their faculties for longer. They are (for the time being at least) better off, and more of them will have a lifelong driving habit. Some will also be attracted to cost-effective longer-term finance, although others will be cash rich (eg benefiting from maturing savings plans and other long-term savings programmes, lump sum pension payments). They will also be responsive to attractive buy-back conditions, as they will often be returning cars in good condition and with low mileage for the car's age. Older people have a tendency to gravitate for security towards affinity marketing schemes (eg Saga), so we can expect some attempts here by manufacturers to try this new dimension of marketing (eg the older people's club, where buyers and sellers are both older!). However, conservatism increasing with age means that it may be hard to get older customers to switch, so the key direct marketing task may be to get them to replace more often and to up-sell (not necessarily larger models, but more highly featured ones).

Disabled drivers will also be growing in number, for the same reasons of increased longevity (whether or not disabled) and increased incidence of the driving habit. This segment is quite small (around a third of a million in the UK), but clearly requires selling to differently. One point that needs to be taken into account is that often the purchaser is not the driver.

Meanwhile, the steady decline – only occasionally reversed – in family formation means that at the other end of the life cycle we can expect to see younger people delaying their purchase of classic 'family vehicles'. Younger people are less likely to be worried about running economies (except for the environmentally-conscious few), and more concerned to make a statement.

Declining birth rates and household sizes mean that customers may be expected to move towards smaller, perhaps sportier versions of cars, but often with the economy/value-for-money attributes more commonly associated with normal family cars.

Women are becoming more important as buyers, despite the motor trade's traditional disbelief that women could have anything to do with car purchase. This has started to affect everything from product design and marketing communications to the evolution of distribution channels. One of the reasons for the success of car supermarkets is that they provide the kind of buying environment women like and are used to through their role as household shoppers. This is evidenced by the fact that in some car supermarkets, women make up well over half of the customers. The implications of this for CRM are clear:

- Customer databases must carry details of all adult members of the household, not just the male.
- Campaigns must be timed to reflect the typical life cycle of the woman car buyer.
- The media used and the creative treatment must be appropriate for women buyers.

Reflecting these demographic, income and asset trends described above, car marketing is becoming more life-stage-oriented. The implications of the above analysis for CRM is that new products will be closely targeted to age groups and lifestyles, but also the marketing campaigns that support them. So we expect there to be a premium on customer information, as manufacturers struggle to influence customers cost-effectively at the right time (and not – as most customers believe – at the wrong time).

The environment

This need for running and service economies is likely to be exacerbated by the environmental commitment of European governments. The mixed feelings about diesels may be abandoned as the new generation of engines hits the market, with halved fuel consumption compared to their petrol equivalents, and dramatically improved emissions and reduced noise levels. With new petrol engines achieving fuel economy close to that of current diesels, the trend towards diesel that exists in some countries may be reduced. However, this depends on governments abandoning their tax discrimination in favour of diesel, due to the reliance of commercial transport on diesel.

Increased congestion will, of course, continue. Most governments will probably deliberately allow road-building or improvement schemes to lag behind the demand for road space, and rely on a variety of economic pressures to reduce the demand – at a minimum self-imposed congestion costs, at a maximum, increasingly severe taxation, road pricing, and absolute restrictions on access. As the demand for peak-hour travel continues to rise, well beyond the capacity of public transport networks to supply it, the naïve call of environmentalists for a transfer of traffic from road to rail will die away. Governments will then resort – as economists have urged them for the last 40 years – to market-based tools to restrict the demand for all types of travel into congested urban areas.

First among these will be pricing of individual access, either on an as-used basis (expensive to administer in megalopolises) or through much tougher and possibly access-based licensing. However, this is unlikely to reduce the demand for cars, or even change the structure of demand much, though it will change use. The structure of demand for cars is more likely to be affected by specific incentives or penalties, such as taxation differentials for engine types and sizes, or very high fuel taxation. Tax incentives for early scrapping (or penalties for late scrapping) may also be introduced to ensure that the car park is modern and therefore less polluting. A particular problem is that there will shortly be many vehicles over three years old whose catalytic converter is no longer functioning. These will have to be replaced, each costing over £1,000, which could be 20–30 per cent of the vehicle's market value.

With an increasing proportion of the population in all countries working in information-intense industries, home working for some or all of the week is becoming increasingly attractive for many companies – helped by developments in cable and mobile telephony. Hot-desking has become much more common. Interestingly, while this may reduce the demand for peak-hour road space, it conjures up an image of the home/car-based worker, spacing work out throughout the day while working from home, and popping out *in the car* to run local errands such as shopping.

Governments are also working on the supply side. One of the reasons for Mercedes' A Class car is that the United States and EU will tax manufacturers more if they only sell large cars. The same pressures apply to the introduction of electric, gas and hybrid vehicles (petrol/gas, petrol/electric). In the long term, the highly efficient but currently expensive fuel cell engine may be viable for the same reason.

From a marketing point of view, the above pressures will affect how the car buyer thinks about car buying. Leaving it to dealers to identify which customers are or will be interested in particular categories of car will be seen by car manufacturers as an increasingly weak form of marketing. Many will be looking to build much stronger, earlier relationships with customers and prospects, so as to ensure that when the brand and model choice is finally made, it is made for the 'right' company, and just as importantly, for the 'right' model. At the moment, 'right' is defined as most profitable, but manufacturers may be more concerned to achieve long-term customer loyalty by ensuring that 'right' becomes 'right for the customer'.

CATEGORY OF CAR PURCHASES

There are many categories of buyers, and they tend to have very different buying patterns. Moreover, these patterns vary by country and over time. Let us have a brief look at these categories.

Private buyers

These are conventionally divided by whether the car is a first car, and by the employment status of the driver (eg student, someone in employment, housewife, retired person, disabled person). There are some typical patterns here. For example, first cars are very rarely new, and increasingly will be bought when the buyer is a student, as participation rates in higher education continue to rise throughout the world. A parent will often buy this car very cheaply, from a used car dealer or a private seller. From a direct marketing perspective, the main implication is that finding out about the first car may be more difficult, and yet more important, because first cars have some influence on subsequent choices. This is why it is so important for car manufacturers to have a small car in their line, and explains the recent emphasis by companies such as Fiat, Daihatsu, Nissan and VW on the micro end of the market, which usually cascade down to provide first cars for students.

Second (and subsequent) car buyers who buy new in the UK tend to be in jobs where they do not get a job car (often public sector workers – although relatively low public sector pay tends to move these buyers towards the used market), or they may be buying a second car for the family. However, as increasing numbers of businesses respond to increasing government taxation of business cars by giving their staff a cash/leasing budget, in some cases without a recommended supplier. We can expect more private purchases in this area. This creates a problem for direct marketing, because customers who change from a company car to a cash purchase may not appear on any marketing database.

The second car in the family has been called disparagingly the lifestyle car, runabout, or shopping trolley, but in fact it may be used for more hours if not more miles than the first car, which may be used just for commuting journeys and family trips. The advent of small off-roaders and people carriers has opened new possibilities to buyers in this market. In better-off households, this car may be bought new.

Corporate buyers

Here, one can distinguish national fleets, car rental and leasing companies, local and central government and other public organizations, business fleets (where users have no choice) and fleets where they do (perhaps from a limited range). In all but the last, the focus of CRM must be very strongly on the fleet buyer and the total package offered. Acquisition cost is of course very important, but cost per mile is the effective budget for most fleet buyers (particularly where this function is outsourced). So, in many respects, fleet buyers are normally best managed using business-to-business CRM techniques. Here, the focus is on information flows and service (logistics, residual values, efficiency of customer service), because purchasing policies are usually clear and available to suppliers. This contrasts with consumer buyers, where the key issues are identification of prospects, gaining information and predicting replacement cycles.

On the other hand, user-choosers are a mix of personal and business behaviour. The key problem for manufacturers is to identify the user-choosers, because in many cases all incentives for these customers to identify themselves to manufacturers are stripped out of the cars. Keeping track of these customers is also a problem.

BEYOND THE BASIC VEHICLE

The product is not just the basic vehicle, but may also include:

- product options;
- finance – loans, payment schedules, guaranteed buy-back prices; insurance;
- servicing and damage repair.

Product options

As manufacturing technology improves, so what were options tend to be incorporated as part of the basic design, although at any one time there is a big difference between brands in what is regarded as standard. Typically, companies such as BMW, Mercedes and

Audi have derived much of their profit by selling additional features which are incorporated as standard in, for example, Far Eastern brands. This is a tribute to the brand strength of the former and the need for the latter to achieve their volume targets by high value-for-money marketing strategies. As customers' needs become more sophisticated, so the need to keep them informed of (profitable) options becomes more important. As one of the German manufacturers expressed it to our researchers, one of the key aims of CRM is to make sure customers consider high-value options early in the buying cycle, so that they fix their price expectations accordingly and then specify the options when they order.

The move towards telematics

Industry executives and consultants said that recent studies indicate consumers are willing to pay small fees for Internet access and information in their cars. Speaking at the eAuto World seminar in Chicago on 20 June 2000, Peter Holland, chief executive of InfoMove, a telematics consulting firm, said consumers were willing to pay about US $6.60 a month for wired emergency response services. He said that a number of studies also indicated that motorists would be willing to pay 96 cents per call for traffic updates and navigation help. Holland said that he expected telematics – which includes in-car information, entertainment and emergency-response systems – to be widespread by 2004 with consumers spending an average of US $15 per month. Holland said that recent consumer studies indicate that 75 per cent of motorists are interested in navigation systems; 73 per cent want auto makers or dealers to be able to remotely diagnose problems; 72 per cent want real-time traffic updates; and 42 per cent would like to be able to download and respond to e-mails while driving. Holland noted that recent studies expected about one million vehicles to have real-time Internet access capability by 2004 at an average cost of about US $700 and commented that this was a low number.

However, bandwidth, flat-rate pricing, clear voice recognition and text-to-speech software and ubiquitous network access are some of the obstacles auto makers and telematics providers must overcome. The other big obstacle to widespread deployment of telematics is the wide disparity between product development cycles for cars and electronic hardware. Currently, new-car development times can range anywhere from 24–60 months, while electronic hardware and software is upgraded every 6–18 months. However, this may be resolved by the use of docking stations in vehicles. Technology providers are encouraging car makers to build common hardware into cars that will allow consumers to plug-and-play whatever technology applications they choose. Technology providers are also encouraging car makers to develop a dashboard cradle that will hold a cellular phone, or PDA, or both. Hardware embedded in the car would then allow consumers hands-free use of portable digital products.

DaimlerChrysler, Ford, General Motors and others are developing telematics systems. Most analysts agree that GM is ahead of the pack with its OnStar system. OnStar currently offers road-side emergency response, navigation and premier services for hotel, dinner and theatre reservations. Later this summer OnStar will launch Virtual Advisor, a new service that will allow users to download and respond to e-mails, get real-time traffic reports and stock quotes. Delphi Automotive Systems Corp, GM's former parts unit, is considered the leader in telematics hardware. Rather than focusing on branding, Delphi's Communiport hardware is adaptable to a number of systems and can provide in-car communications and navigation as well as entertainment hardware and software, such as DVD movie capability and in-car video game ports and screens.

In Europe, Ford, DaimlerChrysler and Peugeot-Citroën are among those well advanced with on-board Internet access systems. Citroën, for example, will soon launch limited production runs of Xsara Windows CE models providing e-mail, voice-activated navigation and related systems. Even at the £2,000 premium Citroën is expected to ask for its Xsara Windows CE models, most cars are likely to go to fleets because of the improved operating efficiencies they offer. Drivers making full use of the technologies in a few years' time could be spending up to US $100 a month with service providers. While satellite navigation and related conveniences in company cars are still mainly the province of the perk car user, the rapidly falling cost of such equipment makes it destined rapidly to permeate throughout the fleet. This is particularly the case given that, much like the mobile phones sector, carmakers will look to subsidize hardware costs in the expectation of ongoing subscription revenues. Few drivers of company cars or vans, once they have experienced the technologies' benefits, are likely to reject them.

Companies and their fleet managers, therefore, will be faced with decisions such as whether to:

- Seek to negotiate the best terms for their entire fleet and then control individual drivers' spending on the services internally.
- Require individual drivers to take out their own service contracts.
- Adopt the potentially divisive approach of allowing access only to selected drivers.

Such policy decisions are much less problematical for commercial vehicle operators, for whom the logistical advantages of such technologies are unquestionable. Ryder, the US van and truck rentals and transport group, is already installing 10,000 interactive communications and vehicle tracking systems in its vehicles under the control of a central monitoring operation – good business for systems provider OmniTRACS Mobile Systems.

Vehicle tracking, not just as an anti-theft measure but to improve operating efficiencies of commercial vehicles, is itself becoming a big business. In the UK, Trafficmaster, a pioneer of so-called telematics technology, which began life as a provider of traffic flow information, is just launching Fleetstar to enable around-the-clock monitoring of vehicles, including journey length, stationary periods and average speed. It coincides with the launch by Global Telematics, a 50–50 joint venture between electronics and defence group Racal and European Telecom, the mobile communications group, of a system for tracking truck trailers separately from their articulated tow vehicles. Since a fleet operator typically will have two to three times as many cargo trailers as trucks, using them more efficiently – by monitoring where trailers are in relation to possible loads – has the potential to cut costs significantly by reducing the size of the trailer fleet.

A third European contender in the field, also UK-based, Minorplanet Systems, meanwhile, has formed an alliance with British Telecom to exploit the field and is fast creating a sizeable customer base, including GE's car and commercial vehicle fleet operations. Soon it will start supplying the first of 25,000 units to Schmitz Cargobull, the European trailer maker, for delivery up until 2003. BT itself is likely to fit the system to some or all of its 53,000-strong fleet.

Such alliances are taking several forms and quickly crossing national boundaries. Trafficmaster, for example, is also to supply US multinational Motorola with real-time digital traffic information in Germany for use in what Motorola hopes will become a Europe-wide navigation system capable of routing drivers automatically around traffic jams.

After-sales service

The car market is a strange market compared with that for similar complex electro-mechanical devices (eg photocopiers, industrial equipment). Increasingly designed-in reliability is clearly reducing the need for a 'service'. In theory, the most advanced new models should only be serviced every 100,000 km or so, with occasional checks for tyre and brake wear. But the existence of a dependent industry – servicing dealerships – which also constitutes the main channel of distribution is leading to restrictive practices, in which recommended servicing is more than the car needs. Car owners are given a variety of incentives (eg free emergency service) or threats (eg warranty invalidity) to ensure that they continue to provide revenue in this way. Governments, whether wittingly or unwittingly, conspire to support this market by insisting on a variety of annual checks for vehicles, rather than taking steps to ensure that the car park is kept up to date by quicker scrapping (and therefore less in need of such checks). Indeed, in countries such as the UK, limitations on the treatment of cars for tax purposes can slow down replacement cycles. The motor industry can only hope that governments will one day see the light, and become much tougher by refusing to allow cars which are unsafe or unclean by modern standards on the road at all, rather than allowing them on the roads if they scrape through a poorly administered annual test.

If this happened, we can see a situation developing in which the after-market for car servicing separates from selling, as they will require very different physical set-ups. In fact, this has already started to happen, as service retention rates are falling. Many specialists have emerged to deal with particular aspects of the after-market (tyres, exhausts, lubrication, body repairs), and in some areas where automotive manufacturers were slow to move, they never really had the market (eg cellular phones, insurance, off-the-road service). Once this service separation happens, the need to maintain the dealer as the prime outlet disappears, and we can see the emergence of the car supermarket and similar channels, as already exist in other areas of similar machinery, whether for consumers or businesses. If this happens, then relationship marketers need to be prepared, as managing the customer through the dealer will no longer be a serious option, and the market will move increasingly to managing 'over' or 'around' the channel, and of course direct distribution.

However, there is a route open to manufacturers to retain a degree of control. An alternative scenario is that all vehicles will be fitted with some form of mobile communication and will download data to the manufacturer about the condition of the vehicle, requirements for repair and service, and the option to book the vehicle in. It will, of course, be used in accidents to assess blame. The installation of mobile communication in vehicles is becoming common for a variety of other reasons, such as:

- crash detection systems installed for some insurers;
- locating commercial vehicles;
- traffic information.

It is conceivable that the market will split, with some vehicles being bought precisely because they are managed in this way (eg commercial fleets), while some consumer customers will prefer not to be 'controlled' in this way.

MANAGING CUSTOMER FEEDBACK – A CASE STUDY

So far in this chapter, much of the emphasis has been on the buying process. However, once a vehicle has been bought, the typical user normally has several years of experience with it. How should this be managed? The following case study demonstrates how it should be managed in practice.

Mitsubishi Motors

In the early 1990s, Mitsubishi Motors was winning business rapidly and customer contact was increasing. To continue expansion and create a more professional image, a dedicated customer services department was introduced. Mitsubishi Motors initiated a feedback cycle between customer, dealer and manufacturer to create a two-way information loop, and turn around demands into answers. The service loop was designed to increase, rather than reduce the level of customer contact with the company. Customers can contact either their local Mitsubishi dealer, or Mitsubishi Motors' centralized customer service department direct. Mitsubishi Motors then passes on specific enquiries to dealers, who follow up personally to complete the loop.

Initially, enquiries were recorded manually and information only fed upwards. To maximize the feedback cycle initiative, in 1997 Mitsubishi Motors implemented Charter 2000, a customer management system from Swallow Information Systems, to allow direct response to the customer. Feedback from dealers to the central service centre at Mitsubishi is also recorded using Charter to help resolve enquiries or problems they are unable to deal with themselves. Mitsubishi Motors uses Charter to record letters, e-mails, faxes, and telephone calls from customers and dealers. The information stored in the knowledge base can then be analysed to produce detailed reports, specific information or to identify trends. Charter 2000 incorporates Business Objects reporting software, which allows exact information from the customer database to be located and presented in a illustrative format. Mitsubishi Motors uses Charter's reporting function to analyse trends in customer and dealer contacts and this then enables them to change working practices for the benefit of the customer. Dealers also receive a monthly update on their progress with specific customer issues.

'Charter is an excellent tool for proactively managing customer issues,' said Sharon Hunt, General Manager – Service, at Mitsubishi Motors in the UK. She adds:

> We use Business Objects to search through the data and identify which products, or which regions are experiencing customer dissatisfaction. We can then provide our dealers with the back-up they need for sales support or pass on recommendations to our marketing department before issues become real problems. Encouraging our customers to get in touch has helped us to second guess problems, and provide our dealers with the right information, before they escalate. As a result, we have been able to implement customer-led service initiatives, and experience a 60 per cent reduction in negative feedback and a boom in repeat business

Role of financial services

The increasing use of financial services is a logical extension of controlled distribution. In general, it should always be easier to get a loan secured on an asset, and the process of validating the connection between the two is made much easier when the provider of the asset also gives the loan. The process becomes even easier if the asset is never transferred, but simply leased for its period of use. However, as motor manufacturers have discovered, not only they can play this game. The explosion of leasing companies, offering deals at effective rates well below those of manufacturer-branded finance, is a sign of how competitive the financial services industry is. The largest companies can obtain models at low cost through bulk-buying, and then lease them using direct selling techniques to large commercial accounts and direct marketing techniques such as 'off the page selling' to small business customers and consumers. With a solid credit-rating industry in Western Europe, we see this as the way forward for financial services.

In the UK, this approach has been given a boost by the decision taken by many large companies to reduce their involvement in managing fleets. In many cases, employers are just given leasing allowances and told to manage the process of car provision themselves, through one or more approved leasing suppliers. This approach may erode the premium achieved by manufacturer-owned finance companies. However, the latter will still have an important commercial advantage, in that they can work closely with their product marketing and sales colleagues to help the latter implement their sales targets by subsidized pricing schemes. However, customers might consider that good car suppliers should not sell their own finance, but either: recommend several alternative sources of finance, rather than trying to get all the finance business themselves; or have a panel of finance companies, to whom they turn for competitive quotes (as banks do with insurance companies).

Meanwhile, manufacturer-owned finance companies continue to expand their services. Volkswagen UK is expanding its range of financial services beyond traditional car finance, insurance and warranty products, following its parent's move into banking. It will be using its UK database of over 1 million customers to launch loans, deposit schemes, savings accounts and credit cards.[1]

However, to an outsider, financial services still seems to be a successful parasite on the brand, achieving good margins thanks to inert customers prepared to pay a premium. Because their car loan and insurance contracts are fixed period, they know precisely the 'replacement date' (renewal) for the policy, and can use CRM techniques to improve loyalty rates. Interestingly, many car loans and leases are terminated early, despite penalty clauses. This gives companies the opportunity of reducing penalties if customers decide to renew with them.

DISTRIBUTION CHANNEL EVOLUTION

The major changes here have been the emergence of car supermarkets and direct distribution.

Car supermarkets

This concept is becoming very popular in the UK, as it already is in the United States. These offer comparison shopping for the same type of car in a number of different stores in the same location. Their aim is to create a classic retail environment, in which customers have a wide range of choice at a fixed price, and can buy in the certainty that they are getting value for money. In the UK, they specialize in cars that are reasonably new (ie up to about five years old), displaying 1,000–2,000 cars per site, receiving around and selling 250–300 vehicles per week per site, and receiving 2,000–3,000 visitors per week. Many car buyers buy service packages. In response to these moves, dealers themselves are changing, taking on multiple new-car franchises, with many dealer companies now being listed companies and moving into related areas, eg bulk crash repair contracting with insurance companies. Such groups now control around one third of car sales.

Direct selling by automotive manufacturers

Car makers are increasingly bypassing dealers in the UK, especially in their relationship with fleet buyers. The major trend is for smaller fleets to buy direct, but many fleet managers with fleets of all sizes who are not currently buying direct are negotiating with manufacturers to buy direct. Fleet managers are increasingly going direct to auctions to dispose of their cars as well. Direct selling experiments are widespread, and the Web is used extensively to support selected dealers.

The manufacturers' response

The manufacturers' response to these developments is very simple, and is of two kinds.

The first, typified by BMW, is to focus even more strongly on the brand and the product, to ensure that demand always exceeds supply. This maintains the manufacturer's bargaining power vis-à-vis dealers. However, this is combined with a very strong partnership approach towards the dealers. As one BMW manager put it to one of our researchers, 'Our job is to make desirable cars and ensure that dealers have something special to sell; the dealer's job is to sell them to the right customers'. For this reason, BMW's investment in CRM is focused mainly on ensuring that the relationship with customers is three-sided, involving manufacturer, dealer and customer in an equal partnership. Tough standards of customer management are enforced on dealers, but to mutual benefit. The manufacturer's aim, for example, in its direct marketing, is to get the right customers to visit dealers and buy or receive service. This strong three-sided relationship is cited by many customers as one of the reasons why they stay loyal to BMW, despite the premium price of cars and service. It is the envy and ultimate aspiration of many other quality brands.

The second response, typified by the mass-market producers, is, it seems, to attempt to take control of the marketing cycle, whether through media advertising, direct marketing, or new media, and to make the dealer subservient. Discounts to dealers are reduced, and returned as a series of incentives if the dealer conforms to the manufacturer's marketing strategy.

To an outsider, the two policies may not seem very different. But the difference in strategic emphasis is clear to both manufacturer and dealer, and sometimes to customers as well.

The longer term

With the end of the Block Exemption, which allows car manufacturers to specify that dealers must sell only their brand, we expect an environment which is more akin to classic retailing. Of course, the dealer will continue to sell and maintain vehicles because the manufacturers have no skills, experience, and premises. Nor in most cases do they have a customer focus. In fact, the trend towards buying direct which we identified above is a classic case of disintermediation taking place because of intermediary failure, but in the case it is a failure connived at by the manufacturers themselves! Once car intermediaries are free to deal with who they like, subject to meeting safety and similar conditions, we see the following possible scenario. CRM by manufacturers will focus less on identifying customers and more on: getting customers to identify themselves by responding to promotions and other solicitations; rewarding customers for loyalty.

Meanwhile, strategic marketing competition between manufacturers will focus on brand, product and price. Competition between intermediaries will become similar to that visible in the retail sector today. Dealers will get bigger territories – in fact, the very idea of a territory may disappear, as it is doing in the United States. It will be up to dealers to decide where they want to locate and what catchment area to try to cover. They will of course become multifranchise.

SUPPLY CHAIN DEVELOPMENTS

Some experience and methodologies can be transferred between product markets, and some cannot. One of the reasons that automotive industry managers are uncertain about what can be transferred is the nature of the automotive supply chain. The car is a very complex piece of machinery that represents most consumers' largest or second largest (after a house) asset purchase and holding. Certainly if depreciation is taken into account, for most consumers who own their own car it represents one of the three most important financial flows in their lifetime (together with house and pension), with at least as high a level of risk. But there are significant differences between these three categories. Most houses are bought used, as seen, from another consumer. The frequency of house purchase varies, but is typically no more frequent than every 6–10 years on average. Pensions may be bought three to four times in a lifetime (and sometimes the employee makes the decision). In an (increasingly typical) two-car family, a gross investment of £10,000–£20,000 is made every 18–24 months. Associated with it is a reliability risk (although the increasing dominance of three-year warranties is reducing the perceived risk). If the car is bought used, the consumer can reduce the risk by buying a three-year warranty (although exclusion clauses are something of a worry to consumers). If the car is bought new, the customer can also specify their particular version. (This is also possible to a lesser extent with housing if bought new – though if bought used, houses can obviously be modified; in pensions, not much can be customized – basically just the payment and term.)

But this degree of customer-specification in the motor industry – most easily measured by the difference between the basic model and top-of-the-range price – creates problems for the supply chain. For while manufacturing flexibility helps companies move towards build to order without penalizing the customer with long delays, volume car manufacturers rely on sales pressure through the dealer channel to achieve their targets. This means that they must commit to producing particular variants. Of course, it is also more economical to do so, as it means that they can achieve purchasing and sometimes assembly economies.

In this situation, CRM techniques can help, by asking or motivating customers to commit early to particular variants. This tendency is already clearly visible in mass-market holidays, where early booking discounts are prevalent. So perhaps as more consumers buy cars on finance, with a clear intention of replacing after, say, three years, it will not be uncommon for consumers to respond to offers of (or indeed demand) early order discounts for their replacement car!

One reason why customers are not prepared to commit in advance in any industry is the thought that they might be able to get the item cheaper if they wait until the last minute, to get a discount from a supplier who is desperate to sell. This happened in the package holiday market. Of course, the closer the attunement between demand and supply (overall volume and particular variants), the less likely this is to occur. As the market moves more towards retailing norms, this is less likely, as selling will be less through manufacturers pushing stock through the chain, and more through intermediaries pulling stock through it, based on their demand. Of course, the increasing 'retailization' of the industry may mean that the advance order relationship is with the retailer, not the manufacturer, as it is with holidays.

Many commentators used to feel that the threat and opportunity of the end to EU Block Exemption would set automotive manufacturers in direct competition with their multi-brand dealer networks. In addition, the Internet is clearly already having an increasing impact on the whole automotive-buying process. New entrants are entering the market to sell both new and used vehicles at discounted prices with the promise of improved levels of customer service, ie Virgin, AutoByTel. A significant challenge for these new Internet-based entrants is the lack of a 'bricks and mortar' distribution infrastructure. Vehicles still need to be test driven, received from the manufacturer, stored, pre-delivery inspected and then delivered to the consumer. Trade-in facilities need to be offered. Many new entrants are therefore developing partnerships with existing dealer groups and inspection and valuation services.

Many manufacturers have recognized that dealers add significant value in the fulfilment and distribution of the vehicle. Although in the UK, there are several manufacturer-led initiatives to market and sell vehicles directly to consumers via the Internet, in each case the dealer plays a significant role in the distribution process. The cost of developing 'a green field' distribution network would be prohibitive for the manufacturers, particularly for those operating in mass-volume segments. Manufacturers are likely to continue to focus on their core business of manufacturing, marketing and selling new vehicles while generating additional revenues from cross-selling complementary products and services, both traditional (ie insurance, finance) and new (ie Internet services, infotainment). One significant opportunity for dealers is to focus on profitable areas such as used vehicle sales and after-market parts and servicing. As a result of the global consolidation of vehicle brands to a small handful of manufacturers, the dealer might have the freedom to offer a broad portfolio of vehicles.

Dealers will soon be forced to make long-term strategic decisions. Do they partner with a new market entrant in a multibrand environment, relinquishing their sales and marketing processes to that Internet-based entity? Do they partner with a manufacturer and increasingly share their processes, technology and knowledge with a single or multi-brand manufacturer and accept that the manufacturer will play an increasing role in managing the relationship with the consumer? Do they attempt to develop their own customer-oriented, multichannel, multibrand retail environments? Or is a combination of these, the optimum mix?

Online browsing and buying

The Internet is affecting the automotive business in many ways. Autobytel, the US Internet car sales organization which expanded into European retailing last year, is to target the fleet sector – operators, dealers, manufacturers and finance providers – with an online auction service expected to start later this year. Autobytel executives claim that the avoidance of unnecessary transportation and other administrative costs should benefit both sellers and buyers. Initially to be confined to dealers, the service may eventually be opened up to private buyers.

Over the past several years, Ford has fallen behind GM in the telematics race. But recently it announced a partnership with Qualcomm to develop technology and services through a new venture called Wingcast, which will be based in San Diego. Americans already make about 70 percent of their wireless calls in vehicles. GM's OnStar system's services include automatic air bag notification, stolen vehicle tracking, emergency services, remote door unlock, roadside assistance with location, remote diagnostics, route support, convenience services and concierge services. GM says it will offer a built-in voice-activated wireless service by the end of this year that can make ordinary phone calls as well as access customized Internet services. GM says 4 million of its vehicles will have the service within three years.

Ford has offered limited telematics services for several years, principally its Lincoln Rescu system and Ford Visteon product. Both are aimed at emergency messaging services. Wingcast, using Qualcomm's CDMA and location technology, will broaden those offerings starting with a core set of products a year from now and more complete services in 2002 and beyond. Ford says more than 1 million of its new cars and trucks will be equipped with the products and services by the end of 2002, 3 million by 2003 and virtually all of its cars and trucks by the end of 2004. In March 2000, Ford announced a deal with Sprint PCS to provide wireless voice and data services to select Lincoln 2001 models, including voice-activated calling, emergency and roadside assistance and Internet content. That relationship will last through 2001 but is subject to review after that.

Ford has just launched a new Web site. Called FordDirect.com, the site will allow customers to browse models, select styles and options, negotiate a price, obtain financing, and schedule the purchase and delivery of the new car or truck. Customers will buy the vehicle through a dealer, who they choose on the site, and they will see both the e-price and the invoice price. Ford Dealer Council, with 4,200 US dealer members, said it initiated the idea for an e-business site, and 95 per cent of the dealers were in favour of selling over it. Ford's move to set up FordDirect and GM's BuyPower scheme reflect concerns among car makers that they could lose sales to large independent Web retailers, such as Autobytel and Amazon.com. The venture is a significant step of cooperation between a vehicle manufacturer and its independently owned and operated dealer network to sell cars over the Internet. Dealers have been very wary of the manufacturers' e-commerce attempts, fearing that eventually the car makers would attempt to circumvent them and sell direct from the factory online. Earlier this year, GM aroused the opposition of some of its US dealer groups amid fears that its Internet initiative would bypass car showrooms. GM has since signed a strategic alliance with Reynolds & Reynolds, the information management group, to develop a Web-based system that will include dealers. Ford is also piloting direct Internet sales in Europe, but the project has yet to be rolled out across the region amid fears that it could alienate dealer groups. So far, the European pilot has been confined to Finland. The UK is expected to go online soon. GM has also developed an Internet-based sales systems in Europe, where Vauxhall, its UK arm, has set up direct sales for some of the group's best-selling models.

The Gartner Group says that 48 per cent of the households surveyed used the Internet at some point in its new-car buying process; 45 per cent used the Internet for information while 3 per cent actually bought their new vehicle online. This compares to less than 25 per cent of households that used the Internet to shop for a car only two years ago. Gartner surveyed 40,000 US households that had made a new car purchase from September 1999 through March 2000. The vehicles referenced were brand new, as opposed to previously owned vehicles that may be new to the purchaser. When the survey households were asked to indicate how likely they were to use the Internet in their next new car purchase, 48 per cent of all households said that they were 'very likely,' and 51 per cent said that they were at least 'likely' to shop for their next new car online. The two most popular new car buying activities on the Web were finding and comparing prices and requesting price quotes. However, Gartner believes that the participation of consumers in online auctions or reverse auctions for new vehicles will grow at the expense of other activities such as reading online car classified ads. In prior years, male new car buyers outnumbered women buyers online. That gap has now shifted as more women than men shop for new cars online. Gartner attributes this to the fact that there is less pressure to make a sale online.

Gartner says that the Internet is evolving from a pure shopping tool to an alternative way of buying a new vehicle. Of the households surveyed, 7 per cent said that they are 'very likely' to buy their next new vehicle online, up from the 2 per cent of households that already have done so during the six-month period covered by the survey. Of the households surveyed, 12 per cent said that they would be 'likely' to buy their next new car online.

Automotive business-to-business Internet exchanges

In the UK a recent development in many industries are business-to-business Internet exchanges (eg letsbuyit.com). It is forecast that 40 per cent of all e-commerce in the future will be through these types of exchanges. A challenge for automotive manufacturers is to avoid becoming a commodity. Should the manufacturer participate if the aim of the exchange is to reduce price? This issue highlights the importance of branding in the automotive industry and indeed the importance of effective prospect management.

Changes in automotive CRM

Spend is shifting towards new media. A significant shift is beginning to occur from above-the-line to below-the-line activity. Manufacturers do not trust dealers with marketing activity and in nurturing long-term customer loyalty. Manufacturers are increasingly monitoring the performance of the 'dealer experience' in both customer acquisition and retention. Dealers are not perceived as effective at capturing and sharing customer information. However, dealers are often included in manufacturer-led marketing, particularly in retention programmes. Loyalty clubs are particularly good for maintaining a dialogue with the customer. Manufacturers are trying to understand 'loyalty' and develop metrics for planning contact programmes based on that understanding. One hypothesis is that the higher the brand value, the higher the capability to manage customer loyalty. If that is the case, then mass-market car manufacturers may need to work considerably harder at managing customer loyalty.

CUSTOMER BEHAVIOUR

How customers buy today

Some of our clients have researched the acceptability of a straightforward CRM approach, in which customers' needs and wishes were understood, and then they were given information, products and services of relevance to them throughout their relationship cycle. This research nearly always showed that what clients want is virtually the opposite of what they get. Information gathering by companies is one-sided and no feedback is given. It is aimed exclusively at current customers. Customers see many customer satisfaction questionnaires but no feedback. If you are not a current customer, it seems that nobody cares about you in the auto industry, and even then, information is gathered from you for the general good of the company, not for your good. Discussions are seen as lacking interaction, compared with similar companies that encourage dialogue by telephone. Customers are beginning to develop benchmarks of companies who treat them relevantly, and none of these benchmarks is in the motor industry. One of the life cycle benchmarks is Procter & Gamble, with its diaper/nappy programme – information, offers, tips, small gifts lasting through the life cycle of the nappied baby!

Research seems to show that most customers would like direct contact with the manufacturer from the beginning of the relationship. Normally, the manufacturer is regarded as more competent and objective than the dealer. Customers hope that direct contact will lead to them being more appreciated as customers, receiving more care and attention and being regarded as part of the family. However, there is a big difference between countries in how customers view dealers versus manufacturers. In some countries, customers just want the dealer to be replaced by manufacturers, who are considered more competent and honest, while in others the manufacturer is considered too remote. However, contact from the manufacturer is often seen as flattering to the customer, and in some cases a new and objective source of information. Service industries are quite active in this approach and provide the benchmark for many customers (financial services, mail order, retail, travel and tourism, public sector, etc).

Research carried out by our clients indicate that customers look for the following in communication with automotive suppliers as follows.

Before the purchase

- The dialogue being opened well before the purchase – six months to two years before. Remember those who consider the next car when they've just bought this one. This is important for prospects with competitive makes – they want to be taken seriously.
- Exploring aspects of the dream.

- Questions about how they use or would like to use a car, not lots of questions that help suppliers categorize customers – though some customers recognize the serious purpose behind this. It's mutual classification: 'Are we right for each other?'
- Information on how the car will be for them, given their individual usage.
- A feeling of participation, particularly if it involves test driving (well demonstrated by Land Rover events and Audi racing). For after-sales service, being part of the family (and so being treated well) is important.
- A clear view of the long-term financial consequences.
- No unsolicited contact by phone.
- Use of electronic media (CD ROM and the Internet) if they themselves are users.

After the purchase

- Customers value additional information and attentive treatment, especially just after the purchase.
- They look for thanks for being a customer.
- They look for suppliers who provide assistance when customers really need it.

Some of the questions customers ask of their supplier – manufacturer or dealer – include:

- Does the supplier take me seriously?
- Does the supplier understand me?
- Does the supplier respond when I give information – or even when I ask for information?
- Is the proposition right for me – in terms of style and content of communication?
- Is the supplier telling the truth?

Much depends on the relationship between the dealer and the manufacturer, and how the customer perceives it. For some customers, the dealer is simply the point of dealing, with the manufacturer as fallback; while for others the dealer gets in the way; and for others the dealer is the preferred contact. The level of trust of the dealer varies greatly within and between countries and between brands.

Automotive companies are rarely seen as having effective customer contact programmes. Where professionalism in contact strategy and execution is observed, it tends to be manufacturers that are seen as more competent by customers. This makes it all the more important, as the market becomes more competitive and less hampered by legislation, that manufacturers do not lose their marketplace 'image' with a set of poorly coordinated programmes. Many manufacturers have (and know they have) already run many poor-quality (mainly poorly targeted and therefore perceived as irrelevant) mailing campaigns. Our view is that many manufacturers need to rebuild their capability in this area, starting with a clear customer management strategy, reduced but more targeted volumes, planned more carefully and executed more professionally, thereby establishing good practice and producing better results.

TOMORROW'S CUSTOMER

To develop a view about the needs and behaviour of tomorrow's customers, we conducted a survey by e-mail among individuals and companies actively working in the customer management, motor and IT industries. Most respondents were senior or middle managers in large blue chip businesses, so their views reflect those of educated ABC1 consumers – more discerning consumers who will often pay more for perceived quality or added value. About half the respondents drove company cars, which they received new. The other half drove their own vehicles – of which roughly half were bought new. A few respondents bought cars for other members of their family, and most of these vehicles were bought used.

The study investigated the recent car buying experiences of the respondents, identifying whether they bought new or used vehicles, or both, how they bought them and whether they bought for themselves or for other family members. The research also investigated the respondents' car buying experience, both at the initial stage of car purchase, and at the later stages of servicing and other customer support. The use of finance for car purchase was investigated, including an assessment of how easy this was to arrange and how effectively the motor retailer assisted this process. Finally, future car buying trends were investigated to identify the selection criteria the respondents' considered most important in choosing a new or used car and to identify what the respondents' thought the car buying experience in the year 2002 would be like. The findings are as follows.

Current car buying experiences

More than half the respondents made their most recent car purchase for their first car based on a dealer visit, whether they were buying themselves or through their company. Press advertising (display and classified) was the other key route to find the car they wanted. Finance played a relatively large part in the purchase of the first cars for all respondents. For second cars, the purchase was made mainly from dealers, although some were made at car auctions.

Almost all respondents stated that they did not have a relationship of any value or significance with the manufacturer of their car, nor with the dealer from which they purchased. Neither did they have any continuing relationship with the finance company that had financed their vehicle. Indeed, comments relating to the finance companies focused more on 'pestering' calls and calls to resolve problems rather than positive issues.

When asked what criteria the respondents would give priority to in selecting their next car, the factors that affect overall safety for driver and passengers received the greatest vote: build quality, reliability, general safety, accident protection, braking, good visibility and comfort. Running costs, ie fuel economy, maintenance economy and low depreciation, were quite important for most respondents. Spaciousness, load-carrying ability and manoeuvrability were also rated quite important. The power of a brand of which the buyer has previously had a good experience, and the availability of a dealer nearby rated quite important. Considered not at all important by most respondents were the availability of a diesel engine or four-wheel drive.

In the year 2002...

The respondents were asked how they thought the way people buy cars would change by the year 2002 across a number of areas of the car buying experience. The questions and our comments on the responses follow:

- *Do you think there will be an increase in the use of inbound telephone to the manufacturer?* Many believed that direct purchase from manufacturers was inevitable – there is no reason not to buy direct. Some respondents believed consumers would still prefer the dealer as middleman.
- *Do you think there will be an increase in the use of inbound telephone to the dealer?* As this is already relatively common, particularly for the buyer to obtain initial materials, there was a strong belief that this would increase by 2002, although a few respondents questioned whether dealers would still exist.
- *Do you think there will be an increase in the use of outbound telephone calls from the manufacturer?* This was acknowledged as a key driver for manufacturer marketing direct to the purchaser by about a third of respondents. It raised questions among several respondents about where this left the dealer relationship with the consumer.
- *Do you think there will be an increase in the use of outbound telephone calls from dealers?* Accepted by the majority of respondents as a normal sales technique already, this was expected to be sustained in the year 2002 although not considered very sophisticated by most respondents.
- *What will be the role of direct mail?* Respondents believed that this would still be important in car selection, reinforcing other marketing communications activities.
- *What will be the role of the Internet?* Considered by some respondents to be already making inroads into the car selection process, the Internet was seen by many as a very powerful future alternative for customers to get information. However, current Internet users were seen as not necessarily the most ideal for the market as a whole.

- *Will other uses of the PC be made for the car purchase?* The PC and in particular CD ROM was cited as an ideal medium for virtual test drives and the provision of more information for consumers, possibly taking the place of hard copy literature.
- *What will be the use of kiosks?* Positioning kiosks in dealer sites was highlighted by some respondents, but many believed the kiosk would not be used to a greater extent in the future.
- *What will be the role of truly interactive digital TV?* This was seen by many respondents as the real threat to the Internet and CD ROM with the benefits of colour and interactivity empowering consumers more in their decision-making process. Some respondents highlighted the advantages of this medium for obtaining information about customers.
- *Will the dealer visit be a feature?* Despite all the new technology on the horizon, most respondents believed the dealer visit and the opportunity to see and drive would remain an essential part of the car buying process.
- *Will the test drive continue?* Many respondents believed that new technologies would become an integral part of the test drive process. The test drive would not disappear but be complemented by other ways of seeing and assessing vehicles before the consumer actually put on his or her seat belt.
- *What will be the role of finance?* Most respondents believed finance, in one form or another, would remain important in the car buying process although there was a general view that there would be a greater move towards interest/capital depreciation and that finance should play an important part in the customer loyalty process.

MAIN CRM STRATEGIES

Despite all the problems faced by automotive manufacturers trying to develop closer relations with their final customers, the efforts to do so are heroic! However, compared with other industries, such as financial service, retailing and airlines, the use of CRM techniques, whether by automotive manufacturers (selling through dealers or direct) or the dealers themselves, is still at a very early stage. The main areas of focus in the industry today are:

- Developing loyalty/affinity through communication programmes, with small incentives.
- Improving the performance of call centres in handling and prioritizing customer enquiries and ensuring that customers have timely information on the product and how and where to buy it.
- Focusing on best prospects.
- Improving the capability of dealers to manage customers. This includes rationalization and quality improvement, to ensure high-quality presentation of the brand and management of the relationship.

There is some difference between established suppliers and new entrants. Established suppliers tend to focus on:

- Maintaining and strengthening the brand.
- Sustaining high-quality nationwide coverage of their dealer base.
- Improving the quality of existing customer lists.
- Reviewing their very large prospect files to identify which current non-customers are worth managing.
- Developing integrated marketing campaigns – covering all media old and new.

New entrants tend to have the following characteristics:

- A relatively low media presence. They are more press reliant, often via dealers, but with some use of door-to-door media.
- Building the brand from a low base.
- Database-building/profiling/targeting.
- Ensuring dealer coverage in the highest potential areas.
- Focus on dealer selection, then building the dealer relationship.
- Building the after-sales relationship.

More established competitors are starting to focus (correctly in our view) on the need to develop a consistent information warehousing infrastructure across their whole business. This is clearly more difficult to achieve because it cuts across organizational boundaries and areas of responsibility. Many companies believe that they need to address the customer information challenge before being able to move on effectively. This usually means starting with a good customer database.

Who sponsors and manages CRM?

One of the problems the automotive industry suffers, like many other industries, is the issue of who 'looks after ' (we avoid the use of the term 'owns') the customer, and at what level of seniority. In general, our research shows that the marketing department may not have full executive management sponsorship of this area. One of the reasons for this is that marketers have not created (or even helped create) the kind of integrated information infrastructure to support customer management. Too often, their first reaction is just to 'get the communication job done' by outsourcing tactically, without regard for the long-term consequences, instead of taking a strategic view (whether or not through outsourcing). Of course, it is also true that other functions, such as dealer operations, sales, product management, and customer service, feel that their jobs are also at risk if their particular part of customer management fails, so they want to control it! We believe that improving the customer database (which may mean outsourcing it) and designing the links to the rest of the business is a priority and a good pragmatic first step. Implementing an integrated information/warehousing environment may be a number of years away for most automotive companies.

However, it is certainly true that there is a new interest in CRM in the automotive industry, driven by real or perceived gains accruing to CRM in other industries. Interestingly, in several companies it appears that much of the financial and management sponsorship for the new interest in CRM is coming top-down from the manufacturer's HQ (via the local MD to the marketing departments). In some cases, a global initiative is under way.

Dealers and manufacturers in CRM

Larger dealers themselves are becoming involved in the world of CRM as they drive their own CRM strategies, encouraged by the ending of Block Exemption. In any intermediated situation, the original equipment supplier can choose between managing customers in cooperation with the intermediary, or in spite of the intermediary, or sometimes a combination of the two (most common!). Whatever approach is taken, once the intermediaries start taking CRM seriously, manufacturers need to respond with an end-to-end strategy of some kind, unless they plan to resort entirely to product marketing and leave the dealers to manage the relationship. In some cases, this may involve re-engineering the total supply chain and marketing process, right through to and including the dealers.

NEW MEDIA

The Internet is now being used more intensively, and the automotive sector is one of the dominant and most visible users. A customer-controlled medium such as the Web is ideal for a situation in which the customers determine the buying cycle, and may change their mind and want new sources of information at short notice. The strength of third party sites such as Autobytel and Cars-Mart has caused the major brands to respond. Thus, GM began a trial of its GMbuypower site, which requires its dealers to reveal their stock to any enquirer, provide their single best price on any vehicle selected, and allows the prospect to reserve the car. The entire sales process is handled by GM, with Delores providing little more than test drive and delivery facilities. The slow move towards offering transactions on the Internet has also started in the UK.

General advantages of the Web

The major advantage of the Internet is that it allows customers to decide when to contact the supplier and how much information they want to give. However, penetration is still relatively low, though growing fast, and the question of its relationship to interactive TV is still unresolved. However, it is an ideal medium for reaching new car buyers, particularly those who work in organizations which have access to the Internet through their own networks (this is already evidenced by the peak in lunchtime usage!). Associated with the Internet is the possibility of using e-mail to manage the relationship with the prospect or customer. Advertising banners are proving a useful medium, comparable with TV but immediately measurable by response.

The Internet can help an automotive company achieve any or all of the following:

- Increased brand awareness.
- Reinforcement of brand values.
- Communication of new product news, previews, other news.
- Allowing customers to explore options: product (eg the build your own Mini – see below), finance.
- Making it easy for customers to see what used car stocks are available (either directly or via third party sites).
- Better and more personalized information access and service to prospects, including collection of e-mail addresses.
- Improved communication with dealers, eg via extranets – allowing dealers to download marketing and service information.
- Improved customer management by dealers using Web-enabled customer databases.
- Improved buying traffic for dealers (dealer location, links to dealer Web sites, direct e-mail or phone call to dealers).
- Prompt delivery of urgent information.
- Access to production schedule so customers can see when their new car is likely to be delivered.
- Allowing customers to find car from used car stocks of many dealers.
- Helping customers submit requests for quotes to many dealers simultaneously.
- Welcoming new customers by e-mail.
- Cost-effective targeting of markets segments that are poorly served by mainstream marketing communications. These include women, ethnic groups, disabled drivers (see Vauxhall's targeting of drivers for Motability). Disabled drivers are particularly suitable for this, as many see the world through their PC.
- Running customer clubs.
- Customizing services at the point of sale (eg providing warranty, finance and insurance).

- Gathering valuable information about customers – not just what car they want, but their needs, family situation, etc – including through online surveys, online focus groups, passive information gathering (signing in to Web site, 'cookies', where users have been, what they have looked at, how long they spend, what other sites they visit).
- Targeting other members of a user's family.
- Online delivery of documentation.
- Cross-selling and up-selling (particularly in accessories and financial services).
- Financial services renewal or resell.
- Complaint handling. This is ideal given the non-confrontational nature of the Internet, and 24-hour availability. It is very powerful if linked to a call centre; and allows subsequent online tracking of compliant resolution or other problems.

Not all consumers are appropriate for communication via the Internet, but this may change with the use of Internet platforms on digital interactive TV. Today the UK audience is typically ABC1, aged 18–34, and male. So CD ROM (currently present in 2.4 million UK households) can be used to achieve improved information delivery and exploration of options. In public locations, in dealerships or car supermarkets, or at car auctions, kiosks can be used for similar purposes.

THE CALL CENTRE

Call centres are now used extensively by the automotive industry at various stages in their relationship with customers. The prime use is during customer recruitment, when the customer calls in response to a media advertisement to obtain a brochure and/or to get details of his or her local dealer(s). Most of these call centres are outsourced. A general complaint of car buyers is the time it takes for a brochure to arrive. The Web is now substituting for this use of the call centre. In some cases, after customers have made contact, their data is passed to a dealer for follow-up, and also in some cases the manufacturers themselves follow up to identify whether the customer is still interested. This follow-up is usually done by mail. In some cases, the call centre has access to the automotive company's customer database, and the agent can therefore check whether customer details are correct. However, in most cases the connection between the two is through batch updating. In general, it is clear to customers that the call centre is not operating in the integrated manner that they are used to, for example, in motor insurance. The clear disjoint between mailing programmes, call centres and dealers is in sharp contrast to the customer experience in many other areas, and this can lead customers to resist attempts to involve them more closely in the brand through CRM activities.

Call centres are also used extensively for the off-the-road service contract that comes with most new cars, but in this case, the service provider usually operates the call centre, and there is usually no feedback to the manufacturer.

The following trends can be seen in the use of the call centre in the industry:

- Increase in inbound calls to the manufacturer – making the move towards direct purchase from the manufacturer much easier
- Increase in inbound calls to dealers (where they continue to exist), particularly to ask for brochures (where the central helpline has failed), to view or book test drives, to enquire about delivery dates and of course to book service.
- Outbound calls from manufacturers may start to rise if they move more towards marketing direct to the customer, but this will require careful handling of customers who believe their relationship is with the dealer.
- Outbound calls from dealers are an accepted current sales technique – but they are used in a rather unsophisticated manner (ie not targeted at hot prospects) in most cases, so this will need to improve to ensure cost-effectiveness.

Call centres can be used to support the phases of CRM, as shown in Table 19.1.

Table 19.1 CRM applications of call centres

Targeting	Outbound telemarketing to prospect list generated from Internet and coupon campaign
Acquisition	Booking test drive, perhaps ordering too
Welcoming	Welcome and introduction call for every purchase
Account management – retention	Replacement cycle calling at timed intervals before expected replacement
Account management – development	Campaigns to cross-sell and up-sell (eg warranties, accessories, financial services) to the buyer and to family members
Intensive care – service problems	Ensure availability to handle complaints, allow easier complaint tracking
Intensive care – customer change	Regular calling cycle to collect data on any changes in needs
Pre-divorce	Extra careful 'listening' in call centre; triggering urgent action; active calling to identify what else can be done to help customer
Divorce	Outbound call to protect brand and offer route back
Win-back	Outbound telemarketing

The business benefits of call centres in the automotive industry are as follows.

Cost reduction

- reduced costs of marketing and selling;
- increased agent productivity and/or headcount reduction;
- improved staff retention through enhanced job satisfaction;
- lower operational costs through reduced call length, hold time and the need for transfers;
- reduced operational and process complexity;
- capture of abandoned calls.

Revenue increase

- leverage lifetime value of customer relationship;
- enhanced quality of customer service and interaction;
- retention of existing customers;
- attraction of new customers;
- access new customer groups;
- exploit cross and up-sell business opportunities.

STRATEGIC CHALLENGES IN CUSTOMER MANAGEMENT

Identifying today's customers and prospects

There is great scope for improving data usage. This can be achieved by moving away from traditional direct marketing towards CRM. Traditional automotive direct marketing tends to have these characteristics:

- Its timing is determined by the supplier.
- It is one way.
- It is transaction focused.
- It involves target volumes from lists.
- It results in little learning by the supplier.

Automotive CRM could have these characteristics:

- Customer timing is known.
- It could involve dialogue over time.

- It could be continuous.
- It could be focused on prospects and customers, finding the best ones to talk to, using data to make contacts more meaningful, and marketing investment more productive.
- It could use predictive algorithms to decide who to talk to and when, based on predictive models of changing value states.

The key variables automotive suppliers need to include and have data on, to understand when customers are likely to buy, include not only data on the car owned, but also the current state of and changes in income and wealth and occupation, and also issues such as ethnicity.

Using today's data more effectively

The automotive industry is a massive investor in IT, including systems for sales and marketing. It is also a massive investor in market research, and a principal source of income for leading market research companies throughout the world. Typical sources of information include:

- new vehicle registrations;
- used car sales;
- after-market sales – service and parts;
- new car buyer studies;
- customer satisfaction indices (product, service, finance);
- advanced product features studies;
- vehicle inspection clinics;
- quality tracking studies;
- measurements of car age and condition;
- advertising impact studies;
- direct marketing enquiry and response data;
- sales promotion returns and analysis;
- customer attitudes;
- complaints;
- warranty claims;
- breakdown assistance data;
- vehicle finance data (products taken, payments made);
- mobile phone sales data;
- dealer attitudes (own and competitive);
- purchasing intentions (from shoppers' surveys).

Very little of this information has a customer's name attached to it, even if the customer would have been willing to have it attached. Automotive companies that give a free off-the-road service on condition that the vehicle is serviced within the franchise at the right time now support this approach with questionnaires. These achieve up to nearly 50 per cent completion, but often this data is not stored on the customer database for access for analysis. The result is that much of the effort that goes into understanding customers is wasted when it comes to managing existing customers. Much data on events in their lives that is within the company already or available from outside is not used to manage them. One of the reasons for this is that the data is collected by so many different departments (eg product planning, product marketing, dealer management within the manufacturer), and even different dealer departments, for many different purposes (eg forecasting, general decision making, individual customer management).

The information listed above is often structured at a local level (but is rarely structured at the macro level). The value of the data is increased by an order of magnitude when 'knowledge' can be derived from all information sources across the organization. This includes information which is obvious (Mrs Jones has had to take her car back to the garage four times this week and has written to the customer services director, so we had better send her a bunch of flowers and a note apologizing). It also includes less obvious findings (eg data mining shows that 95 per cent percent of French teachers like to drive French cars, so let's advertise in the media which advertise jobs for French teachers – in the UK the appropriate section of *The Times Higher Education Supplement*).

Our conclusion here is that automotive suppliers should focus not primarily on the customer database, but on the customer information environment. However, the customer database is still likely to be the central information repository for customer information, acting as a focal point for customer-related activity. This is just an issue of opportunity lost, (if they get this right the manufacturers should win new customers). It is also an issue of damaging existing business (since the customers are being managed badly and leaving), the latter being a priority of the two because it is the less expensive to implement and naturally leads the former.

Data quality and management

In all industries trying to improve how they manage relationships with customers, one of the first problems faced is the generally very poor quality of customer data. In general, the less frequent the interaction between supplier and customer (this includes billing and payment as well as marketing and service actions), the greater the problem. The automotive industry's contact with the private buyer is in a major burst around new car acquisition – say every three to five years, and then when the car is serviced. This situation is complicated by the fact that the data is shared between manufacturer and dealer (and sometimes several dealers). For makes where the manufacturer–dealer relationship is strong and based upon a very clear division of roles (generally the more upmarket brands), the rules and rights concerning creation, access and updating of data are clear. Where the relationship is more adversarial, manufacturers have found data-quality issues harder to resolve. To complicate the situation further, both manufacturer and dealer may have several different relationships with an individual customer (eg sales enquiries – on the phone, at the dealer, at a motor show; car purchase; parts sales; service; accident damage repair; insurance; loans and leases). This means a customer is very likely to appear on several different databases. Although current owners of cars are available to manufacturers (for safety reasons, in case they have to be recalled), this does not necessarily tell the manufacturer who chose the car or who is driving it.

This complex situation can result in customers receiving duplicate mailings, being treated both as an owner and a prospect, or receiving mailings about trading in a car they have long since disposed of. The situation is improving, however. Most motor companies have invested substantially in reducing the number of databases they have – many have created or are considering creating a master customer file, which is used as the basis for all other databases, though few have created a true customer data warehouse.

However, because customers are not given a clear incentive (eg better service, more relevant information, perhaps a loyalty bonus) to identify themselves whenever they are in contact with the supplier, the area of data will continue to be a problem for automotive companies.

MANAGING CUSTOMER VALUE

Perhaps more than any industry, the automotive industry cries out for the application of the customer value management approach (see Chapter 9). This is because so much of what occurs in the industry today is done because it suits the manufacturers or dealers, and so little is done because it suits the customer. Rarely have we come across a situation where the main channel of access of the customer (the dealer) is regarded with distaste by so many customers in so many respects. Rarely have we come across a situation in which customers cry out to be recognized by their suppliers but are so often denied this. As we have already pointed out, when intermediaries fail in their role, new forms of intermediation and indeed disintermediation take place.

However, the finger of blame for this situation points squarely at manufacturers, who have stifled competition between dealers in their attempt to control their brand through exclusive distribution. Fortunately, in Europe, this situation is gradually coming to an end. Where competition is stifled in this way, customer value inevitably suffers, and new intermediaries, dedicated to providing customer value based on classic retail requirements, come to the fore. We therefore advocate the application of customer value management as a matter of urgency to the whole industry!

A CRM METHODOLOGY FOR TOMORROW

The basic philosophy of CRM as applied to the automotive market would indicate that a cycle something like the following should be followed:

1. Identify prospects.
2. Decide target media – choice of direct response media, mutually compatible (using testing).
3. Build awareness – consumers need information before making big decisions.
4. Carry out main mailing – proposition and the sell – need to establish competitive differentiation.
5. Carry out follow-up mailing – give prospects another opportunity to respond (poor timing first time), especially with good performing lists.
6. Gather information – ask why people are not responding. Gather this information – by postal questionnaires (or just letters asking why) to a cross-sample of the target audience, telephone interviews, market research (although this is not as reliable) – to pin down what is causing this inertia. Asking consumers what they think may even bring about a competitive advantage.
7. Use a welcome pack – say 'Thank you' (the two most powerful words in marketing). Offer reassurance, explain company procedures, invite customers to volunteer information, show interest in their needs.
8. Gather information to build profiles of customers to drive the next steps.
9. Issue regular communications for meaningful dialogue with customers (improving customer service, troubleshooting, relationship building). This could be through customer magazines.
10. Cross-sell, up-sell – use profiles to identify cross-sell (other products/ added value services) or up-sell (longer-term commitment) opportunities.
11. Engage in loyalty building – build customer relationships, encourage customer involvement in new product development, offer appropriate rewards to customer for continued loyalty.
12. Analyse the database – use profiles of the most profitable customers to identify new prospects.

Table 19.2 indicates the main automotive marketing and service processes required at each stage of the relationship cycle, and suggests the type of business question that needs to be resolved at each stage, and the systems that can be used to support each stage.

Table 19.2 Managing the relationship cycle through systems

Relationship Stage	Key Marketing and Service Processes	Type of Business Question	Examples of Required System-support
Targeting	Identify current prospects pool and new arrivals	Who are best prospects – individuals and families?	Data warehouse Data mining
Recruitment	Understand how customer wants to buy or be sold to; develop and deliver customer-oriented marketing and sales process	Who will buy? What and when will they buy?	Multimedia to allow customers to raise hands Telemarketing systems, using profiles from data mining Systems integration to ensure dialogue managed professionally Campaign management system for recruitment process
Welcome	Gather information and provide good service	How can we reinforce bond with customer?	Multimedia to deliver further information to customers Telemarketing system connected to database to allow outbound welcome calls Questionnaire results taken back to database
Getting to know	Understand usage patterns and likely replacement cycle	Who will be loyal customers? Who will buy again? Who will buy more?	Outbound telemarketing/mail gathers information to enhance database (needs, family)
Account management – retention and development	Maintain and support service	Who is likely to become dissatisfied?	Multimedia to provide 'Martini' contact – 'anytime, anyplace' Data mining to analyse results
Intensive care	Customer care Keeping in touch	Who are problems likely to hurt? Who might replace early because of problems or customer changes?	Contact management system and complaints management to ensure professional problem handling and good retention management Integration with call centre and mailing systems to ensure future contacts recognize problems Data mining to track reasons for problems
Pre-divorce	Customer care: Keeping 'close to the customer'	Which customers are at risk of switching? Which ones will replace 'smoothly'?	As per intensive care
Divorce	Customer breaks link	Why did they leave?	Data mining to identify when becomes good prospect again Data management to present good prospects into targeting list
Win-back	Marketing campaign	Who should we try to win back? When should we try?	As 'Targeting' above

TECHNOLOGY AND DATA

In Table 19.3 we show the general situation and the main opportunities in the automotive industry today.

Table 19.3 The technology and data situation today

Topic	Current Situation and Issues	Suggested Resolution
Justification of investment in relationship management strategies, processes, technology	Generally act of faith, with a few properly structured pilots and tests Often poor integration with long-term marketing strategy – database and CRM seen as tactical 'fix' to supplement main drive of product marketing and dealer management	Develop model of customer management which is integral part of marketing strategy Base model on audit of current customer management situation and clear view about how customers want to buy in the future
Customer database development	Great strides in basic database Reduction in numbers Good progress in cleaning of data But mostly used for basic direct mailing and call centre support (in a few cases)	Continue current process of reducing number of databases and building 'data cleansing' into all sales and service processes rather than as afterthought Consider reason why customers should cooperate in maintaining their data Consider development of company-wide customer data warehouse Consider outsourcing management of data warehouse (major advantage in dealers perceiving objectivity of third party) Consider using third party data source suppliers as foundation for data warehouse
Data analysis (eg data mining, profiling)	Some progress made with profiling, but generally weak prediction of which prospects likely to become customers, and therefore poor targeting of prospecting mailing and calling	Move to 'prospect pool' methodology, with profile of likely buyers based on full range of market, economic, social and individual factors, and continuous redefining of profile according to latest trends Consider outsourcing of prospect pool management, so best prospects presented to company at any one time
Campaign management systems – selection, campaign implementation	Strategies of contact management focused too late in replacement cycle, due to above poor analysis Systems and processes unable to deliver consistent approach though all communication and distribution channels	Develop improved profiling of new and replacement buyers Implement 'industrial strength' campaign management systems, supporting call centres, mailing selections, the Internet and dealer systems Consider Web enablement to support dealers through extranet
Call centre development and maintenance	Good practice in literature distribution and customer service, but poor integration across different contacts	Move towards unified call centre approach (supported by and supporting customer data warehouse, the Internet and improved campaign management system)

Table 19.3 *continued*

Topic	Current Situation and Issues	Suggested Resolution
E-mail, the Web, intranet and extranet	Non-integrated pilots proving very successful in delivering better information to customers and gaining (for the first time) customer involvement, but still rather counter culture	Implement transparent marketing approach and put it at the forefront of customer and dealer management Web enable all key applications, and provide relevant and secure access to customers and dealers, to enable them to ask all the questions they want to ask, give all the data they want to give, and manage/be managed as they wish

THE WAY FORWARD

In this chapter we have reviewed the main developments in customer relationship management in the automotive industry. In this final section, we summarize our action points for automotive industry management:

- Increasing competition in the automotive market combined with rapid development of new customer management technologies has increased the focus on enhancing the customer relationship. It has exposed the weaknesses of current channels of communication and distribution in managing customers, and has opened opportunities for new channels.
- Some experience from other industries concerning how to manage customers is transferable, and some must be transferred, as this is what customers are experiencing and want. However, which experiences should be transferred should be researched carefully, and determined according to the balance between expected benefits and costs to all parties.
- Despite having access to mountains of data, automotive suppliers and dealers are generally poor at identifying which customers need managing in different ways. Major improvements are required, and these can be achieved through data warehousing and mining, and through giving customers much easier ways of telling suppliers who they are, what they want, what their problems are and when they are ready to buy.
- Most companies would benefit from a thorough review of their customer management situation, practices and opportunities.
- Most companies need to develop a much clearer and shared model of CRM. This should include how far they want to go in managing customers and being managed by them, the role of different channels of communication and distribution, policies on data sourcing and management, and a clear policy on how much they should do themselves, and how much should be outsourced.

Notes

1   Volkswagen in financial drive, *Marketing*, 5 February 1998 p 3

20

Consumer durables

Merlin Stone and Paul Weston

INTRODUCTION

When a customer buys a 'consumer durable' product, contact with the manufacturer may or may not occur. An intermediary usually manages most contact. The contact is typically infrequent – taking place in bursts around the initial purchase or around regular or emergency service. Sometimes there is no contact with the manufacturer. This happens if the customer uses an 'unauthorized' service agent, or if the product (eg a fitted kitchen) is one in which there is no need for it.

The big problem for most manufacturers is how to get repeat sales from customers they may not see too often. Is it worth either the manufacturer or the agent (retailer, dealer, etc) trying to maintain a relationship with the customer. Would it be better for the manufacturer to apply the classic and well-tried product marketing model, by providing some combination of quality, value for money, availability, reliability, image and so on? In this model, customer management by the manufacturer is implicit rather than explicit. If this policy is followed, is it worth the agent maintaining a relationship with the customer? Or would it be better for the manufacturer to partner with the distributor and share data?

Marketing theory uses a variety of typologies to describe products, according to:

- Importance to the customer – typically in terms of the cost compared to the customer's budget.
- Durability – whether the item is 'used up' by the consumer and how quickly, and how long the item lasts physically.

- Obsolescence rate. Once the customer has bought the product, how long does it remain up to date in terms of its technology?
- Fashionability. How long does the product remain acceptable to the customer compared with products which become available later?
- Customization requirements – whether the product requires adaptation to the specific requirements of each customer (eg fitted kitchens and bathrooms, double-glazing, tailored clothing).
- Replacement requirements – whether when the item reaches the end of its life with each customer, it tends to be replaced, and if so whether by similar or different products.
- Typical resale situation – whether at the end of its life with the customer, the product is resaleable and if it is, what is its likely resale value? Also, how does this vary according to the amount of use of the product, time for which it has been owned, etc.
- Whether the products are binary or not – ie whether the customer typically only has one at a time (eg a fitted kitchen) or several (eg fashion items), or whether the product is typically one of a portfolio of products bought by the customer, either at a moment in time or over time.
- Whether there is typically a relationship between the customer's total purchases from the category and his or her loyalty to one manufacturer (eg whether customers follow a policy of single sourcing or having multiple suppliers).
- Typical frequency of purchase and then use.
- After-sales requirements, especially in terms of service, parts and information, and their associated revenues and costs.
- Cross-sell implications, in particular whether the brand is stretchable beyond the product to other products and services (eg automotive branded clothing, and financial services).
- How the supply chain is organized, in particular whether the customer can view what lies 'before' the final stage in the assembly process, and perhaps can configure modules by selecting them from suppliers 'higher up' in the supply chain (see Chapter 8).

These are all interrelated, but not in absolute ways, ie they are related in different ways for different customers. Items that go out of fashion quickly tend to be replaced as soon as they do by customers who are followers of fashion or image conscious. Other customers might replace the same items only when they no longer reliably perform the physical function they were designed for (eg playing music, transportation). Even here, reliability is subjective. There is also a trade-off between product quality after-sales service – for example, some customers may prefer a product for which little or no service is required, but which is perhaps replaced more often. Others may like products with preventative maintenance and other service interventions as part of the proposition. Higher reliability and modular replacement in many products of the engineering industry have reduced the basis for CRM in many product markets.

From a CRM perspective, the key for the supplier is to understand the nature of the different time-lapse buying patterns for these products. Once these are understood, then it becomes possible to determine the answers to the question, 'Should we use CRM techniques?'.

At one extreme of the product spectrum are fast-moving or packaged consumer goods – grocery foods, hygiene products, and the like. At the other are items such as automobiles and houses. The product may also be a service (eg a mortgage, a pension, an annual family holiday, a hospital stay or even a funeral). However, at the heart of whether it pays to manage customers for any product is the value associated with managing the customer. This in turn depends upon the chosen model of customer management. As we have discussed in our previous chapters, different models of customer management require very different systems, data, processes, metrics, skills, etc. Using the wrong model at the wrong time can be extremely expensive and lead to business failure. This is particularly likely if the user of the model has not worked out its value equation. The value equation covers factors such as:

- Whether the gross and net value of the customer is affected by explicit customer management strategies and how they are implemented. This in turn depends upon customers' propensities to be managed.
- Mean and distribution of the cost to acquire and keep customers.
- Mean and distribution of gross and net value that can be derived from each customer, per time period and over the life of the customer, including after-sales revenues and costs.
- Mean and distribution of customer life with the company.
- Whether any of these means or distributions are correlated with each other (eg is a high gross-value customer expensive to acquire and/or to keep)?

The first factor is particularly important. If the value of customers is not affected by how we manage them, this is probably because product or price is king – more on this later. In practice, it is rarely possible to determine all the value equation factors in advance. Usually they can only be established through piloting and testing.

Also, which model is 'the best' depends partly on what the individual supplier can do, in turn dependent on management and systems capabilities and skills. But is also depends on what competitors are doing, and most importantly of all on how customers want to be managed – or perhaps can be persuaded to be managed.

In general, it seems to be true that the classic CRM model works:

- the higher value the product;
- the more customizable it is;
- the more dependent the customer is on the product;
- the higher the potential for incremental revenue (up-selling, after-sales and/or cross-selling);
- the more frequently the product is bought.

However, factors such as a high obsolescence rate can work against CRM. Very high obsolescence rates reduce the probability that a particular supplier will always lead, so customers may wish to go to review all available products each time they buy.

Also, the usefulness of CRM depends upon whether customers feel locked-in once they have made the choice. For example, private educational establishments tend to keep most of their students from beginning to end of course, while many financial services meant to be of longer duration tend to use CRM for retention purposes, although it is less useful for cross-selling.

Table 20.1 illustrates in a simplified way value versus frequency of purchase. Note that the exact position of a product for any individual customer might be different. Similar diagrams could be drawn showing value against incremental revenue potential or any other of these variables, to identify the CRM potential.

Table 20.2 shows how some of the characteristics of these products affect whether and how CRM techniques can or should be used, for three main categories of product – cars, major domestic appliances (eg refrigerators, washing machines) and fitted furniture (eg kitchens and bathrooms).

WHO KNOWS THE CUSTOMER?

Earlier, we referred to the question of whether the customer is 'known' by either product supplier or agent (retailer/dealer, etc). In our previous chapter, we discussed some of the issues involved in sharing customer knowledge. Of course, in many situations, the customer is unknown or imperfectly known by both parties. Take as an example the situation of a department store that has no loyalty card but only a store charge card. It will only know the name and address of customers who either buy on the store card or else give their name and address as part of the purchasing or service process. This process would include:

- Buying items to be installed in or delivered to the home (eg fitted kitchens and bathrooms, electrical appliances).
- Buying of services where contact details are required as an essential part of the process. This includes financial services, and any product where there is a licensing requirement (eg automobiles, television in some countries).
- Contacting by any medium (mail, telephone, via the Web) to check availability (if name and contact details are asked for), make a special order, or just to order from stock.
- Giving customer feedback (requests for information or service, complaints).

In fact, our experience of working with retailers is that the proportion of revenue to which a name and address is attached is much higher than they believe, though in some cases the details are not kept on a central database. In a recent case, we discovered that a retailer believed that it only knew the customers providing less than half of 1 per cent of its

Table 20.1 Value versus frequency of purchase

Value	Frequency of Purchase Very low (every 4 years or less often)	Low (every 2–3 years)	Medium (every 6 months–yearly)	High (weekly or monthly)
Very high	Housing Pension plans Life assurance New private education course	Automobiles Investment plans		
High	Fitted kitchens and bathrooms Funeral	Private in-patient hospital treatment	Packaged family holidays	
Medium	Items of furniture New fixed line telephony supply	New bank or credit card account New mobile phone account New utility supply contract New online service provider Specific domestic electrical appliance (white and brown goods)	Home PC software Visit to private doctor Motor insurance School uniform Men's shoes	Fashionable clothing Women's shoes Automobile fuel
Low		Domestic telephony equipment	Light bulbs	CDs Cigarettes Batteries Blank video or audio tapes Books Newspapers and magazines Grocery foods Dining out Hair-do Entertainment

Table 20.2 How some product characteristics affect time-lapse strategies

	Automobiles	Major domestic appliances	Fitted furniture
Typical time lapse	Bought every 2–3 years, but more often for families with more than one vehicle, and businesses	Every 5–10 years for each appliance, every 2–3 years overall, except at house move, when several may be replaced at the same time	Every 10 years each for kitchen and bathroom. At house move may be both
Life cycle effect	Change in family size, in job, financial assets or in location of house can trigger change	Change in family size, in job, financial assets or house move can trigger change	Change in job, financial assets or house move can trigger change
Typical customer attitudes and behaviour during time lapse	Frequent use, high salience of brand, usually receptive to communication unless poor experience with quality or service. Some highly involved customers consider replacement as soon as car purchased, others are less involved and consider choices only near replacement time	Frequent use, medium salience of brand, usually receptive to communication unless poor experience with quality or service. If performs well may replace like with like	Frequent use, low salience of brand, less receptive to communication because of infrequency of purchase. Likely to be unaware of brand and will approach replacement as totally new purchase decision
Obsolescence	Quite high – new models usually offer better value for money, but most manufacturers keep pace with each other on product, so absence of specific technologies less likely to cause defection	Medium, so new products available at time of replacement may cause customer to completely reconsider choice	Little effect
Customization requirements	Medium, and manufacturers well adapted to this. However, getting loyal customers to specify high-value options a major opportunity	Low	High, so agent's ability to do this with appropriate price/quality is key
Replacement requirements	Often like for like, or life-stage determined (eg capacity for children, retirement)	Usually higher quality/value as income likely to have risen	Usually higher quality/value as income likely to have risen
Typical resale situation	Trade-in normal	No trade-in	No trade-in
Source behaviour	Likely to stick to restricted portfolio of brands, but may go to any agent	Likely to review many sources	Likely to review many sources

Table 20.2 *continued*

	Automobiles	Major domestic appliances	Fitted furniture
After-sales requirements	High	Medium/low	Almost none except just after installation
Cross-sell requirements	Services, perhaps second vehicle	Medium – between appliances	Medium/low – kitchen to bathroom or vice versa
Possible strategies for managing customers to and through replacement	Strong brand advertising in broadcast and printed media, direct mail, the Internet, but rationalized distribution to control costs and maximize coverage	Brand advertising, strong retail presence, relevant magazine advertising, database viable only through lifestyle questionnaires	Retail showrooms, magazine and other low-cost media advertising, Web

revenue. In fact, the figure was nearer 80 per cent, when all the above knowledge was taken into account. Most of this additional knowledge was for asset-related purchase (see Table 20.3) where the unknown figure is therefore only 14 per cent.

In general, and other things being equal, the higher the proportion of customers whose contact details are known, the greater the potential for classic CRM. Note that from an individual product supplier's point of view, this proportion might be low. But a retailer selling a wide range of durable and semi-durable products might be able to put together a very clear view of most of its customers, provided that it collated the data collected as a normal part of the buying and service process.

CHANGING TECHNOLOGIES

Many products in the consumer electronics segment are becoming increasingly sophisticated. There is a high degree of convergence in functionality. For example, the Sony PlayStation 2 and Microsoft X-Box are Web enabled. They have significant processing power in addition to games functionality. Increasingly consumer electronics are becoming network-connected intelligent devices enabling the manufacture to communicate with (and provide new services to) the consumer in a way which has not been economically or technically viable until now. Such technologies will soon be introduced to white goods

Table 20.3 Matrix of known versus unknown customers

			% from Sales or Service Data	
			Unknown	Known
% from charge card data	Known	30%	6%	24%
	Unknown	70%	14%	56%
			20%	80%

products. These include the 'intelligent fridge' and the 'intelligent kitchen bin'. These products can monitor use and where appropriate automatically reorder via the Internet. Combination products are also under development (eg the microwave oven with flat screen display, Internet browsers and e-mail capabilities).

As discussed in Chapter 19, a similar scenario is developing in the automotive industry. Most engine management and dashboard systems now contain a surprising amount of computer processing power. We are about to experience an explosion in the use of Web-based in-vehicle infotainment (known as telematics). The vehicle manufacturer and third parties will provide various information and entertainment services (ie traffic information, e-mail, news reports, etc). Manufacturers will be able to interact directly with car users. If the previous challenge of power utility companies was getting 'beyond the meter', telematics gives vehicle manufacturers the opportunity to get 'beyond the dashboard' and interact with consumers and monitor their behaviour in a way that was never before possible.

The spread of information processing and Web-enabled technology to products beyond computers is known as 'pervasive computing' (see also Chapter 10). When a customer buys a consumer durable product today, contact with the manufacturer is usually rare. In the future, although an intermediary may play a key role in managing the transaction, the manufacturer will be able to develop a dialogue or 'relationship' with the consumer through the product. Though manufacturers will continue to focus on product reliability, they will also aim to differentiate themselves through the services they provide directly to the consumer and the intelligent use they make of the knowledge they acquire.

CUSTOMER MANAGEMENT – MANUFACTURERS OF CARS AND APPLIANCES

In this section we look at the quality of customer management carried out in manufacturers of cars and appliances.

Using CMAT (see Chapter 1), we can examine how durable goods manufacturers perform in customer management. An average score of 40 means 'some commitment and some progress'; 100 would be perfect. Durable manufacturers perform on average about as well as all other companies. In Table 20.4, we show only those areas where there are significant differences that are important for the purposes of this chapter.

MODELLING THE INTERMITTENT BUYING CYCLE

In this section, we discuss the use of CRM techniques to manage the prospecting and re-buying cycle for products bought intermittently. The longer the gap between purchases,

Table 20.4 CMAT comparison of manufacturing with other industries

Topic	Overall Average	Durable Products	Possible Reasons for Difference
Overall customer management planning	28	29	
Planning for customer acquisition	27	22	Suggest too much action, too little thought
Planning for customer retention	30	46	This is good news, probably showing strong focus on replacement
Knowledge management	23	15	Probably reflects product silos, and use of third party distributors
Developing the proposition	31	26	Proposition is product-focused, not customer-focused
Communicating the proposition	33	27	Proposition is product-focused, not customer-focused
Creating the organization	43	38	Organization is product-focused, not customer-focused
Managing your people	39	32	Organization is product-focused, not customer-focused
Managing suppliers	38	26	Suppliers (eg marketing agencies) managed in product-focused way, not customer-focused way
Ongoing process management	30	24	Processes are product/sales volume-focused
Process improvement	30	23	Processes are product/sales volume-focused
Targeting	30	38	Reflects strong focus on customer acquisition activity, but dangerous when combined with poor planning
Welcoming	29	34	Reflects the strong use of welcome packs, operating instructions, etc
Win-back	21	4	If the customer goes, the manufacturer does not usually know it
Measuring the effect of channels	35	46	Very strong manufacturers' focus on intermediary productivity
Measuring the effect of individuals	37	31	Reflects focus of people on volume, not customers
Understanding satisfaction and loyalty	34	64	Almost overdeveloped relative to the rest; could be seen as compensatory activity
Experiencing what customers experience	28	21	Much research and analysis based on product experience, not customer experience across all functions and interactions
Using benchmarks	31	41	Strong manufacturing focus has probably come through
OVERALL	34	33	

and the less often the act of using the product involves the supplier, the more the processes for managing rebuying are similar to those for prospecting. The similarity increases the lower the loyalty rate. If only 40 per cent of customers are expected to rebuy, the other 60 per cent are prospects. The key questions, for both existing customers and prospects, are:

- Which ones can be led towards buying or rebuying the brand?
- When are they most susceptible to being influenced?
- How should they be influenced?

In terms of our relationship stage analysis (see later), many customers probably go into the problem management stage when considering replacement. However, good dialogue management and service can help save them for the brand unless they have been disappointed by product quality or performance or have had one or more very poor service experiences, which they attribute to the brand rather than the dealer. The problem management stage is similar to targeting and enquiry management stages, in that the probability of buying/rebuying the brand is low. This means that companies must be selective about which customers they target for action. Building a dialogue is expensive. Companies should therefore focus on the hottest prospect pool among existing or other customers (ie the warmest 'approachers') and during the time when they are 'open to buy/rebuy'. The automotive and certain other industries (eg clothing fashions, garden equipment) are helped to identify timing by the dominance of anniversaries in buying cycles. These are as follows:

- The anniversary of the purchase itself can trigger thoughts of repurchase among buyers for some products, particularly if this is because the product has been bought on finance. Note that the actual purchase is often not on the anniversary. For example, many durable goods finance agreements do not reach their term, as the item is replaced sooner and a new agreement is taken out.
- Calendar anniversaries – in the case of automobiles, typically yearly plate changes and the New Year.
- Model changes, which themselves are often driven by regular manufacturer design cycles, eg in the automotive industry four years for minor change, eight years for major change.

Customers do move into and out of the 'ready to buy' stage. In some markets, the decision about which brand and model to buy is often made well ahead of the actual purchase (six months is commonly quoted in the automotive industry, with the balance of time normally spent on identifying which dealer to buy from, and perhaps considering options). For other products, the choice of brand may be left open until the last minute. However, managing a customer towards 'a sale' can be made more complicated by the proliferation of product types. This makes it important for suppliers to manage customers towards the product that is right for them. In some cases, it may not be clear which type is 'right'. For example, in the automotive market, a customer with a demand for safety and capacity might consider a large estate, a multi-purpose vehicle or a sports-utility vehicle. When children leave home, the same decision maker may go for a highly featured upmarket saloon. The increasingly niche nature of the market means that users can in theory (ie if we had data and had done good profiling) be targeted better, but of course with poor data and poor analysis, the probability of targeting the right customer falls! For example, if there were only family cars, we would not need targeting other than on basis of timing and brand. Now we have a complex set of categories, predicting crossover becomes important. However, most crossovers can in principle be explained by changes in needs, circumstances, etc.

The difficulties of predicting who is in the market for what can be overcome to some extent by making it easy for the customer to tell the company – something which most surveys show that customers do not yet believe is easy for them. In direct marketing terms, a company could encourage hand-raising to get customers to tell the company what they want and when they want it. The company could then select them into a dialogue programme. Of course, in most product markets all the natural marketing factors come into play, including:

- Brand loyalty.
- Service satisfaction.
- Promotional responsiveness, particularly to incentives to choose particular models or options or to move one category higher or lower.
- Economic effects, eg the natural tendency to want to trade up in good times (the influence of the economic cycle), but increasingly to trade across to more economical models, due to government policy.
- The family as a decision-making unit. In the automotive market this is particularly important given the increasing number of two and three vehicle families, which means that the family is in the market more often, sometimes – though rarely – for just one brand. Similar trends towards having more than one home create additional opportunities for domestic appliances, fitted furniture and the like.

One aim of customer communications is to reach hotter prospects cost-effectively and keep them on the road to purchasing the supplier's brand. This means that when we assess the effectiveness of different media, we should be measuring how far each medium progresses us along that route. Just generating responses is not enough. More responses from customers who are not ready to buy our brand – or susceptible to influence in that direction – are valueless. Ultimately, the contribution of different media and campaigns to each type of sale must be the measure we use. This even applies to the Web, where the key cost can be getting customers to find their way to a particular site.

Today, most manufacturing companies are at best looking at cost per lead, with very few having fully-fledged return on investment models. One of the reasons for this is that so much depends upon the intermediary to convert the lead into a sale. However, with good lead management, there is no reason why a supplier should not reach an accurate figure for cost per sale for each medium, which allows for variations in intermediary performance. Nor is there good reason why a supplier should not have a clear idea about how different media perform against each other. Even where campaigns are integrated, it is possible to test, for example, TV advertising versus TV advertising plus mail, to identify the uplift effect of mail. Silent TV areas can also be used to complete the test matrix.

The mail is good at gaining consideration, and in triggering visits to intermediaries, product tests and purchase. For products where customers make up their minds quite early, mailing should begin earlier rather than later and then keep customers informed and motivated as they move towards purchase. The cost of the greater frequency of mailing involved should be offset by improved targeting. However, we believe that the cost of using any medium for taking customers through to each of these steps should always be measured and kept under review. But, once again, the more targeted, the better, which is why this chapter explains how to develop and use a targeted approach.

We have discussed targeting and timing – conventionally the two most important aspects of a direct marketing campaign. There is still ample room for improvement to the creativity and offer design, to stimulate customers into action 'Now!' However, it is perhaps the poor timing of the approach that holds suppliers back: they are so uncertain that they know the desired timing of customers that it does not make sense for them to use direct marketing to do what it is best at – moving customers to quick action.

Acquisition modelling

In order to focus mailings on customers most likely to be in the market, companies need to build a model to help them in two main areas: to target the customers most likely to buy in the forthcoming period – product type and particular models; and to identify which messages are most likely to influence those customers.

To do this, the following conceptual sets are required:

- classic economic modelling;
- CRM modelling:
  - customer-oriented definition of CRM;
  - customer-controlled contact;
  - relationship stages;
  - customer value management;
  - loyalty/value matrix;
  - strategic relationship-based segmentation;
  - life-stage analysis.

Classic economic modelling

This identifies that the determinants of timing of acquisition and of the general model-type acquired as an additional or replacement asset depends mainly on:

- the financial status of acquirer – income, wealth (and especially changes in them);
- the cost of funding acquisition (which depends on way it is financed);
- the status of any asset replaced (type, age, usability);
- the demand for services of asset (work, leisure, etc);
- replacement policy (eg frequency).

These may all change with time, so customers move into and out of the likely acquiring group. However, the detailed type of acquisition depends upon marketing (including relationship) variables.

CRM modelling

Some of the key issues that apply to durable goods market are listed here:

- Data-bearing contact is the key to relationships.
- Success in managing the contacts and the data that is given or that arises from them is associated with higher customer satisfaction and loyalty.
- Customer-controlled contact is becoming more popular. Not all customers want their contacts with a company managed by the company – some want to manage it themselves, particularly to signal changed needs or problems. Contact methods must provide means for them to do this.
- Customers pass through stages in relationship: targeting, enquiry management, welcoming, getting to know, customer development, problem management and win-back.
- Recognizing the above, identifying the stages the customer is at, and understanding his or her behaviour at each stage, are key to managing and predicting the move to the next stage.
- Managing relationships with customers requires understanding the value the customer requires from each interaction. Driving valueless contacts will not pay off.
- Customers' value and loyalty to the company change and customers with different loyalty/value mixes behave differently, therefore they should be modelled and managed differently.
- There are many approaches to grouping customers. A key one is to identify segments that need to be managed strategically over a particular period. These are groups of individuals, whose characteristics may change greatly over a period, so in classical marketing terms they seem to be changing segments. But they are the same people moving between segments, eg into and out of a prospect pool.

- Customers' behaviour changes radically over a life cycle. But their basic psychological make-up and preferences tend to change more slowly and can be worked on over the long term. The key to modelling the effect of life stages is to see how other changing variables (eg economic, social) change how they express their needs.

The resulting central idea of the above is that manufacturers should avoid the common cross-section error of assuming customers are permanent members of a group, and move to a time series methodology – what we call here approach management. This requires identifying and understanding the specific factors that determine: when a customer is ready to buy – and ready to buy a particular model type; and what makes a customer prepared to switch.

The central idea of prospect approach marketing

Prospects do not suddenly 'appear'. They develop rather over their lives and 'move towards' or 'approach' either: the brand; or the category.

Note that if a market fragments in terms of model types and brands available, customer behaviour becomes apparently more complex. This implies that identifying timing is the key to cost-effective influencing of customers. Note that the approach period could be several years for more expensive products, through building of wealth or income, and may consist of buying used versions of the aspired product. However, for some the approach period may be just a few weeks (eg windfall gain, sudden experience of class, category or brand).

This implies that understanding the nature and slope of approach is key. This requires focusing on:

- customer behaviours and attitudes;
- segments that customers 'pass through';
- customers' relationship management needs;
- value that can be derived from the 'approaching customer';
- translation of approach into purchase;
- cost to manage the approach;
- how the approach varies in different market segments.

So how do we manage it? The essence of our approach is:

- Identifying those who may approach.
- Predicting who is approaching the time – for brand, category and class.
- Allowing those whose approach we have not predicted accurately to signal it quickly.
- Professional management to help those who are approaching to approach more securely and more quickly as well as translating the approach into sale.

To do this, we need to identify:

- determinants of approach (ie what makes a customer get nearer);
- evidence of approach (ie how we know that the customer is getting nearer);
- policy (ie what we will do with the customer who is getting nearer, and how we can get him or her nearer).

Determinants of the customer's approach

These include the following:

- Static or slow-moving personal characteristics (eg family and business history, past patterns of brand and vehicle ownership type, lifestyle, ethnicity, social group, education).
- Dynamic or faster-moving personal characteristics (eg occupation and status, income and wealth, ability to raise finance, business situation – especially for manager and/or owner, demographics – number in the family, ages, etc). As these are faster moving, changes in and expectations about all the above will also be significant.
- 'Market/behaviour' characteristics(eg exposure to and experience of own and competitive brands, categories and classes, responsiveness to brand and competition).

These determinants are the normal marketing and economic determinants of buying behaviour. Extensive data mining experience shows that these determinants are usually fairly obvious, and that it is data, modelling and quantification that yield competitive advantage. In particular, this advantage is gained through knowing:

- who is approaching;
- who responds to approach management;
- the value they require and value they give;
- eligibility and affordability;
- how they respond – timing, content, etc;
- cost-effectiveness issues – who is worth 'approach-managing', and who should be managed by normal advertising and retail proposition.

As being in the state of approaching is a psychological state, until the customer takes action (eg by responding, visiting a dealer) it is worth identifying what different measures we could obtain of approach status. They include:

- expressed awareness of product and brands, attitude towards them, interest, preferences, satisfaction, etc;
- economic and social variables;

- relationship variables (eg response propensities for all kinds of contact, especially the propensity to give data – overall and different types);
- buying behaviour – for the products and services themselves, and in some cases, buying behaviour for associated products and services (eg leisure and holidays, education, housing);
- Special dates (eg purchase anniversaries, registration periods, finance dates).

Modelling approach

The ultimate aim is to deliver an approach score, predicting:

- whether customers are likely to buy;
- when they are likely to buy;
- what they are likely to buy;
- how they will behave after buying.

This score should be the basis on which different approach management propositions should be applied to:

- different score groups;
- groups with the same scores but with different approach management needs;
- groups before and after acquisition (to build loyalty).

Scores above and below target scores for particular product types indicate that there is unlikely to be value to the supplier in trying to manage the relationship towards purchasing a particular type of product or brand. However, the process should take into account possible misclassification, and allow access to those who want to elect in (customer-controlled contact).

The modelling required needs to take into account the many possible approach routes, including movement between and within:

- brands;
- model types;
- used and new purchases;
- single and multiple product owning.

These patterns must be modelled and related back to determining variables, using: discovery data mining; and hypothesis-based analysis. For data mining, the key issues to be addressed will be:

- timely gathering and recording of key data;
- warehousing key data;
- transformation into a sensible basis for mining (eg data reduction).

Warehousing has a major benefit in that it preserves time-slices of data, often overwritten or neglected in the past. Mining should interact with hypothesis-based work. The result will be a variety of approach profiles to be subjected to mail treatment.

In order to quantify the approach profile, data is required on recent acquirers of the brand/model type *and* non-acquirers. The key sources for the latter are:

- acquired databases;
- promotional responses;
- questionnaires.

Note that data based on current interactions with brand may be irrelevant, as current interactions are usually not based on best practice CRM. In practice, it is probably most cost-effective to try to predict the immediate future, ie near-term acquirers, based on recent past data, and then work one's way backwards and forwards slowly, understanding more and more about the recent past and likely near future behaviour (and its predictability); and how to manage it.

Note that the longer away the event (past or future), the bigger the pay-off must be for it to be worth analysing/managing. Typically, this means focusing on the last two or three years' data, predicting those likely to buy within the next two to three years, and then managing them appropriately and measuring the results.

Modelling process

Here is our suggested modelling process:

1. Hold group discussions to confirm key 'state change' determinants of purchasing.
2. Build the sample database.
3. Develop and implement questionnaire to gather missing present *and* past explanatory data (ie changes in likely determinants).
4. Profile brand, category and class acquirers versus non-acquirers of each, using hypothesis-based and discovery mining techniques.
5. Identify key triggers for purchasing for example:
   - age of existing product(s);
   - children growing up or other changes in the family (eg death of relative plus inheritance);

- changes in business, work or leisure profile;
- changes in income or wealth;
- changes in the relationship with the brand/intermediaries.
6. Develop profiles of 'near acquirers'.
7. Evaluate whether and how data on triggers can be collected:
    - directly (eg through behaviour/response);
    - directly via questionnaire;
    - indirectly – via surrogates (eg financial services buying behaviour for income, magazine or club subscription for interest).
8. Build the main database.
9. Examine the status of acquirers versus non-acquirers, say, one year ago.
10. Use statistical tools to 'post-cast' those who did/did not acquire.
11. Recalibrate the model.
12. Identify those whose current status is that of 'one year from acquiring' (ie apply profile of 'near acquirers' to identify individuals who need to be managed towards acquisition).
13. Market to them.
14. Analyse success
15. Recalibrate the model.
16. Extend to include the following two years.

Summary of model

This can be summarized as follows:

Prob{acquiring new product of your brand and model type} = *f{(Prob(acquiring a product), Prob{product will be new ie not used}, Prob(acquiring model type), Prob(acquiring brand)}*

There are four approach velocities that need to be understood separately. Therefore, the model output will be a scoring model, in which each customer will be scored in a time-related way, ie with probability for acquiring at particular times. Note that the same model will apply for used products (eg used vehicles), ie a low probability of new combined with a high probability for acquisition indicates a high probability of used vehicle acquisition.

Customer approach management process

This is our recommended approach:

- Select predicted near-term acquirers or 'approachers'.
- Research their contact management needs.

- Develop contact management strategies attuned to their needs – particularly their propensity to initiate or accept contact and their responsiveness to contact, especially for predicted competitive acquirers, including allowing them to signal when their changes occur, and ways of developing value to and from customers.
- Implement testing of strategies.
- Measure the results.
- Select the best strategies to apply to the next round of predicted acquirers.

MORE DETAIL ON APPROACH MANAGEMENT

In this section, we discuss in detail how to handle certain issues relating to brand, intermediary and family buying.

The brand

For more upmarket brands, affordability/eligibility is an important dimension, but this should already be covered in the types of data gathered or sourced and the type of analysis to be applied to these. There are three key groups of customers to consider – those who are already within the brand (currents), those who have ever bought the brand (returners), and those who have never bought the brand (novices). Suppliers need to identify which data provides the best indicator of each group's likelihood to buy their brand and models within their ranges. Approach propensity is suggested in Figure 20.1.

The curve for those who have a second vehicle or are considering acquiring one is a combination of this analysis (for replacers) and value approach analysis, for first-time second vehicle buyers.

A supplier's market research should indicate determinants of brand loyalty, but this needs to be translated into a dynamic model, ie how customers move towards and away from the brand, rather than their current state. This model must be supported by the acquisition of data to support targeting of those with not necessarily the best state, but with the state most moveable in positive direction.

Novice approach

Novices are usually identified by their absence from the database of current or past owners. The best approach is simply to ask the question 'Do you own or have you ever owned ...?' as part of a dialogue questionnaire. The key need is to identify individual's attitude to the brand and how far that attitude can be influenced. This is likely to be elicited by two

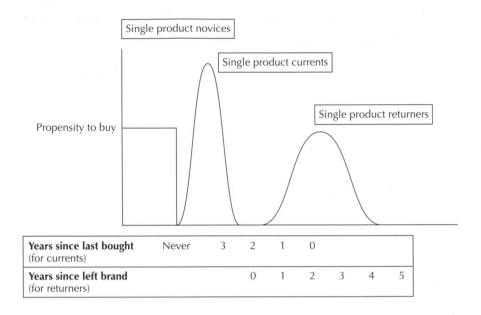

Figure 20.1 Approach curves

approaches: attitudes – answers to questions on brand attributes and preferences, expected consideration; and behaviour – (eg responsiveness to communication, dealer visits, involvement in events).

These should be tracked for these customers over the period of the approach. Small incentives need to be carefully targeted, and different patterns of brand approach must be modelled. This should be aligned with estimates of expected value ie there is no point in encouraging brand approach too early. Different novice dialogue streams must be set up according to forecast value and according to movements in attitudes and behaviour.

Returners

These are customers who have ever owned the brand. If they are recent owners of new vehicles, they should be identified from the company database and/or from sourced consumer databases. If not, they will have to be attracted back into dialogue. They are likely to be two main categories: *portfolio players*, for whom brand is normal part of portfolio but where another brand took last purchase (and in the recent past, where they moved into a particular model type market but the possible absence of the supplier's brand from that type meant they moved elsewhere); and *reluctants*, who had some problem with the brand or product type when they last bought it and need to be persuaded to return to it.

Portfolio players will in principle now have another brand of the same type, and already be in target market for all competitors. They will be relatively easily identifiable through a variety of existing data sources and media. However, higher value of client's brand means that value approach analysis should be applied to them.

For reluctants, the issue with the brand must be identified. This may be an issue with dealer, service experience, inappropriate model chosen (cost, quality, performance), etc. These may be identifiable from past-satisfaction questionnaires, which may have been archived, or they may need to be identified from new questionnaires. The key difference is not in how they are identified – which is the same basic way as portfolio players – but how they are handled by enticing them into dialogue (eg with a different intermediary, for a different product).

For both these categories, we need to identify where possible which product the individuals bought after leaving the brand. This is sometimes available from dealer records (though it may not be entered on the database), or may be available from lifestyle questionnaires. In both cases, failure to respond to attempts to create dialogue should lead to archiving of prospect.

Currents

These are replacers of a sole product. They are owners of another model within the supplier's range, and so should appear on the supplier's database, if there is one. They are more likely to be responsive to promotional solicitations, particularly if they are in the right value class.

The intermediary

This is the most thorny area in manufactured product marketing, and it will remain so. There is usually conflict over ownership of the customer. There is also evidence that starting the dialogue too late, ie in the last six months before purchase, merely influences the choice of intermediary, not brand, but may also influence the choice of extras. Starting the dialogue early will give the brand more control if this is done by the brand – but the same applies to the intermediary. It will also enable secure handling through to the intermediary (eg by early involvement in visits to intermediary, launches and other special events, and test drives). Tracking of these contacts will be absolutely key, via some kind of fulfilment mechanism (eg intermediary stamps voucher, sent back to the centre, in order to obtain an incentive), so the database must track these. However, exposure to fraud is high if the incentive is offered through the intermediary, or involves the cooperation of the intermediary. So there is a need for a customer commitment mechanism, eg in the automotive industry, purchase of sealed test drive kit from a dealer (shrink-wrapped with clear warning of invalidity if seal is broken), for which money is refunded by the central fulfilment house on presentation of evidence of purchase (eg a voucher from inside the kit).

The family

So far, we have assumed that there is only one decision maker per family. This is often so, but there is usually at least one important influencer (a spouse). This person's details must be captured, as he or she affects propensities (eg second income). There may be ethnic, geographical and a variety of other influences at work here.

Sample approach categorization definitions

Table 20.5 gives a more complete categorization for use in targeting.

MANAGING THE FUTURE CUSTOMER

The automotive industry

The motor industry is still very focused on current prospects. If it has ever managed future prospects, it is through service loyalty programmes, in which customers are given small incentives (eg free off-road service) to have their vehicles serviced at franchised outlets. The

Table 20.5 Sample approach categorization definitions

Category	Sub-category	Definition
Value	Current value	Have product(s) of this value
	Near value	Will have product of this value in next 1–2 yrs
	Distant value	May have product of this value in 3+ yrs
Brand	Novices	Have never owned brand
	Currents	Currently own brand
	Returners – portfolio players	Non-currents, have owned and will consider brand, but select by current preferences
	Returners – reluctants	Non-currents, have owned brand, left brand dissatisfied
Type	Type owners	Have type
	Near type	Will have type in next 1–2 yrs
	Distant type	Will have type in next 3+ yrs
Intermediary	Specific attachment	Loyal to specific intermediary
	Open to offer	Will consider several intermediaries
Portfolio	Single product, near	1 product, will replace in next 1–2 yrs
	Single product, distant	1 product, will replace in next 3+ yrs
	Single product, 2nd, near	1 product, will own 2nd in next 1–2 yrs
	Single product, 2nd, distant	1 product, will own 2nd in next 3+ yrs
	2+ products, near	2+ products, replace 1 in 1–2 yrs
	2+ products, distant	2+ products, replace 1 in 3+ yrs
Family	Sole decision maker	Makes acquisition decision
	Spouse/influencer	Influences acquisition decision

assumption is that this will keep the customer 'close to the brand'. Meanwhile, the customer remains on the database anyway because of the last purchase. Often, a change of address recorded through the service database is not updated on the sales database, and the same may apply to an early trade-in. So the customer may be mailed with an offer to replace the vehicle already traded in, and at the wrong address. With this poor practice, it is not surprising that most motor companies have been unwilling to move into managing future prospects. Much of their effort targeted at customers they believe to be current prospects is wasted by the above poor processes.

However, most motor companies are pulling their databases together now, or have recently done so, and this will stop some of this poor practice. This will enable them to focus more on approach management. Some are using questionnaires to establish when customers are next likely to be in the market, but this information is rarely updated, even annually. The obvious way to do this would be a simple satisfaction questionnaire after the first (often warranty-based) service, asking about intentions, brand feelings, interests and activities, and then another questionnaire a year later, replaying to customers what they said last time and asking for an update. These annual questionnaires are usually funded by customer service as a check on quality of intermediary service, but rarely used as an opportunity to tighten the dialogue or to give the customer the chance to express interest. So where does managing the future customer work? There are four examples that we know of, and there may be more (some of these examples are discussed more fully elsewhere in this book):

- credit and charge cards;
- frequent flyer programmes (FFPs);
- telecommunications;
- business-to-business capital equipment.

Credit and charge cards

The average life of a credit card customer is six to nine years until switch (and this life span is falling). The average life of a charge card customer is less, usually around five to six years. Cards may be held for a longer period, but tend to be inactive. These markets are both becoming more competitive. The shorter the life, the more important it is for companies to identify high-potential prospects and get them into the brand. Then, early on in the relationship, they should re-evaluate their customers for their propensity to cross-buy or use more, and then at the end of the relationship identify whether the end has taken place because the customer has moved out of the category (eg moved to debit card, stopped travelling). Given this need, the most advanced companies have identified the profile of high future spenders, and encourage those who fit this profile to spend more by targeted mailings. Likely future patterns of usage are also picked up by some companies through the welcome call. This identifies likely usage patterns and interests. It results in the use of particular communications streams for high-potential individuals. In particular, one charge card company has a good sense of where each individual lies on the value curve (approaching higher value or reaching the down slope). Of course, it has the benefit of being in a continued transaction relationship. But credit card companies also monitor closely the responsiveness of customers to their communications, as often the key to value is not just number of transactions (as value is destroyed for credit card companies by paying off the whole debt each month), but responsiveness to promotions. In this example, the prospect pool for higher-value users is effectively the recent joiners. Knowledge of who is likely to be a valuable customer in the future has helped one credit card company to follow a more discerning policy for dealing with younger customers in trouble. If they are deemed to be of relatively high future value, Barclaycard treat them better, helping them solve their early problems.

FFPs

Until recently, most FFPs were managed entirely by current customer value. As the average frequent flyer lasts three years, and the modal frequent flyer two years, this meant that most flyers were managed best as they were about to stop flying. Now several leading airlines are using data mining techniques to identify future frequent flyers. These are selected from what can be regarded as the prospect pool of relatively infrequent flyers, using profiling by initial patterns of flying, but more importantly according to their location, age, gender, employer and job. Certain international airlines are now treating predicted high future value customers better earlier than their current flying pattern would have warranted.

Telecommunications and utilities

One major telecommunications company can identify likely higher-value small business customers by a combination of their early billing patterns and demographic details on the business (eg type of business). This enables them to focus their customer development and retention work more on higher future value businesses.

The power utilities, following deregulation, are all after each other's customers as they cross into each other's industries (eg electricity into gas). They effectively are faced with a prospect pool of millions of customers, and need to identify which are higher-value ones. Because they are not allowed to use their own billing data to identify high potential customers, they are using postcode-based prospect pools to identify which customers they want to acquire. For the time being they are focusing on likely current customer value (often dictated by size of house). But they are also looking at future value. On the other side of the coin, they want to predict which customers are likely to turn bad. Here, they are more advanced, as utilities are very exposed to bad debt (it is hard to disconnect bad customers). So they are very keen not to acquire customers who may turn bad. They use a variety of finance-based indicators for this (eg credit searches).

Business to business

The heartland of future CVM is really in business to business. This has its origin in the practice of account management, particularly in capital goods (eg IT, machine tools). Here, it is recognized that the customer has an acquisition cycle, and must be managed through it in the way we are suggesting.

The acquisition equation

There is a straightforward equation which summarizes our model:

Probability (acquisition) = f (Good states in some leading and lagging indicators, and positive changes in some leading and lagging approach variables)

Which variables are key can be discovered by statistical modelling and data mining. Focus on leading rather than lagging indicators is important because everyone understands the lagging indicators and they are therefore no source of competitive advantage. This is because customers are approaching the purchase along several different routes (eg they may always have been in the value category but not in the model-type category).

Changes in lagging approach variables = f (Changes in leading approach variables)

Customers should continue to be modelled over, say, the three-year period to see which leading indicators are best predictors of lagging indicators. This will give us competitive advantage in targeting, and help us develop approaches (eg questionnaires) to help define which prospects should be in our pool. The conclusion is that automotive companies could manage future acquisitions better if they identify leading approach variables as early as possible.

Here are some examples:

- Leading approach variable is getting money (or even knowing that you're going to get money), lagging variable is spending the money.
- Leading approach variable is planning to enlarge the family, lagging approach variable is the addition taking place!
- Leading approach variable is having a latent interest in a particular leisure pursuit or holiday type, lagging approach variable is actually taking up the interest or taking the particular type of holiday.

Work on data reduction in mailed questionnaires indicates that psychographic leading indicators can usually be picked up on lifestyle questionnaires, through attitude statements (eg I like ..., I prefer ...) rather than behavioural statements (eg I do ..., I read ..., I buy ...), which tend to pick up lagging indicators. Finally, if customers want to manage their contact with a manufacturer, they are more likely to give the company data as part of that process. Putting it in customer terms, 'I'll tell you what I'm interested in so you can make me the right offer', rather than 'You try to find out what I'm interested in and I'll see if you can make me the right offer'.

CONCLUSION

In this chapter we have investigated some of the issues involved in establishing a relationship with customers who buy higher-value items intermittently. We have suggested that it is not necessarily correct to assume that these customers are managed by CRM techniques. However, using CRM techniques is more likely to work if data is available on the timing cycle and if it is then used to drive a communications cycle which recognizes where the customer is in the acquisition and use cycle.

21

Utilities and telecommunications

Merlin Stone and Steve Dickey

THE CHANGING COMPETITIVE SCENARIO

The utility and telecommunication industries are in turmoil. In just a few years, from being cosy monopolies, on friendly terms with their neighbours, they have been pitched into head-to-head competition with their former colleagues – with some companies becoming multi-utilities, including gas, electricity, water, telecommunications and other services. New entrants, such as retailers and affinity organizations are also involved as utility supply markets and value chains are deregulated. Mobile telephony has turned its sector upside down, with exploding demand and many new applications (see Chapter 10).

After a period when the customer management requirements of the energy and water industries, on the one hand, and the telecommunications industry, on the other, seemed to be diverging, it is apparent that the main difference between the two is the complexity of services and the associated complexity of billing that separate them. These latter factors were expected to lead to lower levels of switching between suppliers and less price competition. In many countries, tough regulation, including the enforcing of interconnect agreements and number transferablity have ensured that competition in wireless telecommunications has been just as tough as in energy. Throughout this chapter, we therefore use the term 'utility' to refer to both sectors, unless specifically stated. The water industry, being still a regulated monopoly in most of the world, has less of a requirement for the customer management techniques, processes and infrastructure discussed in this chapter, but many of the points still apply here too, and nearly always in respect of the unregulated part of a water company's business (eg service contracts).

IT spend has increased rapidly to enable companies to cope with the increasing amount of data, and to provide individualized services such as real-time billing. Pricing is becoming much more sophisticated. Customers may receive increasingly individual pricing (eg loyalty bonuses for length of customer relationship or lack of servicing claims). Customer loyalty activities are more common. However, consolidation is also occurring, just as in other deregulated industries such as railroads or airlines after being deregulated.

The entry of retailers into reselling energy was not the first intermediation in this market. Intermediation has long existed in telecommunications, mainly in the mobile phone market. Retailers benefit not only from a sign-on fee, but also from a share of the subsequent network revenues from the airtime provider. In energy, brokers have always been present. They exist not only in domestic fuel oil, where they negotiate with the major suppliers on behalf, for example, of housing estates or blocks of flats. They have also been around for some time in the public sector, and have recently appeared in ethnic communities.

Naturally, there is a major risk that these developments may lead to a fragmentation of customer service – the same accusations that have been levelled at the UK's railway system in the area of ticketing, pricing and timetables and, in certain sad cases, safety, after accidents have occurred. However, if the truth is to be told, the fragmented situation is the norm under capitalism, because it brings specialization and creates the 'nowhere to hide' situation, where it is on the whole pretty clear who is responsible for what, rather than it being hidden inside an impenetrable monolithic structure. Who would suggest that an airline should own all travel agents, airports, even holiday destination and travel-related financial services? Indeed, in the travel industry, the merging of holiday airlines, package tour companies and travel agents that has occurred has clearly led to a reduction in choice. In railways, although there have been some problems with customer service, there is a strong argument that the focus which breaking up the value chain brings will in the end result in better service. However, there is also evidence that rail traffic is starting to rise faster than would be accounted for by economic recovery, and this is due partly to improvements in the nature and frequency of service (although progress with service is a little patchy!).

Meanwhile, the new utility suppliers have already learnt this lesson. For example, they have discovered that one of the best ways of recruiting customers is to contract the task out to field-marketing companies, who literally walk down the streets 'door-knocking', to propose the switch to every customer on the street (except financially risky ones). As with all of these practices, there are risks, and many training and poor sales-practice issues have arisen. For example, there is a risk that field-marketing companies will recruit for one company, be paid the recruitment fee, and then re-recruit for the competitor!

DATA PROTECTION

Utilities see their customers partly through their customer data. It is this data which has traditionally helped utilities keep customers informed of new developments, but now enables them to focus on the retention of desirable customers, or ensure that customers who have had problems are better treated when they start a new relationship. However, what utilities are allowed to do depends partly on what the government allows them to do with their customer data. This has already caused problems in countries with existing data privacy laws and regulators.

In allowing for competition the regulators have been keen to inhibit use of existing customer data for the marketing promotion of new services, as it was never collected for this purpose. For instance, in the UK electricity companies were 'banned' from using their electricity billing databases as a source of information for trying to sell gas. This restriction has led many to create separate databases or use standalone lists. This has clearly affected marketing costs and capabilities, and the sophistication that they have managed to achieve in their targeting (for many electricity companies the initial recruitment costs for gas customers who were already electricity customers have led them to consider in-area-only acquisitive strategies). It may also have led to a customer perception that these utilities are unable to reference one service together with another that they may be receiving. On a wider corporate level it brings into question one of the potential benefits of acquiring competitive utilities either in a vertical or horizontal integration

The economies of scale that can be achieved by creating multi-utilities – offering one-stop shopping for gas, electricity and water to its customer base – and the potential systems integration to allow a seamless customer interface, ie unified billing systems, marketing databases using centrally held information, etc, is not currently being realized. In the United States, several utilities have begun positioning combined products and services offerings through various alliances. Their experience to date has been to achieve lower than expected customer acceptance as well as higher than expected complexities in making the deals work with their business partners. This is due to the level of uncertainty that exists in the regulatory system and the political decision making. There are clear dangers in committing to an IT strategy and substantial investments towards delivering these benefits, when the 'goalposts' have been moved so much already. A healthy degree of scepticism exists within utility IT departments, and with justification.

The legal debate on this issue is complex and its state seems to change quite often. There is some degree of confusion between what is allowed by the regulations or voluntary code of practice of each industry in each country and what by data protection law. In fact, the latter is usually more liberal, as it allows a company to market almost anything to its customers, provided consent has been sought. However, utility licences issued under the several utility acts prohibit utilities from using their customer databases for marketing non-utility products and services. At one time customers had no choice but to reveal their details to what were monopoly suppliers and the view is that this position should not be exploited. We can expect the current pressures and restrictions to continue for a short time, but certainly expect a degree of liberalization in data use once market share becomes fragmented.

Despite all this confusion, most utilities have decided that if they are going to keep their valuable customers and acquire valuable customers from competitors, they need to invest in a strong combination of customer service, sales, branding and direct marketing. But they also know that they have to adapt this combination to take into account a number of special issues, in addition to those mentioned above. The first of these is the bad customer syndrome.

THE BAD CUSTOMER SYNDROME

Utilities are particularly open to special customer risks – in both consumer and business markets. The simplest is failure to pay bills. One way consumers do this is to move between different utility areas within the same broad region. In the United States, work by Equifax with such companies has resulted in a tracing database and process (Equifax Exchange), which allows debtors to be tracked. When they appear in another area, if they have outstanding debt, this can be dealt with, and the new supplier can ask for prepayment. Members of Exchange find that around 10 per cent of new applicants actually have a concealed history of bad utility debt. The use of this approach results in 3–5 per cent additional revenue, which is immense given the very tight margins that utilities operate on. It also saves the costs of marketing to (and then de-marketing to) high-risk customers.

A related problem is consumer financial distress. When a consumer gets into financial difficulty, typically the first unpaid bill is the utility bill – not the credit card, because failure to settle this leads to rapid barring from this and all other sources of credit. But utilities are usually regarded as 'fair game' for such consumers, and while the debt may finally be settled, this is often only after a protracted and costly period of negotiation and special arrangements. This is more serious for telecommunications suppliers, whose exposure can be much greater than a gas or electricity supplier – how much heat can you use? Mobile phones and cable were particularly vulnerable in their early days.

A more serious threat for energy suppliers is small business bankruptcy. A small factory or office can use a lot of energy, and bankruptcy typically leads to bad debt. With many utilities moving outside their business area for the first time, or faced with the possibility of targeting their own customers for additional sales, they are particularly concerned only to target solvent customers. This objective has caused utilities to be more selective in customer recruitment, using indicators of financial stress that are known and obtainable from third parties.

Finding the good customer

Most utilities have pretty strong credit control functions, and this means that they know what sort of customer they want to avoid on risk grounds – but these are not the only grounds for avoiding certain customers. Utilities therefore need to define which customers they want to attract and retain. This is important for customer service because the nature of a utility's future customer base will determine how far customer service can be used as a retention weapon, and how much extra profit will be contributed by customer service. This requires the business to define different kinds of good customer (to be recruited and retained) and bad customers (to be avoided).

Good customers usually have one or more of the following attributes:

- They buy for value, not just for price, and they don't switch suppliers for small price gains.
- They have good long-term value – not necessarily because they buy a lot, but perhaps because they buy steadily, don't incur high additional costs and don't switch.
- They complain 'reasonably' – ie when something has really gone wrong.
- They are responsive – they respond to marketing communications, and give relevant information when asked. Ideally, they are also prepared to enter into a deeper relationship with the supplier, perhaps involving buying additional products and services.
- They are 'non-bad', ie not risky or fraudulent.

Bad customers, from which a company is unlikely to make much profit, are broadly the opposite.

This looks all very nice, but developing a customer base with a high proportion of good customers takes time. This is because good customers don't 'come on to the market' very often, by definition (they are not price switchers, and don't abandon their existing suppliers easily). If a company is targeting itself to achieve a very large number of customers in a very short time, it tends to attract a much stronger mix of bad customers. This is precisely what will happen to many of the new utility companies. Their margins are often low, and to cover their set-up costs, they need to attract a large number of customers quickly. As the financial services industry has discovered, this can lead to trouble – witness the direct motor insurers who built large customer bases of price-switchers recruited from the *Yellow Pages* – the medium price-switchers go to them for a cheaper quote!

In practice, utilities do not have access to data on switchers in other industries. They have also become timid about passing data between companies in the same group. This means that an electricity supplier which owns a gas company will not tell its own gas company that it has just lost a particular electricity customer! So utilities are forced to take something of a risk on new customers, and focus on using branding, service and incentive techniques to keep the customers they had when competition started, and those they have acquired for their new businesses.

However, it is possible to use third party data agencies to provide a 'prospect pool'. This consists of a list of prospects who have been checked for their quality and creditworthiness and profiled for their propensity to switch. This reduces the cost of customer management, as it ensures that the utility recruits as few bad customers as possible.

Targeting issues – good and bad customers

Immediately after deregulation, bad debts tend to rise significantly. This is because bad customers are suddenly given the opportunity of leaving one company holding the debt while they transfer their 'business' to another. This phenomenon is known as 'debt hopping'. Some customers will in fact move repeatedly from one supplier to another, leaving behind a string of unpaid accounts.

The competitive market brings many new financial and operating risks. Therefore it will be essential for suppliers to minimize these risks in order to protect and maintain future revenues and what are already wafer-thin supply margins. The most significant risks and issues facing them are likely to be:

- Cherry picking, in which case the cost per account increases while the profit per account decreases, if a company is left holding a greater share of low-value, high-cost, or high-risk customers.
- The benefits of a database diminish as customers start switching suppliers and as companies target and take on unknown out-of-area customers, and restrictions continue to prohibit companies from using or exchanging default or debtor information on tariff customers.
- The costs of managing accounts gradually increases due to:
  - increased dependency on credit vetting using third party or bureau data;
  - the impact of debt-hopping and debt assignment;
  - difficulty, time and costs associated with tracing gone-aways and investigating fraud;
  - weaknesses in the licences in dealing with distant purity of supply, rights of entry and revenue protection.

In preparing for the opening up of the supply market, processes need to be in place to measure and minimize risk effectively when the customer seeks to change supplier. This ensures that customers with a history of non-payment, or who bring with them an unpaid final account, can be quickly and easily identified so appropriate terms of supply may be applied to minimize supplier exposure while complying with licence and data protection requirements. While account information associated with a tariff customer may not be shared or exchanged, the introduction of second-tier licences and the contract relationship between suppliers and customers will allow for the disclosure and exchange of information relating to the performance of customers accounts. All suppliers would therefore be wise to ensure that a clause that allows for such an exchange appears in all future supply contracts and agreements.

There are three main approaches to data exchange. The first is to set up a closed user group which would hold and make available to contributing members bill payment histories recorded against contract customers. The second would be to join a recognized credit industry user group run by a credit referencing agency. The third is to establish a closed user group, while at the same time allowing individual contributors the further option of participating in one of the much larger credit industry greater sharing schemes.

Once the problem of avoiding bad debtors is sorted out, utilities then have four other major targeting needs, as follows:

- The *prospect pool*, in which a utility identifies clearly what criteria define a good target customer – usually on another utility's territory, and then contracts to an outside agency to supply it with good prospects. In some markets, customers will be relatively likely to switch in the early years of deregulation, and then the market will settle down. This means that it will be very important to catch as many customers in the first year as possible – hence the desire of all the utilities to go flat out for volume in that first year.

- The *retention pool*. This is for identifying customers who are likely to leave, using profiling and data mining techniques and signalling what sort of actions would be appropriate to help retention. For example, this could be an outbound telephone call or simply a letter reminding the customers that the company is thinking of them.

- The *'lock-in' pool*, ie identification of customers who would be prepared to lock themselves into a supply contract above the statutory period customers are required to give. This is a form of commitment marketing, and may involve some contribution in exchange for benefit (eg improved tariff). Regulatory authorities of course discourage such moves immediately before deregulation.

- *Business to residential cross-over.* Utilities have many small and medium businesses where the directors are also higher domestic consumers. The crossover is normally in both directions for smaller businesses, in the sense that a customer at risk for the business use might be about the same value as the customer at risk as a residential user. In medium-sized businesses, the key need is to identify the director at home and work on acquisition or retention strategies for the business account.

Our advice is certainly that the exchange of information on bad debtors is the top priority, and should be sorted out first, simply because of the extent of financial exposure. This needs to be followed quickly by processes to ensure that any debt transfers work properly.

THE CHANGING FOCUS OF CUSTOMER SERVICE

Work done by one of the utilities has indicated that there are three contributors to reducing the propensity to switch, namely:

- Satisfaction with the brand.
- Satisfaction with customer service – in all its forms. Service is no longer just emergency service, or even preventive maintenance. It includes every contact with the company, during selling and billing, in a retail outlet and, of course, in the home. It covers every medium – telephone, mail, face to face and electronic.
- Satisfaction with the category, ie do customers feel that they have made the appropriate arrangements for energy, telecommunications, water, etc.

Note that a customer may be very satisfied with the brand and customer service but still leave, because another company suggests a better arrangement (not necessarily a cheaper one).

Customer service makes a major contribution to all of the above – before the sale and during the relationship. Let us consider this in terms of the media by which customers are served.

Telemarketing

Utility customers with issues now accept the call centre as the primary communications method for enquiries and service. The speed and the level of interaction it supports means that its importance as a sales and support channel will continue to grow, as it can be used constantly to cross-sell and support retention strategies. The challenge facing utilities is to develop their call centre expertise to meet the expectations of increasingly promiscuous and demanding customers.

So, the importance of call centre performance in maintaining market share in the deregulated environment cannot be underestimated. Call centres have a vital role in the development and support of brand equity through meeting customer expectations of service quality. Failure to handle customers well over the telephone leads inevitably to weakening of the brand. This is one of the areas where the winners in the deregulated market will outperform their competitors. We expect that as utilities focus more strongly on this, they will turn to outsourcing companies who are used to handling high and fluctuating volumes of calls, with committed levels of cost and service.

All utilities will be seeking to differentiate their offer, using tariffing, communications and service. However these attributes alone will not be sufficient to gain sustainable competitive advantage, or develop strong new identities. There is an important link between raising customer expectations supporting a new brand proposition with proactive marketing and the need to sustain the promise with every subsequent interaction. Clearly the role of the call centre in managing these interactions is crucial.

The Internet and interactive TV

A short time ago, scepticism about the importance of the Internet as a service medium would have been justified. However, we are now seeing increasing numbers of companies delivering information to existing customers using this medium. Switching can be done on the Web, and information can be obtained about account status. Customers can get information about how to avoid problems, or how they can get better service. However, those with their eyes on the distant horizon are suggesting that interactive TV will replace the Internet as a device for supporting marketing and service, simply because of its ease of use and likely higher take-up by less well-educated customers.

The role of the customer database

Once upon a time, managing customer service could be done using standard customer service systems, focused on managing the individual interaction. Today, customers expect the organization to have a good memory of past interactions, and to refer to them when appropriate (I'm sorry your trouble has recurred!). This same memory has to be deployed in filtering marketing communications, eg not trying to sell more to a customer who is half-way through having a tough problem resolved. Companies such as IBM, which supplied many of the original utility customer service systems, are now working to integrate these systems with other customer-facing systems to ensure that service can continue to be managed well in an age of heightened customer expectations. This is not easy, because billing systems – which usually provide the master customer record – are under great strain, simply because of the number of additional customer records being created. For example, if I buy gas from a different supplier, I create a new record with the new supplier, but my gas distributor must of course continue to hold a record on me.

The systems requirements for a new market entrant or for a company crossing over into a new (geographic or functional) energy area are not simple. First, the customer sets do not match each other. Typically, an electricity company will have relatively high-quality customer data for customers in its original area, and low-quality data about customers in new areas. It will have a payment history for the first group, none for the second group. It may need to outsource much of its data requirement for the second group. Its new systems will need to be able to handle a variety of different billing arrangements – tariffs, billing frequencies, etc. Utilities do not have a very impressive record when it comes to major system change projects. The size of the system change required to cope with a big increase in the customer base and much greater complexity of administration has caused some utilities severe difficulties. Many problems are caused by billing systems. In addition, because the industry's systems will have to communicate with each other, as one company distributes the power of another company, this could be a further problem, as Coopers & Lybrand, the auditors to the electricity pool, have pointed out.[1] They comment that 'too much emphasis is being placed on delivery to a deadline and insufficient attention is being given to quality.' This looks like a recipe for customer service disaster.

Billing errors

There is no doubt that the risk of billing errors will increase in the new deregulated and competitive environment. There is already strong evidence of frequent billing errors, particularly in the bills submitted to large commercial enterprises. In many cases, companies are being charged for long-disused connections, and may even be billed twice for the same service. In most cases, these bills are simply paid automatically until the purchasing manager decides that it is time for a major review. These commercial billing problems can be traced back to the low quality of many utilities operational databases – they simply have not been updated to reflect physical site changes. In the consumer market, while there are errors, a more serious problem is on the other side – the unbilled. Utility databases are not perfect, and many consumers benefit from free energy, water and telecommunications for years. This may be because of new building, or simply because something went wrong in the transfer process.

CUSTOMER RETENTION AND LOYALTY

The topics of customer retention and customer loyalty have spawned many articles and conference presentations, and indeed whole magazines and conferences. It is a bit like the search for the Holy Grail – or as the MD of one promotional agency expressed it to me last year, a little more cynically, 'My door keeps being battered down by big companies who want "half a pound of loyalty, please".' The disappointing news is that though both loyalty and retention can be helped by promotional schemes (not necessarily supported by plastic cards) in the long term they can only be the result of sensible marketing and service strategies, indeed business strategies. Utilities that have problems in these areas can (or perhaps should?) trace the origin of these problems back to fundamental policy errors, sometimes committed more than 10 years ago.

Before examining these errors, and the origin of good practice, we need spend a little time on definitions. Perhaps surprisingly, both retention and loyalty terms are hard to define except in the most general sense, and there is still considerable debate on this topic. It's probably better to take a more relaxed approach, accepting that both represent something important to utilities, and that each utility company should probably spend some time arriving at its own precise definition.

How do we define retention?

Let's start with customer retention. First, we need to separate customer retention – the empirical fact that can be measured – from customer retention policies. Where the measure is concerned, the least controversial way to define it is that it is something to do with the extent to which a utility's customers stay with it. For example, if a utility had 100 customers at the beginning of the year, how many did it have left of this original 100 at the end?

Like most general definitions, this raises more questions than it answers. Here are six of the most important questions, together with suggested answers:

- If a customer who has bought two of our products (eg gas plus a service contract) stops buying one of them (say the service contract), does this represent weakening retention? If we are a utility that supplies more than one main utility product, eg electricity and water, has a customer who bought both but now only buys one been retained? The usual answer to these questions is to say that a good measure of retention must include some measure of customer development, more commonly known as 'account penetration' or 'share of wallet'.
- Over what period is it best to measure retention? The usual answer to this is: the average length of time between the real decision about which supplier to use, eg three years for cars, five or six years for mortgages. Of course, for utilities, this period is changing quickly, because customers are being given choices that they never had before. Think of gas customers who showed decades of 100 per cent retention, followed by a few months in which 30 per cent or so changed to other suppliers when offered the choice. In this case, monthly retention measurement is necessary!
- Is retention of all customers equally desirable? The short answer to this is 'No'! A key step in retention management is for a utility to decide which customers it wants to retain, ie high value, less problematic (no bad debt, delayed payments). This implies that retention management and measurement capabilities should not be confused with each other.
- How important is customer retention relative to customer development and customer recruitment? The answer used to be simple. Incumbent utilities start with 100 per cent share, and know they must lose share or face regulatory wrath. So although incumbent utilities must focus on customer retention, the wisest concentrate retention efforts on 'best customers'. Similarly, once they have lost some customers, because they can't

guarantee losing only bad customers, they concentrate their win-back efforts on good customers. A new utility inevitably focus on recruitment of new customers. But recruitment and retention are linked in the long term. Recruitment of too many bad customers, as some cable and mobile telephony companies discovered, leads to later (quite early) retention problems – either because you want to get rid of them because they're bad, or because they switch to competitors very easily. Correspondingly, retention of too many bad customers leads to an urgent need to recruit more good customers. Failure to develop good customers leads to the need to recruit more, and so on.

● Most utilities have very high fixed costs, so unlike some companies, they cannot afford to be too indifferent to losing large numbers of lower-value customers, for it is often these customers that make the distribution network viable. So long as these customers have positive value, and can be managed at relatively low cost, they are worth retaining. Utilities should only be indifferent to losing the bad customers among them, particularly bad debtors and constant switchers.

● As customer management strategies for acquisition, retention and development are applied to well-defined groups of customers – or even individual customers – the key to successful customer management strategies is customer data and the systems needed to use that data in customer management processes (eg direct mail, call centres).

So, before agreeing a measure of retention to be used for policy purposes, utilities should review these issues, and agree a measure which can be measured in practice, but which also makes sense strategically.

Managing retention in practice

Once a utility has defined retention, how can it actually achieve its target retention levels? While retention is an outcome of the behaviour of individual customers, customer loyalty relates to what customers think and do (or try to do). Most customer loyalty experts would agree that loyalty is best defined as a state of mind, a set of attitudes, beliefs, desires, etc. Companies benefit from customers' loyal *behaviour*, but this behaviour results from their state of mind. Loyalty is also a *relative* state of mind. It precludes loyalty to some other suppliers, but not all of them, as a customer could be loyal to more than one competing supplier. Apparently disloyal behaviour is often exhibited by loyal customers. For example, a loyal customer, when coming up to a major purchasing decision, may solicit more information from competitive suppliers, for reasons which may include justifying the decision, benchmarking, following formal purchasing processes, or developing a stronger negotiating position. Loyal customers may buy from competitors if you do not have the right product or service, to avoid risk of dependence, or if you have temporary quality problems.

There are also degrees of loyalty. Some customers are very loyal, some less so. Loyalty is therefore developed by approaches which reinforce and develop a positive state of mind and the associated behaviours. The aim is not to make all customers loyal, but rather to improve the loyalty of those customers most likely to respond. Some customers are more likely to respond to incentives, some to differentiated service provided only to loyal customers, while some may only respond to a combination of the two.

The exchange of information is one of the keys to loyalty, and provides a critical bridge between state of mind and behaviour. Loyal customers are more likely to give information to you (because they trust you and expect you to use it with discretion and to their benefit). They also expect you to be able to access that information during transactions with them. The importance of IT as the 'corporate memory' of customer information cannot be overstated. Loyal customers also expect to receive more information from and about you, so 'privileged' communication is an essential element of loyalty programmes.

If the above view of loyalty is accepted, then managing loyalty becomes much more than devising a promotional scheme to reinforce customers who buy more. Anyone from the sales promotion discipline would stress that unless a scheme designed to change behaviour reinforces and adds value to the brand, the changed behaviour will last only a little longer than the scheme, except where the scheme is used to encourage trial by new users. Most customer loyalty schemes, by definition, are not of this kind.

Further, managing loyalty means not only managing behaviour but also managing a state of mind. It means affecting the customer's attitude to doing business with the supplier over the long term – not merely until the next visit or the next purchase. This means that a properly managed approach to loyalty must make the customer want to do more business with the supplier over the long term or, at least, sustain his or her existing level of business.

CRM and customer service

Customer service and CRM are close relatives. CRM – the art of building appropriate and enduring relationships between companies and customers – is the younger relative. But many companies have already discovered that there is no point in investing in ever improving levels of customer service if the underlying customer relationship is unsound. In one airline case we examined, frequent flyers – the company's most valuable customers – were treated worst at the beginning of their relationship, while forming their brand preferences, and best when they were about to stop flying! Not all customers want to get closer to their suppliers – many prefer to buy purely on product or price, and to remain as far as possible anonymous to their suppliers. But in most markets there is a large group of customers who understand that a closer relationship with their suppliers can lead to better value and service. In particular, they understand the role of mutual commitment and are prepared to spend on, say, higher-value service contracts provided this results in a better relationship. However, they will not understand the situation today in most companies, where a stronger service relationship is somehow irrelevant when a billing query arises or if they have to make a complaint. Woe betide the utility if these customers discover that the agent they are talking to on the phone does not even know they have such a contract.

Just to make things a little more difficult for utilities, the goalposts on customer service, customer loyalty and the use of customer information are moving very quickly. This is because customers are being exposed to much better practice in a number of sectors.

The benchmark bill

One of the main contacts between utilities and customers – and for some customers virtually the only – is the bill. It is therefore an important service deliverer. Today, a telecommunications customer gets a great deal of transaction detail, and in some cases is able to specify the frequency of the bill and the type of analysis provided. Also, it seems that the day of the untargeted 'bill stuffer' – which so annoys customers with low propensities to respond – is coming to an end. This is because when they have finished their current round of database development, most utilities will at least be able to differentiate between responders and non-responders and reduce the volume of communication going to the latter.

Retention in practice

The relationship-based customer service culture is not like a suit that can be put on and taken off at will. It takes a long time to develop, and customers take a long time to respond to it. Systems to support it require strategic planning, not last minute crashing together of unrelated systems. Conversely, keeping it going requires a constant focus on indicators of the quality of customer management – mainly market-research-based measures of loyalty, customer-databased measures of retention, as well as system-based measures of complaints and their resolution. The way ahead for most utilities is clear and being marked out by their peers in other industries. For the next year or so, while so many companies are concentrating on customer acquisition, it will seem possible to ignore it. But the whirlwind will be reaped in customer attrition, unless policies start to change now.

SYSTEMS FOR UTILITY CUSTOMER MANAGEMENT

Utilities are one of a group of companies that have very special needs when it comes to IT systems for managing customers. They share much in common with other very large companies, such as major airlines, retail finance (mainly banks) and major retailers, which have extensive networks through which they contact customers. But the competitive utilities have so many special requirements that they need to be treated as a case apart. Below, we list these requirements and their systems implications.

Managing millions of customers

Utilities are in what we call the 'super-database' group. They must manage millions (or tens of millions) of customers in their homes or businesses. This management must include tracking usage, invoicing, collecting payment, and delivering customer service (including emergency service). It must also now include selling additional products and services to existing and new customers – from an expanding range – and defending customers from competition.

Managing customers over the network

Customers have to be managed over the network – both the service network and the sales network. This network includes not only the network of direct connections to customers for provision of the service, but also the extended network of sales and service branches operated by the utilities. So, when a customer calls, whether by telephone or visit, or is called by telephone or a field visit, it is important to be able to identify the customer at whichever point in the network contact has been made. Without this identification, the utility will not have access to data on customers, their needs and history, and will not be able to optimize the outcome of the contact, whether in terms of improved service or increased sales.

A further problem is that, for each named customer (whether domestic or business), several individuals could be in contact with the utility during the sales or service dialogue. These requirements create specific problems for database structure.

Managing customers competitively

Ten or so years ago, the only form of competition these companies faced was at the commodity level (eg gas or electricity; telephone, post or travel). Now, they are all faced with several companies with well-established businesses trying to capture their customer base, while they themselves are returning the compliment to their competitors. The systems capability required here is very different from that required by a monopoly customer service and billing operation.

This issue is complicated by the move away from 'account control'. Formerly, with very few exceptions, utilities could be more or less certain that the customer placed 100 per cent of their business with them. Now, customers may source from many companies. For example, in the telecommunications business, a growing customer could easily be identified by the supplier by increasing use of existing lines and by requests for additional lines. Today, this will no longer always be the case. So new types of information about customers must be obtained just to maintain the utilities' knowledge of customers at its existing level. Further, some of their new customers will receive their service through agents, who in some cases are their direct competitors. This makes customer service and marketing much more complex.

In the telecommunications sector, additional issues are raised by technological developments, in particular in cable, wireless and data communications telephony. This has had two main results. The first is market dividing lines (between entertainment and telephony) being abolished by cable technology, and corresponding new customer behaviour and combined regulatory authorities emerging. The second is a big increase in the variety of options (products, services and supplying companies) for individuals to meet their static and mobile communications needs, by a combination of different technologies.

These developments mean that suppliers are getting an increasingly partial view through their records of purchases of a given customer.

Another issue raised by the arrival of competition is the need for suppliers to differentiate their services from their competitors'. In the days before competition, 'commoditization' – or the inability of customers to distinguish the service supplied by one supplier from that of others – was irrelevant. Electricity was electricity, gas was gas, and so on. Now, maintenance of market share will depend upon being able to persuade customers that the service really is different from that of competitors. Of course, this means not only telling them so, but ensuring that there are some real points of differentiation. Put simply, competitive branding must have firm foundations in service definition and performance.

This points leads to the issue of customer loyalty. It is clear from our researches that the amount of discussion of loyalty in most cases hides a vacuum when it comes to policy – a vacuum which senior utility managers are now trying hard to fill.

Customer contact and customer service

Utilities are distinguished from many other large companies by the factor of 'constant presence'. Their customers use their services constantly, and receive regular reminders of the cost of the service in a way that is divorced from the experience of the service. That is to say, customers receive the benefits of the service over a period, and experience the cost at the beginning (commitment contract) or end (pay for usage). This makes it hard for some customers to relate the service to costs, and leads to the particular phenomenon in the telecommunications market of overestimation by customers of the cost of making calls. In the energy market, this phenomenon is exacerbated by the need to 'de-market' the service in order to encourage energy saving.

Seen from another angle, customer contact consists of a few buying decisions, the timing of which may be difficult to predict, followed by many use decisions. In competitive marketing terms, this leads to a requirement to understand customers' buying cycles and manage contact with them over their cycles. Given the very large number of customers concerned, this leads to a requirement for a database marketing capability that is integrated with all other marketing and with customer service capabilities.

Superimposed on this pattern of purchase, use and payment is the classic customer service contact – either in the form of a regular service (eg for heating systems) or an emergency service (eg to restore network functioning, replace a critical component in a telephony switch, stop a flood or gas leak). In the case of emergency service, safety can be critical, so the need to identify and reach the customer quickly and then solve the problem takes precedence over everything. This accounts for the traditional 'skew' of the energy utilities' customer service systems towards being able to deliver field service quickly for certain types of call.

Regulatory and political factors

Combined with recent deregulation of all these industries, regulatory and political factors have pushed customer care into a very exposed position, where any slip is quickly seized upon by media and politicians. For example, cost pressures force utilities to turn to contractors to manage some aspects of installation and after-sales service. However, some customers still see the privatized utilities as different from the rest of the private sector – in a positive way. Their working practices are seen to be more public-service-oriented, and possibly even worth paying a premium for, and customers are often offended when they discover that the representative sent to deal with their problem turns out to be a contractor. Put simply, in the drive for efficiency encouraged by relentless price formulae, utilities have constraints which their peers do not.

Price control has had two main effects on customer management. It has restricted the extent to which core services can be attuned, through price packaging, to individual customer requirements. In some ways, this reduces the complexity that might otherwise emerge in holding even greater quantities of individualized tariff information. And it has forced a management distinction between regulated and unregulated activities which is directly opposed to the normal marketing tendency to seek to add value to basic services in order to differentiate them and achieve higher profitability. This may have long-term effects in terms of perpetuating the 'utility mindset' (see below) versus the 'competitive marketing mindset'.

The human factor and the 'utility mindset'

In analysing utility management, many commentators use the term 'utility mindset', which refers to past ways of thinking of utility managers, characterized by, among other things:

- lack of customer orientation;
- inability to conceive of or deliver competitive strategies;
- obsession with the technical parameters of customer service;
- focus on prices and costs rather than value.

This mindset is said to have been transferred to customers, through marketing methods focusing on tariffs and means of payment, and service measurements which were internal rather than customer-determined. The utility mindset is hopefully a thing of the past, but organizations and their people, systems and procedures take longer to change. Indeed, many of the systems changes outlined in this section form part of this change.

MAIN FUNCTIONAL REQUIREMENTS

Given the above, the main requirements for customer management systems, in terms of the major functions supported, are as follows:

A central customer data management function

This allows the holding of all the key data about customers and prospects – name, contact details (address, telephone number(s), etc), role in buying/using the product or service in question, any relevant demographic data. In its most advanced form, it includes details of the relationship with the supplier (which products and services bought, how much, payments outstanding, targeting for and responses to marketing and sales initiatives, potential value, etc).

An agent management function

This allows the holding of information similar to the above, but on resellers of the suppliers' products and services, and where appropriate, rules/links which determine/show which agents are responsible for which customers, and which products or services agents are eligible to handle.

A consumption/sales monitoring and billing function

This is closely associated with the central customer filing function and gives the central customer file its accuracy (where existing customers are concerned). The billing function ensures the updating of the customer file on consumption/purchasing history, payments received and outstanding payments, and uses the customer file for ensuring invoices and statements reach customers. Part of this function is meter reading, an area in which paper data entry is being increasingly replaced by hand-held or remotely read terminals.

A maintenance service function

This is for the management of field service or similar operations. It ensures matching of customers' requirements for service to the service resources available and then scheduling and management of the consequent workflow. The function also usually extends to communications with the field force, including in some cases data transfer. The maintenance function may be an integral part of the billing functionality, and the resulting combined functionality usually then falls within the ambit of what is known as a *customer service system*. This is usually closely linked with the inventory management system – particularly that part of it that relates to spare parts.

Product/service/price functionality

This allows identification of all the products and services available, the different prices at which they can be sold, and in some cases the qualification criteria that determine which products are allowed to be offered to which customers at which prices.

An inventory management function

This supports identification of whether the physical inventory required to fulfil a customer's need for products or maintenance is available, reserves inventory items for particular orders/jobs, orders product from suppliers in order to maintain inventory at target levels, and supports inventory audit.

A supplier management function

This allows the company to hold information about its relationships with and liabilities to its key suppliers. This is obviously closely linked to the inventory management function for physical goods.

A sales and marketing function

This supports recruitment of information on prospects and additional information on existing customers (including registering interest in products or services, levels of satisfaction with service) and its addition to the customer file. This information is then used, often after complex statistical and creative analysis, to target customers for marketing and sales initiatives (including targeting customers for loyalty and competitive defence initiatives). The sales and marketing functionality is then used to produce lists of customers for actions in relation to customer dialogue (see below). It is also used to maintain the quality of information on the customer file, by ensuring that data is audited and updated at appropriate intervals. In its most advanced form, this functionality includes within it an online campaign-planning function, to assist managers to determine which campaigns will be run and which customers will be targeted for them, and then to support the implementation and tracking of the actual campaign.

A customer dialogue function

The online part of this function operates in a telephone and face-to-face environment, for managing all direct contacts with customers. For any particular requirement (eg bill payment or query, sale, service request, initial call for or response to a marketing or sales initiative), a script is defined for managing the dialogue. It is supported by interfaces with all appropriate databases and functions above to ensure completion of the dialogue so as to meet customer needs and update the supplier's representation of its relationship with the customer. The environment for call handling usually requires ACD functionality and increasingly computer integrated telephony. The batch part of this function relates to the response handling and fulfilment facilities associated with direct mail, and may therefore be required to work together with the billing functionality.

So far, what has been described above is fairly uncontroversial. Utilities have had most of the above for some time, in some cases for 30 or more years. What has changed, because of the actual or emerging competitive nature of utilities' markets, is the way the different functionalities described above need to work as an integrated overall customer management function to recruit, manage and keep customers.

Address management systems are important. As a 'service' to the customer, utilities may need to hold 'preferred' customer addresses, which in fact are non-standard by postal service definitions(eg they may hold a more prestigious locality of a town). Billing or other customer systems may need to hold pointer files against which an underlying correctly formatted address is held.

The appliance retailing systems may need to hold many individual address possibilities (eg delivery address, installation address, billing address, customer address, etc).

Marketing database systems may be constrained in terms of their capability and address handling ability (especially as the larger systems, in order to handle larger data volumes, are typically non-relational, ie without the complexity of an operation sales system). This causes a huge issue in terms of which address to hold and update.

The uncoordinated dialogue

In most utilities today, the situation is some way removed from the competitive business requirement. In particular, there is a clear division between the service and billing functionality on the one hand, and the marketing and sales functionality on the other.

This results in (at least) two separate but simultaneous customer dialogues. For example, customers who are in contact concerning billing or service are not managed in a marketing and sales relationship, and vice versa. In practical terms, a customer who has responded to a marketing or sales initiative is not visible as such when engaged in a service or billing dialogue, or vice versa. This leads at the very least to some loss of cross-selling opportunities and at worst, to failure to act quickly to retain customers at competitive risk!

This division between these two kinds of dialogue has been recognized as a problem by those utilities that are furthest down the competitive road – the telecommunications companies. They are integrating their systems to remedy this situation, although the sheer size of their markets still means that complete transparency of the two functionalities to each other is unlikely to be achieved just yet.

Key strategic questions influencing functionality

As noted above, the individual elements of this functionality are now well understood. The key questions facing utilities now are:

- What are the best strategies for customer acquisition, management and retention, taking into account the evolving regulatory and competitive situation and the need to grow revenues while controlling costs?
- What are the most important business functionalities required to support these strategies, and when and where will they be needed?
- How are these functionalities best delivered individually, in terms of software and systems?
- How can these functionalities be combined to best technical effect?
- How can they be made to work together in practice, taking into account the processes involved and the people?

- What detailed customer service and marketing policies should be used to maximize exploitation of the new capability?
- How can functionalities and policies be planned and how should these plans be implemented, to ensure that immediate needs are met in ways that do not preclude required functionality for later on?
- What kinds of suppliers can help utilities achieve all this?

It is not the purpose of this chapter to investigate all these questions. Of course, many of these questions can only be completely answered by the utilities themselves, as they know their customers and their competition better than any outsider could. What this chapter does, however, is to consider some of the issues raised by these questions, and their implications for the choice facing the utilities in the area of customer management systems.

Strategies for customer acquisition, management and retention

Here, the key issues are the degree of competitive threat and the consequent balance between acquisition and retention. Where power utilities are concerned, their main focus will be on selective retention of customers and acquisition of new customers in new product or area markets, on acquisition of customers for electricity, gas and their new products and services. New customers may be the focus of intense win-back activity by their current supplier after a period, so customer retention will quickly become a key requirement for these new customers too. This requires *high-quality management of each contact* (marketing, sales, service, billing, etc), but also integration of these contacts into a complete dialogue.

REQUIRED BUSINESS FUNCTIONALITY

We have already identified above the general functionalities required. The current state of play of most utilities is that the customer service and billing functionalities are well established, and now require modification for the supply of additional services (eg other energy products, telecommunications). However, with one or two exceptions, marketing and sales functions are limited compared with those already developed for airlines, retail finance and automotive industries. Within the utilities sector, national telecommunications companies (ie excluding cable companies) have or are developing much stronger functionality, and are or will be able to identify opportunity and risk customers and focus marketing, sales and service attention on them quickly and effectively, and where appropriate integrate this with billing activities. Most energy utilities have a long way to go before they have this capability. It is therefore not surprising that the customer-facing systems of most energy utilities are currently the subject of tenders – the scope of which is complete system renewal. Their marketing capabilities are also the subject of intense review, including their marketing agencies (advertising, direct marketing, PR, etc).

Customer and agent data management

This can be split into four very different kinds of database requirement (but not necessarily different databases as data must be shared across these requirements), as follows:

- The prospect/customer/agent requirement, relating to information on customers and agents (identification, location, characteristics, needs, attitudes, satisfaction, etc) and their interaction with the supplier (enquiries, purchases, invoices, after-sales service, etc).
- The product/service/resource requirement, relating to information about the organization's products and services (identification, characteristics, production/usage/sales – past, current and forecast, resources required or used, inventories, prices, profit/surplus, etc) and the marketing and service resources used to support them (eg media spend, overheads).
- The market requirement (status of the market of which the supplier's activity forms a part, including both the above kinds of data). This requirement is particularly important for suppliers who are dealing with consumers through agents, such as retailers, as direct customer data may be hard to obtain. Also, the agents' concern for category management and their own competitive position puts a premium on analysis of the relationship between supplier, agent and market data.
- The management requirement, which relates to data on the organization's plans for managing the market and schedules (dates, budgets, etc) relating to those plans.

All these requirements have been the subject of much attention and investment as utilities come under pressure to improve customer service, in turn often due to competitive pressures. The process of matching the customer to the product or service is mirrored by the requirement to match information about the two.

There is no doubt that for companies with customer bases the size of most utilities, ie a million or more, the developments taking place in the area of very fast database servers have considerable implications. Until now, accessing databases with very large numbers of customer records, each record containing full details on the customer and all the customer's transactions and contacts with the company, and then delivering that data to the point of use, has posed considerable problems. However, a new generation of database servers is emerging, and the main database software packages are available on these servers. So, utilities can now take on much more comprehensive objectives in terms of making data available at the various points of contact with the customer. This data can now include a variety of types of image, moving way beyond images of bills and correspondence into areas such as transmissible images promoting products and services, network configurations, etc.

Combined with the basic server capability will be the need to manage access and updating of this database by the key business areas that use it, with reach internally, through partners and to customers as required.

Consumption monitoring and billing

This functionality is one of the longest established in utilities. New arrivals such as cable companies often use adapted versions of standard packages (eg US cable TV customer service systems). The real changes required in this area are associated with the need to handle rapidly expanded product lines and *greater variety of pricing schemes* (including tailored packages and pricing), together with the need to work more closely with the marketing and service functionalities to sustain customer care. The prime requirements therefore are for *more flexible and rapid set up procedures for billing routines*, faster access times and sustained integrity of data while the billing functionality is in use for other reasons than actually issuing bills or entering payments received. Meanwhile, in order to contain the cost of billing and payment handling, increasing numbers of utilities that require metering at the point of consumption are moving towards mobile data entry and radio-transmitted data.

Maintenance/service management

This is an area of relative stability in systems requirement. Because of the need for emergency service management, with consequent danger to life and limb if service resources are not deployed quickly, the systems for managing this area are usually among the best available. However, there are two areas of significant change.

The first is the move to contractual arrangements with guaranteed service levels. As an example, British Gas has been particularly successful in selling central heating and other domestic service contracts, but all utilities have opportunities in this area, particularly as they move into each other's markets. This introduces the concept of differential levels of service (eg response time, availability of service), higher engineering skill demands and the requirement to manage these services so as to fall within contractual obligations. In some cases, refunds may need to be made because of failure to meet these obligations or service-level commitments. This has created the need for a more complicated interface with billing and financial systems, as well as with inventory management systems. However, the software requirements in this area are well understood and such software has been in use for many years in many industries, in particular the IT industry itself.

Another major change has been the move to the use of agents (subcontractors) to fulfil installation and contractual and non-emergency service requirements. This has created the need for different interfaces between the service system and the supplier management system. Recent events have exposed the importance of managing this whole area from the customer care perspective, so monitoring of quality levels by direct liaison with the customer (eg an after-service questionnaire) has become an important need. This has created the need for additional data to be held on the customer's file. However, in many cases, this quality monitoring is not integrated with overall customer management through the customer file, because the latter has usually not been designed for holding this data. This 'service dialogue' – one of the key areas of contact between a utility and its customers – is often not well provided for on the customer database. The major challenges are posed by the volume of data that may need to be held and the origins of the customer database in billing and emergency service provision.

Inventory management

Because of their involvement in retailing a wide range of bought-in products and accessories and in field service, most utilities' inventory systems are quite well developed and need little modification for the new environment, other than extension to cope with the much wider range of products they will be supplying. In some cases, utilities have separated their retailing out as a different business activity, or even merged it with other utility-owned retailers or sold it off. Unless the inventory system continues to be shared, this creates the need for the two inventory systems to interface with each other, unless trading becomes completely arm's-length and one operation becomes the supplier of the other. In this case, the main inventory management system can revert to a spares and tool inventory management system.

Supplier management

This is an area of radical change. One reason for this is the use of service agents. The other is the entry by utilities into a variety of new product and service areas – in particular other types of energy and new or different telecommunications services involving changed supply chains. This requires new links between billing, service and sales and marketing systems at the least, and possibly other systems.

One of the problems that this may cause is that *the utilities will focus their concerns on the technical implementation of these links and not on how to attract and keep customers* for these new product areas. In systems terms, this relates to the link with sales and marketing systems.

The required functionalities for this area are well understood – it is the combination that poses the challenge.

Products/service/price

Here, the explosion in numbers of products and services, packages, tariffs and customized pricing rates, and the need for much more frequent data maintenance (including deletion of obsolete elements), combined with 100 per cent accuracy, will be the major systems challenge. Management reports will be required to keep this area of functionality under very tight review, in the light of changing costs, sales and profitability and competitive activity. This implies that the presentation of this possibly very complex data for senior management review will become absolutely critical. The development of customer management scorecards can help to address this issue.

Sales and marketing

Here, the protected environment in which non-telecommunications utilities have existed for many years is visible in the state of their systems, which in some cases cannot handle the most basic required functionalities (eg online selections). Fortunately for them, the requirements for managing large numbers of companies in a competitive sales and marketing environment have been very well explored by their peers in parallel industries – particularly in retail finance, the telecommunications companies and the automotive industry – all industries that have long-term relationships with their customers. The required functionalities are now embodied in the most advanced packages, which combine sales and marketing functionality, including the handling of customer dialogue (see below) and the associated areas of computerized telephony and direct mail management systems. However, the size, depth and complexity of the utilities' requirements usually imply substantial customization of these packages and adaptation to interface with most of the other business functions mentioned above.

An additional requirement, which has recently been the focus of increasing attention as the volume of customer data available for analysis has exploded, is for an analysis capability which will enable utilities to make sense of this data, by helping them answer questions such as:

- Which customers are most at risk of loss to competition?
- Which new customers are likely to be the worst payers?
- Which customers are most likely to stay loyal?
- Which customers are most responsive to different types of marketing promotions?

One requirement which has received little attention until recently is that of delivering information direct to customers using the utilities' own networks. Our research shows little in the way of plans to use the best of telecommunications and computing technology to market utility services to customers. The view seems to be that what is being provided is a smart pipeline for others to use. However, there are signs that this requirement will be taken more seriously over the next few years.

Customer dialogue management

Here, as we have already mentioned, the need for a high-quality emergency service dialogue has placed the utilities in a favourable position, despite the age of some of the systems which support this dialogue. Extremely rapid access to customer details is the norm for utilities. However, once this idea is extended into full dialogue, ie including sales, marketing and full customer care, the same speed of response is not required for every sub-function. The appropriateness (eg which product or service is offered to which customers) and quality of the response and the integrity of its handling become more important. In adapting existing sales and marketing dialogue packages to meet utilities needs, it will therefore be important to take a realistic stance on performance requirements if quality is not to be sacrificed.

Combining hardware and software to best technical effect

Until recently, despite the so-called advent of open systems, the mature state of the mainframe database software and hardware market and the restriction of data used to character-based data, meant that it was possible to focus evaluation in this area on the applications software alone. Several developments have changed this:

- The first moves of major computer suppliers in the area of massively parallel processing, which speeds up existing database software by many times, and enables storage of image data to be handled much more easily and reliably.
- The increasing understanding of what the term 'client-server' implies in this environment, in particular where the server is a very large customer database server.

- Developments in transmission technologies, which facilitate the delivery of high volumes of data to the point of contact with the customer – here, video on demand in the home is not an irrelevant development for companies that need to manage very large numbers of customers.

This means that the many utilities who are redesigning their systems to cope with a multi-product competitive environment may need to take 'two bites at the cherry'. The first will be largely based on existing available packages and 'legacy' hardware, where the focus must be on minimizing the adaptation of the existing packages to preserve and optimize exploitation of their functionality, while focusing on their ability to work with other packages which support new functional areas such as sales and marketing. Here, the critical inter-working between packages seems to be between sales and marketing packages (including that aspect of dialogue management) on the one hand, and billing and service packages on the other.

Scalability and flexibility

The change from managing a slowly increasing customer base for one core set of product offerings to managing a fluctuating customer base, with different types of relationship (distributor, supplier, generator) for different products is a quantum leap for utilities, and for their systems. In some cases, this has required more or less complete replacement of older systems.

MAKING IT WORK IN PRACTICE

Although there is much evidence to show that, increasingly, customers' interface with large suppliers may be directly through a terminal rather than through a member of staff using a terminal, for most customers their contact with utilities will be with a member of staff. This will be mainly on the telephone and sometimes in the field (service and meter reading) or over the counter (where retailing has not been sold off). Staff will be required to handle increasingly complex and varied transactions, covering a number of business functions. The route that seems to be marked out for non-field contacts is that of multiskilled staff supported by very high-quality scripting – with varying degrees of structuring to meet the type of customer involved (from major account to domestic consumer). For the largest business accounts, close attention will need to be paid to how team-working is established and maintained between calling sales and service forces and remote customer contact teams operating via the telephone. This may lead, as it has in telecommunications, to the establishment of different kinds of customer service centres focused on different types of account, with varying degrees of integration of sales and service roles.

MARKETING AND CUSTOMER SERVICE POLICIES

As utilities move into new markets – new products and services as well as new geographic areas – they will need to go back to basics to understand the requirements of new and existing customers. These requirements are likely to change rapidly under the influence of competition. The key areas for policy developments are likely to be the following:

- Extended customer research programmes, incorporating frequent checks on levels of customer care, with data stored on the customer database for use in targeting of remedial and cross-selling actions.
- Redefinition of service objectives into broader customer care objectives, adapted to the needs of consumers of different products and services.
- Redefinition of market segmentation, away from product/tariff usage (number of connections, type of tariff, size of account, method of payment) to segments which enable greater focus on the business of acquiring and retaining customers (eg loyal customers versus price sensitive customers).
- Competitive attack and win back programmes, tightly targeted for maximum effect and to reduce the costs of giving poorly targeted incentives.
- Much improved integration of media advertising, direct marketing and customer care initiatives, enabling focus on critical market segments for maximum effect.
- Customer loyalty programmes involving incentives of increasing value as customers remain loyal.
- Focus on giving access to certain systems to customers big and small, to view consumption, product and service options, etc.

All of these will have major systems implications, of which only some can be handled by existing systems or newly acquired packages.

IMPLEMENTATION REQUIREMENTS

One of the best strategies for utilities – perhaps for all but the very largest – is to use packages in their first phase of database development or redevelopment. They should then develop from these packages a more integrated approach with improved functionality (including the ability to support the full range of marketing and service initiatives described in this chapter) for the tough competitive period that lies ahead. In order to obtain this result, utilities should ensure that any packages chosen are customizable in all key respects. By following this approach, utilities will get the most important benefits and learning now, allowing them later, when they are faced with the much greater data handling requirements of expanded and more competitive markets, the additional benefits of: integrating the tried and tested functionality of these packages with additional software developments; and exploiting new computing and communications technologies.

Supplier choice

What kinds of supplier utilities should go for is, of course, a very controversial issue, and depends on the extent to which a utility wishes to contract out the accountability for achieving the systems development that will keep it competitive and cost-effective.

Customer and market management systems, most broadly defined, normally result from the work of a range of suppliers, typically including:

- hardware – ranging from mainframes to PCs and including operating system, networking and printing provision;
- telecommunications – to connect sites, customers and suppliers;
- database and integration software (often called middleware);
- transaction software – defined as anything that handles the flow of product and service to the customer and payments from the customer;
- marketing and sales software – defined generally as software designed to support the acquisition and retention of customers (in some cases this overlaps with transaction software);
- analytical software – to analyse integrated data (eg against a data warehouse);
- data providers – who provide data about the external world (eg markets) to match with company data, enhance it and in some cases to help interpret it;
- facilities managers (including bureaux) – to carry out work done by some of the above and by the company's managers (marketing and/or systems);
- marketing service suppliers, whose work is conditioned by the type of systems used by their clients, and whose ability to devise and help implement marketing strategies and actions to exploit the systems capability is becoming an important criterion for supplier selection;
- consultants – mainly to help develop strategy and define requirements and projects;
- systems integrators – to integrate the whole!

What is clear, however, is that no single supplier has all the software and skills required to take major utilities through the next few years. For some utilities, a consortium-based approach may be the best, with systems integration and project management by a company used to handling all the accountabilities involved in managing implementation of such complex and mission-critical systems. Additional key contributions are made by package software companies, hardware suppliers and consultants with experience of working in the new competitive utility environment.

CONCLUSION

In this last section, we have summarized very briefly some of the key issues involved in the development of the next generation of the utilities' customer management systems. Our main conclusion is that utilities need to take a phased approach. They have an urgent need to increase the functionality of their systems in order just to be able to handle the basics of a multi-product, competitive environment. Following this first phase comes a second phase, the objective of which is to develop systems which provide competitive advantage in every area of customer contact. But the two phases must be managed as an integral proposition, with clear objectives for each phase being determined at the beginning, and partnership sourcing arrangements established with key systems suppliers, ensuring continuity of development.

The concentration on regulatory requirements from systems has pushed the priorities of what is generally a two-fold marketing issue – retention and acquisition (including cross-sell) – to the bottom of the list. The lack of integrated systems has left individual systems which in order to achieve the marketing objectives need remarrying. This is often achieved by using an external systems integration supplier and packaged database solutions given the IT resource and mindset that may exist within the organization. The downside of the development is that in order to create the 'super-database' there are a number of compromises made in terms of data storage (often categorizing data during preparation to allow faster access) and in terms of the available functionality.

The lack of integrated systems for many utilities provides a real headache in terms of how to handle change and updates. The data cycle has huge implications for the marketer and the immediacy and accuracy of marketing response. The inability of systems to deliver in this area has negative PR and marketing implications. The power of the marketing database, and of building integrated systems is that they can be distributed to different levels within the organization – perhaps summarized marketing information in an executive information system, or individual-level data accessible by a customer service operator. Tools and methods exist for delivering this level of integration, but as yet – to our knowledge – no one has delivered it completely in utilities!

Notes

1 Electricity choice may bring chaos, auditors warn', Simon Holberton, *The Financial Times*, 17 September 1997 p 30

22

Where next for CRM?

Merlin Stone

In reviewing the contents of this book, we can certainly say we have covered a lot of ground. There is of course no implication that companies who want to manage customer relationships better should do everything recommended in this book, or indeed in our previous two books. Selectivity is the key to success in all management, and the same is true here. So we thought it would be appropriate to end with a few warnings and some suggestions as to how some aspects of CRM will develop in the next few years.

IS IT ALL WORTH IT – FOR YOU OR YOUR CUSTOMERS?

Customers like to do business with suppliers because they offer good value. Of course, most customers would like to get the maximum value from us while returning the minimum value to us, just as the Consumers' Association would advise them to do. However, many customers understand that buying at lowest cost can lead to poorer service, or even product quality problems. In most markets it is suppliers that create the expectations that lead to customer behaviour. So if all suppliers tell their customers that it does not matter how much they buy from each supplier, they will always get roughly the same price incentive, then customers will happily carry on as before, pocketing the incentives from the different suppliers. On the other hand, if all suppliers tell their customers that the more they buy with one supplier, the better they will be treated, then customers for whom being treated better is important will tend to concentrate their spend.

This raises the question of what the opportunities are for being treated better (or less badly in some cases). In grocery retailing, opportunities exist, but they are limited. Examples include self-scanning and privileged delivery conditions. However, as treating one customer better can mean treating another worse, such privileges have to be managed carefully. In other areas of retailing, the opportunities are greater. For example, in a retailer that sells complex items or services, queues may form (eg because of seasonal or life event purchasing, or the arrival of new items). Here, privileged queuing can be an important benefit, though it should only be done if customers' responsiveness to this makes it worthwhile and if the distribution of value between customers makes it sensible to offer queuing privileges to the very highest-value customers. This is similar to the priority wait-listing usually offered by airlines to their highest-value flyers. This is a back-handed tribute to their yield management and capacity planning, but also a clear demonstration of the value of concentrating one's spend in order to obtain top status. Although new digital marketing and service technologies make it easier for customers to find alternatives, as long as these alternatives rely on some kind of physical delivery, the prospects of queues exists. Even if queues can be abolished by auctioning (bidding for places in queues), privileged auctioning is also possible (opening it only to customers of highest value, for example). Yield management and loyalty management can go hand in hand. Putting it another way, the economic basis of CRM is vital, however you decide to do it.

Knowing who your individual customers are and being able to address them directly is only worthwhile if: you have got a proposition that you can only offer to them via the database; and that proposition ensures that they give you more value than they otherwise would, by buying more, more profitable items, staying longer, or costing less to manage.

Any looseness of thinking in this area makes marketers vulnerable, because it makes the investment in creating and maintaining the customer database yield questionable and probably negative returns.

FROM DATA TO VALUE

A closely related question is the value of data. Today, as our reasons for having customer databases have proliferated, so understanding the value of particular data items has become more complex. In fact, paradoxically, the more we focus on the objective of increasing the net value of our customer base, the more difficult it becomes to be certain about the value of particular data items. There are various reasons for this, including:

- We have discovered so many different ways of developing (and destroying) customer value, so that data items which might not be useful for one way might be useful for another.
- We can do it through many media, so data items that do not help us with our customer management through one medium might help us through another.
- Many companies subscribe to the idea of developing new customer value, but many have no agreed definitions of the different types of customer value they are trying to develop.
- Some companies that have developed definitions of customer value are not measuring it.
- Even if they do measure customer value, their measurement processes do not include predictive work associating marketing, sales and service actions which use data with increased or maintained customer value.
- Finally, even if they measure it, they may have no reliable business processes for translating potentially valuable data into actual value.

The result of all of this is that the effectiveness of CRM is often called into question by finance directors.

Agreeing a model for measuring and then improving new customer value is essential for the survival of CRM. Such a definition must be predictive. The value of a customer depends not only on how long the customer is likely to stay or buy more. It also depends on whether the customer is likely to create negative value, for example, by claiming early on insurance, by having bad debt, or just by being an intensive user of free services. Data sets on negative value have in many companies been kept separate from marketing data on positive value, and both of these are kept separate from customer service data on cost to serve.

Some companies have succeeded in identifying which data items were good predictors of short-term value changes (eg a burst of buying, likelihood of attrition). The term 'lifetime' value is misleading because most companies are not capable of predicting with reasonable reliability the value of a given customer next year. This applies not just to value to the particular company, but also category value – value to any company based on category spend. But some companies can. They have found the valuable data that is indicative of future value. The very best practice companies monitor changes in the value of these variables to detect changes from predicted value. They have even developed proper processes for deploying when the variable changes value. These processes ensure that when predicted value rises, the company gets a larger share of a growing cake (or at least maintains share), and when predicted value falls (eg attrition or 'wallet share' decline), the fall is arrested as far as possible.

Put simply, really valuable data is data that tells you not what customers are buying or doing now, but what they are likely to do in the future. The reason this kind of data is valuable now is that most companies do know what the customer did in the past, and even what the customer is doing now. So the competitive value of data depends on whether it tells you what the customer will do.

However, the competitive edge has shifted yet again. In some industries, prediction of next year's value is not the issue – prediction of tomorrow (or even today's) value is. The reason for this is that smart data analysis – whether of high-volume retail transaction data, or of answers to questions posed by call centre operators – really does give knowledge about what the customer is likely to do next. In the world of e-business, this has been extended to where the customer will click next. In the area of mobile/wireless customer data, the issue will be how we can motivate customers to give us data while they are shopping, not when they get home or when they receive a call or a questionnaire from us. So the idea of 'value immediacy' is changing some of our conventional notions of data value. Of course, at the core of all of this will be the focus on traditional variables, such as customer identification and location, response propensity and net value. We should never lose sight of these, because they are what make money for us. However, in the future they will take very different forms from those they take today.

BUSINESS INTELLIGENCE

'Business intelligence' is a lovely phrase. Of course, it almost sells itself – for what company would knowingly refuse the offer to become more intelligent – provided the price is right? However, there are many large companies whose behaviour in this area could be classified as 'choosing stupidity'. What do we mean by 'stupidity'? 'Wilful ignorance' would be my definition – knowing you have information and deciding not to use it.

The lessons that we have learnt from applying the disciplines of business intelligence to marketing include recognizing:

- the number of ways in which information arises;
- the many tools that can be used to distil actionable knowledge;
- the work that sometimes has to be done to organize this information so that it can be translated into knowledge.

Let us suppose that we move a marketing or a sales process from one locus of interaction, say a mailing campaign or a call centre, to an e-channel (eg the Web or a WAP phone). What happens? Instead of a more or less structured interaction managed by us, we may have a series of explorations by the customer, as he or she investigates the different ways we can serve him or her. Of course, these explorations may simply be an 'e' version of what customers do when they talk to the call centre operator or when they respond to a mailshot. But the difference is that a much higher proportion of these interactions are with our IT systems. This means that in principle they are storable and analysable. It is this thinking that has given birth to the ideas of Web-mining and even – in the greatest detail – click-mining.

So far, we could say that this is just a difference in order of size. There are already famous case studies of companies that apply online mining to very high-volume call centres, typically to adjust the promotion or the product/service offer to data given by the customer during the interaction. These case studies make very good reading, but they are rare. More importantly, good operators can compensate (to some extent) for basic systems by applying their own expertise, eg finding out the kinds of variation on the offer that are likely to appeal to the customer. This contrasts with the 'business intelligence' route of inferring from a complex set of data, derived from the company's experience with thousands or more of previous customers.

The difference between this situation and the e-business situation lies in speed and complexity. E-business adds channels of communication to existing ones, and often does not substitute for them completely. So, to communication face to face, mail and telephone are added e-mail, Web and mobile. In some cases a substitution is made (eg Web for telephone) but in many cases a human being is often a destination for escalation. The problem IT planners face is that business managers developing e-business concepts often only partly visualize what they will be like when working – so much of their business intellect is devoted to getting there!

Take for example, the interaction with earlier stages of the value chain, whether in terms of decision making, such as campaign management, or the classic value chain definition, such as parts and component suppliers for manufacturers, or product suppliers for retailers. The e-business models being developed by many 'real' companies (ie not those whose presence is only virtual) are often only partial. Thus, a retailer considers how flows of information between it and its consumers will change, but relies on existing (possibly even e-based) flows between itself and its suppliers. However, the retailer's suppliers would like to know about the 'product explorations' the retailer's customers make, and which customers make them. Of course the information is valuable, but a far-sighted retailer might take the view that you make more money by dealing with product manufacturers who know what excites which customers where, rather than by trying to rival the manufacturers' expertise. Similarly, a far-sighted marketing director might take the view that if campaign design is outsourced, so marketing agencies ought to be connected through the client to the customer – in real time.

Putting it simply, one of the challenges of e-business intelligence is that intelligent businesses tend to succeed when they work with other intelligent businesses. In the e-world, this means rapid and clear connection to the information flows that form the foundation of intelligence. Only a few of the best companies are taking this view.

THE SINGLE CUSTOMER VIEW

Many companies base their CRM on the idea of a single customer view. This single view is, in theory, held on one database or several databases linked in real time, accessible by all staff who have contact with customers and by customers, when the latter are interacting directly with systems (eg over the Internet or through interactive telephony of some kind). The theory says that when a customer interacts with the company (responding to a promotion, buying a product or service, making a complaint or an enquiry), or the company interacts with the customer in similar ways, relevant aspects of the data are accessed. This allows the company to optimize the contact (from both company and customer point of view) in various ways, such as:

- Minimizing the time because details given previously can be accessed, and so do not need to be asked for and keyed in again.
- Improving quality because the scope for incorrect keying is reduced.
- Ensuring relevance of treatment (eg service action, product/price offered), because details of customers' needs can easily and quickly be matched with features and benefits of products and services.
- Improving security, because the customer can be asked to give PIN numbers, passwords, special account numbers and other confirming details.
- Reducing fraud, because exceptional patterns of customer behaviour (and that of staff interacting with customers) can be identified more easily.

However, in practice most companies are a long way from achieving this, and many are actually going backwards. This is because there are strong forces working against the achievement and use of a single view. These include:

- Mergers and acquisitions when different companies that share some of their customers come together. It is usually very difficult to bring their customer databases together, because they are resident on different systems, cover different data items and the data in them is of varying quality. The sources of the different data items are not always clear, nor are the terms under which they were collected – the latter raises particular data protection problems.
- Proliferation of channels of interaction. Most companies are increasing the number of channels through which they communicate with customers and distribute their products. In particular, the Internet, mobile telephony and digital television have in the last few years been added to fixed-line telephony, direct mail, counter service, kiosk-type devices (eg ATMs, ticketing machines) and other 'classic' methods of interacting with customers. Unless the same data set about customers is available and immediately updateable through each of these channels, then the view of the customer through one

channel will not be the same as that through another. This applies particularly with respect to updating data concerning recent interactions.

- Introduction of new products and services with different systems needs (eg in terms of the amount of data about customers, how the data is used), coupled with slow response of IT departments to these needs, leading to management responsible for the new product or service to declare independence and set up a separate database.
- Internal politics – usually in the form of simple refusal by one department to moderate their required view of their customers in favour of the corporate view.
- Customer failure or unwillingness to cooperate: many customers may be unable or unwilling to cooperate in the process of interacting in different ways. This behaviour can range from forgetting key data items (eg PIN numbers), to making errors in keying data in, or simple refusal to cooperate. For example, a customer using the Internet for the first time to interact with an established supplier will usually, if not correctly identified, end up creating a new customer record. This can also apply if he or she uses different computers to access the Internet, as the cookie on the first computer that identifies them as a previous customer will not be on the second computer.
- Costs of maintaining a single view: the costs of setting up and maintaining a single view are substantial. The figures depend upon the initial position, the amount of data that needs to be integrated, cleaned, and maintained. But for a large company, the figure is normally millions if not tens of millions of pounds, with system licence fees, system maintenance and data maintenance also in the area of at least a million pounds a year.
- Data protection – our research shows that most companies are poorly compliant with new (and old) data protection legislation, and many are becoming less, not more, compliant, for the reasons listed above.
- A severe shortage of staff skills for any of the complex tasks involved in developing, delivering and using such systems.

The result of all this is that most companies achieve at most a less fragmented view of customers, usable only for some types of interaction, for some products or services, for some customers, in some channels. They do this at high cost, and because the achievement is only partial, it increases the likelihood that when new channels or products are added, or further mergers or acquisitions take place, additional customer views will be created. The main exceptions to this are companies who have a simple business model. These are simple because of two reasons. Their interaction with customers does not normally need to be supported by a lot of data about them, their needs and past interactions with the company (like many retailers, low-cost airlines). Also, they need the data, but interact with customers in simple ways (eg using direct marketing only via call centres, mail, the Internet), like many mail order, credit card and general insurance companies.

One of the results of this customer data chaos is that many companies are deeply non-compliant with recent data protection legislation. This non-compliance is visible in: the multiple sources of customer data with no secure process for maintaining the data to the appropriate quality or allowing customers to obtain copies of it; and the absence of a secure process for reviewing what data is held and moving towards compliance with the law.

This chapter takes the view that this focus on trying to obtain a single view of the customer has been very damaging to the business achievement of many companies. Enormous IT budgets have been spent in the attempt. The energies of many marketing, sales and service management and front-line operations have been sucked into planning and implementation to support the attempt. This has been particularly damaging in companies selling to consumers (rather than to businesses), where the number of customers is so much larger, the costs of creating and maintaining the databases so much greater, and the customers' requirement for being managed in a relationship is so much less. Many such companies have had two or three attempts at creating the single view, only to abandon them to save costs or limit their scope in order to extract at least some business value.

What we see here is just an example of a wider problem in business. The idea that a company can have a single, completely up-to-date view of any entity, accessible quickly and easily by all those involved in managing that entity occurs in other areas. The entity may be a unit of inventory, a geographical area, a member of staff, a department, a factory and so on. In most cases, companies have developed sensible compromises to managing these. Getting a 'single view' of any entity which is truly independent (ie a customer) is very hard to do if there are lots of them, if the company's interactions with them are complex, relatively unstructured and at varying intervals.

This has already been realized by personnel departments, who are increasingly using smart cards for security and stored value purposes. Many governments and public sector bodies have followed the same path. Both are much more sensitive to the legal, technical and social risks of big centralized databases.

An alternative strategy is to give customers smart cards that, through data given by them and through the cards' use in transactions, builds a profile of them and their interactions with the company. The same card can do this for several companies. Costs can be shared, and (subject to customer preferences and data protection laws) relevant data about one company's view of the customer can be given to another. A key barrier to using smart cards as an essential device for managing consumers has been the absence of card-readers in locations where consumers are managed – in the home, at the workplace, on the Web, in the store, etc. This barrier is now being removed. Most households of interest to consumer marketers will have a digital TV set-top box by the end of this year, with a second smart card slot. Software to support different applications can be downloaded directly by the TV operator. This opens up a vista of mass-market advertisers being able to address most of their customers directly, in a personalized fashion, including the delivery of personalized coupons in digital form, collapsing the costs of the redemption process and significantly reducing fraud opportunities. Credit card companies will be introducing smart cards, with strong incentives for retailers to install readers, funded mainly by fraud reduction. Kiosks are appearing in many locations, funded by suppliers of services and products made available through them, whether in post offices, transport sites (ticketing, parking, etc) or retail stores. Governments around the world are using smart card technology as the key to consumer access for public facilities and services. Bluetooth technology will allow short-range communication between digital devices, so even if there is no smart card reader, a consumer who inserts a smart card into another device (a dual-slot mobile, a personal organizer) will be able to communicate with other devices (eg point of sale terminals, vending machines). At home, even a single card reader (eg digital TV) could be used as a device to distribute and receive smart card data to other devices (eg PCs, mobile phones).

Some of this is distant, but much of it is very near. Companies who deal with millions of customers through many channels for many interactions will realize that a sensible technology for managing customers has been around for some time, whose acceptance is exploding, and which allows lower-cost, more customer-friendly and higher-quality methods of improving relationships with customers – whether independently or in cooperation with other companies.

THE CRM/IT INTERFACE

One of the major risks in CRM is complete project failure. The subject of why so many big, systems-supported change projects fail is one that exercises many boards of directors. Understanding why is not easy, and it is made harder by the fact that when change projects fail, there tends to be a rise in the attrition rate among the senior and middle managers associated with them. Along with the managers disappears the corporate memory of much of what happened – particularly the management decisions – who made them, why and on what evidence or business case they were based.

John Maynard Keynes observed how many apparently practical men of affairs were slaves to the scribbling of long-dead theorists.[1] The same seems to be true of those who plan IT. In many academic textbooks and courses, the idea is proposed that first a business must clarify its strategy and plans. From these it develops a brief for the IT department. There is absolutely no evidence that this approach works better than the two main alternatives.

The first alternative is for a team composed of IT and its 'internal customers' to work together to develop a feasible approach, taking into account what the business needs and what it is possible to do – cost-effectively – with the support of systems. In CRM, this approach has worked for many companies. It works very well when the business is less complex. Complexity is expressed by, for example, the number of significantly different products, the numbers of channels of distribution used, the number of significantly different market segments addressed, or the number of ways of managing customers (eg whether they are managed using a comprehensive highly customized CRM approach or using a simple best-value-for-money approach for all customers). Where the business is complex, the number of different 'internal customers' for the services of IT in supporting customer management may be too great for this approach to work. The joint IT/business team becomes unwieldy, and may have conflicting objectives.

This leads to the second alternative, which may seem surprising to some. Here, IT communities are led by senior managers with strong experience on the business side. They look with a degree of cynicism at the complex requirements being thrown by internal clients 'over the wall' to the IT department. They have seen it all before. They are used to dealing with complex wish-lists of features and functions for which the business case is shaky. They have noted the tendency of senior functional managers to move on up or out of the organization, such that by the time the system is delivered, a new senior client is in place asking for a different system or a radical reconfiguration of existing systems. This wise IT manager therefore develops a view about the overall systems requirements for managing customers, based not just on what internal clients are asking for, but also upon data from the 'outside world' about what works where. IT directors often talk to their opposite numbers in competitive companies. They form a view about what is feasible, with what speed, and at what cost. They understand that, for example, CRM strategies often involve two steps forward and one step back, because of implementation problems, changes in key staff, etc. They develop an understanding of when it is wise to slow down the process of developing new customer-facing applications in favour of making existing ones work – better or sometimes at all. They develop a realistic view about what should be outsourced and what can be done in-house, whether development or operations. They understand how much successful CRM implementation is due to solid programme management rather than brilliant conception. They pay close attention to what is really happening at the interface with customers, rather than the myths that so often exist at board level. This includes evidence on what customers experience and what they think about it. A recent meeting with a client reinforced this point. Finally, these wise IT managers realize that the chances of building a stable IT strategy on a detailed but unstable customer management strategy are pretty slim. However, they also realize that, to achieve a solid advance in the way their company manages customers, they need to manage the functions which are responsible for customers (marketing, sales and service) sensitively but challengingly. This means asking gently for evidence that the assertions these functions make about what they are doing are correct, or that the business cases they propose as justification for major systems changes are based on realistic projections as to how customers will react when faced with the proposed new approaches to customer management.

THE FUTURE

The classic (and still improving) model of direct marketing, which focuses so clearly on customer data, targeting, media choice, contact strategies, timing, offer development, creative expression of the offer and response management, has had a dramatic effect on marketing in areas such as financial services, utilities, automotive, telecommunications and retailing, and is starting to affect packaged consumer goods. Marketing to small and medium enterprises has also been transformed. The CRM fashion has created many cases of exaggerated expectation. What does the future really hold for CRM?

Systems

- We will have abandoned the naïve idea that it is possible to meet all customer management requirements with one system, or even suite of systems from one manufacturer. Customer management simply takes too many forms.
- We will have rejected the idea that choice of customer management systems depends on full articulation of marketing and service strategies, and an associated business case. In real life, strategies are deeply unstable.
- IT directors will have finally realized that they need to provide a steadily growing range of capabilities to their internal customers, rather than a single system. Flexibility will be more important than optimized performance for fully defined requirements.

Direct marketing techniques and media

- The wireless revolution will finally allow customers to contact suppliers and suppliers to contact them wherever both sides wish (provided permissions have been given). However, companies will still want to promote to customers and to 'push' them to do things.
- Customers will want (as they will be able to properly for the first time) to give permission for certain contacts and refuse others.
- Customers will also want to compliment, complain, request information and track progress. Companies will want to respond and clarify.
- The differences will be that new sets of data will help (or hinder if badly managed) companies to do what they want to do, while the technology will have allowed dramatic acceleration of the process.
- Companies will receive much more information about the kinds of contacts customers make with them, when and where, as well as about their failed or half-attempts. If companies design response mechanisms properly, they will know very quickly whether

the contact was worthwhile. This will even work in intermediated channels, provided the right processes are established between suppliers, intermediaries and customers. However, these new techniques and media will be recognizable cousins of existing approaches, and work alongside them.

- Mail will be used to explain complex notions to customers, to fulfil enquiries, and increasingly to deliver products to customers.
- Voice telephony will focus on areas such as handling complex and/or new types of enquiries, setting up new complex relationships and ending difficult relationships – where the human touch may be necessary.

The brand

In theory, the notion of the customer-oriented portal/agent makes a lot of sense. In some ways, it is the most modern version of the intermediary. For the customer, having to give and maintain only one set of data sounds a dream. Why specify my requirements to many suppliers when I can specify them to one, which will show me the best deal I can get? This is what new high-worth individuals have done for decades with financial services, and what consumers are increasingly doing with travel, through sites such as Travelocity. Yet in parallel, highly specific businesses such as EasyJet are showing that you should concentrate on just getting customers to give the new data (their next travel request). If you wish, you can allow them to store with you the minimum previously existing data (credit card details), you can easily get most of your customers booking on the Web. Even in this example, customers are often happier to rekey what they see as confidential data rather than store it. Consider too the problem of remembering your different PIN numbers, even if you were to use only three of four such agents. My bet, in consumer markets, is that we shall see the big brands, with their enormous advertising and promotional budgets, continue to use publicly available data (postal address file, electoral roll and their derivatives) as their basis for dialogue management,. Customers will be given strong incentives to come to suppliers' heavily branded Web sites, using Internet or wireless technology. These suppliers simply cannot afford to lose this particular battle for customer access, and most customers don't want them to, as evidenced by their responsiveness to direct approaches using today's technology.

MAKING IT WORK – PROFITABLY

Throughout this book, we have produced lots of evidence showing where CRM works and where it does not, and why. We have also suggested many ways of improving CRM. We end with a simple exhortation – CRM works for many companies, for some of their customers. With good thinking, good planning, good preparation and good programme management, and good integration of systems – with each other and with management activity – you too can make it work – profitably.

Notes

1 Keynes, J M (1936) *General Theory of Employment, Interest and Money*, Macmillan, London

Index